ASPIC AND OLD LACE

TEN DECADES OF COOKING, FASHION AND SOCIAL HISTORY

Diane L. Barts

Costumes Illustrated by Mrs. Edward J. Meehan

Northern Indiana Historical Society —— South Bend, Indiana
1987

COVER PHOTO:
On July 27, 1906, a group of young ladies gathered to be photographed prior to a formal luncheon given by Mrs. George Ford. Seated L - R: Hilda Stedman, Margaret Stephenson, Gertrude Oliver, Mrs. George Ford, Helen Leach of Orange, New Jersey, Mildred Apgar of Trenton, New Jersey, and Violet Witwer. Standing L - R: Estella Brick, Nell Fountain, Bessie Haughton, Helen Matthews, Gertrude Myers, Grace Cummins, Ada Sawyer, Margaret Myers, and Louise Studebaker.

INTRODUCTION

On October 26, 1867, members of the community were invited to attend a meeting to organize an historical society. The mission statement of the organization formed at that meeting, the Northern Indiana Historical Society, makes the same commitment today that it did when the by-laws were drafted 120 years ago. The statement reads: "The mission of the Northern Indiana Historical Society is to institute and encourage historical inquiry and research; to collect and preserve historical materials of the St. Joseph River Valley Region; and to disseminate historical information to the community." The Society was formally incorporated on February 29, 1896. During the week of February 5, 1900, the Society held its first public exhibition of the fine old treasures in the possession of the Society, its members and their friends. In 1907 the Commissioners of St. Joseph County, Indiana generously provided the Society with a new home -- the County's second courthouse built in 1855. The Northern Indiana Historical Society continues to reside in the 1855 courthouse, which has been designated a landmark and has been included on the prestigious National Register of Historic Places. Today, the Northern Indiana Historical Society proudly maintains and exhibits a collection of over 200,000 objects, and continues to provide the region with quality educational programming and publications.

The collection of more than 3,000 historic costumes maintained by the Northern Indiana Historical Society is highlighted in "Aspic and Old Lace." Included in the collection are costumes dating from the early 19th century, and hundreds of accessories such as hats, shoes and jewelry.

Eleven of the costumes in the collection are illustrated in the book. We thank Norma Lou Meehan for the many hours she devoted to creating the illustrations. We also thank Pat Potts for the hours she spent working with Norma Lou in selecting the special costumes for illustration and writing the costume descriptions.

We are indebted to Diane Barts for her hard work and commitment to writing this book. She devoted more than two years to collecting recipes, having them tested, writing the narratives, and finally assisting the printer with the book design. She has made an outstanding contribution to the history of our region, and we thank her!

The Society also wishes to express its appreciation to Tom Mason Printing Co., Inc. for their assistance and patience. Without their expertise, this book would never have become a reality.

We invite you to read "Aspic and Old Lace" and to try all of the excellent recipes. The narratives, illustrations, advertisements, photographs, as well as, the memories of those who contributed the many recipes will provide a look at the rich heritage of the St. Joseph River Valley Region of Northern Indiana and Southern Michigan.

Dr. Stanley M. Koscielski
President, Board of Trustees

Mrs. Kathleen Stiso Mullins
Executive Director

TRUSTEES AND STAFF

ACKNOWLEDGEMENTS

I would like to extend my most heartfelt thanks to Kathleen Stiso Mullins for her patience, hard work, and moral support; without her efforts, this book could never have become a reality.

My thanks go to Norma Lou Meehan who used her considerable talents to design the cover and sketch the costumes from the Museum collection. Thanks, also, to Costume Curator, Patricia Potts, who chose the gowns to be sketched and provided the descriptions for each costume.

A special thanks to the many people who contributed to the project including:

The Staff and Volunteers of the Northern Indiana Historical Society
The many ladies who tested recipes, and their friends and families who were forced to blaze new culinary trails
The St. Joseph County Extension Office
Charles Lamb and The University of Notre Dame Archives
Dr. Thomas J. Schlereth, University of Notre Dame
The South Bend Community School Corporation
The South Bend-Mishawaka Area Chamber of Commerce
Mr. Arthur S. Irwin
Mr. Milton Kouroubetis
Mr. and Mrs. Frank Sindlinger
The Staff of the **South Bend Tribune**
Dr. James M. Wilson
Mrs. J.M. Studebaker III
Patty Williams and Betsy Cockshott of Tom Mason Printing Co., Inc. who made countless changes
and corrections without screams, tears, or threats of bodily harm.

Diane Barts

RECIPE TESTERS

		The Advanced Foods Class of Penn High School:	
Mrs. Lola Lyons	Mrs. Louise Barts		
Jerry & Sheri Wiener	Mrs. Margie Canfield	Tracy Bair	Nicky Calhoun
Ms. Cheryl Haas	Mrs. Wava Apelgreen	Kim Bridges	Corrina Griggs
Mrs. Sharon Love	Mrs. Sharon Deneen	Dawn Coleman	Tammy Hills
Mrs. Jan Frieden	Mrs. Beth Lamon	Christina Hills	Tammy Kline
Mrs. Sharon Gumz	Mrs. Mary Renshaw	Renae Johnson	Kathy Long
Mrs. Susan Weaver	Mrs. Eleanor Carr	Beverly Kraus	Rod McAller
Mrs. Faye Philippsen	Mrs. Karen Curtis	Regina Long	Tracy Taylor
Mrs. Carol Collins	Mrs. Anne McGraw	Laura Suetkamp	Kristie Worm
Mrs. Georgianne Compton	Mrs. Shirley Mason	Stacey Vandenhandle	Susan Morton, Instructor
Mrs. Doris Purucker	Mrs. Gail Jaskowiak	Jamie Brantley	
Ms. Rita Mitchell	Mrs. Barb Hocker		
Mrs. Mary Rohleder	Mrs. Claralu Blake		
Mrs. Elie Olson	Mrs. Nadine Collier		
	Mrs. Sue Mullett		

RECIPE CONTRIBUTORS

Mrs. Marlene Abrams
Mrs. Janet Allen
Mrs. Roy Allen
Mrs. Charles (Wava) Apelgreen
Miss Janet Apelgreen
Miss Lena Armbruster

Mr. and Mrs. David (Christine) Bainbridge
Mrs. John Bamber
Mrs. Wayne (Judy) Bartholomew
Diane Barts
Mrs. Roger (Louise) Barts
Mrs. Thomas E. (Louise) Bath
Mrs. J.B. Birdsell
Mrs. Robert (Claralu) Blake
Mrs. Lester (Aileen) Borough
Mrs. Maxine Bowers
Mrs. Lee (Jill) Brummett
Mr. John Charles Bryant
Mrs. Joel (Lou Ann) Bullard
Mrs. D. William (Ruth) Bungert

Mrs. Paul (Ellen) Cahill
Mrs. Marge Campbell
Mrs. David (Margie) Canfield
Mrs. Eleanor Carr
Mrs. H.L. (Margaret) Carrington
Mrs. George Earl (Florence) Carroll
Mrs. J. Oliver Casaday
Mr. James Lewis Casaday
Mrs. Edward Chambers
Mrs. Rose Cira
Mrs. Schuyler (Ellen) Colfax
Mrs. Walton (Carol) Collins
Mrs. Ronald (Georgianne) Compton
Mrs. Glady Conant
Mrs. Frank Coppes
Mrs. Alexis (Mary) Coquillard
Gloria Crepeau Cudney
Mrs. J. Oliver Cunningham
Mrs. Robert (Karen) Curtis

Mrs. Kenneth (Amy) David
Sally Day
Mrs. Patrick (Sharon) Deneen
Maryanne Denisi
Mrs. Arthur DeWispelaere
Mrs. Arthur (Dagny) Diamond
Linda Haines Dillard
Mrs. Bipin (Linda) Doshi
Mrs. William (Anna) Dumke

Mrs. Frederick C. (Lilla) Elbel
Mrs. Andrew (Magda) Eperjesi
Mrs. Anne C. Erdman
Mrs. Ronald (Nancy) Eversole

Martha Jane Fields
Mrs. Mary Fischer
Mrs. George W. (Florence) Ford
Mrs. Daniel W. Fowler
Mrs. John C. (Jan) Frieden
Mrs. C.W. Frink

Mrs. Thomas (Jean) Gast
Mrs. H.M. Geleske
Mrs. Holly Grant
Lucy Green
Mrs. Stephen (Sharon) Gumz

Mary Haag

Cheryl Haas
Mrs. Dennis (Shirley) Hagye
Mary Ellen Handwork
Mrs. Betty Hans
Mabelle Hartfield
Miss M. Geraldine Hatt
Mrs. Harold (Carolyn) Heath
Dr. Lillian Holdeman
Mrs. Mary Jo Hruska
Mrs. Charles (Florence) Hurcomb

Mrs. John (Gail) Jaskowiak

Mr. Edward Kalamaros
Mrs. Bernard Kamm
Mrs. George E. (Marjorie) Keller
Mrs. Karen Keller
Rev. Mary H. Kendzora
Karen Kiemnec
Mrs. Harry (Betty) Koehler

Mrs. David (Stephanie) LaDow
Mrs. Margaret Lamb
Mrs. Lester (Beth) Lamon
Mrs. Dennis (Joan) Laughlin
Mrs. Judd (Mary Lou) Leighton
Mrs. John R. (Virginia) Lionberger
Mrs. Michael (Sharon) Love
Mrs. A.T. (Betty) Lynch
Mrs. Harrison (Lola) Lyons

Mrs. Della Mann
Mrs. Glenn A. (Maxine) Mann
Mrs. Tony (Edith) Mathia
Mrs. W.F. (Deborah) Mayers
Mrs. Eleanor Mays
Mrs. Joseph McKown
Mr. David P. McLellan
Mrs. Edward J. (Norma) Meehan
Mary Jane Micinski
Mrs. Robert C. Miller
Mrs. Spiro (Marilyn) Metros
Mrs. John J. (Bonnie) Molloy, Jr.
Mrs. Ralph Mowsier
Dr. and Mrs. James (Kathleen Stiso) Mullins

Mrs. Robert H. Nickerson
Mrs. Franz Nyberg

Mrs. Erich (Alice) Oetting
Virginia Gilberg O'Hair
Mrs. John (Jane) Olcott
Harriet Oliver
Joseph D. Oliver Family
Mrs. Ronald (Pat) Olsen
Mrs. Donald (Elie) Olson
Mrs. George Omacht
Mrs. Eveline O'Neal
Maybelle Otterson
Mrs. Kayane Oxian
Mrs. Mannig Oxian

M.E. Parrott
Mrs. A.J. (Sarah) Paul
Mrs. Eva Peirce
Mrs. John N. (Muriel) Perkins
Mrs. Eric (Faye) Philippsen
Mrs. John (Lola Mae) Philippsen
Mr. Ted Poledor
Miss Mary M. Post
Mr. and Mrs. Philip (Patricia) Potts

Mrs. Ervin (Bertha) Purucker
Mr. and Mrs. Ervin (Doris) Purucker
Miss Annajane Puterbaugh

Mrs. Kathy A. Rastetter
Mr. and Mrs. Claude (Mary) Renshaw
Mrs. H.J. Rickert
Karen Ripy
Doris Roberts
Mrs. Michael (Gail) Rohleder
Mrs. Paul (Mary) Rohleder
Mrs. Harvey (Margaret) Rostiser
Mrs. Louis N. (Janice) Rugee

Mrs. Helene Sailer
Mrs. Jean Savarese
Mrs. Arthur (Emma) Schlorch
Gladys Scoville
Mrs. H.J. Shreiner
Mrs. Bertha Sindlinger
Mr. and Mrs. Frank (Maureen) Sindlinger
Miss Jenny Sipocz
Mrs. Ethel Haynes Skeen
Charlotte Smith
Mrs. Ralph Sollitt
Miss Nina Solloway
Mrs. Helen E. Moore Spears
Mrs. Pauline Stigall
Mrs. Glenn (Fannie Mae) Stoneburner
Mrs. Ruby L. Stratigos
Sue Stratigos
Mrs. Brian (Carolyn) Straup
Edith Studebaker
Mrs. George M. (Ada) Studebaker
Mrs. J.M. (Lillian) Studebaker III
Mr. Art Sumption

Mrs. Charles (Mary) Taylor
Fannie Taylor
Miss Mary Taylor
Miss Thaddessa Taylor
Mrs. E.W. Thompson
Jeannie Tiniti
Mrs. Herb (Betty Ann) True

June Urbanski

Mrs. Paul (Edna) Van Dusen
Mrs. Tobi Van Dyke
Mrs. Robert (Helen) Veith

Jennifer Warlick
Mrs. Stephen (Susan) Weaver
Mrs. L.B. Weber
Mrs. Margaret Whipkey
Mrs. Melvena Whitaker
Mrs. Daniel (Nancy) White
Mrs. Eugene G. (Annette) White
Mr. and Mrs. Jerry (Sheri) Wiener
Mrs. Marianne Wilcox
Mrs. Margaret W. Wilder
Mrs. Charles Williams
Mrs. James Lee Wilson
Mrs. James M. Wilson
Irma Wiseman

Mrs. G. Toms (Margie) Yarger
Mrs. John (Millie) Yoder

Mr. Daniel Zakrowski

TABLE OF CONTENTS

Mrs. Schuyler Colfax

1870's

Mrs. Schuyler Colfax wore this extremely heavy gown at the inauguration of her husband as Vice President of the United States in March, 1869. The two piece dress has an ornate pattern of jet and crystal beading, black cut velvet and lace over heavy white silk. A black cut velvet decorative apron forms a bustle in the back over a skirt of black beaded lace against white. The bodice is beaded lace and cut velvet.

CENTENNIAL

The 1870's saw an adolescent America struggling to come of age. Once again whole after four painful years of Civil War, a lean and lanky nation was stretching powerful arms from coast to coast drawing East and West together via the transcontinental railroad. The sweet smell of money was in the air; young lungs were filled with the promise of untold prosperity, the stench of unbridled greed.

This was an era of conspicuous consumption -- and the more conspicuous the better. Newly acquired wealth was quickly put on display for all to envy and admire. There was a flurry of building as mansions began to spring up in cities across the country. Ladies vied with one another to possess the most ostentatious and extravagant clothing; this attempt to out do one another buried women's dresses under a profusion of frills, flounces, tassels, and trim.

Paris couturier, Charles Worth, put an end to the stiff crinolines of the 1850's and the awkward hoop skirts of the 1860's by designing dresses which showed fullness only at the back of the skirt. The hallmark of feminine beauty was still the tiny waisted "hour-glass" figure (18 inches was the most desireable dimension for a chic waistline). Now, however, tapes were sewn into garments which pulled the front and sides of the skirt close to the body while the rear became a cascade of puffed material tumbling to the floor and spilling out into a train. Unfortunately, this concentration of yards and yards of fabric put a terrible strain on ladies' backs. As a result, pads or metal frameworks were added to help support the weight of the cloth and the bustle was born.

As 1876 approached, America was preparing a gala celebration -- the Philadelphia Centennial Exhibition. This city, from which our independence had first been proclaimed 100 years before, was a perfect setting for an event which was to pay homage to the accomplishments of the past and offer a glimpse into the wonders of the future. Some of the new innovations on display were Alexander Graham Bell's telephone, Elisha Graves Otis' elevator, and Charles E. Hires' root beer.

For the housewife, life had changed very little since the Revolution. For those who were unable to afford domestic help, life was an unending series of back-breaking tasks. Knuckles were rubbed raw and red as women hunched over wash boards and laundry tubs. Heavy metal flat irons had to be constantly reheated to press the family's clothing. Melvin Bissel invented the carpet sweeper in 1876, but most women were still forced to drag their heavy rugs from the house, throw them over a clothes line and beat them furiously. Wood had to be chopped, water had to be pumped, blackened lamp chimneys had to be scrubbed.

Food preparation, which consumed a large part of every woman's day, was revolutionized in the 1850's when wood burning stoves first began to appear. After centuries of cooking over an open hearth, women gladly said goodbye to the dangers, soot, and stifling heat of the fire place. Unfortunately, this would prove to be the last major improvement in kitchen technology until the turn of the century.

Although food was plentiful, a family's diet was still dependent upon seasonal availability. Meat had to be smoked or salted while fruits and vegetables were dried or stored in root cellars. Refrigerated railway cars went into operation in the 1870's, but since ice was still a luxury, the produce they brought in was generally far too expensive for the average consumer to afford. Despite these difficulties, however, oysters were an extremely popular delicacy of the period.

As Chicago was building a new city upon the rubble of the Great Fire of 1871, so, too, was America building a new nation upon the devastation wrought by the War Between the States. The western Indians were still a potent force as General Custer discovered, much to his mortification. However, the invention of barbed wire, the slaughter of the buffalo, and the steady flood of people pushing westward was signaling the end of an era. Soon all that would remain of the "Wild West" would be disembodied legends -- caricatures that were once great men and women. In the East, ambitious men were building an industrial empire. There was more merchandise available to consumers than ever before: the department store was being developed by men such as John Wanamaker and Marshall Field; Frank Woolworth opened his first "5-and-10 cent" store; goods could even be ordered by mail with the help of Montgomery Ward & Co. Ice cream sodas and sarsaparilla, sewing machines and Ebenezer Butterick's paper patterns all joined with the piano to make life more pleasant and satisfying. The rush to the cities was on; never again would America be the innocent rural child staring at the world with wondering eyes.

A dose of Raspberry Vinegar will undoubtedly perk you right up. This recipe has been in Miss Hatt's family since the 1850's.

RASPBERRY VINEGAR

To **4 qts. red raspberries** put enough **vinegar** to cover and let them stand 24 hours. Scald and strain it (bring this mixture to a boil). Add **1 lb. sugar** to **1 pt. juice**. Boil 20 minutes and bottle. It is then ready for use and will keep for years.

To one glass of water add a great spoonful. It is much relished by the sick. Very nice.

Miss M. Geraldine Hatt

NORTH COAST CLAM CHOWDER

1 large potato, boiled and peeled
3 slices bacon, diced
1 medium onion, chopped
2 cans minced clams with juice
Freshly ground black pepper
½ tsp. celery seed
3 cups milk or Half and Half

In a soup kettle, brown the bacon till lightly browned. Add the onion and cook till limp. Drain the fat. Add the potato, salt, pepper, and celery seed; stir. Drain the clams, reserving the juice. Add the clams to the chowder and simmer several minutes till hot. Add the juice and simmer until hot. Add the milk and heat; do not boil. Serve in a warm bowl. Dust the top with cayenne pepper for added zip. Good on a cold rainy day.

Mrs. A.T. (Betty) Lynch

1868 was an important year for Schuyler Colfax. Not only was he elected Vice-President of the United States, but he married for the second time. His new bride was Miss Ellen Wade, the niece of Senator Ben Wade of Ohio.

AMBER SOUP

Ingredients: A **large soup bone** (2 pounds), **a chicken, a small slice of ham, an onion, 2 sprigs of parsley, ½ a small carrot, ½ a small parsnip, ½ a stick of celery, 3 cloves, pepper, salt, a gallon of cold water, whites and shells of 2 eggs and caramel for coloring.** Let the beef, chicken, and ham boil slowly for 5 hours; add the vegetables and cloves, to cook the last hour, having first fried the onion in a little hot fat, and then in it stick the cloves. Strain the soup into an earthen bowl and let it remain over night. Next day remove the cake of fat on the top, take out the jelly, avoiding the settlings, and mix into it the beaten whites of the eggs with the shells. Boil quickly for ½ a minute; then,

placing the kettle on the hearth, skim off carefully all the scum and whites of the eggs from the top, not stirring the soup itself. Pass the soup through a jelly bag; it should be quite clear. The soup may then be put aside and reheated just before serving. Add then a large tablespoon of caramel to give a rich color and slight flavor.

Mrs. Schuyler (Ellen) W. Colfax

When Thomas Jefferson returned from serving his country in France as Minister Plenipotentiary, he brought back with him a French governess, Annette, to care for his children. Julienne Soup is a recipe she brought with her.

JULIENNE SOUP

6 cups beef broth
2 carrots, cut in julienne strips
1 medium potato, peeled and cut in julienne strips
1 small turnip, peeled and cut in julienne strips
1 small onion, cut in thin wedges
½ tsp. dried marjoram, crushed
¼ tsp. salt

In a saucepan bring the broth, carrots, potatoes, turnips, onion, marjoram, and salt to a boil. Cover and reduce heat. Simmer till vegetables are tender, 15-20 minutes. Top with seasoned croutons, if desired. Serves 8.

Mrs. Anne C. Erdman

Mary Schuyler Mathews was born in South Bend in 1840. Eighteen years later, she married Elijah Cowles and moved to Nebraska. Her half-brother, Schuyler Colfax, was the publisher of an early South Bend paper, "The Saint Joseph Valley Register." In later years he became a prominent politician: a Congressman; the Speaker of the House of Representatives; and Vice President of the United States in the administration of Ulysses S. Grant (1869-1873).

DEVILED EGGS

Hard boil **6 eggs.** Peel. Cut in half lengthwise. Drop whites into salted water. Mash yolks with **two generous tablespoons of butter.** Add **1 tablespoon finely chopped onion. Salt and pepper to taste.** Sprinkle on **cider vinegar to taste.** After stirring, beat (fork) vigorously to fluff. Fill shells. Put into the storm cave to cool until supper time.

Mrs. Oetting still devils eggs this way, but she adds **1 tsp. of prepared mustard.** In season she substitutes chives or green or red peppers for the onion.

Mrs. Erich (Alice) Oetting
From her grandmother,
Mary Schuyler Cowles, who was the
youngest half sister of Schuyler Colfax.

Mrs. Anne Erdman is director of food management and operation at Lake Michigan College in Benton Harbor, Michigan. In her never ending quest for information on colonial cooking, she discovered that Thomas Jefferson was a man who truly enjoyed vegetables. His garden contained 19 varieties of lettuce. He also took special interest in developing a salad dressing from sesame oil.

SALAD OF MIXED GARDEN STUFF

1 head Bibb lettuce
1 bunch watercress
1 small head endive
1 small head iceberg lettuce
1 small head chicory
A few sprigs of tender spinach leaves
1 Tbsp. chopped chives or scallions
Monticello Dressing

Wash the salad greens in ice water; drain and pat completely dry. Tear apart and place in the refrigerator to crisp. Toss with Monticello Dressing to serve.

Monticello Dressing: Combine **1 small clove of garlic** (crushed), **1 tsp. salt, ½ tsp. white pepper, ⅓ cup olive oil, ⅓ cup sesame oil, ⅓ cup tarragon or white vinegar.** Place in a covered jar and shake well before pouring over salad.

Mrs. Anne C. Erdman

My husband's grandmother, Johanna Mainer Elbel, arrived in South Bend in 1852 from Arzberg, Bavaria. She was 18 years old. She carried with her on the boat a large copper Turk's-head mold used in making this special bread, which became a favorite recipe of the family. Unfortunately, she left no directions for mixing, assuming that her descendants would be good cooks! Just follow the procedure for making any yeast cake or coffee cake.

GUGELHUPF

4 cups flour
3 cakes yeast
1 cup milk (at 70 degrees)
¾ cup sugar
1 cup butter
5 eggs
1 tsp. salt
1 cup raisins
¼ cup sliced almonds

Let the dough rise 1½ hours. Use a 3-quart mold. Bake for 50-60 minutes at 350 degrees.*

* (Ed: In Germany this coffee cake, more commonly spelled Kugelhopf, was often served for Name Day celebrations [the birthday of the saint for whom a person was named].

For those who don't want to try to figure out the directions -- Grease a mold or tube pan. Sift the flour before measuring. Scald the milk; cool and pour over the yeast which has been crumbled to help it dissolve more quickly. Beat in 1 cup of flour to make a sponge; let this mixture rise until double in bulk in a warm place. Cream the butter and sugar. Add the eggs one at a time, beating after each addition. Add the salt and the sponge. Stir in the remaining flour and the raisins; beat until the batter is smooth and elastic. The almonds may be mixed into the batter or spread into the bottom of the mold or tube pan with the dough placed on top of the almonds. Put in a warm place and let rise until doubled. Bake as indicated.)

Mrs. Frederick C. (Lilla) Elbel
From Johanna Mainer Elbel

POTATOES SUSAN

6-8 good sized potatoes
1 small onion, minced
3 Tbsp. butter
½ tsp. salt
½ tsp. pepper

Put part of the butter in a small (10 inch) French skillet over moderate heat. Peel the potatoes and slice very thin. Soak in cold water and dry well. Put several fanned-out slices in the center of the skillet and continue to place the potatoes (overlapping) so they cover the skillet surface. Continue until about one-half of the potatoes are in the skillet, then spread the minced onion on top of the potatoes. Salt and pepper. Place the remaining potatoes in an overlapping pattern on top of the onions. Salt and pepper. Cook the potatoes about 15-20 minutes in a 325 degree oven, until the bottom is well browned and crusted. Loosen any potatoes that are stuck with a spatula. Toss the potatoes in mid-air (if you are dexterous) to turn, or set a plate on the potatoes and turn them (being careful not to disrupt the shape). Cook the other side about 10-15 minutes, or until the potatoes are cooked.

M. E. Parrott

1870 RECIPES

Boston Baked Beans was a hearty dish that was popular throughout the colonies. It was a particular favorite with those whose religion restricted work on the Sabbath; the beans could be made a day ahead and served either hot or cold on Sunday.

Over the years, Midwestern taste buds have become accustomed to baked beans made with a spicy ketchup and brown sugar sauce. This early American recipe is quite different; it's mild flavor may not be for everyone, but it does provide an authentic link with America's New England forefathers.

BOSTON BAKED BEANS

3 lbs. dry pea beans or navy beans (6 cups)
1½ cups dark molasses
1 Tbsp. dry mustard
1 tsp. salt
½ tsp. pepper
½ lb. salt pork, diced
1 large onion, chopped

Rinse the beans. Combine the beans and (6 qts.) cold water in a large kettle. Bring to boiling and simmer for 2 minutes. Remove from the heat. Cover and let stand for 1 hour. (Or, add the beans to water and soak overnight.) Bring the water to a boil once again and simmer till the beans are tender, about 1 hour. Drain, reserving the liquid. Combine the molasses, mustard, salt, pepper, and 3 cups of the reserved cooking liquid. In a 6 qt. bean pot, mix the beans, salt pork, and onion. Stir in the molasses mixture. Cover and bake in a 300 degree oven for 3½-4 hours, stirring occasionally. Add more of the reserved cooking liquid if needed. Serves 15.

Mrs. Anne C. Erdman

CORN FRITTERS

½ can corn (cream style)
1 egg
4 Tbsp. milk
½ cup flour
Pinch of salt
1 tsp. baking powder

Mix all ingredients. Drop from a spoon into hot oil or lard.

Irma Wiseman
From her grandmother,
Mary Jane Riley Bainbridge
(first cousin to
James Whitcomb Riley)

This old German recipe has been used by the Elbel family since 1852. Aunt Laura's Potato Pancakes were a favorite with the large Elbel family of 6 sons and 2 daughters back in the days when potatoes were the backbone of every meal.

AUNT LAURA'S POTATO PANCAKES

MIX WELL:
6 raw potatoes, peeled and grated
¼ cup flour
1 onion, chopped fine
1 egg
1 tsp. salt
¼ tsp. pepper

Form patties and saute in ¼ inch of fat or drop by spoonfuls into a hot skillet (with the same level of fat).*
* (Ed: Bacon drippings give the pancakes a nice flavor. Mix the pancakes immediately after grating the potatoes, or the potatoes will darken.)

Mrs. Frederick C. (Lilla) Elbel

Table Etiquette

It is ridiculous to make a display of your napkin, to attach it with pins to your bosom, or to pass it through your button-hole. Never use the tablecloth instead of a napkin.

The napkin should be touched to the lips in the interval between partaking of greasy food and drinking; otherwise the rim of the glass will not be inviting to look upon.

In conversation at the table, be careful not to speak while eating a mouthful; it is indecorous in the extreme.

In carrying food to the mouth the handle of the fork should not be kept against the palm, as conveying it in that position gives the effect commonly expressed as "shovelling". A firm hold upon both knife and fork does not necessitate gripping them as if they were endowed with the ability to fly.

Never use your knife to convey food to your mouth, under any circumstance; it is unnecessary and glaringly vulgar.

Never pick your teeth at the table.

Reaching over another person's plate or standing up to reach distant

articles, instead of asking to have them passed is a violation of conventional propriety. When at a formal dinner, it is indelicate to take bread, even when it is within your reach, instead of calling upon the servant.

Do not gnaw bones at the table.

Whoever is given to "loading up" a fork or holding upon it a quantity of food pending its deposit in the mouth, had best dine by himself until such gaucheries are overcome.

Throwing the head far back, thrusting the spoon or fork far into the mouth, turning the bowl of the spoon over in the mouth, or draining a glass in a single draught are sins against the social gods; they are coarse and repulsive habits.

Ladies should never dine with their gloves on unless their hands are not fit to be seen.

Persons of good breeding never eat fast or in a noisy manner. Neither do they look or act as if very hungry, or as if anxious to get at certain dishes.

The Indians taught the colonists the importance of planting squash to revitalize the soil after growing corn. Pumpkins and squash were used interchangeably, and were welcome additions to the colonial diet.

BAKED GLAZED SQUASH

2½ lbs. butternut squash
⅓ cup packed brown sugar
2 Tbsp. butter
¼ tsp. paprika
½ tsp. salt
Dash of pepper

Slice the squash in 1-inch thick slices; remove the seeds. Arrange the squash rings in a 13 x 9 x 2-inch baking pan. Cover with foil. Bake in a 350 degree oven until almost tender, 45-60 minutes. Meanwhile, in a saucepan, combine the brown sugar, butter, paprika, salt, and pepper; cook and stir till bubbly. Spoon the mixture over the squash. Continue baking, uncovered, till the squash is tender, about 15 minutes more, spooning the mixture over the squash occasionally. Serves 8.

Mrs. Anne C. Erdman

Early pies were baked in large black Dutch ovens. These kettles were placed on trivets over hot coals which had been raked out onto the hearth; additional coals were then piled on top of the lid to provide more even heat. The pies were really more steamed than baked; as a result, the crusts were often soggy. Early meat pies are not very glamorous by modern standards, but they were nourishing and could be easily adapted to make use of whatever meats or vegetables were available.

BEEF STEAK PIE

1½ lbs. beef round steak, cut into 1-inch cubes
¼ cup all-purpose flour
1 large onion, chopped
2 Tbsp. lard
2 cups water
1 tsp. salt
¼ tsp. dried thyme, crushed
⅛ tsp. pepper
2 cups potatoes, diced
Pastry Top
Salt and pepper
Milk

Coat the beef cubes with the ¼ cup flour. In a large saucepan or skillet, cook the beef and onion in lard until the beef is browned and the onion is tender. Add the water, 1 tsp. salt, thyme, and pepper. Cover and simmer for 1½ hours.

Add the potatoes; cover and simmer for 20 minutes longer. Prepare the pastry top. Transfer the meat mixture to a 1½-qt. casserole. Season to taste with salt and pepper. Cut slits in the pastry top. Place the pastry top on the hot meat mixture, turn the edge under and flute. Brush with milk. Bake in a 450 degree oven until golden brown, about 15 minutes. Serves 6.

PASTRY TOP: Stir ¾ cup all-purpose flour and ¼ tsp. salt together. Cut in ¼ cup lard until the mixture resembles coarse crumbs. Sprinkle 2-3 Tbsp. cold water over the mixture (1 Tbsp. at a time) and gently toss with fork. Form into a ball. Roll on a lightly floured surface to a circle ½-1 inch larger than the casserole.

Mrs. Anne C. Erdman

HOW TO KEEP COOL IN HOT WEATHER:

Sit in a room covered with matting or without any carpet, and keep the floor wet with pure water and a watering-pot. On hot nights, place a double wet sheet on the bed and a woolen blanket over it, and it will cool the bed which is heated through the day, and does not cool as fast as the evening air. Wear wristlets and anklets of wet flannel. If chambers open upon the hot roofs of piazzas or porticoes, cover them with clean straw or hay, and wet them with a watering-pot.

This is an old family recipe brought over from Sweden in 1873 by my grandparents. We always have it for our Christmas Eve supper, along with other Swedish foods.

SWEDISH POTATO SAUSAGE

3 lbs. ground lean pork
5 lbs. potatoes (raw)
5 medium onions
2 Tbsp. salt
½ tsp. pepper
1 tsp. allspice
1½ tsp. ginger
6 yards casings

Soak casings in water overnight. Run cold water through the casings by holding one end over the faucet. If there are holes in the casings, cut off there, otherwise cut in about 18 inch lengths. Grind the potatoes and onions medium fine. Mix with the pork and seasonings. Stuff loosely in the casings. Tying the ends is not necessary if 1½ inches of casing are left empty at each end of the sausage. Put in boiling water and simmer uncovered for 45 minutes. To serve, brown in the oven (or in a frying pan using a small amount of oil). Make about 6 pounds. Freezes well.

Doris Roberts

1870 RECIPES

17th and 18th century cooking is a hobby with Mrs. Erdman. Chicken Virginia is her favorite dish; it has a unique flavor and an attractive appearance when served.

CHICKEN VIRGINIA WITH GRAPE SAUCE

3 chicken breasts, boned and halved
4 Tbsp. butter, melted
12 fresh mushrooms
6 slices Viriginia ham, thinly sliced

GRAPE SAUCE:
¼ cup butter
¼ cup all-purpose flour
½ tsp. salt
2 cups chicken stock or canned chicken broth
2 Tbsp. lemon juice
2 Tbsp. sugar
2 cups seedless grapes

Preheat the broiler. Line the broiler pan with foil; place the chicken in a single layer, skin side down. Brush with butter. Broil the chicken breasts 3-4 inches from the heat for 15 minutes; turn and brush with butter. Lower the pan to 7-8 inches from heat; broil 10-15 minutes longer or until chicken is done.

Saute whole mushrooms in the remaining butter. Serve each half chicken breast on a slice of ham. Spoon the grape sauce over the meat and garnish with sauteed mushrooms. Yields 6 servings.

GRAPE SAUCE: Melt ¼ cup butter in a saucepan and blend in flour and salt. Stir until smooth. Gradually add the chicken stock, stirring constantly until smooth and thick. Stir in lemon juice and sugar. Add the grapes just before serving. Makes 3 cups.

Mrs. Anne C. Erdman

Animals and poultry were only used for meat after they were no longer useful for other purposes such as eggs, milk, wool, etc. As a result, most of the meat which reached the colonial table was quite tough. It was necessary, therefore, for cooks to cut meat and poultry into bite sized pieces to help facilitate cooking and eating (people did not use forks, only spoons and knives).

CHICKEN IN HERB SAUCE

½ cup chopped celery
¼ cup butter
¼ cup all-purpose flour
1 tsp. snipped chives
¾ tsp. dried rosemary, crushed
¼ tsp. dried chervil, crushed
¼ tsp. dried tarragon, crushed
1 cup milk

1 cup chicken broth
2 cups cubed cooked chicken
Toast points or frozen patty shells, baked

Cook the celery in butter till tender, about 10 minutes. Stir in the flour, chives, rosemary, chervil, and tarragon. Add the milk and chicken broth. Cook and stir till thickened and bubbly. Stir in the chicken. Season to taste with salt and pepper. Heat through. Serve on toast points or in patty shells. Serves 4.

Mrs. Anne C. Erdman

FILLETS OF SOLE MORNAY

1½ lbs. fillets of sole (you can also use flounder)
1 small onion, sliced
6 peppercorns
6 Tbsp. water
½ bay leaf
Salt to taste

Wash the fillets and dry with paper towels. Fold the ends of each fillet under so they all appear to be the same length and place them into a lightly greased shallow baking dish. Sprinkle with a little salt. Add the onion slices, peppercorns, bay leaf and water. Cover with buttered paper and bake for 10-20 minutes in a moderate oven (350 degrees), or until the fish flakes easily. Reserve the fish stock for the sauce.

MORNAY SAUCE:
2 Tbsp. butter
2 Tbsp. flour
1¼ cups milk
Salt and pepper
3 Tbsp. grated Swiss or Parmesan cheese

Melt 2 Tbsp. butter in a small saucepan; remove the pan from the heat and blend in the flour. Pour in the milk. Season lightly with salt and pepper. Return the sauce to the heat and bring slowly to a boil, stirring constantly. Strain the liquid from the fish and add it to the sauce; cook for 2-3 minutes longer. Remove the sauce from the heat; stir in the cheese, a little at a time, reserving 1 Tbsp. Arrange the fish in a gratin or flameproof serving dish. Cover with the Mornay Sauce and sprinkle with the reserved cheese. Brown the dish lightly under the broiler. Serves 4.

M. E. Parrott

TO PRESERVE EGGS

Pack eggs in a jar small end downward, and then pour in a mixture of four quarts of slacked lime, two tablespoonfuls of cream tartar, and two of salt. This will cover about nine dozen for several months.

The recipe for Hot Water Gingerbread has been in Mrs. Lynch's family since the 1840's. It can be traced to her grandmother who emigrated from Maine, sailed round the Horn, and helped to settle the town of Mendocino, California.

HOT WATER GINGERBREAD

2½ cups flour
2 tsp. soda
½ tsp. baking powder
2 tsp. cinnamon
2 tsp. ginger
½ tsp. cloves
½ tsp. nutmeg
2 eggs
¾ cup molasses (dark)
¾ cup brown sugar (dark)
¾ cup cooking oil
1 cup hot water

Sift the dry ingredients twice. Beat the eggs. Add the sugar, oil, and molasses to the eggs and beat till smooth. (Hint: Measure the oil first and then measure the molasses in the same cup so the molasses will come out easily.) Quickly stir in the hot water and add this mixture to the dry ingredients. Beat till smooth. Pour into a greased pan 9 or 10 inches square. Bake for 30 minutes at 375 degrees. Serve warm with whipped cream.

Mrs. A.T. (Betty) Lynch

CIVIL WAR GINGERBREAD

Sift together and set aside:
2¾ cups flour
2 tsp. baking powder
½ tsp. cloves
½ tsp. soda
1 tsp. ginger
2 tsp. cinnamon

CREAM:
½ cup sugar
½ cup shortening
1 tsp. salt

Blend in **1 cup molasses.**
Add **2 eggs** and beat well.
Add flour mixture alternately with **1 cup hot water** till all is used. Blend well. Bake at 350 degrees for 50 minutes.*
*(Ed: Bake in a greased and floured 13 x 9-inch pan.)

Miss Janet Apelgreen

The recipe for Funeral Pie comes from my Rugee relatives in the Deep South (Mooresville, Alabama). It was used by the Negroes on their plantation before the the Civil War.

FUNERAL PIE

3 cups water
4 cups raisins
1 cup sugar
2 Tbsp. cornstarch
½ tsp. grated lemon peel
3 Tbsp. lemon juice
1 tsp. salt
1 Tbsp. butter or margarine
Pastry for a 9-inch 2-crust pie

Heat the water to boiling; stir in the raisins. Cook until tender, about 5 minutes. Mix the sugar and cornstarch; stir into the raisins. Heat, stirring constantly, till boiling. Boil and stir for 1 minute. Remove from the heat. Add the remaining ingredients. Pour the filling into the pie shell; cover with the top crust and cut slits into it. Bake at 400 degrees for 35-40 minutes. Cool.

Mrs. Louis N. (Janice) Rugee

HOUSEHOLD HINTS

A sink should be scalded out every day, and occasionally with hot lye. On nails, over the sink should be hung three good dish-cloths, hemmed, and furnished with loops -- one for dishes not greasy, one for greasy dishes, and one for washing pots and kettles. These should be put in the wash every week.

Flour should be kept in a barrel, with a flour-scoop to dip it, a sieve to sift it, and a pan to hold the sifted flour, either in the barrel or close at hand. The barrel should have a tight cover to keep out mice and vermin.

Rye should be bought in small quantities, say forty or fifty pounds at a time, and be kept in a keg or half-barrel, with a cover.

Molasses, if bought by the barrel or half-barrel, should be kept in the cellar. No vessel should be corked or bunged, if filled with molasses, as it will swell and burst the vesssel, or run over.

Sweep carpets as seldom as possible, as it wears them out. To shake them often is good economy. In cleaning carpets, use damp tea leaves, or wet Indian meal, throwing it about, and rubbing it over with the broom. The latter is very good for cleansing carpets made dingy by coal-dust.

Indulging in large quantities of cold drinks, or eating ice-creams, after a meal, tends to reduce the temperature of the stomach, and thus to stop digestion.

The fittest temperature for drinks, if taken when the food is in the digesting process, is blood-heat. Cool drinks, and even ice, can be safely taken at other times, if not in excessive quantity. When the thirst is excessive, or the body weakened by fatigue, or when in a state of perspiration, large quantities of cold drinks are injurious.

To clean rusty and blackened knives , cut a small potato in half, dip one-half in brick dust and rub the knives. Rust and stain will disappear like magic from their surfaces.

Diluted laudanum is excellent to apply to sores or wounds to heal them. If the wounds are fresh and of great extent, care must be taken to not use it full strength nor too freely, as enough might be aborbed into the system to cause too profound a sleep to be desirable.

1870 RECIPES

During her lifetime, Sarah Ervin saw a great deal of history. As a girl of 12, she helped to make bandages for wounded Civil War soldiers. In 1941, she was still doing her part, knitting scarves for soldiers overseas. She and her husband, B.F. Ervin, were held in such high esteem, that virtually the entire community of Desoto, Iowa turned out to help them celebrate their Golden Wedding Anniversary on February 12, 1924.

LITTLE SWEET GRANDMA'S COOKIES

2 cups brown sugar
1 cup shortening (lard is best)
4 beaten eggs
1 tsp. baking soda dissolved in 2 Tbsp. water
4 cups flour
½ tsp. nutmeg
½ tsp. cinnamon
½ tsp. salt

Mix the ingredients in order given. The dough may be sticky (it's best if the dough is refrigerated for several hours before rolling out). Add just a little flour. Roll out onto a floured board and cut with a cookie cutter. Bake in a 350 degree oven until nicely brown, about 15 minutes. (Experiments with this recipe indicate that the eggs may be reduced to 3 and the flour to 3 cups.)

These cookies are better when placed in a pottery cookie jar for a few days and allowed to season.

Dr. James Mullins
From his great-grandmother,
Mrs. Sarah Melissa Cutter Ervin

Most families have a few very special recipes which have been passed down from generation to generation. Often, basic recipes are adopted by good cooks and altered to suit their family's tastes. An excellent example of this can be found in a cookie recipe treasured by two families. Although quite similar, they each bear the distinctive imprint of a strong lady.

From Miss Nina Solloway: *This very old recipe has been handed down several generations from my great, great grandmother, Barbara Koterba, whose daughter, Baatta Koterba Ackerman was born in 1837.*

When my Father was a little boy, he was especially fond of these cookies, so his Grandmother Baatta Ackerman always quadrupled the recipe just for her grandson, Johnnie.

SOUR CREAM COOKIES

1 scant cup lard
2 cups sugar
1 cup sour cream
2 eggs
Pinch of salt
1 tsp. soda
Flour enough to roll dough and cut the cookies

Cream the lard and sugar; add the eggs and salt. Stir the soda into the sour cream and add to the mixture. Add enough **flour** to roll out and cut the cookies (**between 4 and 5 cups**). Bake 10 minutes at 425 degrees.

From Mrs. Dennis (Joan) Laughlin: *This cookie recipe is from my husband's grandmother, Ida Mae Reichelderfer. We still have the handwritten recipe she sent to her daughter, Frances, who in turn made these Sour Cream Cookies for her children.*

Ida Mae was widowed with 2 girls (ages 1 and 3 years old) when she moved to Fort Wayne, Indiana to open a grocery store. It proved to be a very successful business and supported the 3 of them in a comfortable life style. Ida Mae died in 1961 at the age of 96.

SOUR CREAM COOKIES

Take **2 eggs, 2 cups sugar, 1 cup shortening**, (I use half butter and Spry), **1 cup sour cream**, salt, nutmeg (2 tsp.), and **2 tsp. soda** (level measure). I use **flour*** enough to make a rather stiff batter. You can make drop cookies or add more flour and rollout and cut. I added **½ cup chopped nut meats,** that is just as you like. Makes about 7 dozen.

*(Ed: About 3 cups of flour works for drop cookies. Bake for 12 minutes in a 350 degree oven).

Mrs. Nyberg's parents both came from Scandinavia. Her mother was born in Sweden in 1853, and came to America at the age of 16. Her father emigrated from Norway to work in James Oliver's plow factory. It is said that Mr. Oliver valued Scandinavian employees because they were such good workers; he tried to recruit as many of them as possible.

NORWEGIAN PEPPERKAKAR

⅓ cup butter
¼ cup Karo syrup
⅔ cup sugar
½ tsp. soda
1 tsp. cloves
1 tsp. ginger
2 tsp. cinnamon
1 egg, slightly beaten
1 Tbsp. orange peel, grated
2 cups flour (or barely enough to handle with hands)

Melt together the butter, syrup, and sugar. Add the soda and spices; let cool a little. Add the egg and orange peel. Then add the flour. Let stand over night in the refrigerator. When rolling out, take a small amount at a time keeping the rest in the refrigerator. Roll almost paper thin.*

*(Ed: Try baking in a 325 degree oven. Because of the thinness of the cookies, watch carefully so they don't burn).

Mrs. Franz Nyberg

ITEMS OF INTEREST CONCERNING NOTRE DAME

It takes three barrels of flour a day to supply the bread used by the students and the Community.

40,944 pounds of beef, mutton and pork have been sent to the kitchen during the months of October, November and December.

Seven hundred hams and shoulders have been purchased during the same months, and a much larger number procured from the farm have been disposed of, moreover, four thousand fowls a year, three hundred and twenty pounds of green coffee a week, or, forty-six pounds a meal; sixty pounds of tea a week; two hundred and fifty pounds of sugar a day; nine hundred pounds of butter a week; two barrels of fish for a meal and two hundred dozen of eggs a meal.

These figures are not at all exaggerated, and will be better understood when it is known that six hundred are fed at Notre Dame every day.

The food expenditures of St. Mary's are not included in the above.

Reprinted from *The Scholastic Year,* May 7, 1868.

Downtown South Bend was a busy place in the 1870's.
This photograph shows the east side of Michigan Street, north of Washington Street.

James
Lewis
Casaday
Collection

1880's

This carefully detailed two-piece sapphire blue silk damask morning gown has a large bustle formed from a pannier on the right hip, and a long train with many pleats. Tiers of pleats cascade down the left side of the skirt, while the right side is bordered with heavy metallic beading in a floral design and helps to form the bustle. The train buttons onto the skirt. Circa 1882.

HUSTLE BUSTLE

Out of the maelstrom America loomed as an Eden in the 1880's. Immigrants by the thousands, seeking refuge and renewed hope, clamored ashore in search of the promised land. Soon these dreams were to be embodied in metal and stone as the Statue of Liberty slowly raised her torch to light the way to the new world.

Social advancement was the consuming passion of the decade. For immigrant and native-born families alike, life was a constant struggle to better themselves. Those who had recently found a measure of financial success were now interested in acquiring the burnished glow of old money.

In order to vault toward the dizzying heights of social prominence, however, it was absolutely vital to first become genteel. Toward that end, people increasingly relied upon etiquette books to help them smooth their rougher edges. Women were generally far more interested in gaining a toehold in society than men; wives eagerly contrived to step forward and give their husbands a swift kick up the social ladder.

In Europe, Americans traditionally had a reputation for being unkempt, uncouth, and uncommonly in a hurry; this was especially true at meal time. People freqently consumed three large meals a day. Since the time spent in eating could not be used to generate income, it was not unusual for these gargantuan repasts to be devoured in under ten minutes. Heartburn was a national affliction; this, however, was more often attributed to the workings of the Almighty than to poor eating habits.

A few minor innovations were making life easier for housewives. The Dover egg beater was a tremendous asset in preparing dishes requiring whipped cream or meringue. Baking powder became a more reliable leavening agent, and cookbooks bulged with wonderful new recipes for light and fluffy baked goods. Can openers were being touted as necessary kitchen equipment even though canned food was generally far too expensive for most families to afford. Lastly, the ice box, which had previously been a bit of a luxury, now joined the wood-burning stove as a must for every up-to-date kitchen.

The grocery store was just beginning to emerge under the leadership of the Great Atlantic & Pacific Tea Co. Unlike modern supermarkets, there was no self-service, and shoppers were forced to go elsewhere for their meat and produce. Among the new products making their debut were shredded wheat, malted milk, and a delicious concoction by druggist John L. Pemberton called Coca Cola.

In 1880 the work force was dominated by men. It was a commonplace belief that once a woman became employed she could no longer be considered a lady. The truly refined lady cared for her home and family, exercising her intellect and imagination in only such carefully defined areas as painting, dressmaking, and needlework. By the end of the decade the invention of the typewriter and adding machine allowed a few pioneering women to enter the business world, but only in a very minor capacity.

The bustle epitomized the fashions of the period: uncomfortable; impractical; and restrictive. The size of the bustle varied from year to year reaching its most outrageous proportions toward the middle of the decade. In true Victorian fashion, dark colors predominated, and the popularity of heavy fabrics such as brocade, velvet, and silk often gave ladies an appearance vaguely reminiscent of their favorite settee. Bodices were closely fitted and heavily boned; women on occasion had their clothes made a bit too small so that they would be properly confining and painfully chic.

Fashion design was dominated by Parisian couturiers who ruled as feudal lords. Since their clients were primarily ladies of leisure, there was no pressing need for designers to create clothing which allowed for freedom of movement. Nevertheless, the faintest hint of change was in the air as women slowly began to embrace a more active way of life; boating, tennis, riding, and even golf began to draw ladies out-of-doors. Since each activity required a totally different costume, women now sought to expand their wardrobes to include a variety of sporting attire.

The 1880's were a time of turbulence cloaked in the romantic mantle of a Strauss waltz. The formation of the American Federation of Labor gave hope to the working man, yet strikes, violence, and injustice continued for decades. Reform was begun in the civil service, but only after President Garfield was assassinated by a disappointed office seeker. The gun fight at the O.K. Corral and the Oklahoma land boom rang down the curtain on the great American frontier; it would be declared officially closed by the 1890 census. Progress, like a coquettish woman, often makes men pay dearly for her favors.

Like many young men of his day, 19 year old John Mohler Studebaker was lured West by the discovery of gold in California. After an arduous journey, Studebaker arrived in Hangtown in August 1853, with only 50ᶜ in his pocket. After deciding that prospecting was far from a sure thing, he accepted a job making wheelbarrows for Joe Hinds. Five years later, he returned to South Bend with $8,000 and bought his older brother Henry's interest in the struggling H and C Studebaker Wagon Factory. With his brother Clem doing the blacksmith work and J.M. doing the wood work, the business soon began to prosper.

In trying to sell one of the firm's wagons to a farmer, Henry Stull, J.M. met and fell in love with Mr. Stull's daughter Mary. They were married on Jan. 3, 1860 during an Indiana snowstorm.

FISH CHOWDER

The fish should be boiled in enough water to cover, and then cooled in the same water. Then the fish should be boned and broken in small bits with silver forks.

9 potatoes, peeled and diced
9 slices of bacon, diced and fried
1 large onion, sliced and fried in bacon grease
3 tomatoes
1 cup diced celery
1 large carrot
Enough fish to equal the rest of the ingredients
**   (boned and picked up)**
1 qt. sweet cream
Seasoning

Serve hot in soup bowls with crisp crackers or hot buttered toast.

Mrs. J.M. (Lillian) Studebaker III
From Mrs. J.M. (Mary Stull) Studebaker

COLESLAW

1 cup vinegar
Piece of butter the size of a walnut
1 egg
1 tsp. mustard
1 tsp. sugar
1 tsp. salt
1 tsp. flour
½ tsp pepper

Boil the vinegar and melt the butter in it. Pour over a mixture of the remaining ingredients; stir it well, then put it back on the stove to boil again about a minute. Pour the whole upon the chopped **cabbage.**

June Urbanski

OLD FASHIONED BEEF STOCK

5 lbs. beef knuckle
3 qts. cold water
1 medium onion
2 carrots, sliced
1 medium turnip, diced
½ tsp. whole black pepper
4 pieces celery, cut into ½-inch pieces
5 whole cloves
1 small bay leaf
3 sprigs parsley
1 Tbsp. salt

Have the beef knuckle cut into several pieces. Cut the meat from the bone and cut into cubes. Brown. Put the meat and bone in a soup kettle, add water and let stand for 1 hour. Bring to a boil. Skim the foam from the top and reduce heat to simmering.

Cook slowly 4-5 hours. (Add vegetables and seasoning during the last hour of cooking.) Strain the stock. Chill. Remove the layer of fat after the stock is chilled. Makes about 2 quarts.

Mrs. Walton (Carol) Collins

This is great way to use up mashed potatoes. These Potato Puffs are unusual - light and delicious. Use them as an interesting addition to breakfast, lunch, or supper.

AUNT TONY'S POTATO PUFFS

2 eggs
1 cup cold mashed potatoes
½ tsp. salt
1 tsp. baking powder
½ cup flour

Beat the eggs until light; add the potatoes. Sift the flour, baking powder, and salt; stir into the egg and potato mix. Drop from a spoon into deep hot fat and fry brown like doughnuts.

Mrs. Frederick C. (Lilla) Elbel

My husband's great grandmother made these buns as a young girl in Slovenia (Czechoslovakia). Later, in 1903, she brought the recipe to America. It is a tradition to serve this bun on Easter and Christmas along with turkey and ham for sandwiches. For my husband and our entire family, the holidays would not be the same without Krofi.

KROFI

4½-5 cups flour
½ cup milk
½ cup sugar
1 tsp. salt
½ cup margarine
½ cup warm water (105-115 degrees)
1 Tbsp. sugar
2 pkgs. dry yeast
2 eggs, beaten slightly

Sift 4 cups of the flour into a large bread bowl and set aside. Next, scald the ½ cup of milk. Stir in ½ cup sugar, salt and margarine. Cool until lukewarm.

Measure the warm water into a large warm bowl. Add 1 Tbsp. sugar. Stir the sugar and water mixture. Sprinkle in the yeast and stir until dissolved. Allow to sit 1 to 3 minutes until it begins to foam.

Add the yeast mixture to the milk mixture. Then add the slightly beaten eggs. Take the large bread bowl containing the flour and make a well in the middle of the flour. Add the yeast, milk, and egg mixture. Stir with a wooden spoon until a dough is formed.

Sprinkle flour on a kneading board. Knead the dough for 8-10 minutes. (Add flour until the dough is no longer sticky.)

Place in a greased bowl, turning to grease the top of the dough. Cover and let rise in a warm place until double in bulk.

Punch down and let rise again, until almost double in bulk.

Turn onto a floured surface. Roll to ½ inch thickness. Cut with a 3 inch round biscuit cutter. Cover with a towel and let rise another 15 minutes or until almost double thickness.

Fry the biscuits in shortening at 350 degrees for 1½ minutes or until golden brown. Turn often during frying.

Mrs. Kathy A. Rastetter
From her husband's
great-grandmother

Polish immigrants began to flock to the South Bend area in the 1870's and 80's. Drawn here by the need for work, the Poles soon found jobs in local industry: the Studebaker Brothers Manufacturing Company; James Oliver's South Bend Iron Works; and the Singer Manufacturing Company. (For a time, ¾ of Singer's sewing machine cabinets were made in South Bend.)

SWEET-SOUR CABBAGE

1 32-oz. pkg. kraut
3 Tbsp. bacon grease or lard
¼ cup white vinegar
⅔ cup sugar
1 tsp. salt
¼ tsp. pepper
2 cups water

Rinse the kraut with 3 quarts of water; drain in a strainer. Melt the grease in a covered cooking utensil (I use a frying pan). Add all the ingredients and stir well. Cover and simmer for 1 hour, stirring occasionally.

Mrs. Mary Fischer
From Mr. John Lawecki

Mrs. Cira can trace this recipe back to her Grandma DeCola. It has been a family favorite for as long as she can remember.

ITALIAN BREADED STEAK

1½ to 2 lbs. sirloin steak, ¼ of an inch thick*

BREADING:
2 cups fine bread crumbs
¼ cup Parmesan cheese, grated
Salt and pepper to taste
Clove of garlic, minced finely
2 Tbsp. chopped parsley, fresh or dried
    (fresh tastes better)

Cut the steak into serving pieces. Dip in oil (Wesson or olive), covering both sides of the meat. Press into the bread crumb mixture on both sides and lay in a pan (broiler pan covered with foil paper). Spray lightly with oil and put in an oven preheated at broiling temperature (about 4-6 inches away from the flame). Brown the meat on one side and then turn and brown again like you would broiled steak. Serve on a warm platter with **lemon wedges** that you use to squeeze on the steak.

*Sirloin steak is the best cut of meat for this recipe, but cubed round steak or T-Bone may also be used.

Mrs. Rose Cira

POTATO PAPRIKASH

2 lbs. potatoes, sliced lengthwise (approx. amount)
1 large onion, diced
1 Tbsp. paprika
2 Tbsp. oil, chicken fat, or lard
1 lb. smoked sausage, cut in circles
    (smoked ham or hot dogs may also be used)
Salt and pepper to taste

Dice the onions and saute in the fat till light brown. Add the paprika, salt, and pepper. (If desired, slices of tomato and green pepper may also be added.)

Add the potatoes, sausage, and enough water to barely cover the potatoes. Cover the skillet and cook until the potatoes are done.

Mrs. Andrew (Magda) Eperjesi

HAM OMELETTE

Remains of **boiled or fried ham** - cold, minced fine, and seasoned

2 or 3 eggs
1 cup milk
Flour to make a good batter - about 4 Tbsp.
2 Tbsp. butter
Chopped parsley
Pepper and salt

Heat the butter to a boil in a frying pan. Mix the eggs, milk, flour, parsley, pepper, and salt into a batter and pour it into the frying pan. As soon as it begins to "form," lay the minced meat in the middle. Fry rather slowly, taking care that the batter does not burn. When done on one side, fold the edges of the pancake over to the middle, enclosing the meat, and turn with a cake spatula. When both sides are of a delicated brown, put the cake "turner" under it and slip over to a hot dish. Send around a little gravy in a boat.

Mrs. Betty Hans
From the Ransom's family
Receipt Book from 1886

EGGS

In shaking an egg, if it makes a sound, it is not a good egg, and should be rejected. The water test consists in putting them in water deep enough to cover; the "good eggs" will lie flat at the bottom, while the "bad eggs" will stand upright, like many other unsound things in the world. The "candling" process consists in looking through the egg at a light, or holding it between you and the sun. If it shows up clear and spotless, so that the yolk can be perceived, it is good; otherwise it is not.

RECIPE FOR MAKING HENS LAY

Shell Indian corn, put it in a pot with some red pepper, (if you have no red the black will do) boil it till it is soft, feed the hens on it.

This recipe was brought to America in its basic form by my Scandinavian ancestors from a recipe originally prepared on top of and in a wood-burning stove. It has been updated for use on a gas or electric stove.

SWEDISH MEAT BALLS

2 large eggs, beaten
1 cup milk
½ cup finely crushed bread crumbs (dry)
1 Tbsp. butter
⅔ cup finely chopped onion
1 lb. ground beef (round steak)
½ lb. ground lean pork
1½ tsp. salt
⅛ tsp. cardamom
¼ tsp. allspice
¼ tsp. nutmeg
⅛ tsp. cloves
⅛ tsp. ginger (optional)
2 Tbsp. butter
3 Tbsp. plus 1 tsp. flour
½ tsp. monosodium glutamate
¼ tsp. freshly ground pepper
1 10½-oz. can beef broth
½ cup heavy cream

In a large bowl, mix together the eggs, milk, and bread crumbs. Heat in a large, heavy skillet over low heat 1 Tbsp. butter; then add the ⅔ cup chopped onion, cooking over medium heat until golden yellow and soft (stirring occasionally). Add the onions to the bread crumb mixture. Also add the beef, pork, salt, cardamom, allspice, nutmeg, cloves, and ginger (optional). Mix well. Place the meat mixture in the refrigerator until the meat can be shaped into balls.

Heat in the skillet 2 Tbsp. butter and saute the meatballs until browned. Remove the meatballs to a casserole or crock pot. Add 2 Tbsp. drippings in a skillet; then add the flour, ½ tsp. monosodium glutamate, and pepper. Heat until the mixture bubbles and the flour is slightly browned. Add the beef broth gradually, stirring constantly, until the mixture thickens slightly. Bring to a boil and add the cream. Pour the gravy over the meatballs in the casserole and bake for 30 minutes in a 325 degree oven, or cook in a crock pot on high heat for 15 minutes, then on low heat for another 10 minutes. Serve hot at the smorgasbord.

Makes about 3 doz. 1-inch balls, or 30 1½-inch balls.

Virginia Gilberg O'Hair
President, GFWC Progress
Club of South Bend

Banquet given in honor of the Golden Jubilee of the Ordination of The Very Reverend E. Sorin, C. S. C. Founder of the University of Notre Dame May 27th, 1888

E. Sorin c s c
Founder Notre Dame

Courtesy of the University of Notre Dame Archives.

TURTLE SOUP.

FISH, SAUCE TARTARE.

HORS D'OEUVRES VARIES.

ROAST SPRING CHICKEN.
PETITS POIS A LA FRANCAISE.

FILET DE BOEUF AUX CHAMPIGNONS.
POMMES DE TERRE PARISIENNE.

ASPERGES A LA CREME.

CHARLOTTE RUSSE.   ASSORTED CAKES.
VANILLA ICE CREAM.
STRAWBERRIES.   FRUITS.

CANDIES.   NUTS.

CAFE.

This is a speciality of our Family. It was brought to this country from our former home in Barbizon, France.

BREAST OF CHICKEN WITH SAUCE CHAMPIGNON

**Breasts of three 3-lb. chickens, freshly killed
Salt and pepper, freshly ground
8 oz. sweet cream butter
2 lbs. button mushrooms
1 tsp. shallots or onions, chopped very fine
1 pt. extra heavy sweet cream
2 oz. dry sherry**

1. Skin the chicken breasts and sprinkle with the salt and pepper. Place in a frying pan with 4 oz. of the butter and cook slowly until the chicken is golden brown (10 minutes on each side should do it). Remove the chicken from the pan and keep warm.
2. Use the same pan without washing it. Place in it the remaining 4 oz. of butter, the mushrooms, and the onions.
3. Cook for 10 minutes over a very high flame.
4. Lower the flame; add the sweet cream and sherry and let this sauce simmer until it thickens.
5. Place the breasts on a very hot platter. Pour the mushroom sauce over them and serve with wild rice. Makes 6 servings.

M. E. Parrott

1880 RECIPES

This dish is a reflection of the past glories of the old Ottoman Empire which covered vast stretches of Eastern Europe and the Middle East before it was dismantled following World War I. Dolma is an Arabic word which means "something stuffed." The Oxian family brought this particular recipe from their home in Armenia.

DOLMA

3 green peppers
3 firm tomatoes
3 medium squash (zucchini)
1½ lbs. ground lamb shoulder or ground chuck
½ cup rice
3 medium onions, chopped fine
½ cup parsley, chopped
½ cup dill, chopped
Salt and pepper, to taste

Wash all the vegetables. Scoop out the centers of the green pepper. Cut the squash in half and scoop out the centers. Do the same to the tomatoes, but add the pulp to the meat. Knead the meat with the rice, onions, parsley, salt, and pepper (to taste). Fill the hollows of the vegetables, not too full, with the meat mixture. Arrange side by side in a baking dish. Add a little water (start with about ¼ cup; add more later if needed), cover, and bake in a medium oven for 1½ hours.*
*(Ed: Bake in a 350 degree oven for 1-1½ hours.)

Mrs. Kayane Oxian

SPICE CAKE

1 cup sugar
½ cup shortening
1 egg
¾ cup sour milk
1½ cups flour (or more)
1 tsp. baking soda
¼ tsp. cloves
½ tsp. allspice
¼ tsp. nutmeg
½ tsp. cinnamon

Cream together the sugar and shortening. Mix the spices and baking soda with the flour. Add the flour mixture and the sour milk. Stir until thoroughly mixed. Bake in the oven.*
*(Ed: This makes a small 8-inch cake [2 layers]. Bake in a 350 degree oven for 25 minutes. Be sure your cake pans are well greased and floured. An 8-inch square baking dish would also work well.)

Mrs. Paul (Edna) Van Dusen
From her grandmother,
Mrs. Mary Ann Hooton Rodgers

The Daily Times.

FRIDAY, JUNE 12, 1885.

Ducks at Bert & Stover's.

Strawberry sherbet at E. Jonquet's.

Bananas and oranges at E. Jonquet's.

Chickens for Sunday at Bert & Stover's.

Old papers, very cheap, at THE TIMES office.

All kinds of poultry at Bert & Stover's.

To-day the streets received their weekly clean up.

Dressed chickens, for Sunday, at Bert & Stover's.

Go to Heller's for a smooth shave and a clean bath.

There are now seventeen prisoners in the county jail.

Apricots and peaches, three for 5 cents, at E. Jonquet's.

Imported jersey suits for boys at Moses Livingston's.

The choicest cuts in the market at Rockstroh Bros'.

Would it not be well to occasionally flush the sewers?

Pine-apple sherbet Saturday and Sunday at Jonquet's.

Hose Company No. 4 will picnic at Chain Lakes on Sunday.

All kinds of fresh, smoked and salt meats at Bert & Stover's.

Dodd's string band will play at No. 7's festival on Friday evening.

Heller's 115 North Michigan street, is the place to get a good bath.

Singing by the Hoosier quartette at No. 7's festival on Friday evening.

Butter only brings from six to eight cents in this market, and sells at ten.

Buggies and wagons at cost for this month at Joe Seafer's, E. Water street.

Old papers in any quantity and at exceedingly low prices at THE TIMES office.

For pure lake ice, leave orders at L. Nickel, jr., & Co.'s, or at Bert & Stover's.

The iron-work of the Rockstroh, Klingel and Vinson buildings arrived yesterday.

Mr. Will Reed, of the East Side, boasts over a new daughter since yesterday.

Leave orders for Beck & Son's ice at L. Nickel, jr., & Co.'s, or at Bert & Stover's.

Eugene Jonquet w terday, and while tl 400 pineapples, 50 bu and also apricots, p store.

Frank Johnson, w other day under su robbed the farmer, charged, as there w convict.

We are pleased to ments have been ma to Maxinkuckee Lal June for the benefi nies Nos. 1 and 6.

The new postal la out of newspapers year after year and t for the same, an offe same as any other th

To-morrow is sho mense crowd of peop The festive and inno ant will hold high lemonade accompani

A buggy agent ca terday to take in th expect to sell a doll made a sale twenty he thinks he has don the circumstances.

Dr. A. G. Miller tr tions of the lungs, tl and spleen, dyspepsia complaints, piles, &c. males and females opposite postoffice.

From present indica ral society will clear 500 on their spring that the one in whose entire management placed, certainly und

Invitations are out Isabella Hyatt, daugl R. D. Hyatt, and Ge Dr. Robert Harris, of emony will take place June 18, 1885, at tl 118, E. Wayne street

Boss Walters, sher ty, and Ed. Harter a Manchester, were in endeavoring to inte and others in a trotti Manchester, on July $1,000 and there are

One hundred man of elegant ready mad

(Published in South Bend)

GRANDMA'S FEATHER CAKE

¾ cup butter
1¼ cups sugar
4 egg yolks
½ cup water
2½ cups cake flour
2 tsp. baking powder
4 egg whites, beaten stiff
½ tsp. lemon extract
1 tsp. vanilla

Cream the butter and sugar. Add the egg yolks. Sift the flour; measure and sift 3 times with the baking powder. Add the flour and water alternately to the butter mixture. Add the lemon extract and vanilla. Fold in the beaten egg whites. Bake in a medium oven* in layers or a sheet. Test with a straw.

This cake was served plain, without frosting, but any favorite frosting may be used.

*(Ed: For a greased 13 x9-inch pan, bake in a 350 degree oven for 30 minutes.)

Mrs. Thomas E. (Louise) Bath

This very old recipe is from my grandmother who lived in Pennsylvania. It was my father's favorite pie. The cake or "sponge" rises to the top as it bakes.

GRANDMA KENDIG'S LEMON SPONGE PIE

1 lemon, pulp and juice
    (take out the seeds - use no rind)
1 cup sugar
2 egg yolks, well beaten
3 Tbsp. flour
¾ cup milk
1 Tbsp. melted butter, cooled
Stir together and then add:
2 egg whites, beaten stiff

Fold the egg whites in. Pour into an unbaked pie crust. Bake at 250 degrees for 45 minutes.

Mrs. John (Millie) Yoder
From her grandmother,
Mrs. Emily Strawbridge Kendig

With a family of 10 children, Mrs. Molloy's mother spent a great deal of her time in the kitchen. She, like many other clever housewives, had to find palatable alternatives to fresh fruits and vegetables. Since citrus fruits were generally unavailable in the Midwest during the 1880's, Mock Lemon Pie might often have appeared on the family dinner table.

MOCK LEMON PIE

Make and bake a good crust (Fills 1 8-inch pie shell)

1 cup sugar
2 Tbsp. vinegar
1 Tbsp. cornstarch
1 Tbsp. butter
Yolk of 1 egg
⅔ cup water (hot)
1 tsp. lemon extract

Cook until thick, stirring constantly. Add the flavoring. Pour into the shell.

MERINGUE:
2 egg whites
4 tsp. sugar

Beat the egg whites until stiff; add the sugar. Spread over the pie and put in the oven to brown slightly.

Mrs. John J. (Bonnie) Molloy, Jr.
From her mother,
Mrs. Mida Lee Massie and her grandmother,
Mrs. Woodward

ROLLED ALMOND WAFERS

¼ cup butter
½ cup confectioners sugar
⅞ cup bread flour
¼ cup milk
½ tsp. vanilla
Finely chopped almonds

Cream the butter. Add the sugar gradually, then the milk drop by drop. Add the flour and flavoring. Spread the mixture very thinly on a greased baking sheet. Sprinkle with almonds. Bake slowly.* Cut in 2-inch squares while in the oven by drawing the pan to the front. Turn each square upside down and roll into cylinders. This leaves the nuts on the outside. The cookies may be filled with whipped cream.

*(Ed: Bake in a 325 degree oven until lightly browned; watch carefully. The cookies can be rolled over the handle of a wooden spoon to give a cylindrical shape.)

Mrs. Frederick C. (Lilla) Elbel

GRANDMA'S ITALIAN "S" COOKIES

3 cups flour
1 cup sugar
1 cup shortening (I now use Butter Crisco)
2 eggs, beaten
3 tsp. baking powder
1 Tbsp. vanilla

Mix the ingredients well by hand. Pick up the dough, about the size of a walnut, and roll between the palms of your hands. Form into the shape of an "S". Place on a lightly greased sheet and bake in a 350 degree oven for 15 minutes.

When cool, ice with a thin glaze (spread it on with a brush) and sprinkle with colored sugar or colored sprinkles.

These cookies can be made ahead. If placed in cookie cans they will stay crisp and very good for weeks. Everyone enjoys them, children especially.

Mrs. Rose Cira

HOUSEHOLD HINTS

Shaking pepper, from a pepper- box, round the edge of the floor, under a carpet, prevents the access of moths.

Beef and mutton are improved by keeping as long as they remain sweet. If meat begins to taint, wash it, and rub it with powdered charcoal, which often removes the taint.

Never allow the cogs of a Dover eggbeater to be put in the dish pan. Wash the lower part carefully and dry before putting away. If the cogs are allowed to get wet, the grease will come off on the hands, and the beater will wear out in half the usual time.

For sleeplessness, eat a cracker or something to set the stomach at work and relieve the brain.

A simple remedy for neuralgia is to apply grated horseradish, prepared as for table use, to the temples when the face or head is affected or to the wrist when the pain is in the arm or shoulder.

To cure fever and ague, take equal parts of turpentine and laudanum, shake thoroughly, apply to the spine with a sponge or cloth beginning at the hair and pressing down the whole length. Use twice a day and just before the chill comes on, never known to fail.

A wash for teeth and gums may be made by taking the juice of half a lemon, a spoonful of claret or port wine, ten grains of sulphate of quinine, and a few drops of cologne water; mix well, and keep it in a closely stopped bottle for use.

To renovate black silk, wash in cold tea or coffee, with a little sugar in them. Put in a little ink if very rusty. Drain and do not wring, and iron on the wrong side.

Fold a newspaper across the chest and attach with safety pins under the cloak or coat when exposed for a long time in cold winds, as in sleighriding.

In a restaurant you may ask the usher to send a waiter to you if the service is slow or the attendant negligent, but not even in this public place does a well-bred man call out "waiter," and he who commits such a blunder beneath a private roof might as well hope for future canonization as for present social success.

Ladies of good taste seldom wear jewelry in the morning; and when they do, they confine themselves to trinkets of gold, or those in which opaque stones only are introduced. Ornaments with brilliant stones are unsuited for a morning costume.

Raising the dress when tripping over the pavement, a lady should raise her dress a little above her ankle. With the right hand, she should hold together the folds of her gown, and draw them towards the right side. To raise the dress on both sides, and with both hands, is vulgar. This ungraceful practice can only be tolerated for a moment, when the mud is very deep.

The most appropriate morning dress for a lady upon first rising is a small muslin cap and loose robe. It is not in good taste for a lady to appear at the table in the morning without being laced at all; it gives an air of untidiness to the whole appearance. The hair papers which cannot be removed on rising (because the hair would not keep in curl till evening), should be concealed under a bandeau of lace or of the hair. They should be removed as soon as may be.

When the chest is scientifically laced as tight as can be borne, it often causes the blood to rush to the face, neck, and arms, on taking exercise or remaining in a heated room. Young ladies at parties frequently become so suffused from this cause, that they present the appearance of a washer-woman actively engaged over a tub of hot suds. Tight lacing also causes an extreme heaving of the bosom, resembling the panting of a dying bird.

Nickel's was one of the best restaurants in early South Bend. The proprietor, Louis Nickel, was a believer in trust and integrity; there were no checks in his restaurant. When a customer had finished with his meal, he would walk up to the counter, tell Mr. Nickel what he had eaten, and wait while Mr. Nickel figured out what was owed.

SPICED CHERRIES

3-6 qts. tart cherries (3 qts. makes 12 cups cherries)

Pit and cover the cherries with **vinegar** in a large crock. Let stand overnight with a spice bag of **1 stick of cinnamon and 6-8 whole cloves.** The next day, drain off the vinegar and remove the spice bag. Measure the fruit, return to the crock, and add equal cups of **sugar.** Stir. Let stand for several days, stirring often, until the sugar is completely dissolved (this may be 3-5 days). Put in jars and seal.

This is delicious when served with many meats, especially veal.

Mrs. Louis N. (Janice) Rugee
From her husband's grandmother,
Mrs. Louis (Katherine Rockstroh) Nickel

Early cooks never wasted a thing. Even corn cobs could be used to make a tasty jelly. (It tastes like apple jelly, by the way.) Be sure to wait until the farmers have harvested the field corn, then go to the elevator and ask for clean corn cobs without any kernels. If you use the cobs from red corn, the jelly will have a nice color.

CORN COB JELLY

12 clean corn cobs
8 cups water
1 box Sure Jell*
3 cups sugar

Boil the corn cobs in water for 30 minutes. Strain. Measure 3 cups of the liquid, adding water if necessary. Add the Sure Jell and bring to a boil. Add the sugar and boil for 2-3 minutes. Seal in heated jars.

*(Ed: Before products such as Sure Jell were available, housewives had to depend on the natural pectin in fruit to make their jellies. One way to test for pectin is to combine 1 Tbsp. cooked fruit juice, 1 tsp. sugar, and ½ tsp. Epsom salts. Stir this mixture until the salts dissolve and allow to stand for about 20 minutes. If the juice contains sufficient pectin to make jelly, the mixture will form into a gelatinous mass or large flaky particles. If the fruit juice does not have sufficient pectin, use equal amounts of fruit juice and apple juice [which is naturally rich in pectin].)

Miss Janet Apelgreen

L. Nickel, Jr. & Co.'s Restaurant
South Bend, Indiana

Mrs.
Maude
Perley
Coquillard

1890's

*This unique Parisian gown
has a jacket of apple green,
pink and mauve moire silk
flocked in black, with leg-of-mutton
sleeves. Large apple green satin lapels
are embroidered with tiny flowers and
rhinestones. The skirt of deep olive
green satin is trimmed in ropes of
jet beading and sequins.
This was worn by
Maude Perley Coquillard,
whose husband, Alexis,
was a wagon maker
and nephew of
Alexis Coquillard,
co-founder of
South Bend.
Circa 1898.*

ONLY A BIRD IN A GILDED AGE

In 1893 the city of Chicago was transforming the marshlands along the Lake Michigan shore into an enchanted land, the great "White City" of the World Columbian Exposition. Although the nation was in the grip of one of the worst depressions in its history, the plaster of Paris walls continued to rise, temporary monuments to American progress and technology. Visitors to the Fair that year probably saw Columbus' discovery of the New World as no more wonderous than their own exploration of the "future world" -- a dazzling display of mechanical wizardry and electrified miracles.

These modern conveniences, such as automatic dish washers and electric stoves, might be breath-taking to see, but they were too expensive and unreliable for most people. Man was still cheaper than machine. "Gracious living" was society's battle cry, and a staff of at least 5 to 10 servants was generally required to assure one's ascendancy to a fashionable level of idle opulence.

Even in this time of financial hardship, entertaining was done on a lavish scale. Grand dinner parties were an especially popular way of making people aware of one's rising social status. Guests were expected to arrive promptly at 8, a very chic hour to dine.

Keeping in mind that anyone serving more than 10 courses would be accused of putting on airs, the hostess would probably begin the meal with oysters on the half shell. In rapid succession, guests would be plied with soup, fish, a meat course, and several different vegetables, cooked to the point of total disintegration. Sherbet would then be served to cleanse the palate and give the stomach a breather before the intrepid diner was confronted with a roast of either poultry or game (a totally ruthless hostess would serve both). Dessert, fruit, and finger bowls were a proper finale, followed by coffee. At this point the gentlemen would retire for cognac and cigars, and soon all the guests would be sent lurching home, firm in the knowledge that they had truly partaken of the "good life."

As advertising techniques improved, so did the public's awareness of brand-name merchandise. When Campbell's developed a formula for condensed soup, they cleverly packaged their product in eye-catching red and white labels. A cereal empire was founded when Charles W. Post began marketing Grape Nuts in 1898, and the National Biscuit Co. asked ladies to buy only those soda crackers labeled, "Uneeda Biscuit." The names Quaker, Hershey, and Borden soon became as familiar to shoppers as Heinz and his "57 Varieties."

A semblance of order was beginning to creep into kitchens across the country. Fannie Merritt Farmer made history when she published *The Boston Cooking School Cook Book* in 1896. Her advocacy of standardized measuring cups and spoons took recipes from pinches and dabs to the precise measurement of ingredients and won her the undying gratitude of generations of women. On a different front, a triumph of kitchen organization was introduced by the Hoosier Manufacturing Co. Their free-standing kitchen cabinets offered ladies the priceless luxury of storage space and began the evolutionary movement toward the modern kitchen.

Although the automobile was invented in the 1890's, it was a vehicle with 2 wheels, not 4 which won the hearts of America. The bicycle gave women a taste of freedom, and like Eve and the apple, once tasted, things would never be the same again. Young ladies could now go riding off into the country with their favorite beaus, free from the noise of the city and the supervision of anxious parents. Floor length skirts made cycling difficult, so hem lines gradually crept upwards, offering gentlemen a tantalizing glimpse of well-shaped ankles. A few adventurous ladies discarded their skirts completely and happily pedalled away in provocative bloomer costumes. By 1892, people were so smitten with cycling that everyone was lustily singing about the flirtatious Daisy and a "Bicycle Built for Two."

By the early 1890's, the emphasis in fashion had changed from the back of the skirt to the bodice. Women traded in their bustles for gored skirts which fit closely at the hips and then flared out toward the floor, giving the appearance of a bell or morning glory. To balance these skirts, lapels widened and sleeves grew larger, culminating in the popular "leg-of-mutton" style. In order to accentuate this hour-glass silhouette, waists continued to be tightly corseted.

In 1898, amid the echoes of "Remember the Maine," Americans were swept into a war with Spain. In a conflict which was over almost before it began, the United States proved herself to be a growing military and industrial power, ready to interest herself in world affairs. When the guns had been stilled, Cuba, Puerto Rico, Guam, and the Philippine Islands found themselves under the protection of the "Stars and Stripes." With flags unfurled in a cloudless sky and a Sousa march ringing in her ears, America was marching boldly forward into a new century.

1890 RECIPES

The children in my family always looked forward to Grandmother's Fruit Soup. This was a wonderful treat during the holiday season and added a festive touch to many special occasions.

SWEDISH FRUIT SOUP
(Fruktsoppa)

1 cup prunes
½ cup raisins
½ cup currants
½ cup dried apples
2 qts. cold water

Cover and let soak overnight. In the morning add:
Juice of ½ lemon
1 small stick of cinnamon
Cook, covered, over low heat for 1 hour. Add:
½ cup dark corn syrup (or ½ cup sugar)
Cook 30 minutes longer.
This can be served warm or chilled. Serves 12 (¾ cup per serving).

Mrs. Tony (Edith) Mathia
From her grandmother

TO WASH CORSETS
Choose a clear, sunny day; make a strong solution of good soapsuds and a small amount of ammonia, spread the corsets on a clean board or table and scrub with a good stiff brush until thoroughly clean. Apply clear water in the same way to rinse them and hang immediately in the sun. Do not wring out. Let them drip dry, and the shape will not be changed.

This endive recipe was given to my mom by a mid-wife, Mrs. Schank, who helped the doctor deliver us kids. When a baby was born, she would stay with my mom and cook and take care of her for a week or so. Endive salad is a Pennsylvania Dutch recipe and was always served with Pot Pie.

DRESSING FOR ENDIVE

1 large head or bunch of endive, washed and drained well.

About **4-5 slices of bacon** cut in small pieces and fried. Enough **flour** in drippings to make a paste. Add about **1 Tbsp. of sugar,** along with **vinegar** and **water** (about ½ cup each) to the paste -- use your own judgment. If the paste needs to be thinned, use a little more vinegar or water to taste.
Cut a fresh **large onion** and put on the drained endive which has been placed in a large bowl. Cook **2 fresh potatoes** which have been chunked and peeled.
Add the cooked cold potato to the endive-onion mixture. Just before you are ready to serve, pour the warm dressing over the endive. Toss and serve.

Mrs. Thomas (Jean) Gast

This old recipe comes from the Keller family which settled here, in German Township, around 1835. It makes a large bowl of potato salad, full of bacon and just a bit sweet.

GERMAN POTATO SALAD

Boil **potatoes** in the jackets; when done, drain and allow to dry in the pan. Let sit ½ hour. Peel and slice and let sit another ½ hour. Layer the potatoes with the dressing and serve while warm. (Onions, sliced very thin, optional).

DRESSING:
1 lb. bacon, cut up and fried out. Add **2 Tbsp. flour** and cook 3 minutes. Add **½ cup vinegar, ½ cup sugar, ½ cup water.** Stir and serve immediately.*
*(Ed: After the bacon is fried out, you may wish to drain off some of the fat. Also, the quantity of potatoes used is left up to the cook; 15-20 medium to small potatoes does make a nice size bowl, however.)

Mrs. George E. (Marjorie) Keller

SPOON BREAD

1 cup white cornmeal
2 cups boiling water
2 cups milk
1 tsp. salt
1½ tsp. baking powder
2 eggs, beaten
1 Tbsp. melted butter

Scald the cornmeal with boiling water, stirring constantly to keep from getting lumps. Add the milk, salt, and beaten eggs. Beat well. Add the melted butter and the baking powder. Pour into a greased 2 qt. baking dish (I prefer an oblong Pyrex casserole). Bake uncovered at 350 degrees for approximately 1 hour, or until set.

Mrs. Ronald (Nancy) Eversole

POTATO BALLS

One pint of hot mashed potatoes, seasoned with **salt, pepper, celery salt,** chopped **parsley** and **butter.** Moisten if needed with a little **hot milk or cream.** Beat **1 egg** lightly and add part of it to the potatoes. Shape into smooth round balls. Brush over with the remainder of the egg and bake on a buttered tin until brown. (Be careful not to get them too moist.)*
*(Ed: When tested, 2 Tbsp. of milk was used to 1 pt. of potatoes. Bake in a 375 degree oven until brown. For a little added flavor try sprinkling the balls with nutmeg. Serves 2 to 3 persons.)

Edith Studebaker

When this photo was taken in 1891, Sindlinger's Meat Market had already begun to establish itself as one of the finest butcher shops in the area. Frank Sindlinger, Sr., wearing a white apron, stands behind the counter on the right of the picture. Courtesy of Mr. Frank Sindlinger.

DATE BREAD

1½ cups of chopped dates, sprinkle with **1 tsp. soda.** Pour over this **¾ cup of boiling water.** Cool.

Beat **1 egg yolk,** add **¾ cup light brown sugar, 1 tsp. salt** and **1 tsp. vanilla.**

Combine with the date mixture. **Add 1½ cups flour** and **1 beaten egg white.**

Sprinkle with **1 tsp. baking powder** and add **¾ cup of walnuts.**

Bake in a moderate oven ¾ to 1 hour, depending on the size of the pan used. (Two medium loaf pans are satisfactory.) Test with a toothpick for dryness before taking out of the oven.*

*(Ed: When tested, the date bread was baked in a 350 degree oven for 35 minutes; it made 1 loaf.)

Mr. David P. McLellan
From his grandmother,
Mrs. Anne Pease McLellan

This recipe is to my knowledge four generations old. In those days, we used our own canned tomatoes. Today, by using store bought canned tomato sauce, it's much easier and faster to prepare.

STUFFED ITALIAN FLANK STEAK

1 flank steak, 1½-2 lbs. (Have the butcher score it.)
1 clove garlic, minced
2 cups fine bread crumbs
¼ cup grated Parmesan cheese
½ tsp. salt
Pepper to taste
2 Tbsp. fresh parsley, cut

1 onion, cut thin
2 small stalks celery, cut thin
Saute the onion and celery in a little oil.

Pour the onion and celery over the above ingredients (except the steak). Mix well. The stuffing should be moist; if not, add more oil.

Spread the filling onto the steak. Roll up like a jelly roll and tie with string. Brown in oil on all sides. Set aside while preparing the sauce.

SAUCE:
1 large can (15 oz.) **tomato sauce**
1 large can Hunts crushed tomatoes
1 small can (6 oz.) **tomato paste**
2 cans of water (I measure it in the tomato paste can.)
1 onion, chopped
2 cloves garlic
2 Tbsp. sugar
Salt and pepper to taste

Saute the onion and garlic in a little oil. Add the sugar, tomatoes, tomato paste and sauce, water, salt and pepper. Let this come to a boil and add the meat roll. Lower the heat to simmer and cook until the meat forks done, stirring occasionally.

1 lb. linguini
When the meat is done, cook the linguini according to package directions; drain.

To serve, place the linguini on a platter and cover with the sauce. Sprinkle with **Parmesan cheese.** Slice the meat roll and place the slices on the linguini. Decorate with parsley and serve. Serves 4-6.

This is very good! I hope you will like it; we all do.

Mrs. Rose Cira

TO CLEAN THE TEETH

Castile Soap and Cigar Ashes applied with a soft rag is one of the best tooth preparations known.

GRANDMOTHER STUDEBAKER'S VIRGINIA HAM

1 Virginia ham*
2 Tbsp. ground allspice (heaping)
2 Tbsp. cinnamon (heaping)
1½ cups ground coffee
2 cups sugar
1 cup vinegar
2 cups molasses

Cover the ham with water and add all the ingredients. Boil until done (20 minutes to 1 lb.). Skin the ham. Mix **1 cup brown sugar** and **1 Tbsp. mustard.** Cover the ham and stick with **cloves.** Bake for 1 hour.

*(Ed: A Viriginia ham has been heavily cured and smoked, but is uncooked. Midwesterners will probably have to go out of their way to obtain one today.)

Mrs J.M. (Lillian) Studebaker III
From Mrs. J.M. Studebaker

The dining room of the J.M. Studebaker residence, Sunnyside, was photographed by Charles Grant Davis in the early 1890's.

In the 1890's, John M. Studebaker's home, Sunnyside, was a city showplace. Built in 1881, this rambling brick home dominated the Studebaker farm, which lay east of the St. Joseph River on the outskirts of South Bend (on what is today East Jefferson Blvd.). Unfortunately, this lovely home, like so many other fine, old houses, is no longer standing.

SWEDISH MEATBALLS
(Kotteullar)

1 lb. ground round steak
½ lb. ground pork
1½ tsp. salt
⅛ tsp. pepper
¼ tsp. nutmeg
A few grains ginger (optional)
1 tsp. sugar
Mix together.
1 medium potato, cooked
½ cup dry bread crumbs
1 egg yolk
¼ cup hot milk
⅓ cup flour
1 cup milk
2 Tbsp. butter

Mash the cooked potato through a sieve. Add the bread crumbs, egg yolk, and hot milk. Add to the meat mixture and mix well.

Shape into small balls and roll in flour. Melt the butter in a skillet; add the balls and fry until brown. Place in a covered pan and bake in a moderate oven (350 degrees) for 15 minutes. Add 1 cup milk and bake 5 minutes longer.

Mrs. Tony (Edith) Mathia
From her grandmother

WHITE BEAN PLAKI
(Lupia Plaki)

1 cup dried large white beans (Great Northern), soak
    if necessary
4 cups water, approximately
Salt to taste
2 medium carrots, diced
½ cup diced green pepper
1 medium stalk celery, diced
2 medium cloves garlic, finely chopped
6 Tbsp. finely chopped parsley
2 medium tomatoes, chopped (or ½ cup tomato sauce)
Freshly ground black pepper or cayenne to taste
⅓ cup olive oil or sunflower oil
1 lemon sliced (NOT the rind)

In a heavy saucepan, combine the beans and the water. Cook over moderate heat for 15 minutes.

Add the salt, carrots, green pepper, celery, garlic, parsley, tomatoes, pepper, and lemon. Cover and cook 30 minutes. Add the olive oil and cook 20 minutes, or until the vegetables are tender, adding more water if necessary. Serve.

Mrs. Mannig Oxian

This Pot Pie recipe is very old. My grandmother made it, and my mother was the only one in her family (4 girls and 1 boy) who could make it; she was proud of that. She taught me the Pot Pie recipe, and now I'm the only one in my family who makes it.

My father's mother also made Pot Pie, but they were even poorer than my mother's family. They called it ''Poor Man's Pot Pie'' because there was no egg used. (I've made it that way and it's not quite as good.)

POT PIE

2½ cups flour
½ tsp. salt
1 egg, beaten
½ cup water
4 large Tbsp. shortening

Mix the flour, shortening, and salt together (as you do in making pie crust). Add the egg, slightly beaten, and the water. Sprinkle flour on a table or board and rub a rolling pin with flour. Roll the dough very thin (I separate the dough into two parts to roll it) and cut into squares. Drop piece by piece into boiling **broth.** Stir carefully as it's cooking. Let cook about 20 minutes. (Broth is stock from a big soup bone and short ribs. Stock from ham or chicken may be used as well, but beef broth is best).

Mrs. Thomas (Jean) Gast
From her grandmother,
Mrs. Gertrude Wills

A round or oblong dining table is the best, as it can be more readily arranged and decorated than a square one.

In laying the table, allow at least two feet of space for each person; a little more if possible.

Footstools placed under the table will prove a source of great comfort at meal time.

SAUCE ALMONDINE

¼ lb. butter
¼ cup slivered almonds
Juice of ½ lemon
2 lbs. vegetables

1. Render butter in a skillet and brown until dark, but not black.

2. Fry finely slivered almonds in the butter. Add the juice of ½ lemon to the butter.

3. Boil the vegetables in slightly salted water until soft but not too soft (about 20 minutes depending on their thickness).

4. Drain the vegetables. Lay on a flat, hot platter and pour the brown butter over the vegetables. Sprinkle with almonds. Salt very lightly.

M.E. Parrott

1890 RECIPES

Whenever Mrs. Purucker wanted to prepare a very special family dinner, she'd serve her Filled Noodles, wilted lettuce salad, and a sponge cake. It's true that this recipe is time consuming, but you can taste the love in every bite.

FILLED NOODLES

Make a rich beef broth from **2-3 large soup bones** (with some meat on them). Strain and set broth aside.

FILLING:
1½ lbs. ground beef (You may add to this the meat from the soup bones, finely chopped.)
4 heaping cups white bread (2 days old), diced in ½-inch cubes
1 tsp. salt
¼ tsp. pepper
½ tsp. freshly grated nutmeg
3 Tbsp. minced parsley
3 Tbsp. celery leaves, finely cut
1 Tbsp. chives, finely cut
1 small onion, minced
3 well-beaten eggs
¼ cup milk

Mix together thoroughly in a large bowl. The mixture should be light and separated (not stuck together as in a meat loaf). Set aside.

NOODLE DOUGH:
4 eggs, slightly beaten
1 tsp. salt
1 Tbsp. water per egg
3 cups flour

Mix the noodle ingredients. Work in extra flour, if needed, until the dough can be rolled out.

Take ⅓ of the dough and roll into a rectangle (not quite as thin as for noodles). Spread ⅓ of the filling over the noodle dough. Fold the long edge of the dough over about 1 inch, then fold again so that the edges meet at the center. Finally, fold one half over the other to form a roll. Divide the roll into 4-inch sections and cut with a knife. Press the edges together to seal. Repeat with the remaining dough and filling. Cover the noodles with a towel and let dry for 1 hour.

About half an hour before serving, heat the broth to boiling. Put 3-4 noodles into the broth (depending on the size of the kettle -- do not crowd) and boil for approximately 20 minutes. (Cut 1 large noodle in half to make sure that the noodle dough is cooked firm in the center; if not, continue cooking for 5 minutes or until done.)

Serve in a soup bowl. Ladle some of the extra broth over the noodle.

Mrs. Ervin (Bertha) Purucker
From her mother,
Mrs. Andrew (Louise) Armbruster

THE USES OF THE CHAFING DISH

Oh, I am a festive chafing dish,
  I foam, and froth, and bubble.
I sing the song of meat and fish,
  And save a deal of trouble.
In kitchen realm and dining hall.
  The housewife now is able,
When I respond unto her call,
  To cook dinner on the table.

Oh, I am a festive chafing dish,
  Comely, quaint and cosy,
In Circles rather revel-ish,
  My mission somewhat rosy.
I'm ever ready at command
  To do the best of cooking,
Am always sure to be on hand,
  And, best of all, good looking.

Entertaining played an important part in the life of Mrs. George M. Studebaker. As the daughter-in-law of Clement, one of the 5 brothers who founded the Studebaker Corporation, she commanded a place of social prominence in the community. Like many other sophisticated hostesses of her day, Mrs. Studebaker knew how to use a chafing dish. With it, she could serve her family or friends an elegant meal quickly and easily (even on the cook's night off).

LOBSTER A LA NEWBURG

One lobster*, 1 cup sweet cream, 1 large Tbsp. butter, 1 saltspoon salt, dash of cayenne pepper, ½ glass sherry, yolk of 1 egg, 1 tsp. flour. To prepare in a chafing dish, do not cook directly over the flame, but use the hot water pan. Melt the butter, then add the seasoning and cream. When very hot, put in the lobster, stirring gently. When almost to a boiling point, turn in the sherry. After that is mixed, add the flour which has previously been smoothed with cream. The last thing, add the egg, stirring continuously and serve.

*(Ed: 1 lobster is equal to about 1½ lbs. of lobster meat. Since people seasoned their food differently around the turn of the century, adjust the salt, pepper, and sherry to your own taste before serving.)

Mrs. George M. (Ada) Studebaker

People who give dinners — Thanksgiving or otherwise -- may be glad to have the following authoritative dicta in regard to the correct serving of wines:

Sauterne with the oysters.
Sherry with the Soup.
Rhine wine with the fish.
Champagne with the entrees and roast.
Madeira with the vegetables.
Burgundy with the game.
Port with the sweets.
Cognac and liqueurs after the coffee.
Sauterne is served in light green glasses.
Sherry, claret, champagne, Madeira, Burgundy and port in white glasses.
Rhine wine in red glasses.
Cognac and liqueurs in small white glasses.
Sauterne, Rhine wine, champagne, are served in the bottle.
Sherry, claret, Madeira and port in decanters.
Burgundy in bottle laid in wicker basket.

The Ladies' Standard Magazine, November, 1894.

PEACH SHORT CAKE

Three eggs, the yolks beaten with **1 cup of pulverized sugar,** and **2 Tbsp. of sweet milk.** Beat the whites to a froth, then thoroughly mix with the yolks and sugar. Mix **1 heaping tsp. of baking powder** with **1 cup of flour** and mix lightly with the other ingredients. Bake immediately in 2 layer tins in a moderately hot oven.* When cool, put together with **peaches,** slightly mashed and sweetened, and **1 pint of whipped cream,** sweetened and **flavored with almond.** Put a thick layer of peaches and cream on top. (Canned peaches are just as good as fresh ones.)

*(Ed: Be sure to grease the baking pans. Bake in a 375 degree oven for about 12-15 minutes, or until the cake tests done.)

Mabelle Hartfield

NUT PIE

1 cup powdered sugar
1 large cup dates, sliced
2 Tbsp. flour
1 large cup quartered walnuts
2 eggs
1 tsp. baking powder

Mix the flour, baking powder, dates, and nuts. Beat the whites and yolks of eggs separately. Add the sugar first, then the beaten yolks, then whites, then add flour, etc. Put in a well buttered pan and bake one-half hour.* To be eaten with **whipped cream.** This is better the second day.
*(Ed: Bake in a 325 degree oven for about 30-35 minutes.)

Harriet Oliver

MAPLE FROSTING

1¾ cups pure maple syrup

Boil the syrup to 240 degrees using a candy thermometer. Pour over **4 stiffly beaten egg whites** and beat until the frosting is the right consistency to spread.

Mrs. John (Jane) Olcott

Lena Armbruster was the cook for the J.M. Studebaker household for 16 years, until her death in 1898. Of all the recipes she must have known, this is the only one which can be directly attributed to her. This delicious yellow cake makes 3 large 9-inch layers.

AUNT LENA'S CAKE

Cream together **2 cups granulated sugar** with **1 cup butter, 4 well beaten eggs, 1 cup sweet milk, 3 tsp. baking powder** sifted 3 times with **3 cups of flour.** Add the milk and flour alternately. **1 tsp. vanilla.**
(Ed: Bake at 350 degrees for 25 minutes.)

Miss Lena Armbruster

1890 RECIPES

In days past, wedding guest were invited to take home little individual boxes of wedding cake. Since the bride's cake was too delicate to be transported easily, these white beribboned boxes contained slices of dark, fruit-rich groom's cake. Supposedly, if a young woman slept with a box of wedding cake under her pillow, she would dream of her future husband.

This cake has been in Mrs. Miller's family for almost 100 years. Today, this recipe is used for the marriage of each grandchild.

MRS. CASPER'S GROOMSCAKE

2¼ lbs. butter
3 lbs. dark brown sugar
3 cups buttermilk
15 eggs, separated
6 lbs. seedless raisins
6 lbs. currants
4 lbs. dates, cut fine
1½ lbs. citron
1½ lbs. candied pineapple
1½ lbs. candied cherries
1½ cups brandy
3 tsp. soda
3 tsp. cinnamon
3 tsp. nutmeg
3 tsp. allspice
3 lbs. white flour, sifted

Cream the butter; add the sugar and egg yolks. Mix in the flour, spices, and fruit. The stiffly beaten egg whites are last. Bake in a springform pan. Put a pan of water under the cake and bake in a 350 degree oven. Bake for 2 hours. Cover with brown paper and bake for 4 hours. Remove the water and bake 1 hour more.

Mrs. Robert C. Miller
From her mother

A variation of the simple pancake can be found in the culinary history of most countries; Hungary's contribution to good eating is the dessert, Palacsinta. With every bite, one is reminded of the grandeur and elegance of the old Austro-Hungarian Empire.

PALACSINTA

2 cups flour
1 Tbsp. sugar (heaping)
3 cups milk
4 eggs
Pinch of salt

Combine the flour, sugar, eggs, salt, and 1 cup of milk, stirring until smooth. Gradually add the rest of the milk. (It's best to use a whisk to make the batter creamy.)

Put a teaspoon (or less) of oil into a small skillet before you pour in the batter; repeat this each time you add batter to the skillet. Tip the hot skillet with a rotary motion to spread the batter evenly (make paper thin). Brown the palacsinta lightly on both sides (it only takes a few minutes on each side). Remember to stir the batter before making another palacsinta.

Spread one of the fillings on each palacsinta and roll up. Serve plain or topped with a favorite sauce.

FILING VARIATIONS:
1. JAM FILLING
   Spread each palacsinta with your favorite **jam** and serve warm.
2. WALNUT FILLING
   2 heaping Tbsp. finely ground walnuts
   4-5 heaping Tbsp. sugar
   Mix the nuts and sugar together.
3. COCOA FILLING
   1 heaping tsp. cocoa
   5 heaping Tbsp. sugar
   Mix together.
4. COTTAGE CHEESE FILLING
   2 cups cottage cheese
   1 egg yolk
   2 Tbsp. sugar
   ½ cup sour cream
   ½ cup raisins (optional)
   Mix together.

Mrs. Andrew (Magda) Eperjesi

TO PRESERVE A WIFE

Select one "who looks well to household ways," and after you have bestowed "all of your worldly goods" upon her, give her a share of your daily earning; remember, that she is just as anxious to get rich as you are. Cultivate the art of listening without impatience, and also of smiling at a twice-told tale or joke. Don't lose your temper if she does not get sleepy the same moment you do. Don't expect her to get up and build the fires in the morning. Tell her quite often that she makes better bread and pies than your mother ever did. Assure her that she is ever young and fair to you, and you will be "happy forever after."

Thomas S. Stanfield came to the St. Joseph Valley with his parents in the spring of 1831. After studying law, he became active in politics and served in the legislature. In 1852, at the age of 36, he was chosen Judge of the Circuit Court. Twice a year he covered his circuit of 11 counties in a horse and buggy. He continued to be active in the community until his death in 1885.

His granddaughter, Nelly, combined recipe book and diary in a note book dated June, 1896. On the back of the recipe for The Queen of Puddings were the comments, "Early this morning we intended to go walking, but on account of Tom's [Nelly's brother, Thomas E. Stanfield] getting hurt we had to stay at home. I went up to Grandma's, came home, helped make cake and get dinner. At two we went to our writing lesson and then went to see the new steamboat."

THE QUEEN OF PUDDINGS

1½ cups white pulverized sugar
1 Tbsp. butter
5 eggs, separated
2 cups of fine dry bread crumbs
1 qt. fresh rich milk
Flavor with lemon, vanilla, or rosewater
Jelly or fruit

Rub the butter into the sugar and then beat together with the egg yolks which have been beaten light. Then, put in the breadcrumbs which have been soaked in the quart of milk. Flavor to suit the taste. Bake in a buttered pudding dish.* After the custard has set, take it out of the oven and spread with **jelly or fruit** (fresh or preserved). Cover this with a meringue made of the **5 whipped egg whites** and **½ cup of sugar.** Shut the oven and bake until the meringue begins to color.

*(Ed: Bake in a 350 degree oven for about 1 hour, or until a knife comes out clean when inserted into the center of the pudding. Lower the temperature to 325 degrees and bake another 10-15 minutes for the meringue. The tartness of cherry pie filling is very good when spread between the pudding and meringue.)

Miss Mary M. Post
From her mother,
Mrs. C.F. (Nelly Peebles Stanfield) Post

Mother brought this recipe with her when she was married in 1897.

OLD FASHIONED STEAMED PUDDING

1 cup beef suet, cut fine
1 cup molasses
1 cup buttermilk
¼ tsp. cinnamon
½ tsp. salt
1 tsp. soda
3 cups flour, sifted then measured
1 cup raisins

Mix the ingredients and put into a round pan. Set over boiling water in a steamer for 1 hour. Be careful that the pan does not boil dry. When done, set back and prepare the topping.

TOPPING:
1 cup brown sugar
Butter the size of a walnut
3 cups water

Let heat. Thicken with **3 Tbsp. corn starch.** Eat hot over the pudding. It can be rewarmed.

Mary Haag

These cookies are a form of lebkucken (a spice cake or cookie which generally includes some form of candied fruit). They have always been served in our home during the Christmas season. Be sure to keep them in a tightly covered metal container to allow the flavors to blend.

BROWN COOKIES

Beat **5 whole eggs** with ½ **lb. pulverized sugar** to a foamy mixture. Add ¼ **lb. chopped almonds** and ⅛ **lb. finely cut citron,** also the **finely cut peel of ½ lemon** and a **½ tsp. cinnamon** and a **dash of cloves.**
Sift the spices and ½ **lb. flour** with a **tsp. (1) of baking powder.**
Drop with a teaspoon onto a greased cookie sheet. Sprinkle with colored sugar.
NOTE: Warm the eggs before you try to beat them--at least to room temperature, or they will not beat well. Beat the eggs until very thick, almost to the point of forming soft peaks.
Be sure to chop the citron and lemon peel into small pieces [1/16-⅛ inch]. Also, be sure to use only the yellow part of the lemon peel. The almonds should be very finely chopped, as well.
Bake in 350 degree oven for about 15 minutes.

Mrs. Ervin (Bertha) Purucker
From her mother,
Mrs. Andrew (Louise) Armbruster

1890 RECIPES

Date Pudding is an old family recipe used at Christmas time. You can make it a week ahead and keep it in the refrigerator.

DATE PUDDING

1 cup chopped dates
1 cup boiling water
Pour boiling water over the dates. Fix this first and let stand.

1 cup sugar
1 Tbsp. butter
1 egg, beaten
1 tsp. vanilla
Cream the butter and sugar. Add the well beaten egg and vanilla; mix well.
Add the date mixture and **½ cup chopped nuts.**

1½ cup flour
1 heaping tsp. baking powder
¼ tsp. salt
Add the flour, baking powder and salt, sifted together. Then add:
1 level Tbsp. baking soda dissolved in
¼ cup boiling water

Bake at 375 degrees in a 9 x 13-inch pan for 45 minutes or until done. Serve with **whipped cream.** Serves 12-15.

Mrs. Glenn A. (Maxine) Mann

DATE PIN WHEELS

2¾ cups cut-up dates
1 cup sugar
1 cup water
1 cup chopped nuts (optional)
Boil until soft.

1 cup shortening
1 cup light brown sugar
3 eggs, well beaten
4 cups flour
½ tsp. salt
½ tsp. soda

Chill thoroughly after mixing ingredients together. (If eggs are small use less flour, usually about 3 cups.)
Divide the dough into two parts. Roll each into a rectangle about ¼ inch thick. Spread each with the date filling and roll as if for a jelly roll. Chill overnight in the ice box. Cut into slices with a sharp knife. Bake in a moderate oven till brown.*
*(Ed: Bake in a 350 degree oven for about 10-15 minutes, or until lightly brown).

Mr. David P. McLellan
From his grandmother,
Mrs. Anne Pease McLellan

SPRINGERLE

4 large eggs
Powdered sugar (1 pound)
Flour (1 pound)
Butter (size of walnut)
Baking powder (½ tsp.)
Anise seed

Beat the eggs until very light; then beat in sugar. Add the softened butter and anise seed. Sift the flour and baking powder. Add to the egg mixture. Retain some of the flour to use on the board when rolling dough. Roll dough about ⅜ inch thick; use a springerle board and cut out cookies. Lay the cookies on a cloth (on an ironing board) to dry overnight. Bake in a 350 degree oven for about 10 or 12 minutes until delicately brown. Keep in an air tight container; place a piece of bread in the container to help keep the cookies from drying out.

NOTE: Butter- about 1½ Tbsp.
Anise seed - about 1 heaping tsp.

(When rolling out the cookies, be sure that your dough isn't rolled too thin. Be sure that the springerle board is floured, then press the board onto the dough. Remove the board and a clear imprint should be visible in the dough (about ¼ inch thick). Use a knife to cut around the imprints and lift the cookies onto the cloth to dry.
Be sure that you have enough flour in your dough or you will have trouble rolling it out, and the board will not leave a clear imprint.)

Mrs. Ervin (Bertha) Purucker
From her mother,
Mrs. Andrew (Louise) Armbruster

Those Deadly Pies.

I loathe, abhor, detest, despise,
Abominable dried apple pies.
I like good bread, I like good meat,
Or anything that's good to eat;
But of all poor grub beneath the skies
The poorest is dried apple pies.
Give me the toothache or sore eyes,
But don't give me dried apple pies.
The farmer takes his gnarliest fruit,
'Tis wormy, bitter, and hard, to boot;
They leave the hulls to make us cough,
And don't take half the peeling off.
Then on a dirty cord 'tis strung,
And in a garret window hung;
And there it serves, a roost for flies,
Until it's made up into pies.
Tread on my corns and tell me lies,
But don't pass me dried apple pies.

SEVEN BARKS ALMANAC.—April, 1892.

BREAD AND BUTTER PICKLES

1 gal. sliced cucumbers (large)
6 large onions, sliced
Stand 3 hours in salt water.
1 qt. vinegar
1 tsp. black pepper
2 cups sugar
1 tsp. celery seed
1 tsp. turmeric powder

Cook ½ hour. Fill jars and seal.

Mrs. George W. (Florence Burt) Ford
From her mother,
Mrs. Annetta Matilda Burt

Historical Society members picnicking along the St. Joseph River, near Niles, Michigan on September 5, 1895. (L-R): William B. Starr, Mrs. George Baker, Isaac Hutchins, Mary Chapin, Mrs. Otto Knoblock, Mrs. Howard Stanfield, Howard Stanfield, Otto Knoblock.

HOUSEHOLD HINTS

Those who have studied the philosophy and physiology of cooking object to the close covering of any kettle or stewpan while its contents are cooking. All will recall the frequent deadliness of the chicken-pie when the crust has been made without a vent to allow for the escape of the steam and gases generated. The same effect, in lesser degree, may be noticed in the cooking of many, if not all, vegetables, in the boiling of beef, or in any other closed cooking.

All oyster-eaters may not know that the way to determine if an oyster is alive, as it should be when served raw, is to squeeze a few drops of lemon juice on the thin or "whiskered" edge of the candidate. If the edge does not curl up slightly, that oyster should be declined.

When eggs are scarce, cornstarch is a good substitute; one tablespoonful of the starch is equal to one egg.

To clean a frying pan, rub with a hard crust of bread, and wash with hot water and washing soda. Never scrub it or the next food fried in it will be likely to stick.

The stove should have a thorough cleaning inside and out every two or three weeks. Many times it is blamed for not drawing or baking well when it is clogged with ashes.

Gargle for sore throat can be made by mixing one teaspoon cayenne pepper, 1 teaspoon of black pepper, 1 teaspoon pulverized alum, and 1 pint of cider vinegar. Boil all together 3 minutes; after boiling add 3 tablespoons of sulphur and 1 tablespoon borax. If is is too strong pour water into a little of it and use real often.

A kitchen servant, being much troubled with roaches and water bugs, which the ordinary remedies for such evils would not reach, caught three common garden toads and put them in the kitchen, and the roaches and water bugs were annihilated at once. The toads feel perfectly at home in the kitchen.

To clean cut glass, a soft brush is necessary. In drying it, a good plan is to pack it in plenty of fine sawdust, as this will absorb the moisture where the cloth cannot reach.

To warm beds after supper, place one or two bricks in the oven for each member of the family. Remove them an hour or so before bedtime, stand them on end on top of the stove, and slip the covers over them. These are preferable to flatirons, as they are more convenient, and are far cheaper than hot-water bottles.

Keep a stock of matches on a high and dry shelf in a covered earthen jar or tin box with a tight lid where they will be out of the way of children and safe from rats and mice. These animals are fond of phosphorous, and will gnaw match heads if they can, and often set them on fire. To hold burnt matches, a wineglass suspended with a bit of ribbon and hung on the gas jet or near the stove will be found useful.

Mrs. John M.
Studebaker

1900's

*Mrs. John M. Studebaker wore
this elegant gown on the occasion
of her fiftieth wedding anniversary,
January 3, 1910. The underdress
is of heavy gold satin. The
polonaise-style overdress of gold
chiffon features a panel and borders
of heavy gold lace passementerie.*

EDWARDIAN ELEGANCE

As the Panic of 1893 trailed off into the mists of bitter memories, a host of new ideas began to blossom forth--flourishing in a world suddenly wrenched free from economic hardship and Victorian restraints. Change came slowly, often grudgingly, but the voices of a dynamic group of men and women would not be stilled: Carrie Nation swinging her hatchet in the name of temperance; Igor Stravinsky and Pablo Picasso; Teddy Roosevelt "bullying" the world with his "Big Stick"; Frank Lloyd Wright and Sigmund Freud; Upton Sinclair exposing political and social corruption in his novel, *The Jungle*. With the untold potential of a new century stretching before them, these people and many others accepted the greatest of all challenges; they bravely sought to reform, reshape, and redefine the world in which they lived.

After years of vulgar extravagance and dissipation, the "pillars of Society" had finally begun to crumble, forcing Americans to look elsewhere for social guidance. Ladies of the theater became the fashion trend setters. The leading actresses of the day were dressed by the most famous couturiers, while ladies everywhere rushed to copy the large brimmed hats which had been popularized by the operetta, "The Merry Widow". Surprisingly, though, the single greatest social influence of the day was a high-spirited, serenely beautiful woman who drew life from the pen of Charles Dana Gibson.

Everyone wanted to look like, dress like, be like the "Gibson Girl". She was the total embodiment of the "new" woman. Whether in a drawing room or on a tennis court, she was always in control, proving that a lady could be daringly independent, yet still retain her femininity.

This was the era of the "S" shaped or "Pouter Pigeon" silhouette. The foundation of this rather grotesque glorification of the mature woman was a diabolical corset which tightly constricted the waist while thrusting the bosom forward and the hips back. Elegant ladies, parasols in hand, could be seen promenading in elaborately trimmed gowns with long, flowing skirts and high boned collars. Light, airy fabrics such as chiffons, laces, and crepe de Chine were extremely popular; unfortunately, they wrinkled easily sometimes necessitating 5 or 6 complete changes of costume during the course of the day. Women gave a great deal of thought to their wardrobes since this was still considered a crucial measure of their family's social and financial success.

For many, fashion's stranglehold was becoming increasingly intolerable. With the Women's Suffrage movement steadily gathering strength, it seemed only natural to work toward freeing the body as well as the spirit. While most ladies were not quite ready to throw away their corsets, they were eagerly adding more shirtwaists and tailored suits to their wardrobes. A growing number of women were now working outside the home, creating an unprecedented market for ready-made clothing and demure little tea rooms (it was considered unthinkable for ladies to eat luncheon in a saloon).

American eating habits were slowly entering a period of modernization. Breakfast no longer had to be an uncomfortably heavy meal thanks to the introduction of dry cereals such as Dr. Kellogg's cornflakes. Bakery bread, refined sugar, and an increasing number of canned and ready-to-eat products such as Campbell's Pork & Beans and Nabisco's Fig Newtons, Saltines, and Zu Zu Ginger Snaps, were tremendous time-savers for overworked housewives. Home canning was also becoming more popular now that glass jars could be machine-made rather than blown by hand. While open bins and barrels were still prominent fixtures in every grocery store, shoppers could feel a little more comfortable about the food they ate with the passage of the Pure Food and Drug Act in 1906.

S & H Green Stamps, window screens, and aluminum pots and pans were only a few of the many innovations which were making an impact on people's daily lives. Gas fixtures were giving way to electrification, making possible such practical gadgets as electric perculators and the Hoover suction vacuum cleaner. Although audiences were still flocking to amusement parks, stage plays, and vaudeville shows, motion pictures were here to stay, especially after the great success of the first movie Western, "The Great Train Robbery." Henry Ford's Model T was bringing motoring to the masses, and the Brownie dollar camera was there to give families a permanent record of their travels. One popular destination for tourists in 1904 was the St. Louis World's Fair; here America was introduced to a delectable new treat, the ice cream cone.

Even a cataclysm as devastating as the great San Francisco earthquake could not shake America's fervent optimism. There was a wonderful sense of order and stability to life during the century's first decade -- a secure springtime which will sadly never come again. In 1903 the Wright Brothers gave mankind the gift of flight, proving once again that any man could rise as high as his vision and determination would allow.

1900 RECIPES

CHICKEN-CORN SOUP

1 medium stewing chicken, trim excess fat
Water to cover

Cook until the meat falls off the bones. Remove the chicken from the broth; strain the broth. Remove the meat from the bones; discard the bones. Cut the chicken into bite-size pieces. Skim the fat from the broth. Return the chicken pieces to the broth.

Add **4 cups whole kernel corn** (fresh or canned). Heat the soup until the corn is tender. **Salt** and **pepper** to taste.

Just before serving, add **2 coarsely chopped hard boiled eggs.**

If desired when cooking the chicken, add one or all of the following:

medium onion
shredded carrot
stalk of celery
pinch of dill weed

Mrs. Michael (Gail) Rohleder
From her grandmother,
Mrs. Susan Y. Sides
of Highspire, Pennsylvania

A festive atmosphere always seemed to surround birthdays in turn of the century America.

TO SOFTEN THE HANDS

Keep on the toilet stand near the soap a dish of oatmeal, and rub it freely on the hands after washing. This will cleanse and soften the skin.

TOMATO SOUP

1 qt. tomatoes, cut up
1 pt. hot water
1 Tbsp. salt
1 Tbsp. sugar
4 cloves
Pepper to taste
1 Tbsp. butter
1 Tbsp. chopped onion
1 Tbsp. chopped parsley
1 Tbsp. corn starch
A few celery seeds, if you like

Put the tomatoes, water, sugar, salt, and, cloves with the pepper, on to boil in a porcelain kettle. Put the butter in a stew pan or small pan, and when it bubbles, put in the onion and parsley. Fry for 5 minutes, being careful not to burn. Add the corn starch and when well mixed, stir into the tomatoes. Let it simmer 10 minutes.* Strain and serve.

*(Ed: If you have the time, allow the soup to simmer longer than 10 minutes; the flavor will be even better.)

From the handwritten
cookbook of Mrs. Eva Peirce

SPECIAL DRESSING
(For Grapefruit Salad)

Juice of 2 lemons
Juice of ½ orange
½ cup oil
½ cup powdered sugar
½ glass currant jelly

Beat together.

Mrs. Louis (Janice) Rugee
From her mother-in-law,
Mrs. S.B. (Louise Nickel) Rugee

BLACKBERRY SYRUP

Procure perfectly ripe high vine **blackberries.** Set them on a moderate fire till they break to pieces. Mash and strain through a flannel bag. To each pt. of juice put **one lb. white sugar, ½ oz. powdered cinnamon, ¼ oz. mace** and **2 tsp. of cloves.** Boil the whole together for a quarter of an hour. Then strain the syrup again and to each pint of it put a glass of **French brandy.** Put it in bottles and seal it tight and keep in a cool place. This mixed in cold water in the proportions of a wine glass of syrup to ⅔ of a tumbler is good for a summer drink.

From the handwritten
cookbook of Mrs. Eva Peirce

The recipe for Boston Brown bread has been in the Williams family for at least 75 years. It was served at family gatherings and "Round-Up" times in Montana.

BOSTON BROWN BREAD

1 cup molasses
1 cup brown sugar
3 cups sour milk
2 tsp. salt
1 tsp. soda
2 eggs
4 cups graham flour
2 cups white flour
Raisins, nuts or stewed prunes.

Mix the molasses and brown sugar. Add the eggs and mix well. Add the salt and soda to the white flour and sift together. Add the graham flour and white flour mixture alternately with the sour milk (to the molasses mixture). Then add the raisins, nuts, etc. to taste. Bake in a loaf pan in a moderate oven (350 degrees) for 45 minutes.*

*(Ed: This is probably best baked in 3 loaf pans. If 2 loaf pans are used, the baking time will have to be increased. If you have difficulty finding graham flour, try whole wheat.)

Mrs. Charles Williams

MOTHER'S BREAD CAKES

Soak **6 to 8 slices of stale bread** (brown or white) in enough **buttermilk to cover - about 1 qt.** Add **3 eggs,** a **pinch of salt, butter the size of a walnut** (melted), a **level tsp. of soda,** and enough **flour** to make a thick batter - about 1 pt. Have the griddle hot (greased slightly) and try one. If not light, add 1 level tsp. baking powder.

Mrs. J.M. (Lillian) Studebaker III
From her mother,
Mrs. Lillie G. Bartlett

This coffee cake was a special treat for Sunday breakfasts. Later my mother would make it when her grandchildren visited at the lake. After her death, I began to make it when our children came home for college breaks. Now I make it for my grandchildren when they visit us. Our son remarked to his son on a recent stay, "When you're grown, I hope you will remember this the way I do now, when my Nana made it for me!"

NANA'S COFFEE CAKE

SIFT TOGETHER:
1½ cups flour (fluffed pre-sifted)
3 tsp. baking powder
¼ tsp. salt
¾ cup sugar

ADD:
¼ cup shortening
  (butter, margarine, or Crisco)
1 egg, lightly beaten
½ cup milk
½ tsp. vanilla

Add to the dry ingredients and beat until smooth.

TOPPING:
½ cup brown sugar
2 tsp. cinnamon
2 Tbsp. melted butter
2 Tbsp. flour
½ cup nuts

Mix the topping ingredients together like a pie dough.

Place half of the dough into a greased 8-inch or 9-inch baking pan. Sprinkle half of the topping over the dough. Add the remaining dough and topping. Bake at 375 degrees for 25 minutes. Serve from the pan when cool.

Mrs. Edward J. (Norma) Meehan
From her mother,
Mrs. Helen Lower Booth

1900 RECIPES

The Polish side of my family always has its yuletide celebration on Christmas Eve. Pierogi have always been an important part of our holiday meal -- so important, in fact, that the ladies always make 250-300 of these yummy potato-filled pouches. Every year someone starts a contest to see who can eat the most Pierogi; my very thin mother holds the record with 23. She just has to win over all the male teenagers.

POTATO PIEROGI

DOUGH:
- **2 cups flour**
- **½ cup sour cream**
- **1 egg**
- **¼ tsp. salt**
- **¼ cup warm water**

Mix the dough and let it rest in a covered bowl for at least 10 minutes. Do not use an electric mixer.

FILLING: (For 2-3 batches of dough)
- **5 lbs. potatoes** (This should fill at least 75 pierogi.)
- **1 large onion, finely diced**
- **½ cup butter**
- **Salt and pepper, to taste**
- **5 slices of American cheese**

Pare and cook the potatoes. Brown the onion in the butter. Drain the potatoes; put the slices of cheese and the onions with butter over the potatoes. Mash the potatoes and then add salt and pepper. Cool to lukewarm or cooler. (If the mashed potatoes are too warm, they will melt the dough.)

Divide the dough into quarters. Roll ¼ of the dough out onto a floured surface. Roll the dough thin. (Be sure to keep turning the dough over so that it won't stick to the surface. This dough is very elastic.) Cut into 3½-inch circles. After cutting the rounds, place them on a towel, being sure to keep them from touching. Put the scraps back into a covered bowl to rest. As you are rolling and cutting, keep turning the rounds which have already been cut; the dough needs to dry out slightly on both sides (they should still be soft, but not sticky). When you fill the pierogi, fill in the order they were cut out.

To fill, place a generous teaspoon (not a measuring spoon) of the filling on half of each round. Fold over with floured fingers; pinch the edges together to seal. Place the filled pierogi back on a towel. While you are filling the pierogi, turn the ones which have already been filled so that one side does not dry out more than the other.

To cook, fill 2 Dutch ovens ⅔ full of water. Add ½ tsp. salt to each and bring to a good boil. Gently drop 6 pierogi into each pot. Gently stir with a soft rubber spatula, being careful not to break open the pierogi. Cook 10-14 minutes, or until they float to the top. (The dough will be a white color.) As the pierogi are done, place in a large bowl and drizzle with melted butter so they won't stick together. Place a plate over the bowl and keep warm. As you layer pierogi, continue to drizzle melted butter between the layers. (If your cooking water becomes cloudy, start over with fresh water. Add more water to the pans as necessary.)

Serve with melted butter or ½ butter and ½ oleo (either dip the pierogi into the butter, or drizzle the butter over them.) Serve with Polish sausage.

Pierogi can be made ahead and then frozen (be sure to freeze before cooking). To freeze, fill the pierogi and place them on wax paper sprinkled with flour (over a cookie sheet). Being sure to keep the pierogi from touching each other, place wax paper sprinkled with flour between each layer of pierogi. To cook the frozen pierogi, do not thaw. Place them into boiling water and follow the steps for cooking.

HINTS: For each batch of dough, you should get 25-28 pierogi. If not, roll the dough thinner. Make each batch of dough in its own bowl; never double the recipe. Leftover pierogi can be fried in butter until golden brown, or microwave them on HIGH for 2-3 minutes. Store any leftovers in a covered dish; drizzle melted butter between the layers.

Mrs. David (Christine) Bainbridge

Sweet & Sour Cabbage is one of the mainstays of a "Polish dinner". It is generally served as an accompaniment with fried chicken, Kielbasa sausage, home-made noodles and freshly baked pies.

SWEET & SOUR CABBAGE

1 medium head of cabbage, cut like for slaw, but thicker

Bring enough **water** to a boil to cover the cabbage. Cook till tender. Drain off all the water and put the cabbage back into the pot.

Mix together and pour on cabbage:
- **¼-⅓ cup cider vinegar**
- **Dash of salt and pepper**
- **¼ cup sugar** (or enough to taste)

Serving: Enough for 4-6 people.

Mrs. Eleanor Mays

ESCALLOPED SALMON

One can salmon, ½ cup butter, 1 Tbsp. flour, 2 cups sweet milk, and **2 eggs.** Mix the butter in the milk; when boiling, thicken with flour and stir in the beaten eggs. Place a layer of salmon in a baking dish, then a layer of dressing. Sprinkle with a few **bread or cracker crumbs** and season with **salt and pepper.** Continue these layers until all ingredients are used, finishing with crumbs on top. Bake half an hour.

Mrs. Helen E. Moore Spears
From her grandmother

My maternal grandfather, Edward Moore Parrott, was an Episcopal minister in the village of Lake George, New York. It was very important that the whole family put in an appearance at church every Sunday morning, so my grandmother needed to think of creative ways to feed her large, hungry family Sunday dinner after church even though she hadn't been home to cook it. This recipe for Round Steak Casserole was one of her answers to the problem. She put it all in a Dutch oven in the wood stove before church and voila, instant dinner when they got home.

ROUND STEAK CASSEROLE

3 lbs. round steak, cut into 1½-inch cubes
1 tsp. salt
½ tsp. pepper
½ cup flour
2 Tbsp. cooking oil
1 cup cut-up carrots
½ cup sliced onions
½ cup cut-up celery*
1 large can stewed tomatoes

Roll the round steak cubes in a mixture of flour, salt, and pepper to coat. Brown the meat in hot cooking oil in an electric frying pan. After browning, remove the meat and layer it with the carrots, celery, and onions in a 2½-quart casserole dish. Meanwhile, pour the tomatoes (undrained) into the frying pan; heat and mix with the round steak leavings. Pour the hot tomato mixture over all. Cover the casserole and bake in a 350 degree oven for 2-2½ hours until the meat is tender.

This tastes delicious served over baked potatoes which can be baking at the same time. Serves 4-6.

*You may increase the amounts of carrots, celery, and onions if you like.

Mrs. Claude (Mary E.) Renshaw
From her grandmother,
Mrs. Edith Minor Parrott

POTATOES AND HAM

8 good sized potatoes
2 Tbsp. flour
2 Tbsp. butter
Salt to season
1 tsp. brown sugar
1½ cup milk
1 large slice smoked ham, cut medium thick

Slice the potatoes thick. Place in a casserole and sprinkle with flour and salt. Dot with butter. Place the ham on top. Sprinkle with the sugar and cover well with milk. Bake in a moderate oven from 1 to 1½ hours.*

*(Ed: Bake for about 1 hour at 325 degrees. Be sure to test the potatoes to be sure that they are done.)

Mrs. L.B. Weber

My mother compiled her handwritten cookbook before her marriage in 1904. She had a great deal to learn about cooking, but through years of practice she became famous among her friends for her entertaining. At the turn of the century, croquettes often appeared on dinner party menus. My mother usually served her Veal Croquettes with fresh peas and her special biscuits.

VEAL CROQUETTES

Get a **solid piece of veal.** (Off the loin of the veal is the best.) Cook until it is very tender by putting it in a large kettle and keeping it covered with **hot water** - - never add cold water to cooking meats. **Salt** the water when you put in the meat. Let your meat get perfectly cold or your croquettes will be spoiled. Chop the meat very fine; season with **pepper** and **salt.** Moisten with **white sauce** - - just enough so you can roll the croquettes into round or oblong shapes and dip in **egg** and **finely rolled cracker crumbs.** (Mother always made her croquettes oblong for company.) Use a frying basket. Put in four at a time and fry in **hot lard** until a light brown, 3 minutes is usually enough. These may be made the day before they are to be used. When you need them, place them in the oven and warm them through. They will keep for several days in a cold place, but are best at first. When taken from the frying basket, spread on wrapping paper placed in pans if you are going to use them immediately and are going to put them in the oven to keep warm.

Miss Annajane Puterbaugh
From her mother,
Mrs. Myron David (Jessica Faulknor) Puterbaugh

The Joseph D. Oliver residence, Copshaholm, was designed by Charles Alonzo Rich of the New York architectural firm of Lamb and Rich. Copshaholm bears a resemblance to another home designed by Lamb and Rich, Teddy Roosevelt's Sagamore Hill.

LIVER DUMPLINGS
(A Main Dish)

8 oz. beef liver
4 oz. pork sausage
1 tsp. sweet marjoram
1 tsp. salt
¼ tsp. pepper
1 medium onion
1 egg
2 heaping Tbsp. flour
1 cup seasoned croutons

Mix the liver, pork, seasonings, and onion; grind them together. Add the egg and flour. If too thin, add more flour as needed.

Prepare a large pot of broth (use bouillon cubes, if necessary). When the broth is boiling, add the croutons to the liver mixture and drop by tablespoonfuls into the broth. Cook about 10 minutes or till done. Serve with a green vegetable.

NOTE: Leftover dumplings may be sliced cold and browned in butter. They make delicious hors d'oeuvres.

Mrs. Bertha Sindlinger

It is a tradition in the Oliver Family to serve Hunter's Lunch before Notre Dame football games. Try it at your next tailgate party.

HUNTER'S LUNCH

3 lbs. round steak, ground
½ lb. salt pork
1 large can (28 oz.) tomatoes
1 lb. fresh mushrooms
4 chopped onions

Brown the round steak and salt pork in a large pan. Add the onions. Stir in the tomatoes and mushrooms. Cook this one hour or until thick. Then add **1 can pimientoes** and **1 can peas.** Cook **1 lb. spaghetti** for 20 minutes, drain. Then add **½ lb. American cheese.** Put the spaghetti on a platter; pour on the first mixture and sprinkle some cheese on top. Brown in the oven a few minutes. Serve.

From the Joseph D. Oliver Family Cookbook.

CHICKEN POT PIE

2 cups chicken
6 eggs
Salt to taste
Flour
6 small potatoes
3 chicken bouillon cubes

Stew the chicken until tender, then remove the chicken pieces and set aside to cool. Add the bouillon cubes to the left over water and set aside. When cool, remove the meat from the bone and cut into bite-size pieces. Put the meat back into the broth.

Break the eggs into a bowl. Mix the whites and yellows together with a fork. Add salt, then add the flour until the dough is no longer sticky (a rollable consistency). Take one small ball at a time and roll out onto a board. Roll it very thin and cut into 3-inch squares. Continue until all the dough is used.

Pare the potatoes and slice ¼ inch thick. Heat the broth. Add alternate layers of dough and potatoes until all is in. Cook until the potatoes are tender. This also can be made with pork, beef, or onions instead of chicken.

Mrs. Michael (Gail Arner) Rohleder
From her grandmother,
Susan Yegar Sides
of Highspire, Pennsylvania

CHICKEN PAPRIKAS

3½-4 lb. chicken
1 medium onion, chopped
3 Tbsp. fat
1 tsp. paprika
1 cup water
1 tsp. salt
2 Tbsp. flour
1 pt. sour cream

Debone the chicken or cut the chicken into pieces. Brown the onion in fat in a large pot; add the chicken, salt, paprika, and water. Simmer until the chicken is tender. (When using left over chicken, simmer until the chicken is hot.) Mix the flour with the sour cream until smooth in a separate bowl. Add to the chicken before serving.

HUNGARIAN DUMPLINGS:
3 eggs, beaten
3 cups flour
1 Tbsp. salt
¼ tsp. baking powder
½ cup cold water

Mix all the ingredients and beat with a spoon. Drop by ¼ teaspoonful into boiling salted water. Cook until the dumplings rise to the top. Drain; rinse in cold water.

Karen Kiemnec
From her grandmother,
Mrs. Joseph (Theresa) Szabo
of Hazelton, Pennsylvania

This photograph gives us some idea of the elaborate private parties held at South Bend's finest hostelry, the Oliver Hotel. This table is set for the Campbell-Hager wedding reception which was held on January 8, 1902.

MENU

Blue Points
OLIVES　　SALTED NUTS　　RADISHES

Consomme, Alphabet　　　　Mock Turtle, Anglaise

Boiled Oregon Salmon, Shrimp Sauce
POTATOES, DUCHESS　　　　　HOT HOUSE CUCUMBERS

Fresh Crab Meat, Newburg en Casselots
Braised Veal Sweetbreads a la Goddard

Orange Sherbet, Bigerade

Prime Ribs Beef au Jus
1906 Spring Lamb, Mint Jelly　　　　Roast Chicken, Giblet Sauce
NEW POTATOES IN CREAM　　MASHED POTATOES　　GREEN PEAS
SOUTHERN BEETS　　FRESH ASPARAGUS, HOLLANDAISE

Head Lettuce and Tomato Salad

Red Cherry Pie　　Strawberry Shortcake, Whipped Cream
Incubator Ice Cream in Nest　　Walnut Cake
Edam, Roquefort and American Cheese

Mixed Nuts　　Easter Eggs
Cafe Noir

75¢

Easter Greetings, 1906 — The Oliver Hotel.

The recipe I remember so well was the one for Vinegar Gravy. Mother would fix country smoked ham with Vinegar Gravy, butter beans, sweet potatoes, fresh bread and butter, fresh milk, and mock lemon pie; this was a good Sunday dinner.

VINEGAR GRAVY

2 cups water
Enough **vinegar** to make it sour
Enough **sugar** to just leave it tart
Thicken with a **cornstarch or flour paste**
A little **cinnamon**
(Very good with ham.)

Mrs. John J. (Bonnie) Molloy, Jr.
From her mother,
Mrs. Mida Lee Massie

TO CLEAN WALL PAPER

Brush down the walls with a hairbrush or dust cloth, then cut a loaf of yeast bread two or three days old once vertically through the middle, and again crosswise. Hold these pieces by the crust and rub the wall downward with long, light strokes. Do not rub across the paper, or rub harder than is necessary. An ordinary coarse grater held in the left hand will be found convenient to rub off the surface of the bread as it becomes soiled. Clean thoroughly as you go.

This dark, rich cake has been in my family since the turn of the century. We always serve it during the Christmas season.

MOLASSES CAKE

2 cups sugar
5 cups flour
1 cup shortening
1 cup molasses
2 cups sour milk
1½ tsp. baking soda
1 tsp. nutmeg
1 tsp. cloves
1 tsp. cinnamon
½ cup dates, chopped
½ cup candied cherries, chopped
½ cup candied pineapple, chopped
¼ cup nuts, chopped

Mix all the ingredients together. Pour into greased and floured loaf pans. Bake in a 300 degree oven for 1½ hours. Yields: 3 medium or 6 small loaves.

Mrs. John (Gail Parent) Jaskowiak
From her great-grandmother

GRANDMOTHER'S POUND CAKE

1 cup butter
1 cup dark brown sugar
4 eggs, separated
3 Tbsp. sherry, brandy, or rum
  (Mrs. O'Neal uses rum.)
2 cups flour
½ tsp. vanilla
Pinch of salt

(Set oven at 325 degrees. Bake in a loaf pan.)*

*(Ed: Beat egg whites until stiff; beat egg yolks until lemon colored. Cream the butter and sugar; add the egg yolks. Alternately add the dry and liquid ingredients. Fold in the egg whites. Bake for about 1¼ hours.)

Mrs. Eveline O'Neal
From her grandmother,
Mrs. Earlina Harbor

BLITZ TORTE

½ cup butter
½ cup granulated sugar
4 egg yolks
1 cup flour
1 tsp. baking powder
½ tsp. flavoring
5 Tbsp. water

Cream butter and sugar. Add the beaten egg yolks.
Sift the flour and baking powder together; add alternately with the water. Add the flavoring. Pour into a greased, shallow pan and cover with the following:

4 egg whites, well beaten
1 cup powdered sugar
¼ tsp. baking powder

Sprinkle with **chopped nuts** and **coconut.** Bake in a moderate oven for 25 minutes.*

*(Ed: Use an 11 x 7-inch pan and bake at 350 degrees.)
Mrs. William (Anna) Dumke

STRAWBERRY FLUFF ICING

1 cup sliced strawberries
1 cup granulated sugar
1 egg white

Beat well together with a Dover egg beater.

Miss Mary and Thaddessa Taylor

THE FORMAL DINNER

It is customary to send out dinner invitations two weeks in advance of the dinner. An immediate answer is required so that the hostess may know how many are to be served.

Obviously, a formal dinner cannot be given without perfectly trained servants.

Upon arrival, the guests remove their wraps and then proceed to the drawing room where they are first greeted by the hostess and then the host. It is well for the hostess to indicate to each gentleman as he is received, whom he shall escort to the dining room. It is usual to place table diagrams in a hall or dressing room; once in the dining room, the hostess does not direct people where to sit.

When the last guest has arrived, the butler announces dinner. The host then offers his arm to the lady of honor, and they proceed into the dining room. Each gentleman, in turn, enters the dining room with his appointed lady. The hostess is the last to enter. After she assures herself that all her guests are properly provided with escorts, she takes the arm of the gentleman of honor.

Place cards may be used at each cover to direct the guests. When the host reaches his place at the table, he seats the lady he is escorting on his right, and the other gentlemen do likewise. When all the ladies are seated, the gentlemen take their places. As soon as all the guests are seated, ladies remove their gloves.

A dinner napkin containing a roll is at each cover. The first course, usually oysters on the shell, is served at once. Servants should stand at the left of the host or hostess with tray in hand; portions are placed by the host or hostess on the tray and then passed by the servants to each guest. There must always be a plate in front of each guest from the time the table is set until dessert is served.

Interesting talk is as much a necessity to a successful dinner as excellent food.

When dinner is over, the hostess bows slightly to the lady on the right of the host and then slowly rises. When everyone is standing, the gentlemen offer their arms to their partners and escort them to the drawing room. After taking their leave of the ladies, the gentlemen may adjourn to the smoking room. If there is no smoking room, the ladies leave the dining room alone. After coffee, liqueurs, and cigars, the gentlemen rejoin the ladies.

The guest of honor should rise to leave first. After the first guest leaves, the others follow.

Dinner guests should make calls upon their hostess within ten days after the entertainment.

AN ETIQUETTE PUZZLE

Can you detect the common breach of table etiquette in each one of these pictures? The answers are on page 46.

The Ladies' Home Journal, January 1904.

TOMATO RUFFLE

½ lb. bacon
1 qt. tomatoes
1 qt. sliced onions
1 Tbsp. sugar
Salt and pepper

1. Cook the bacon until brown and crisp. Add the onions, and when they are brown, add the tomatoes. Season to taste with sugar, salt, and pepper; cook 10 minutes.
2. Make a thickening of **2 Tbsp. flour** and **4 Tbsp. water.** Stir this into the onions, tomatoes, and bacon until the mixture thickens. Cook a few minutes longer.
3. Serve on crisp toast or crackers. (It is also very good on spaghetti or macaroni.)

Mrs. Wayne (Judy) Bartholomew
From her grandmother

The recipe for Dark Secret is taken from Mrs. Skeen's handwritten cookbook which dates from the turn of the century. This very rich, sweet dessert, while great when served alone, is sensational when teamed with whipped cream and bananas.

DARK SECRET

1 cup dates
⅔ cup sugar
1 Tbsp. flour
1 cup walnuts
3 eggs
Salt

Bake ¾ hour in a slow oven.* Serve with bananas and whipped cream or ice cream.
*(Ed: Beat the eggs with a fork until well blended; mix in the dry ingredients. Add the dates and nuts. Bake in a greased dish [about 7 inches in diameter] at 325 degrees.)

Mrs. Ethel Haynes Skeen
From Mrs. E.A. Ridgely

PLYMOUTH ROCKS

One and one-half cups granulated sugar, one cup butter, three eggs, three cups flour measured after sifting, **one teaspoon soda** dissolved in a **tablespoon warm water, one teaspoon cinnamon, one-half teaspoon allspice;** mix and add **one pound dates chopped fine, one** and **one-half pounds English walnuts** broken into pieces; drop on buttered tins and bake.*

*(Ed: Bake in a 350 degree oven for 15-18 minutes. Makes about 6-7 dozen.)

Mrs. C.W. Frink

CLIFFORD TEA COOKIES

1 cup butter
2 cups brown sugar
2 eggs
1 tsp. baking soda
1 tsp. salt
1 cup walnuts
4½ cups flour

Mix the ingredients together till they form a sticky dough. Roll the dough into a long loaf shape. Let stand overnight in the refrigerator. Slice the dough into ¼-inch slices and put on an ungreased cookie sheet. Bake in a 350 degree oven for 15 minutes or until golden brown.

Mrs. Michael (Gail Arner) Rohleder
From her grandmother,
Susan Yegar Sides
of Highspire, Pennsylvania

ROCK COOKIES

1½ cups caramel sugar
1 cup butter
3 eggs
1 large cup of English walnut meats
1 pound dates, chopped fine
½ tsp. each of cinnamon, cloves, and nutmeg
1 tsp. vanilla
1 tsp. soda dissolved in 1 Tbsp. hot water
2½ cups flour

Chop the nuts and dates. Cream the butter and sugar. Beat eggs well. Mix all together and spread thin in a baking pan. Sprinkle with granulated sugar. Bake in a moderate oven. Cut into squares.*
*(Ed: Bake in a greased 15 x 10 x 1-inch jelly roll pan at 350 degrees for about 25 minutes. They make a delicious spicy date brownie which would be great for picnics or snacks.)

Mrs. J.B. Birdsell

BREAD PUDDING

Break **stale bread** into small pieces. Make a custard of **1 cup milk, 2 Tbsp. sugar,** and **1 egg.** (Use 1 cup milk for each cup of bread.)
Put the bread into a greased baking dish. Add small lumps of **butter.** Sprinkle with **nutmeg,** then add the liquids. Bake for 45 minutes at 325 degrees. Cool and serve with cream.
(**Raisins** may be added.)

Mr. Art Sumption
From his wife's mother,
Mrs. Pearl Ferris Williams

HOUSEHOLD HINTS

Underdone vegetables are unpardonable. Boil potatoes ½ hour, less time, if very small; medium sized onion, 1 hour; peas and asparagus, 20-25 minutes; green corn, 20-25 minutes; cabbage and cauliflower, 25-30 minutes; carrots and turnips, 45 minutes, when young, 1 hour in winter; beets, 1 hour in summer, 1½ or 2 hours in winter; lima beans, if young, half an hour, 45 minutes if old.

A few kernels of coffee burned on coals act as a deodorizer.

To keep lemons, wrap each one separately in tissue or soft paper, and place them in stone jars; put a plate over each jar and keep in a cool, dry room. They should be looked over about once a week; take out any that show signs of decay. Most of them will keep in a perfect state of preservation for weeks and months.

To insure success with salt-rising bread in cold weather, keep the night yeast in a box of hay. A small wooden box with a close-fitting lid is best for this purpose. Put hay into the bottom of the box and around the sides. In the middle of this set your yeast, then cover with hay. This will keep the yeast from a chill. Good bread will be the result.

Look carefully to the stale-bread remains of each day. Keep a wire basket, set in a tin pan in the pantry, to receive all scraps left on plates, toast crusts, or morsels from the bread jar. Never put them in a covered pail or jar; they will mold. Stale bread may be utilized in croutons, dressings, croquettes, etc.

While house cleaning, dress appropriately for the work. Some housekeepers wear a divided skirt or bloomers made of four widths of heavy dark skirting. These are gathered into bands and buttoned about the ankles and waist. They are valuable protectors for skirts, and facilitate climbing stepladders, scrubbing floors, etc. Pull the sleeves of the dress up as far as you want them to go, and put elastic bands on the arms over the sleeves. Wear a dust cap, a big apron, and loose gloves.

A basin of cold water placed in an oven when it is too hot, will soon lower its temperature.

A hot shovel held over varnished furniture will take out white spots.

Furs may be cleaned by rubbing damp corn meal through them and allowing it to dry. Afterwards remove by shaking and brushing. The coarse furs, as bear, buffalo, etc., may be scrubbed with warm suds made of pure white soap and pure water, and their appearance will be very much improved by combing with a coarse comb. To improve the luster of furs, heat corn meal in an iron skillet to a rich brown but without burning. While still hot sprinkle it over the fur and rub with a flannel cloth. Afterwards remove by shaking and brushing.

An old pair of stockings may be converted into useful sleeve protectors by cutting off the feet and hemming the cut edge. These may be drawn over the sleeves of a clean gown if necessary when washing dishes. They are also useful in other kinds of housework.

Before laying the linoleum on a rough floor, cover the floor with a layer of sand, or sawdust, or old newspapers, to prevent its being worn by the cracks, and give the linoleum a coat of paint and varnish three or four times a year. When thus treated it is practically indestructible.

Professional hairdressers do not advocate shampooing the hair oftener than once a month. A thorough brushing once or twice a week is regarded by them as sufficient for cleanliness and is much more beneficial to the hair and scalp.

Don't take any kind of a bath within two hours after eating a hearty meal. Don't bathe early in the morning on an empty stomach unless you are vigorous and strong enough to stand it. The best time for you may be two or three hours after breakfast. Don't neglect the weekly hot water bath, followed by a change of clothing to keep the body clean and healthy.

"Pull Smartly"

To Pull Candy. — The best way to pull candy is to grease the hands thoroughly with butter to prevent sticking, or they may be covered with flour. The work should commence as soon as the candy is cool enough to bear the hands. Work with the tips of the fingers until it grows cool. Continue to pull until it is of a light golden color, or white, according to the recipe. Pull smartly, either by the help of another person or over a hook. Finally, draw out in sticks on waxed paper, or other smooth surface, which may be dusted with flour and cut with shears into sticks.

Household Discoveries and Mrs. Curtis's Cook Book — 1908.

As a child, we would "pull taffy" on the cold back porch on a crisp winter day. We usually tried to have French Chewing around at Christmas time.

FRENCH CHEWING

5 cups granulated sugar
2 cups light cream (Half & Half)
2 cups Karo (light)
1 Tbsp. unflavored gelatin, dissolved in water (the original recipe called for 1 Tbsp. crystal flakes).
¼ stick paraffin
Butter, the size of a walnut

Cook all the ingredients but the gelatin until the soft ball stage. Add the gelatin and continue to cook to the hard ball stage. Pour onto a buttered plate until cool enough to handle. Pull, preferably in a cool room, until white and porous. It will be stiff. Pull out into a rope and lay on wax paper. Cut into bite size pieces. This must be stored in a cool place or it becomes sticky.

Mrs. Robert (Claralu) Blake

The Philadelphia
HOUSE OF PURITY

The Philadelphia as it looked on opening day in 1901.

Courtesy of Milton Kouroubetis.

The Philadelphia opened for business on October 5, 1901, at 116 North Michigan Street in South Bend and was operated by the Poledor family at that location for more than 70 years, until displaced by an urban renewal project.

It was launched as a candy store by Eustice Poledor on his hard-earned savings from flower sales and shoe shines. Shortly after establishment of the candy store, Eustice summoned his brothers and sister, Andrew, Pendel and Georgia from Greece, and in 1903 they began serving lunches.

The name for the business, The Philadelphia, has two derivations, and both are interrelated. One is that it was named after the city of Philadephia, Pennsylvania, where Eustice Poledor earned his first money selling flowers and shining shoes after arriving in this country almost penniless from his native Greece. Secondly, the word, Philadephia, is Greek for brotherly love, which symobolized the love of Eustice, Andrew, Pendel and Georgia for each other as brothers and sister.

Any success The Philadelphia may have had can be attributed to the principles of quality in product, employees, suppliers and patrons. As one of The Philadelphia mottos said, "None Better."

To thank the South Bend area for allowing The Philadelphia to serve its people and to bring back some old memories and nostalgia, the following have been taken from The Philadelphia's recipe book.

Mr. Ted Poledor

PEANUT BRITTLE

    4 lbs. granulated sugar
    3 lbs. corn syrup
    2 qts. water
    ¼ oz. salt
    2 oz. bicarbonate of Soda
    3 lbs. spanish peanuts (raw)

Place sugar, corn syrup and water into a cooking kettle. Cook to 240° F.
Add peanuts.
Cook to 310° or until batch is golden brown color.
Set kettle off fire.
Add salt and soda. Stir until soda is well mixed into the batch and the batch puffs up. When batch has puffed up, stir again and let the batch puff up a second time.
Pour onto an oiled metal table or marble slab. Quickly spread the batch. When the batch is firm enough to handle, cut into 2 or 3 pieces. Turn pieces over and stretch the brittle so that the finished product will be thin.
Care should be exercised in handling this product due to high heat which could cause burns.

CHOCOLATE SYRUP

    5 lbs. granulated sugar
    11 oz. cocoa powder
    2½ lbs. corn syrup
    50 oz. water
    ¼ oz. salt

Place sugar, cocoa and salt into cooking kettle. Mix dry.
Add corn syrup and water. Cook to a boil until syrup starts to foam and rise.
Remove from fire.
After syrup has stopped foaming, return to fire and bring to a boil again.
Remove from fire and let it cool.
Bottle and store in refrigerator.
This syrup is good on ice cream and for making chocolate milk.

Answers To Etiquette Puzzle

1. Fork tines in wrong position
2. Cutting lettuce with knife
3. Resting knife on plate edge
4. Dipping radishes in salt-cellar
5. Holding glass in left hand
6. Taking soup from spoon tip
7. Cutting bread on tablecloth
8. Sexes wrongly grouped
9. Spoon left in cup
10. Picking teeth at table

This old family recipe is usually served by Mrs. Mann for holiday celebrations. This delicious pie would make any occasion a special event.

DRIED APRICOT WHIPPED PIE

1 lb. dried apricots

Cover with water. Cook and puree. Add:

3 tsp. lemon juice
3 egg whites, beaten stiff
¾ cup sugar

Beat the egg whites until stiff; gradually add the ¾ cup sugar. Add the apricot puree and lemon juice to the egg whites and stir well. Fill a <u>baked</u> pie shell. Bake at 350 degrees for 20 minutes until brown. Serve with whipped cream.

Mrs. Glenn A. Mann

BISCUIT TORTONI

¾ cup sugar
¾ cup coffee
1 pint whipped cream
3 well beaten eggs
8 or 10 macaroons, ground
Almond flavoring, to taste

Boil the sugar and coffee until it spins a thread.* Mix with the eggs and beat until cool. Add the whipped cream and macaroons. Freeze.
*(Ed: Cook until the mixture measures 230-234 degrees on a candy thermometer.)

Mrs. Janet S. Allen
From her mother,
Mrs. Edward W. (Betz Orem) Crouse

SPICED PEACHES

6 lbs. (½ peck) peaches, peeled
3 lbs. sugar
1 pt. cider vinegar
⅛ cup whole cloves
2 sticks cinnamon bark

Boil the sugar, vinegar, and spices (which have been placed in a cheesecloth bag) for 12 minutes or until clear. Add the peaches (only enough for 1 can at a time) and cook until tender. Lift out of the pan and put into sterilized fruit jars. Cover with boiling syrup and seal.

Mrs. Ervin (Bertha) Purucker

I brought this recipe back from Groff's Farm Restaurant in Mt. Joy, Pennsylvania. It's an old fashioned dessert which tastes like tapioca pudding.

BETTY'S CRACKER PUDDING

1 qt. milk
2 eggs, separated
⅔ cup sugar
1 cup grated coconut (fine or med. shred)
2 cups broken saltine crackers (not rolled into crumbs)
1 tsp. vanilla

In a heavy 3-qt. pot, heat the milk almost to the boiling point. In a bowl, beat the egg yolks and sugar together until frothy. Gradually add to the hot milk. Reduce the heat to medium. Crumble the crackers into the milk. Stir constantly until the mixture comes to a boil. Add the coconut and stir until the pudding bubbles thickly. Remove from the heat and add the vanilla. Fold in the egg whites which have been beaten stiffly. Serve warm or cold. Serves 6 to 8.

Maryanne Denisi

This flavorful dessert was served by both my mother and grandmother. Traditionally it has been a part of our Thanksgiving and Christmas celebrations.

PERSIMMON PUDDING

2 cups persimmon pulp
2 cups sugar
2 eggs, beaten
1 tsp. soda
1½ cups buttermilk
1½ cups flour
⅛ tsp. salt
1 tsp. baking powder
1 tsp. cinnamon
1 tsp. vanilla
2 Tbsp. milk
5 Tbsp. butter

Mix together the persimmon pulp, sugar, and beaten eggs. Add the soda to the buttermilk and stir until the foaming stops; add to the persimmon mixture. Sift the flour, salt, baking powder, and cinnamon into the mixture; beat well. Add the vanilla and milk; blend into the batter. Melt the butter in a 9 x 13-inch pan, then pour it into the batter, leaving just enough to grease the pan. Beat the mixture well. Bake in a slow oven (325 degrees) for 1¼ hours, or until set. Serve cold topped with whipped cream. Serves 12.

Mrs. Robert (Claralu) Blake
From her grandmother

Miss
Violet
Witwer

1910's

Mrs. Dodd, one of the most
well-known and admired seam-
stresses of South Bend, designed
and made this lovely pale aqua silk
shantung dress and matching long
jacket. The bodice is white
silk voile trimmed in lace, satin
and tassels. The entire outfit
is trimmed in intricately arranged
soutache braid, embroidery, lace, and other
passementerie. Worn by Violet Witwer. Circa 1912.

FROM BUTTERFLY TO BREADWINNER

From off the North Atlantic the winds of sudden and violent change were beginning to blow. On the night of April 14, 1912, the luxury liner, Titanic, sank taking with her 1,500 lives and the unquestioning faith of a generation. The supreme self-assurance which had named Titanic "unsinkable" was now forced to share her fate. The second decade of the new century was to be a time of transition -- the creation of a new world, not gently born of calm and reasoned thought, but churned and swept gale-like into existence by brutal disillusionment and the pain of battle.

Industry was redesigning the American way of life. Telephones were now commonplace sights in homes across the country. Automobile manufacturers were making faster, more reliable cars, while Kodak cameras transformed sober-faced ladies and gentlemen into grinning, posturing pin-ups. The wash day burden was lightened when Rinso, the first granulated laundry soap, was developed for use in electric washing machines. The hum of the assembly line continued to play its siren's song; as large numbers of domestic servants began to heed this seductive call, a void was created in many homes -- a void which could be filled, ironically, only by the manufacture of still more labor-saving devices.

A crusade was launched to make kitchens more efficient. The hulking black stove of the 19th century was getting a face lift as white porcelain panels were added to the exterior. The invention of the oven thermometer in 1915 revolutionized food preparation by giving women control over baking temperatures. Electric refrigerators were on the market by 1916, but their $900.00 price tag put them out of the reach of most families. Electric frying pans and toasters joined with new heat resistant Pyrex dishes to allow housewives to use their time in the kitchen more effectively.

In 1908 fashion entered a period of radical change. The distorted silhouette of the Edwardian era was on the way out, along with high boned collars and ruffled petticoats. The new fashion visionary was French couturier Paul Poiret. His "natural" figure encouraged women to free themselves from heavily boned corsets, allowing the size of their waists to increase while narrowing the hips. Often times the waist line disappeared completely as skirts fell "pillar-like" from an Empire waist. Poiret's tunic jackets added the finishing touch to this straighter, more youthful silhouette.

Unfortunately, Poiret followed this act of liberation by creating one of haute couture's most bizarrely restrictive styles. The hobble skirt, which first appeared in 1910, was cut so tightly about the ankles that fashionable ladies found movement virtually impossible. This extreme style quickly faded, but a modified form remained, slit to the knee and perfect for dancing the sultry, slinky tango.

Ragtime melodies swept America into a dancing furor, giving birth to such colorful steps as the fox trot, grizzly bear, lame duck, and bunny hug. The king and queen of this animal empire were Vernon and Irene Castle, the most famous dance team of the era. Irene Castle's influence on fashion was tremendous. Her bobbed hair, loosely fitting gowns, and corsetless figure were an inspired preview of the 20's flapper look.

Like the inexorable pounding of waves upon a distant shore, greed and arrogance were propelling the nations of Europe ever closer to war. When Archduke Franz Ferdinand of Austria was assassinated in Sarajevo on June 28, 1914, world events were surging out of control; by August 3rd, The Great War was a bitter reality.

The United States managed to remain neutral during the early years of the war, but embattled Europe, desperate for food and supplies, was anxiously reaching out. A spirit of self-sacrifice began to sweep through America. The need to care for the "other mother's son" became so compelling that enforced rationing was never necessary in this country. As German U-boats continued to indiscriminately sink neutral shipping, public opinion steadily turned against the Kaiser and his allies. Finally, on April 6, 1917, America, too, was in the fight.

With thousands of doughboys shipping out to the battlefields of France, women became an important part of the work force: running streetcars; working the farms; laboring in the munitions plants. The ladies who weren't employed outside the home were called on to express their patriotism by tending home gardens, knitting sweaters and socks for servicemen, and of course, always conserving. Through hard work and selfless determination, women proved their worth; they were no longer mere frail, helpless butterflies.

On November 11, 1918, the world breathed a collective sigh as an armistice was signed. President Woodrow Wilson hoped to build a peace by somehow creating perfection in a hopelessly imperfect world. His mystic dream of a "war to end all wars" was sadly doomed to failure -- the last futile gasp of 19th century idealism.

SKI TEA

Bring to boil **25 cups of water.** Add spices which are tied in a small bag: **1 heaping tsp. cinnamon** and as many **whole cloves** as desired. Put **5 bags orange pekoe tea** in and steep for 3 minutes. Remove the bags and add the juice of **6 oranges, 3 lemons,** and **1½ lbs. of sugar.** Serve piping hot in cups. (Don't use an aluminum pan.)

Mrs. John (Jane) Olcott

My grandmother, who is in her 80's, brought this recipe from the Naples region of Italy.

ITALIAN SHORT RIB SOUP

4 or 5 beef ribs
Water
Onion, peeled
Garlic clove, sliced
Potato, quartered
1 can (6 oz.) tomato sauce
Salt and pepper to taste
Rice or pasta (Optional)

Wash the meat and cut off any fat. Put it in a pan; cover with water and bring to a boil. As soon as a foam forms on the surface, dump all the water. Clean the pan and add fresh water to cover the ribs; bring to a boil.

When the water has come to a boil, add the onion, garlic, and potato and continue cooking until the meat is done (about 1 hour). Add the tomato sauce and salt and pepper to taste. Rice or pasta may be added to the broth if desired. Serves 2-3.

Sue Stratigos

BANANA BREAD

4 whole bananas
¼ lb. butter
2 cups sugar
4 eggs
4 cups flour
2 tsp. soda
1 tsp. vanilla
1 tsp. lemon
1 cup pecans

Mash the bananas and let stand. Cream the butter and sugar; beat in the eggs. Add the bananas. Sift in flour and soda. Beat smooth and add the flavorings and nuts. Bake in a slow oven about 1 hour.* Makes 2 nice loaves.
(*Ed: Bake at 325 degrees.)

Misses Mary and Thaddessa Taylor
From Mrs. Nelle Boger

GERMAN POTATO SALAD

Boil **5 lbs. of red potatoes** in the jackets. Peel when cooled. Slice with an egg slicer and marinate over night in **1 cup of salad dressing** (French, Italian, wine vinegar and oil, or Catalina). Season with **pepper** and **Lawry's seasoned salt.**

Cut **1 lb. bacon** into 1-inch pieces; saute. Add **2 medium onions** (sliced). When the onions are transparent, drain off the grease. Add equal parts: **1 cup brown sugar, 1 cup cider vinegar,** and **1 cup water.** Add **1 Tbsp. cornstarch.** When thickened, add the sliced marinated potatoes and heat through. Serves 12 for dinner or 24 for a buffet or salad bar.

Mrs. Jean Savarese
From her grandmother,
Mrs. Emily Zielke

Nicholas Bakouses in his grocery store -- 1916.

Courtesy of Milton Kouroubetis.

KENTUCKY CORNBREAD

¾ cup cornmeal
¼ cup flour
½ tsp. salt
½ tsp. baking soda
2 tsp. sugar
1 cup buttermilk
2 Tbsp. bacon drippings (optional)*

Mix the dry ingredients. Stir the buttermilk and bacon drippings into the dry ingredients. If not thin enough, add a little water. Heat a well greased cast iron corn stick pan or a No. 6 cast iron skillet in a 400 degree oven for about 3 minutes or until very hot. Spoon the batter into the stick pan, filling two-thirds full, or pour into the skillet. Bake at 400 degrees for 25 minutes or until lightly browned. Makes 8 cornsticks or 8 servings of cornbread.

*(*Ed: If you don't want to use bacon drippings, you may substitute butter or margarine.)

Mrs. Ronald (Nancy) Eversole

PANCAKES

Beat **5 egg yolks.** Add **2 cups milk, 2 level cups flour, 1 tsp. baking powder, 2 tsp. sugar, ½ tsp. salt,** and **2 Tbsp. melted butter.** Blend well. Beat **5 egg whites** separately and fold them into the above mixture. Pour onto a hot griddle. Flip when bubbles appear. Serve warm with syrup. Yield: 20 small pancakes.

Mrs. Michael (Sharon) Love
From her grandmother,
Mrs. Hilda P. Anderson

YORKSHIRE PUDDING

Take **2 eggs,** well beaten; add **1 cup of milk.** Stir into **1 cup flour,** sifted with **1 tsp. salt.**

In a heavy bottom (11 x 7 x 2-inch) pan, put **½ cup drippings from a roast.** Warm gently.

Dust **½ cup currants** with **2 tsp. flour.** Add to the pudding mixture. Pour into the pan. Bake at 450 degrees* for 25-30 minutes. Serve at once.

*If the pan is not heavy, watch the temperature and reduce to 375 degrees after 15-20 minutes or the bottom may burn. Serves 4 or 5.

Mrs. Joel (Lou Ann) Bullard
From her mother-in-law
Clara Preston Bullard

When ladies often entertained at afternoon tea, this was a favorite recipe of my husband's mother, Mrs. Fred W. Keller. (Fred W. Keller was mayor of South Bend from 1914-1918.) There is a surprise in each crispy ball.

SWEET POTATO PUFFS

2 cups mashed sweet potatoes
1 egg, beaten
½ tsp. salt
¼ tsp. pepper
8 marshmallows
½ cup crushed corn flakes

If the mashed potatoes are unseasoned, add salt and pepper. Add the beaten egg. If the mixture is dry, moisten with milk. Form into 8 balls with a marshmallow inside of each. Roll in corn flakes. Deep fry in hot **Crisco** when it browns a cube of bread in 40 seconds. Fry until brown, and drain on absorbent paper.

Mrs. George E. (Marjorie) Keller
From her mother-in-law,
Mrs. Fred W. (Edith) Keller

This recipe belonged to my great-aunt. Her husband was the international distributor for The Studebaker Corp. here in South Bend from 1917 until his death in 1943.

ELMA'S RED CABBAGE

1 large head red cabbage, shredded
2 cups water
½ cup vinegar
½ cup bacon drippings
½ cup red wine
2 tsp. salt
½ tsp. pepper
2 large apples, peeled and diced

Combine all the ingredients in a large pan. Bring to a boil, reduce the heat and simmer for about 1½ hours.

Mrs. Ronald (Nancy) Eversole
From her great-aunt,
Mrs. Ernest (Elma) Hoyt

FRENCH POACHED EGGS

Grate some **cheese** on a saucer and sprinkle a bit of **pepper** on it. No salt is needed, as the cheese is salty. Grease a frying pan with a little lump of **butter** then put some **milk** in it. Lay **2 or 3 eggs** in it like eggs for frying (don't break the yolks). Cover the eggs with the grated cheese and cook slowly like fried or poached eggs, lifting a little **milk** on a spoon over them to melt the cheese on them. Serve on **rye toast.**

Mrs. Glady Conant

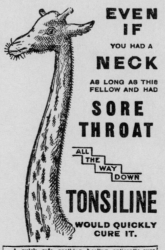

The South Bend Daily Times, Thursday, February 1, 1910.

PAPER INDICATES OVEN HEAT

To judge an oven's heat, try the oven every ten minutes with a piece of white paper. If too hot the paper will blaze up or blacken. When the paper becomes dark brown, darker than ordinary meat pie crust, the oven is fit for small pastry. When light brown, the color of nice pastry, it is ready for tarts. When the paper turns dark yellow, you can bake bread, large meat pies, or pound cakes. If it is just tinged, the oven is fit for sponge cake and meringue.

1910 RECIPES

Mary Diamond grew up in Berrien County, Michigan and came to South Bend in 1916. She reared four children, and all of them remember only this dressing on Thanksgiving. My husband remembers grinding the vegetables in an old grinder -- the blender is a great improvement.

TURKEY DRESSING

Dry sufficient white bread to produce **5 cups of ground crumbs.** The bread may be ground in an old fashioned grinder or a blender.

    1 lb. pkg. carrots, cleaned, pared, and ground
    1 onion, ground
    1 large potato, peeled and ground
    5 stalks celery, cleaned and ground
    1 cup butter, melted and cooled
    2 Tbsp. salt
    1 tsp. rubbed sage
    1 tsp. black pepper
    2 eggs
    1½ cans (12 oz.) **evaporated milk**

Grind the dry ingredients and vegetables; mix in a very large bowl. Break the eggs into a bowl and stir with a fork until mixed, then add to the ground mixture. Add the milk and melted butter. Adjust the milk as needed to produce a mixture which is the consistency of stiff mashed potatoes.

This recipe yields enough dressing to fill a 16 lb. turkey plus 1 casserole. Be sure when filling the turkey to leave room for expansion. I leave room to fit my hand in above the dressing. Truss the bird.

The casserole should be refrigerated until ready for baking. Using a baster, ladle some of the turkey juices onto the casserole. Bake about 45 minutes.

Mrs. Arthur (Dagny) Diamond
From her mother-in-law,
Mary Keitzer Diamond

WARNING MR. TURKEY

Good morning, Mr. Turkey!
I'se come to talk to you;
You'se most awful big and gobbly,
An you kinda scares me too!

But I'se got somethin' to tell you
That I think you ought to hear;
It is this, dear Mr. Gobbler—
Thanksgiving's awful near!

It surely comes next Thursday—
That is just what mama said.
An' if you're here that morning,
Mr. Turkey, you'll be dead!

An' it made me feel real sorry,
What I heard my mama say;
So I came right off to tell you—
Mr. Turkey, run away!!!

Woman's World November 1912

It's hard to believe that anything as good as sauerbraten could meet with public disfavor, but during World War I, it was unpopular to be German. Even sauerkraut was quickly renamed "Liberty Cabbage."

SAUERBRATEN

    4 lbs. beef (chuck, rump, or round), **rolled and tied**
    1 pt. vinegar
    Water
    4 bay leaves
    12 peppercorns
    4 cloves
    1 bunch carrots, cut in strips
    6 onions, sliced
    1 Tbsp. sugar
    12 gingersnaps
    Salt and pepper

Wipe the meat with a damp cloth and sprinkle thoroughly with salt and pepper. Place the meat in an earthen dish and add vinegar and enough water to cover. Add the bay leaves, peppercorns, and cloves; let stand tightly covered for 5 days in a cool place. (Today, place the meat in the refrigerator.)

Put the meat in a Dutch oven and brown well on all sides. Add the carrots, onions, and 1 cup of the spiced vinegar. Cover tightly and cook over a low flame about 3 hours or until the meat is tender. When the meat is cooked, add the sugar and crumbled gingersnaps; cook for 10 minutes longer. This makes a delicious gravy. If necessary, more of the spiced vinegar may be added.

Mrs. Harry (Betty) Koehler
From her mother-in-law,
Mrs. Othelia Koehler

Chicken in a Jug is an old family recipe from Mrs. Borough's home state of Alabama. Cook and serve the chicken in a jug or bean pot. It's an attractive and different way to present your main course, and the jug keeps the chicken warm while you dine.

CHICKEN IN A JUG

    Chicken pieces
    Olive oil
    Salt
    Pepper, freshly ground

Rub cut-up chicken pieces (any amount) with oil. Season with salt and use a liberal amount of pepper. (When you think you have enough pepper, use more.) Put the chicken in a brown glazed jug or bean pot. Put foil over the top of the jug, then place the lid on the foil. Do not add any liquid. Bake in an oven for 3 hours at 300-325 degrees.

Mrs. Lester (Aileen) Borough

TEN FOOD COMMANDMENTS

1. Thou shalt not waste a single ounce of food, for upon it rests the fate of America and the world.

2. Thou shalt save wheat so that thy foreign brothers may not starve for lack of it.

3. Thou shalt use meat sparingly, for the herds of Europe are depleted and meat is ammunition for fighters.

4. Thou shalt not complain when butter is not offered thee—thy French and English Allies have almost forgotten the taste of it, for they know that fat is used for high explosives fired against the Hun.

5. Thy sweets and confections must be few for sugar is no longer grown in the land of war—America's crop must supply many nations.

6. Thou shalt cherish every drop of milk, for fodder is high and cows are few. Babes like thine own are dying for lack of this perfect food.

7. Thou shalt eat poultry, vegetables, fruits and those perishables which spoil on the high seas.

8. Thou shalt refuse to keep in thy employ men or women who are food wasters.

9. Thou shalt sacrifice joyfully, that our men and the men and women behind the lines may eat and live.

10. Thou shalt rejoice when the conflict is over, for thine is a part of the victory. *The Delineator, November, 1918.*

Here is a recipe handed down to my wife by her mother. Her dad was born in Cornwall, England.

CORNISH PASTY

1½ lbs. good steak
4 large potatoes
1 medium onion
Salt
Pepper
Butter
Enough pie dough to make 4 shells

Roll out one-quarter of the dough. Slice 1 potato very thin. Alternate small cubes of steak, potatoes, and a little onion. Season and add several dabs of butter. Fold the dough over and seal edges - shape of half of a pie.

Bake at 400 degrees for 30 minutes, then at 275 degrees for 30 minutes.

Mr. Arthur Sumption
From the recipe book of Ila Sumption

HUNGARIAN GOULASH

1 oz. salt pork
1 pound round steak
Flour
Salt and paprika

1 cup tomatoes
½ stalk celery
1 small onion
1 blade mace
1 bay leaf
3 whole cloves
3 whole peppercorns

Fry the salt pork until a light brown. Add the beef, cut into two-inch pieces and sprinkle with flour. Cover with water and simmer for 2 hours. Season with salt and paprika.

Then cook a sauce of the vegetables and spices for 20 minutes in water sufficient to cover them. Thicken with flour, using a tablespoonful moistened in cold water to each cup of liquid, and season. Serve the meat on a platter with the sauce poured over it.

Potatoes, carrots, and green peppers, cooked until tender and cut into small pieces or long narrow strips, are usually put over the top.

Mr. Daniel Zakrowski

SCALLOPED POTATOES

Peel and boil **10-12 medium potatoes** till firm, but fork tender. Cool, then slice ¼ inch thick.

Butter a 10 x 12-inch baking dish.

Layer the sliced potatoes and dot with **butter.** Sprinkle with **salt** and **pepper** and **¼ cup flour.** Top with **6-8 pieces each of sliced Velveeta, sliced Colby or Cheddar cheese,** and **diced ham.***

Repeat the layers of potatoes, spices, butter, flour, cheese, and ham.

Pour **2-3 cups of milk** over the top (be sure that the flour moistened).

Bake at 350 degrees for 1 hour. (Check during baking to see if more liquid is needed.)

*(Ed: Since the term "pieces" is not a standard measure, adjust the quantities of cheese and ham to your personal taste. This dish is absolutely delicious; a meal your whole family will love.)

Mrs. Michael (Sharon) Love
From her grandmother,
Mrs. Hilda Anderson

Meat Savers - *Peas, beans, lentils, and peanuts.*
Cereal Savers - *Potatoes, sweet potatoes, bananas.*
Sugar Savers - *Sweet potatoes, and all fruit.*

1910 RECIPES

This is another time-saver from my mother-in-law. It uses oleo instead of butter, is cooked on top of the stove instead of using a double-boiler, and never curdles.

HOLLANDAISE SAUCE

3 Tbsp. margarine
2 Tbsp. lemon juice
2 egg yolks
Dash of salt and cayenne pepper
2¾ Tbsp. boiling water

Melt the margarine in a small saucepan on top of the stove. Add the remaining ingredients. Beat with a hand beater until the right consistency. Serve immediately. It is great with fresh vegetables.

This makes a small amount, but it can be doubled.

Mrs. Louis N. (Janice) Rugee
From her mother-in-law,
Mrs. S.B. (Louise Nickel) Rugee

During the war years, women were called upon to perform many tasks which had previously been done only by men. Kate Buckley seems quite at home driving a tractor with an Oliver plow in tow.

Ruth Goewey married a young naval officer in June 1918. Her wedding gown is now one of the many lovely dresses in the Historical Society costume collection.

AUNT NELLIE'S SPICE CAKE

1½ cups dark brown sugar
⅔ cup butter
2 eggs, separated
2½ cups flour
½ tsp. soda
2 tsp. baking powder
¾ cup sweet milk
1 cup raisins, or ½ cup raisins and ½ cup currants
1 tsp. lemon extract
Pinch of cloves
½ tsp. nutmeg
½ tsp. cinnamon

Beat the eggs separately. Cream the butter and sugar. Add the beaten egg yolks. Dust the raisins with about ½ cup of the flour, then add the dry ingredients alternately with the milk and lemon extract. Add the raisins. Lastly, fold in the beaten egg whites. Use greased paper in a tube or large shallow pan. (Aunt Nellie used an enamel milk pan.) Bake slowly at 325 degrees for 50 minutes to 1 hour. Frost with a powdered sugar and butter icing.

Mrs. D. William (Ruth Goewey) Bungert
From her Aunt Nellie

PINEAPPLE, BUTTERSCOTCH SKILLET CAKE

¼ lb. butter
1 cup brown sugar
8 or 9 slices pineapple
1 cup white sugar
3 eggs (beat whites separately)
1 tsp. vanilla
8 Tbsp. pineapple juice
1⅛ cups flour
1 tsp. baking powder
Pinch of salt

In an iron skillet, melt the butter and brown sugar. Lay the pineapple slices in this and simmer.

In a mixing bowl, add the white sugar and egg yolks, flour and baking powder (sifted together 3 or 4 times.). Add the vanilla and pineapple juice. Beat well. Lastly, fold in the stiffly beaten egg whites. Pour this into the skillet over the pineapple and bake in a moderate oven.* When slightly cool, turn out onto a plate and serve with whipped cream.

*(Ed: Bake in a 350 degree oven for 30 minutes - using a 10-inch skillet. A 20 oz. can of pineapple should give you enough pineapple and juice for this recipe.)

Mrs. Robert H. Nickerson

My mother, Lillian Clair Rodgers, married Paul Phenias Runnels on the 25th of December, 1907, and together they raised a family of eight children. As you can see by the name of the cake, with eight children she didn't have time for failures. This recipe was written for baking in the oven of a wood-burning stove

NEVER FAIL CHOCOLATE CAKE

Add as in order into bowl:
1 whole egg
½ cup cocoa
½ cup shortening
1½ cups flour
½ cup sour milk
1 tsp. vanilla
1 tsp. baking soda
¼ tsp. salt
1 cup sugar
½ cup boiling water

Do not stir until the last item is added, then stir until thoroughly mixed. Bake in an oven.*

*(Ed: Use a greased 8 x 8-inch pan. Bake at 350 degrees for 35-40 minutes.)

Mrs. Paul (Edna R.) Van Dusen
From her mother,
Mrs. Lillian Clair Runnels

CHESS PIE

1½ cups sugar
½ cup butter or margarine
¼ tsp. salt
3 eggs
1 Tbsp. vinegar
1 Tbsp. cornmeal
1 tsp. vanilla

Cream the butter and sugar. Add the salt. Add the eggs one at a time; beat well after each. Add the vinegar, cornmeal, and vanilla. Beat well. Pour into an unbaked pie shell. Bake at 350 degrees for 45-50 minutes, or until the filling is set.
Variation: Add **1 cup coconut.**

PIE CRUST:
2 cups flour
1 tsp. salt
1 cup shortening
½ cup milk
1 Tbsp. vinegar

Mix the flour and salt together. In a 1 cup measure, mix the milk and vinegar; set aside. Cut the shortening into the flour and salt. Blend the milk and vinegar into the flour mixture with a fork. Chill before rolling. This dough can be rolled very thin. It is very good for unbaked pie shells.

Mrs. Ronald (Nancy) Eversole

Mary and Thaddessa Taylor were the granddaughters of Lathrop Taylor. In 1827 Mr. Taylor came to this area as an Indian trader, and together with Alexis Coquillard, platted the town of South Bend four years later. Mr. Taylor remained an active and prominent member of the community until his death in 1892.

APPLE PUDDING

Butter a baking dish and fill it about ⅔ full of **sliced apples** over which put a **cup of sugar** and some **cinnamon** and dots of **butter,** if wanted richer.
Put in a mixing bowl **1 cup flour, 1 cup sugar,** and **1 tsp. baking powder.** Add **1 unbeaten egg.** Mix with a fork, then place these crumbs on top of the apples. Bake to a golden brown.* Serve with cream.

*(Ed: Bake in a 325 degree oven for about 25 minutes.)

Misses Mary and Thaddessa Taylor
From Adelle Studebaker

A BAKER'S SECRET
Don't draw hot water from the tank when baking. If you do the oven will cool off.

1910 RECIPES

South Bend turned out to cheer her Doughboys as they marched down Michigan Street.

My mother obtained this recipe from her sister, Evea Darling Miller, sometime after 1915. Although America was not yet in The Great War, a great deal of food was being sent overseas to feed the starving people of Europe; consequently, many staples were soon in short supply here at home. Mother also used this recipe during the difficult times following World War I: as an economy measure during the Depression and as a way to cope with the rationing of the Second World War.

EGGLESS, BUTTERLESS AND MILKLESS CAKE

1 cup sugar
½ cup lard
½ cup raisins
½ cup nutmeats
1 tsp. cinnamon
¼ tsp. cloves
¼ tsp. nutmeg
1 cup water

Boil 3 minutes and cool. Add:

2 cups flour
1 tsp. baking powder
1 tsp. baking soda dissolved in 1 Tbsp. water

Bake at 350 degrees until a straw comes out clean.*

*(Ed: Grease and flour a small tube pan, about 4-5 cups, or a loaf pan. Bake for 35 minutes for the tube pan and a bit longer for a loaf pan.)

Mary Ellen Handwork
From her mother,
Mrs. Etta Darling Carr

This delicious orange whip would be the perfect ending for any special meal. It is a Jewish variation of the famous Italian dessert, Zabaglione.

ORANGE LIQUEUR WHIP

6 egg yolks
6 tsp. superfine sugar
3 Tbsp. orange juice
2 tsp. lemon juice
Grated rind of ½ orange and ½ lemon
3 Tbsp. orange-flavored liqueur

Beat the yolks and sugar with an electric blender, egg beater, or whisk until thick and white. Beat in the orange juice, lemon juice, rinds, and liqueur. Transfer to a basin standing in a pan of almost boiling water. (A double boiler may be used instead.) Continue to whisk vigorously until the mixture fluffs up and has the texture of a whisked sponge or mousse. Immediately remove from the heat and stand in a basin of cold water. Continue to whisk until cool. Spoon into 6 tall glasses. Serve cold.

Mrs. Tobi Van Dyke

DELICATE PUDDING

½ cup rice
1½ cups water
2 cups milk
4 eggs
½ tsp. vanilla
½ cup sugar
½ tsp. salt

Boil the rice in the water. When it's nearly done, add the milk and salt and cook until it is soft. Add the yolks of the eggs, beaten with the sugar; cook until thickened, stirring constantly. Take from the stove and stir in the beaten whites of 2 eggs and the vanilla. Pour into a 2½ qt. baking dish.

Make a meringue of the remaining **2 egg whites** with an additional ½ **cup sugar.** Spread over the top of the pudding and set in the oven over a medium flame to brown.

Mrs. Ervin (Bertha) Purucker

The armies fighting in our defense cannot be maintained through this winter unless there is food enough for them and for the women and children at home.

The Soldiers Need	The Folks at Home Can Use
Wheat	*Corn, oats, barley, and rye*
Butter and lard	*Cottonseed oil, peanut oil,*
	Corn oil, and drippings
Sugar	*Molasses, honey, and syrups*
Bacon, beef	*Chicken, eggs, cottage cheese,*
mutton, and pork	*fish, nuts, peas, and beans*

FILLED SPONGE CAKE

1¼ cups flour
Pinch of salt
5 eggs, separated
½ tsp. cream of tartar
5 Tbsp. cold water
1¼ cups sugar
1 tsp. lemon or vanilla flavor

Sift together the flour and salt. Beat the egg whites until foamy. Add the cream of tartar and beat until stiff. (Beat the whites before the yolks so that you don't have to wash the beaters.) Beat the yolks (in a cold bowl) with the cold water until foamy. Add the sugar gradually and continue to beat.

After you have added the sugar to the yolks, add the flour and salt mixture and beat. Then fold in the egg whites with a large spoon. Pour into an angel food cake pan and bake at 325 degrees for 60 minutes. (Rinse your cake pan in cold water before you put in the batter.)

FILLING FOR SPONGE CAKE:
2 bars German Sweet Chocolate
1 Tbsp. sugar
3 Tbsp. water
4 egg yolks, unbeaten
4 egg whites, beaten stiff
1 tsp. vanilla

Melt the chocolate, sugar, and water in a double boiler. When melted and mixed, beat with a spoon, then add 1 egg yolk, unbeaten, one at a time (beat after each addition). Be sure to take the pan off the burner when adding the yolks. Lastly, fold in the egg whites and vanilla. Let this cool before putting into the cake*.

When the filling is cool, cut off about 1 inch from the top of the cake. Tear out the inside of the cake to within ½ inch of each side and 1 inch from the bottom. Put the cooled filling into the cake and replace the top. Frost with **whipped cream** to which you have added **1 tsp. confectioners sugar** and **1 tsp. vanilla.**

Use the rest of the sponge cake pieces with a custard recipe, or just enjoy eating them.

*(Ed: The filling will be soft, so be sure that it is cool before it is put into the cake. Keep refrigerated before serving.)

Mrs. Harry (Betty) Koehler
From her mother-in-law,
Mrs. Othelia Koehler

HOUSEHOLD HINTS

When serving afternoon tea, try using slices of orange instead of the inevitable lemon. The flavor is very delicious, especially when combined with green tea. Fresh sliced cucumbers also give an agreeable flavor to hot tea if a dash of rum be added to the beverage.

In making coffee, if you will add a dried prune it will improve the flavor and give the coffee a richer color. Some who cannot use coffee without, can use it with the prunes added.

In frying pancakes, after one panful has been cooked use no more grease, but slice a raw potato and rub the pan each time before putting in more batter. Pancakes fried in this way are more easily digested and it is a saving of lard in these hard times.

Spirits of turpentine should always be kept on hand. It is one of the best known remedies for a wound. If a rusty nail is run into the flesh, turpentine should be applied at once, as it gives immediate relief, and will prevent lock-jaw.

If hair is falling out, give your hair a good egg shampoo. Beat up two eggs, rub well into the scalp, let stay on until dry, then rinse out with lukewarm water. When hair and scalp are dry, rub into scalp with tips of your fingers a little coal-oil, which will destroy any germs, and give strength to the roots of the hair. A little yellow vaseline on the scalp, put on the same way, will make the hair grow. Apply vaseline at night two or three times a week. Shampoo every two weeks for a while, then once a month will be enough. Brush your hair well every morning, 120 strokes are not too many.

To dry-clean shirtwaists, put 4 ounces of corn meal into a 24-pound flour sack or a pillow slip. Put the waist into this, and rub or knead gently so that the meal will come in contact with all parts of the fabric. Leave it there for a day or two, then shake and dust thoroughly, and press with a hot iron.

For mud stains on (colored goods), let the mud dry thoroughly, and then remove as much as possible by brushing. When fully dry cover with a mixture of salt and flour and keep in a dry place. If the stains are extensive place the garment in a large paper flour sack with a quantity of salt and flour well mixed, shake vigorously, tie up the sack, and allow it to hang behind the stove for a few days. Afterwards shake out the dust and press.

Ovens in all houses should be well scrubbed out after cooking, with hot soda water and soap. Any hard substance which is caked on the baking sheets should be scraped off with an old knife. It is really very simple to have the oven scrubbed out while it is still hot, after baking a joint, etc., and many disagreeable smells are avoided by this practice. For the purpose a long brush such as is used to clean carriage wheels, is useful. With it the back wall of an oven can easily be reached and the danger of burnt hands avoided.

1910 RECIPES

Before the days of electric refrigeration, our family had a delectable treat in store for winter birthdays. Now, in winter, whenever I knock great pointed slabs of ice from the roof, I remember when my mother collected buckets of icicles, got out the hand-turned freezer, bought rock salt, and prepared the caramel custard for her "famous" dessert. Today, there is no reason why it couldn't be frozen in an electric ice cream freezer.

WINTER BIRTHDAY CARAMEL ICE CREAM

1 qt. milk blended with
¼ cup flour and
2 beaten egg yolks

Cook over boiling water in a double boiler, stirring constantly until a thick custard is formed; keep hot.

Melt **¾ lb. brown sugar,** without water, in a heavy iron skillet; while hot and liquid stir into the hot custard.

Cool. Beat the **2 egg whites** and whip **1 pint whipping cream.** Stir and fold into the cooled custard and freeze.

The tricky part is caramelizing the sugar. Care must be taken to stir it constantly and not burn it. If it is mixed with something cooler, it is likely to explode.

Martha Jane Fields
From her mother

Molasses was the primary sweetening agent in America until the latter part of the 19th century. As a by-product produced during the refining of sugar, it was both affordable and plentiful. It was used for cooking, baking, as a syrup, and, when teamed with sulphur, as a medicine. Take a bite of these mellow Molasses Cookies, close your eyes and savor the taste of a simpler time.

MOLASSES COOKIES

A. Cream Together:
    ½ cup lard or butter
    ½ cup brown sugar
    ½ cup molasses
    1 egg

B. Sift Together:
    2⅓ cups flour
    1 tsp. ginger
    1 tsp. cinnamon
    ¼ tsp. salt

Add mixture B to mixture A alternately with **6 Tbsp. of cold water.** Then dissolve **2 tsp. of soda** with **2 Tbsp.of hot water** and add to the above. As a final ingredient, add **1 cup raisins.** Drop onto a greased cookie sheet. Bake at 375 degrees for 10-12 minutes.

Mrs. J. Oliver Casaday

CRUMB COOKIES

1 cup dry bread crumbs
1 cup chopped nuts
½ cup sugar
1 egg
(Salt)

Mix and drop from a spoon tip. Bake in a medium oven, 375 degrees until brown.*
*(Ed: Bake about 10 minutes.)

Miss M. Geraldine Hatt
From her aunt,
Mrs. Jerome Cooney

The concession wagon was a welcome sight outside the Notre Dame Fieldhouse in 1914.
Courtesy of the University of Notre Dame Archives.

GRANDMA'S CRACKER JACK

1 cup sugar
1 Tbsp. vinegar
¼ cup light Karo syrup
½ cup butter
¼ tsp. salt
2 Tbsp. hot water
6 qts. popped popcorn

Heat everything but the popcorn in a heavy saucepan. Boil until a little dropped in cold water becomes brittle.

Pour over the popcorn; stir to coat.

You may add food coloring to the syrup before pouring over the popcorn.

Mr. David Bainbridge
From his grandmother,
Mrs. Doris Haas Labadie

LEBKUCHEN

¼ lb. almonds, ground
6 eggs, beaten light
1 lb. powdered sugar
¼ lb. citron, cut up
1 lemon peel, cut up
1 tsp. nutmeg
1 tsp. cinnamon
½ tsp. cloves
1 tsp. allspice
½ tsp. cardamom seed, ground
2 tsp. baking powder
2½ cups sifted flour

Mix the above and put into 3 round cake pans. Use brown paper in the bottom of the cake pans. When you remove the cake from the pans, hold a damp cloth on the paper for a few seconds to loosen the paper before pulling if off.*

Bake this for 20 minutes at 350 degrees — 10 minutes on the lower shelf, then 10 minutes on the upper shelf.

*(Ed: If you don't have time to cut brown paper to fit the bottom of the pans, simply grease and flour them instead. For 3 8-inch cake pans, bake about 5 minutes longer than the stated time. This makes an absolutely delicious treat: part cookie - part brownie. It will keep for weeks.)

Mrs. Harry (Betty) Koehler
From her mother-in-law,
Mrs. Othelia Koehler

MUSTARD MIXED PICKLES

1 qt. small whole cucumbers
1 qt. large cucumbers, sliced
1 qt. green tomatoes, sliced
1 qt. small button onions
1 large cauliflower
4 green peppers, cut fine

Make a brine of **4 qts. water** and **1 pt. salt.** Pour over the mixture of vegetables and let soak for 24 hours. Heat just enough to scald the mixture and turn into a colander to drain.

Mix **1 cup flour, 6 Tbsp. ground mustard,** and **1 Tbsp. tumeric** with enough cold **vinegar** to make a smooth paste, then add **1 cup sugar** and enough **vinegar** to make 2 quarts in all. Boil until it thickens and is smooth, stirring all the time. Add the vegetables and cook until heated through. Seal in jars.

Miss M. Geraldine Hatt
From Mrs. Edward Dubail

PEPPER RELISH

1 doz. red peppers, cut fine
1 doz. green peppers, cut fine
1 doz. onions, cut fine

(These should be cut and not put through a grinder.)
Pour boiling hot water over the above and let stand 15 minutes. Drain and add:

1 qt. vinegar (5%)
4 cups sugar
1 Tbsp. salt

Cook 20 minutes and can.

Makes about 8 pints, depending on how big the peppers and onions are.

Mrs. Harry (Betty) Koehler
From her mother-in-law,
Mrs. Othelia Koehler

GUIDELINES FOR KITCHEN PATRIOTS

All the blood, all the heroism, all the money and munitions in the world will not win this war unless our allies and the armies behind them are fed. They will not be fed unless we take care; indeed, if we are not prudent we, too, shall go hungry. Protect our supplies, then, that we may be fed, that your sacrifice of life and money be not in vain. Lest we lose the Great Cause, stand guard, each day, in your home, over your supply of food.

Use meat and vegetables grown in your own locality as far as possible and thus avoid needless transportation.

Serve no white bread with dinner.

Serve no butter with lunch or dinner.

Use less fried meat - it is usually poorly cooked and is quite indigestible.

Do not use breakfast cereals made from wheat.

Use potatoes in many forms.

Use tough cuts of meat in stews - they cost less and are of better flavor.

Plan your meals at least three days in advance. This helps you to buy to better advantage and gives variety in material and preparation.

Trim your own meat and melt the fat.

Don't let a scrap get into the garbage pail.

If there are bits of bread left, dry and grind or pound, using the crumbs in place of flour.

Use cornstarch or rice flour for thickening sauces and gravies and in puddings. (Use half as much as you would of flour.)

Bread made of mixed flours is better body-building material than that made from one grain alone.

The Food Administration asks everyone to maintain rigidly a minimum of at least:

Two wheatless days each week and 1 wheatless meal each day; the wheatless days to be Monday and Wednesday.

One meatless day each week which shall be Tuesday and 1 meatless meal each day.

One porkless day each week in addition to Tuesday, which shall be Saturday.

We will make every endeavor to see that the country is provided with a supply of household sugar on the basis of 3 lbs. of sugar for each person per month. Do not consume more.

In this winter of 1918 lies the period when there will be tested in this great free country of ours the question as to whether or not our people are capable of voluntary individual self-sacrifice to save the world.

Cookbook For Kitchen Patriots — 1918.

Mrs. J.M.
Studebaker II

1920's

The stuff dreams are made of --
This skyblue silk organza ankle-length
gown is woven with silver threads.
Three layers of scallop-edged skirt are
trimmed with silver lace and hang
handkerchief-style. Large appliqued
decorative baskets of flowers of multi-
colored pastel ribbon adorn the skirt,
bodice and lower back. The bodice is
generously trimmed with silver lace
and wide panels over the shoulders
which hang blouson style in back.
Worn by Mrs. J.M. Studebaker II.
Circa 1920.

POSTWAR WHOOPEE

The 1920's were a time of sweeping cultural and social changes. Children who had heard stories at their grandfather's knee of long ago Civil War battles were unprepared for the crushing realities of trench warfare. Caught in the aftermath of World War I, anxious youth, stripped of its innocence, cast longing eyes to the security of times past, but sadly found the world too changed. Since there was no going back, Americans threw open the throttle and roared blindly into the future.

Jazz set the tone for a decade dedicated to the pursuit of passion and pleasure. Even though Prohibition was the law of the land, the hip flask and cocktail shaker came perilously close to supplanting the eagle as our national emblem. "Good time" girls quickly threw away their corsets and their inhibitions in an attempt to prove that they were as good and as bad as any man. With the increasing popularity of petting parties, cigarettes, lip rouge, and boot leg whiskey, it's little wonder that parents feared that the end of civilization was near at hand.

The full-figured, mature woman was no longer the ideal; the modern young sophisticate now sported the boyish figure of an immature girl. The straight chemise dress, cloche hat, and bobbed hair with a "kiss curl" over each ear soon became the flapper uniform. Hemlines marched upward revealing women's legs for the first time in centuries and quickly made stockings an important fashion accessory. Silent movie stars such as Clara Bow and Gloria Swanson began assuming the role of fashion trend setters, popularizing such seductive creations as slinky evening sheaths and lounging pajamas.

The simple, basic lines of the chemise were a blessing for many ladies of moderate income. Now it was possible to make stylish clothes at home and use only about a third of the material which would have been needed at the turn of the century. One of the major proponents of elegant simplicity was Coco Chanel. Her comfortable, well-cut fashions opened the world of couturier clothing to all women, while her perfume, Chanel #5, has continued to be an enticing presence since 1925.

After years of trying to achieve a voluptuous figure, it was not easy to assume the conformation of a walking stick over night. In a world that suddenly saw curves as excess fat, there seemed to be only one recourse for the pleasingly plump -- dieting became very chic. Eating heavy meals was now considered more folly than fashion. In years past, coleslaw was one of the few raw vegetable concoctions which seemed to be acceptable for human consumption; now luncheons and afternoon teas featured interesting salads and dainty sandwiches.

The "New Nutrition" movement was one positive product of the search for trimmer bodies. The word, vitamin, soon became a part of everyone's vocabulary. Parents were shown that fruit juices, milk, and green, leafy vegetables were a vital part of good nutrition. Canned food, now no longer only for the rich, provided a welcome diversity in people's diets, although many women still believed that tin cans in the trash were the sign of a lazy housewife.

To many people, however, beauty was only skin deep. A tanning craze, billed as "sunbath hygiene", swept America. The pale, porcelain skin of the past was definitely out. The pursuit of health and beauty required women to throw away their parasols and wear increasingly more revealing swimwear so that the body could be exposed to the curative rays of the sun. In 1921, Atlantic City sought to capitalize on this quest for the body beautiful when it launched a contest for swim-suited lovelies and the Miss America Pageant was born.

A modern kitchen and bathroom were now the desire of women everywhere. Electricity was powering countless appliances including automatic toasters which now boasted timers. Wonderful new electric irons with adjustable thermostats became the most popular appliance of the decade. Thanks to technology, housework no longer had to be a full time job.

Women began to assume a new role in American life. The Great War had given ladies a sense of independence and they definitely wanted more. The efforts of tireless suffragettes were finally rewarded in 1920 when women walked to the ballot box for the first time and cast their votes in the presidential election.

"Flaming Youth" dominated a decade of perpetual motion: flailing arms to a Charleston beat; Jolson's "Jazz Singer" gave movies a voice; Rockne, Ruth, and Red Grange; sleek roadsters and rumbleseat romance; Jack Dempsey's flashing fists; Coolidge and Capone, G-men and bath tub gin; ticker tape fury to welcome home the greatest hero of them all, Charles Lindbergh. Speculation stoked the fires of prosperity to a white heat until October, 1929, when the flame went out.

The 1926 Notre Dame football team was photographed as they prepared to board the South Shore. Coach Rockne is lost in the crowd, about three rows back near the steps to the first train car.

For over half a century, Knute Rockne has been one of the most dominant figures in college football. During his 13 years as head coach, Rockne transformed the University of Notre Dame from an unheralded Midwestern school into a national institution. He managed to build one winning football team

after another by emphasizing machine-like precision and uncompromising sportsmanship. Rockne's untimely death in 1931 may have temporarily dimmed the light, but his career continues to be the standard against which other players and coaches measure success.

MRS. ROCKNE'S SWEDISH COFFEE CAKE

Cream **½ lb. butter** with **2 cups sugar**; add **3 eggs** and beat well. Combine **3 tsp. baking powder** with **3 cups flour**. Add **1 large can evaporated milk** alternately with the sifted flour mixture. Pour the batter into 2 greased pans: one 13 x 9-inches and one 9 x 9-inches*. (I use an 8 x 8-inch pan for the small cake; it makes it a little higher.) Sprinkle the following topping over the batter. Bake for 30 to 35 minutes at 350 degrees. (This coffee cake freezes well.)

TOPPING:
- **¾ cup brown sugar**
- **¾ cup coconut**
- **4 Tbsp. flour**
- **4 Tbsp. melted butter**

*(Ed: This coffee cake can also be baked in three 8-inch round pans. It probably serves 12 - 18 people.)

Mrs. Mary Fischer
From Mrs. Knute (Bonnie) Rockne

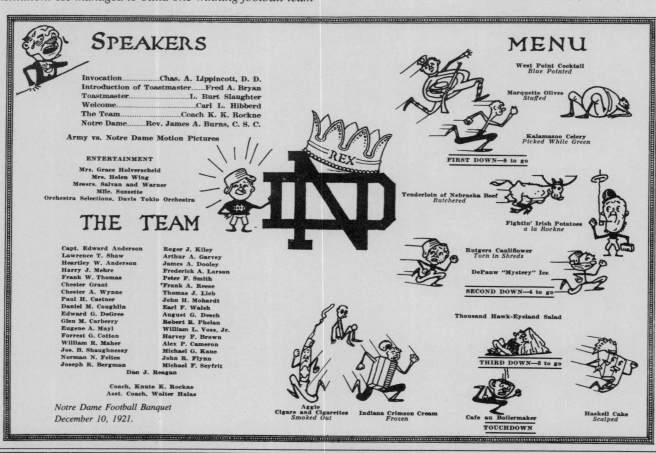

For many years, my mother was the secretary to Mr. Hubbard, the president for the First Bank and Trust Co. After the birth of her second child, she decided to remain at home. In order to use her secretarial abilities, she worked as a volunteer at the First Christian Church sending out the weekly bulletin, the "Friday Caller." She devotedly performed this task for 57 years. This recipe for Irish Soda Bread was given to Mother by Betty Kryder, a member of the office staff at the church.

IRISH SODA BREAD

4 cups sifted flour
¼ cup sugar
1 tsp. salt
1½ tsp. baking powder
2 Tbsp. caraway seed (This is what gives the bread its flavor, don't leave it out.)
¼ cup (½ stick) **margarine**
2 cups dark seedless raisins
1⅓ cups buttermilk
1 egg
1 tsp. baking soda

Sift together the flour, sugar, salt, and baking powder. Cut in the margarine with a pastry blender until like coarse meal. Stir in the raisins and caraway seed. Beat together the buttermilk, egg, and soda. Stir this into the flour mixture until just moistened. Turn out onto a floured board and knead gently until smooth. Place in a 1½ qt. greased round casserole. Cut a cross on the top of the bread about 1½ inches deep, running to almost the ends of the loaf. Bake at 375 degrees for 50 minutes. Cover with aluminum foil and continue baking for another 10 minutes, until the loaf is brown and sounds hollow when rapped with the knuckles.

Mary Ellen Handwork
From her mother,
Mrs. Etta Viola Darling Carr

MOM'S HAM SAUCE

1 tsp. dry mustard
¼ tsp. powdered cloves
¼ tsp. cinnamon
2 Tbsp. white vinegar
8 oz. currant or crab-apple jelly

In a small saucepan, mix the mustard, powdered cloves, and cinnamon with the vinegar and jelly. Heat over low heat till the jelly is melted, stirring constantly.

This can be served poured over hot ham or as a side dish to be served with ham; it is good either hot or cold.

Mrs. Walton (Carol) Collins
From her mother,
Mrs. Hubert (Jeanne) Huebner

At Christmas time, our family traditionally gathers on Christmas Eve for our main holiday dinner. Because of our Scandinavian heritage, we think it is especially nice to have a smorgasbord to honor our family traditions. The crowning glory of each dinner is a Swedish Almond Tea Ring which has been decorated for the holidays with red and green candied cherries and a powdered sugar glaze.

SWEDISH ALMOND TEA RING

3 - 3¼ cups all-purpose flour
1 pkg. active dry yeast
1 cup milk
6 Tbsp. butter or margarine
⅓ cup granulated sugar
½ tsp. salt
1 egg
1 recipe Almond Filling

In a larger mixer bowl, combine 2 cups of the flour and the yeast. In a saucepan, heat together the milk, butter or margarine, granulated sugar, and salt just until warm (115-120 degrees), stirring constantly until the butter almost melts. Add to the dry mixture in the mixer bowl. Add the egg. Beat at low speed of the electric mixer for ½ minute, scraping the bowl constantly. Beat for 3 minutes at high speed. By hand, stir in enough of the remaining flour to make a soft dough. Knead on a lightly floured surface till smooth, about 3 - 5 minutes. Shape into a ball and place in a greased bowl, turning to bring up the greased side. Cover and let rise in a warm place, free from drafts, until double in bulk (about 1 hour).

Punch the dough down. Let rest for 10 minutes. Roll to an 18 x 12-inch rectangle with a rolling pin (on a lightly floured surface). Spread with the Almond Filling. Roll up from the long edge jelly-roll style. Pinch to seal the edge. Place seam side down on a greased cookie sheet and shape into a ring. Pinch to seal where the edges meet. Cut with kitchen shears every ¾ inch to within ½ inch of the inner edge. Gently pull the slices alternately to the left and right (overlapping). Let rise in a warm place, free from drafts, until nearly double, about 45 minutes.

Bake in a 375 degree oven for 20 - 25 minutes. When cool, you may decorate with candied or maraschino cherries, whole or sliced almonds, other candied fruit or raisins and a sugar glaze. (A very simple glaze may be made by gradually adding milk to 1 cup powdered sugar while stirring constantly, until the mixture is a drizzling consistency.)

ALMOND FILLING:
Cream together ⅓ **cup granulated sugar** and **2 Tbsp. butter or margarine** until light and fluffy. Stir in ¼ **cup ground almonds** (may be made by placing chopped almonds in a blender - frequently push the almonds toward the blades; do in small batches for best results), and ¼ **tsp. almond extract.**

NOTE: When I make this recipe, I double the Almond Filling mixture. More calories, but great.

Mrs. Karen Keller

1920 RECIPES

I was given this recipe by a cousin, Ruth Uhl, who passed away in November 1984, at the age of 84. Both she and I are descendants of the Crepeau and Barnard families who settled in St. Joseph County before 1876. The following is a recipe that she usually served to company and which I had the pleasure of enjoying many times at her home.

GLORIFIED GINGER BREAD

Mix as for pie crust:
- **1 cup sugar**
- **2 cups flour**
- **½ cup shortening**
- **½ tsp. cinnamon**
- **½ tsp. ginger**
- **1 tsp. nutmeg**

Take out ½ cup of the above mixture - set aside.
Add the remaining to the mixture:
- **1 egg**
- **2 Tbsp. molasses**
- **1 cup sour milk** (or 2 Tbsp. vinegar to sweet milk)
- **1 tsp. baking soda**
- **½ tsp. salt**

Mix well and pour the batter into a well greased pan. Sprinkle the remaining ½ cup of the first mixture over the top. Bake for 25-35 minutes at 350 degrees.

Gloria Crepeau Cudney
From her cousin, Ruth Uhl

CHINESE BEETS

- **3 cans** (14 oz.) **beets, drained** (reserve liquid)
- **1 cup sugar**
- **2 Tbsp. cornstarch**
- **1 cup vinegar** (cider)
- **24 whole cloves**
- **3 Tbsp. catsup**
- **3 Tbsp. oil**
- **1 tsp. vanilla**
- **1½ cups beet juice** (add water to make 1½ cups if needed)

Cook all ingredients, except the beets, over medium heat until thick. Add the beets; heat through and serve. (You can use whole, chopped, or sliced beets.)

Mrs. Harrison (Lola) Lyons

BAKING POWDER DUMPLINGS

- **1 cup flour**
- **2 tsp. baking powder**
- **¼ tsp. salt**
- **½ cup milk or water** (scant)

Sift the dry ingredients. Stir in the milk or water and mix to form a smooth batter. Drop a teaspoonful at a time into boiling soup or broth. Cover the kettle; let boil for 5 minutes. Serve at once.

Mrs. Harold (Carolyn) Heath

As a young bride (in 1932) I completely lacked any cooking skills and found the recipes in the cookbooks of the day rather puzzling. In some desperation, I resurrected the cookbook I had used in the 7th grade in the William Bell School No. 60 in Indianapolis. There I found, among others, this recipe for Corn a la Southern. This dish, a kind of souffle, has become a real family favorite, handed down to children and grandchildren; it is always enjoyed and in demand.

CORN A LA SOUTHERN

- **½ cup cracker crumbs**
- **1 pt. scalded milk**
- **2 Tbsp. melted butter**
- **1 16-oz. can cream corn**
- **1 tsp. salt**
- **2 Tbsp. sugar**
- **Pepper**
- **3 well beaten eggs**

Add the cracker crumbs to the scalded milk and melted butter; mix well. Add the corn and seasonings and mix well. Add the beaten eggs and again mix well. Pour into a buttered casserole and bake at 350 degrees until firm, at least an hour.*
(*Ed. A 2-2½ qt. casserole works well. This serves 6-8.)

Mrs. H.L. (Margaret) Carrington

RED CABBAGE

1 head of red cabbage, sliced (sprinkle with **salt**). Pour hot water over it and let stand about 10 minutes. Fry **4 slices of diced bacon** and **1 small diced onion** to golden brown. Peel and core **1 large or 2 small apples** (about 1 cup); dice. After draining the water off the cabbage, add the apples, bacon, and onions; barely cover all this with boiling water. Add ½ **cup vinegar, salt** and **pepper** to taste. Simmer about 1 hour or so. At last add **2 Tbsp. of grape jelly or brown sugar.** (More jelly or sugar may be used if you like it a little sweeter.)

Mrs. Ervin (Bertha) Purucker

*The **Moderne** was established in 1929, by Nicholas J. Kalamaros. This popular restaurant, located at 110 W. Washington, had dining facilities, a candy counter, and soda fountain on the main floor. The ice cream was made in the basement, while the candies, which were the store's specialty, were made on the third floor. The restaurant closed in 1963, when Mr. Kalamaros died.*

RICE PUDDING
"Ala Moderne"

¼ cup rice
⅓ cup water
1 qt. milk
¼ cup butter
5 Tbsp. sugar
1 slice lemon
1 Tbsp. vanilla
3 eggs
1 cup raisins
Cinnamon

Over a high flame boil rice until it reaches the boiling point; then lower the flame and cook on medium heet until the rice absorbs all of the water. Add the milk, butter, sugar, lemon.

Over a high flame let come to a boil. Lower to medium flame and cook for 40 minutes, stirring occasionally. Remove from flame. Beat eggs well on beater for 8 minutes. Add to mixture slowly, and beat for 2 minutes longer. Replace on stove, add raisins, and continue beating and cook 2 minutes longer.

Pour contents into dish or pan, sprinkle with cinnamon and serve cold.

Mr. Edward Kalamaros

HOT POTATO SALAD

5 cups diced, cooked potatoes
½ lb. bacon, diced
⅓ cup vinegar plus enough water to make ½ cup total
½ cup chopped onion
1 slightly beaten egg
1 tsp. sugar
¼ tsp. pepper
1 tsp. salt

Cook the bacon until crisp. Remove and reserve. Combine ⅓ cup bacon drippings with the vinegar, water, egg, sugar, salt and pepper. Heat and stir until thickened. Add the potatoes, onion, and bacon. Toss and heat through.

Mrs. Robert (Helen) Veith
From her mother,
Mrs. Fred (Hattie) Ruppert

GNOCCHI
(Potato Dumplings)

3 large potatoes (boiled with jackets on)
1 cup flour
1 egg
1 cup spaghetti sauce
2 Tbsp. grated cheese

Peel the potatoes while hot. Mash well adding the flour and egg. (This will be like a dough.) Roll the dough into long strips (like bread sticks). Cut the strips into 1 inch pieces and make a print with the tines of a fork in each.

Drop into boiling salted water or broth. When they come to the top, remove from the water and drain. Place in a casserole by layers: after each layer of gnocchi, put a layer of sauce. Sprinkle with grated cheese. Serve this with your favorite meat. Serves 4-6.

Mrs. Arthur (Emma) Schlorch
From her mother,
Mrs. Catherine Savio Fenoglio

ROAST LEG OF LAMB
"Ala Moderne"

Leg of lamb - 5-6 lbs.
Salt & pepper
Olive oil
1 large lemon
4 cloves of garlic
1 cup water
Potatoes as needed
Tomatoes as needed

Wash off the entire leg of lamb and place it in a roasting pan. Spread salt, pepper, olive oil and lemon over the entire leg. Make incisions in the lamb in several places and insert cloves of garlic

Cover and cook for one hour in oven at 350 degrees. Add one cup of water to the gravy, and baste roast during cooking, until meat is well browned.

Potatoes and tomatoes may be added to the gravy during the last 45 minutes of baking as needed and desired.

Savory Short Ribs is one of Mrs. Keller's treasured family recipes. It was one of her mother's favorite dishes and brings back fond memories of Mrs. Keller's own childhood days. Short ribs were a very popular cut of meat in the 1930's and 1940's: they were an inexpensive meal during the Depression years and a meat which used few ration stamps during World War II.

SAVORY SHORT RIBS

¼-½ tsp. oregano
Salt
Pepper
2 bay leaves
½ cup chopped onions
½ cup chopped celery
6 short ribs

Brown the meat in a little salad oil (in a heavy pan). Add the seasonings and ½-1 cup water. Add the onions and celery. Cook 1½ hours or until the meat is tender. You may add carrots and green beans toward the end of the cooking time.

Mrs. George E. (Marjorie) Keller
From her mother,
Mary Cookingham Bidwell

SALSA VERDE
(Green Sauce)

5 hard cooked egg yolks
1 can (2 oz.) anchovies (use the oil)
1½ cups finely chopped parsley
1 clove garlic, chopped
⅛ tsp. pepper
Oil and vinegar to taste

Mash the yolks and anchovies to make a paste. Add the parsley, garlic, oil, vinegar, and pepper to make sauce consistency.

The flavors combine to make a sauce that lends itself to steak, boiled meats, chicken, fish, and vegetables.

Mrs. Arthur (Emma) Schlorch
From her mother,
Mrs. Catherine Savio Fenoglio

My father, M.P. Reed, used to prepare this every Sunday evening for the "gang" of high school students who would drop into our house for a get-together. It never curdles and never fails.

WELSH RAREBIT

1 cup sharp cheese
1 egg
½ tsp. salt
¼ tsp. dry mustard
1 Tbsp. flour made into a smooth paste with a bit of milk
1 cup scalded milk

Melt the cheese in a double boiler. Beat the egg and add. Blend in the salt, mustard, and flour paste. Add the milk after mixing well. Beat for 2 minutes with a hand beater until creamy (while still over the heat).

This may be made in advance and reheated later.

Mrs. Louis N. (Janice) Rugee
From her father,
Mr. M.P. Reed

MOMES BEEF MOUSSE

COMBINE:
2 eggs
1⅔ cups evaporated milk
2 cups fine soft bread crumbs
ADD:
2 lbs. ground beef
½ cup grated cheddar cheese
2 Tbsp. chopped green pepper
2 Tbsp. minced onion
2 tsp. salt
Pepper

Pack the mixture into a loaf pan or an 8 x 8-inch square pan. Cover with strips of bacon (about 3 or 4). Bake in a 350 degree oven for 45 minutes to 1 hour. Drain off juices. Let stand for 5 minutes or more before slicing. Prepare mushroom sauce.

MUSHROOM SAUCE:
Clean and slice ½ lb. fresh mushrooms. Saute, covered, in 2 Tbsp. butter for 5 minutes. Add:
1 can (10½ oz.) cream of mushroom soup
3 Tbsp. cream
2 Tbsp. Sherry (optional)
1 Tbsp. chopped parsley (or parsley flakes)

Heat the sauce gently and serve over the sliced Beef Mousse. Serve with Claret wine.

Mrs. John N. (Muriel) Perkins
From her daughter's mother-in-law

GRAPE JELLY

Wash the **grapes** and boil for about ½ hour. Strain the juice. Measure equal amounts of juice and **sugar** and boil (usually about ½ hour per cup). Seal in jars.

I never use preservatives, so I get the natural taste.

Mary Jane Micinski
From her grandmother

GRANDMA'S MEAT LOAF

1 lb. pork
1 lb. veal
2 lbs. beef
½ loaf stale white bread or crackers
1 large onion
½ cup water
4 or 5 eggs
Parsley, nutmeg, salt, and pepper to taste

Grind the well trimmed meat. Grate the hard bread, or if crackers are used, roll them. (If stale bread is used, soak the same in the water.) Mix the bread with the meat; add the seasonings and the finely cut onion and parsley. Add the well beaten eggs. Form into a loaf. Lay 2 or 3 strips of **bacon** in the bottom of a baking pan. Place the meat loaf on the bacon and then lay strips of bacon over the top of the meat loaf. Bake in a moderate oven, 350 degrees. Baste occasionally to make juicy.

Mrs. Ervin (Doris) Purucker
From her mother-in-law,
Mrs. Ervin (Bertha) Purucker

The Chicago South Shore and South Bend Railroad was understandably proud of its 2 new dining cars in 1927. Today, the South Shore is struggling to remain in business; it is the last electric interurban train in this country.

*The social upheaval following World War I produced a great deal of anxiety. The old rules which had governed 19th century society were viewed as stuffy and out-dated, but a new set of guidelines had yet to emerge. In 1922, the void was filled by Emily Post's **Etiquette: The Blue Book of Social Usage**. With this book in hand, a modern hostess could confidently plan an elegant luncheon featuring Chicken Divan (which, incidentally, was named for the Divan Parisienne Restaurant in New York where the recipe was first introduced).*

CHICKEN DIVAN

6 whole chicken breasts, cooked and boned
2 cans (10¾ oz.) cream of chicken soup
1 cup mayonnaise
1½ tsp. lemon juice
½ tsp. curry powder
1 cup sharp cheese, grated
2 pkg. frozen broccoli
Bread crumbs

Cook the broccoli and place in a buttered 9 x 13-inch baking dish. Bone the chicken and lay on top of the broccoli. Mix the soup, mayonnaise, lemon juice, curry powder, and half of the cheese. Pour this mixture over the chicken. Sprinkle with buttered bread crumbs and top with the remaining cheese. Bake at 350 degrees for 30-45 minutes. Serves 6-8. (A tasty side dish may be made by cooking rice in chicken broth and adding ½ tsp. curry powder.)

Mrs. Claude (Mary) Renshaw
From her mother-in-law,
Mrs. Mary K. Renshaw

The Volstead or National Prohibition Enforcement Act was the teeth behind the 18th Amendment, which outlawed the manufacture, sale, or transportation of alcoholic liquors. From the time it went into effect on January 16, 1920, until its repeal on December 5, 1933, Prohibition was one of the most widely violated laws in history. The enforcement apparatus created by the Volstead Act was never able to cope with the rising power of the bootleggers.

VOLSTEAD RAREBIT

2 cups sharp cheese, grated and firmly packed
2 Tbsp. butter
1 tsp. cornstarch
½ tsp. dry mustard
½ tsp. Worcestershire
Paprika (to taste)
¾ cup milk (instead of beer)

Melt the butter in a double boiler. Blend in the cornstarch, mustard, Worcestershire, and paprika. Add the cheese and milk. Cook and stir until smooth. Serve on toast or crackers.

Mrs. John (Jane) Olcott

1920 RECIPES

It was important for children to learn proper table etiquette at an early age.

Courtesy of the South Bend Community School Corporation.

My mother and father both came from the area around Turin, Italy. As a second son, my father was supposed to be a priest. When he decided that the priesthood was not the life for him, he went to his father to obtain permission to come to America; his father promptly said, "No." Undaunted, he next approached his uncle who approved the trip. Father came over and got settled and then sent for his sweetheart so that they could be married in the United States.

STUFFED TOMATOES

8 large firm tomatoes
1 stick butter
1 onion, chopped
¼ cup fresh mushrooms, chopped
½ cup rice
2 egg yolks
2 cups broth
Salt and pepper
1 pinch of nutmeg

Choose the same size tomatoes. Scoop out the centers without breaking the skin. Brown the onion in butter; add the tomato pulp, rice, mushrooms, salt, pepper, and half of the broth. (Bouillon may be used.) Cook slowly for 10 minutes. Remove the rice mixture from the heat when still firm and allow to cool. Add the beaten egg yolks and nutmeg to the rice mixture and blend. Fill the tomatoes. Place the stuffed tomatoes in a roasting pan with the remaining broth. Bake, uncovered, at 350 degrees for 20 minutes, basting with the broth.

Emma Schlorch
From her mother,
Mrs. Catherine Savio Fenoglio

STRAWBERRY MERINGUE CAKE

2 cups sifted cake flour
4 tsp. baking powder
½ cup butter
1 cup sugar
4 egg yolks, well beaten (reserve the whites for the meringue)
¾ cup milk
1 tsp. vanilla

Sift flour once, measure, add the baking powder, and sift together 3 times. Cream the butter thoroughly; add 1 cup sugar gradually and continue creaming until light and fluffy. Add the egg yolks. Add the flour alternately with the milk; beat after each addition until smooth. Add the vanilla. Bake in 2 well greased layer pans (9-inch) in a moderate oven (350 degrees) for 25 minutes.

FILLING AND TOPPING:
½ cup sugar
4 egg whites, stiffly beaten
¼ tsp. almond extract
1 quart fresh strawberries
½ cup sugar

Beat the egg whites until stiff. Fold in ½ cup sugar and the almond extract. Pile the meringue lightly on top of each layer and return to a moderate oven for 15 minutes, or until the meringue is a light brown.

Wash and hull the berries. Reserve a few choice berries for garnish. Crush the remaining berries with ½ cup sugar. Spread the berries between the cake layers. Garnish the top with the whole berries and serve at once.

(Ed: If you do not intend to serve this dessert at once, you might consider serving the cake and then passing the strawberries to your guest in a sauceboat or elegant bowl. Hostesses with a flair for the dramatic might enjoy assembling the cake at the table and then serving their guests. Other fruits such as peaches or blueberries might be substituted for the strawberries; when using fresh peaches, be sure to add a little sugar to keep the fruit from turning dark.)

Misses Mary and Thaddessa Taylor

SMILE AT THE ONIONS

You all know how we cry when peeling onions. To defy this put on your old motor-goggles or, if you haven't any, buy a cheap pair at the ten cent store. Then you can smile at the onions. It is especially a wonderful help when pickling.

BURNT SUGAR CAKE

½ cup butter
1⅔ cup sugar
1 cup burnt sugar mixture
4 eggs
4 tsp. baking powder
2¾ cups flour
¼ tsp. salt

Cream the butter by itself until it is soft, then combine the butter and sugar and cream together until the mixture is light and frothy. Add the egg yolks and cream about 2 minutes longer. Sift the flour and baking powder together 3 times.

Take 5 Tbsp. of the sifted flour and baking powder and add to the creamed mixture and cream again about 1 minute. Now add the burnt sugar mixture and the remaining dry ingredients alternately to the creamed mixture and beat all together hard. Lastly, fold in the stiffly beaten egg whites. Do not beat after the egg whites are folded in. Bake in greased and flour-dusted layer cake pans in a moderate oven. Set layers together with white icing. Nuts may be added to the icing.

BURNT SUGAR:

The burnt sugar mixture is made by taking **½ cup granulated sugar, ¼ tsp. cinnamon, ¼ tsp. nutmeg, ¼ tsp. cloves,** and placing them in a skillet. Set the skillet over a low heat and stir constantly until the mixture is melted and then gradually allow it to burn to a rich, dark brown. Add **½ cup boiling water** to the syrup after it reaches this stage; allow it to simmer slowly until all particles are dissolved.

Pour this mixture into a measuring cup and fill the cup to the top with cold water. This gives you the burnt sugar mixture for the cake, and it should be cold before adding it to the cake batter.

Mrs. Harold (Carolyn) Heath

PEANUT COOKIES

1 cup sugar
1 cup butter
2 eggs
2 cups peanuts
2 cups flour
⅓ cup milk
1 Tbsp. baking powder

Cream the sugar and butter. Add the eggs, lightly beaten. Then add the peanuts. Lastly, add the flour, baking powder, and milk. Drop from a spoon onto a buttered cookie sheet and bake in a quick oven.*

(*Ed. Bake at 400 degrees for about 12 minutes.)

Mrs. Janet S. Allen

Studebaker
Diamond Jubilee Dinner

Menu

Hors d'oeuvres

Celeri farci   Noix salees

Poisson Blanc a la Jumbo
(Maitre d'hotel)

Filets Mignon aux champignons
"Clou du Salon"

Pommes de terre Idaho au Four

Pointes d'asperges   Vinaigrette

Tarte aux pommes
"faite a la maison"

Cafe "Gourmet"

Petits fours   Biscuits chauds

Tuesday, January 4, 1927 — The Oliver Hotel.

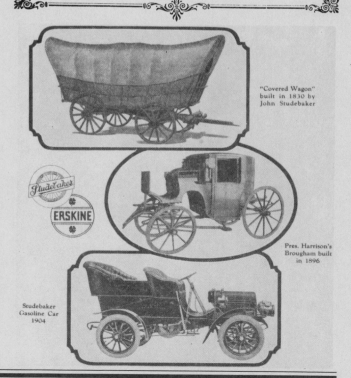

"Covered Wagon" built in 1830 by John Studebaker

Pres. Harrison's Brougham built in 1896

Studebaker Gasoline Car 1904

CLAIRE DUDEK'S RHUBARB PIE

Pastry for a 2 crust pie
1 cup sugar
2 Tbsp. flour
⅛ tsp. salt
2 eggs, beaten
3 cups rhubarb, cut up

Preheat the oven to 425 degrees.

Mix the flour, sugar, and salt together. Beat into the flour mixture the two eggs. Add the rhubarb.

Turn into a pie plate lined with the bottom crust. Roll out the top crust and place over the rhubarb mixture.

Bake at 425 degrees for 10 minutes. Turn down the oven to 325 degrees and continue baking for 25-30 minutes.

Mrs. Kenneth (Amy) David
From her mother,
Mrs. Claire Dudek

SPONGE CAKE

9 eggs, separated
2 cups granulated sugar
Juice of 1 lemon
2 cups flour

Beat the egg whites until stiff peaks form. Beat the egg yolks until thick and lemon colored. Beat 1 cup sugar into the yolks and 1 cup into the whites. Then beat the yolks into the whites. Add the lemon juice. Sift the flour twice and fold slowly into the egg mixture with a wire whisk. Pour into a large tube pan which has been greased and dusted with flour. Bake very slowly 1¼ hours.* (Do not bake as long if it is baked in a flat pan.) Invert the pan to cool. Remove the cake from the pan when cool and dust with powdered sugar.

*(Ed: Bake about 1 hour at 325 degrees.)

Mrs. Ervin (Bertha) Purucker

My mother came from Italian parentage in the Turin area. Her Sunday dinners were always wonderful, a real labor of love. She would start the preparation on Friday and Saturday for a Sunday meal which featured either breaded veal steak, breaded fried chicken or a veal roast. With this, there was a pasta or rice dish and sometimes potatoes. There were always 2 vegetables (a must), a variety of relishes, and either home-made bread, or rolls and breadsticks. For dessert there was a variety of sweets (cakes and cookies), fruit and cheese, wine, and finally coffee. Our meals were never rushed; food was prepared to be enjoyed.

PESCHE AL FORNO
(Baked Filled Peach Dessert)

6 peaches
12 macaroons, crushed
2 Tbsp. milk
1 egg, beaten
3 Tbsp. sugar
1 tsp. almond flavoring

Wash the peaches, cut in half, and remove the pits. Scoop out some of the peach pulp and place in a bowl. Mash with a fork. Add the crushed macaroons, milk, sugar, and almond flavoring. Mix well. (An almond liqueur may be added if desired.) Add the egg and mix well again. Butter a baking dish. Put the peach halves in and fill the centers with the filling. Put a dab of butter on each peach and bake at 350 degrees for 25 minutes.

Mrs. Arthur (Emma) Schlorch
From her mother,
Mrs. Catherine Savio Fenoglio

FORK COOKIES

1 cup brown sugar
1 cup granulated sugar
Scant cup of shortening
2 cups coconut
2 cups rolled oats
½ tsp. salt
1 tsp. soda
1 tsp. baking powder
2 cups flour
2 eggs

Mix well and make into balls. Press down with a fork. Bake in a moderate oven.*

*(Ed: Bake in a 350 degree oven for about 12-15 minutes. Use a greased cookie sheet. For extra flavor you might want to add 1 tsp. of vanilla. The size of the balls will determine the number of crisp, tasty coconut cookies this recipe will yield.)

Mr. David P. McLellan
From his mother, Mrs. Agnes McLellan

Vice President Calvin Coolidge succeeded to the Presidency on August 2, 1923, at the death of Warren G. Harding. That Thanksgiving, the Coolidge Family's housekeeper made public the recipe for the family's favorite Mince Meat pie; it was then published in the Indianapolis Star.

COOLIDGE MINCE MEAT

GRIND FINELY:
  1 lb. boiled beef
  1 lb. suet

COMBINE:
  ½ peck apples, pared and chopped
  1 lb. currants
  ½ lb. citron, chopped
  2 lbs. seeded raisins
  1½ lbs. sugar
  2 qts. wine or grape juice
  Boil 5 minutes, stirring constantly. Add the meat and suet, and the following spices:
  1 Tbsp. salt
  2 tsp. cinnamon
  1 tsp. allspice
  1 tsp. cloves, ground
  2 tsp. nutmeg
  Bring to a boil, stirring constantly, and cook 5 more minutes. Makes several quarts.

Mrs. Ralph Mowiser

This recipe, which was served at the Renshaw family reunion in 1984 in Tempe, Arizona, comes from Florida where my mother-in-law grew up. It is best to use Key limes which come from the Florida Keys, but regular limes also make a delicious pie.

HONEY'S UNEQUALLED KEY-LIME PIE

  1 graham cracker crust (9-inch)
  1 can Eagle Brand condensed milk
  ½ cup lime (or lemon) juice
  3 eggs, separated
  ¼ cup sugar
  ¼ tsp. cream of tartar

Separate the eggs. Beat the yolks until sort of frothy. Add the condensed milk and mix. Add the juice and blend in. Pour the mixture into the pie crust.
Beat the egg whites until soft peaks form. Add the sugar and cream of tartar gradually; beat until stiff peaks form. Spread over the top of the pie (to the edge and touching the crust). Bake in a 350 degree oven for 15-20 minutes.

*Mrs. Claude (Mary) Renshaw
From her mother-in-law,
Mrs. Mary K. Renshaw*

DANISH PUFF

In a bowl, put **1 cup flour** and **1 stick soft butter** (½ cup). Mix with your hands until crumbly. Add **2 Tbsp. cold water;** mix well. Divide in half. Spread onto an ungreased cookie sheet (shape like a long oval or any other shape you choose).
Put **1 cup hot water** and **1 stick butter** in a pan and bring to a boil. Add **1 tsp. almond or vanilla extract.** Dump the mixture into a mixing bowl. Add **1 cup flour** and mix well. Let it cool. Add **3 eggs,** one at a time, beating after each addition. Divide in half and spread over the crust. Bake for 10 minutes at 400 degrees and 40 minutes at 350 degrees.

FROSTING:
  1½-2 cups powdered sugar
  ½ stick butter (¼ cup)
  1 tsp. vanilla
  Dash of salt
  Enough milk to spread

Mix the ingredients together. (The more butter you use, the creamier the frosting will be.) Sprinkle with crushed walnuts.
NOTE: Use only butter in this recipe. It gives a much richer taste.

Mrs. Paul (Ellen) Cahill

TO MEASURE MOLASSES

First dip the cup in cornstarch and the molasses will turn out of the cup without sticking, leaving it smooth and clean.

To make really good ice cream, you need a hot summer day. Children and adults would take turns cranking the ice cream maker, while poking down the ice and salt surrounding the ice cream compartment with a broom handle. Mrs. Deneen remembers that if the proper amount of help was not offered, "we were reminded that if you don't crank, you don't get to lick the paddle."

HOMEMADE ICE CREAM

  2 quarts whole milk
  3 cups sugar
  7 eggs
  1 large can (12oz.) evaporated milk
  2 Tbsp. vanilla

Beat the eggs slightly and add the milks, sugar, and vanilla. Follow the ice cream maker's directions.
Variations: 2 cups mashed ripe fruit, such as peaches or strawberries, plus at least ½ cup chopped fruit; chocolate chips; or chocolate mints, which have been broken up.
If fruit is added, it makes almost a double batch.

Mrs. Patrick (Sharon) Deneen

1920 RECIPES

This dessert was a favorite with the ladies in my mother's bridge group. Each month when this group got together, they would try to outdo one another with their cooking and baking.

GRAHAM TORTE

CRUST:
> 5 eggs, separated
> 2 cups sugar
> 1½ cups graham crackers, crushed
> ½ tsp. salt
> 2 tsp. baking powder
> 1 cup walnuts, chopped

Separate the eggs; beat the yolks till light yellow. Add the sugar and cream together. Mix the graham crackers, salt, and baking powder and add to the yolks. Add the nuts and fold in the beaten egg whites. Bake in 2 round cake tins (preferably with removable bottoms) lined with well-greased paper. Cook in a slow oven until brown.

FILLING:
Cook together **1 cup milk, 1 cup sugar,** and **1 Tbsp. cornstarch** that has been wet with a little **milk.** Cook for several minutes, then add **1 beaten egg.** Remove from the fire, add **vanilla** and cool. When ready to serve, put the filling between the layers of the crust and top with **whipped cream.**

Mrs. Louis N. (Janice) Rugee
From her mother,
Mrs. M.P. (Gertrude Miller) Reed

CHOCOLATE BIRD NESTS

FOR EASTER:
> 1 box shredded wheat biscuits (10-12)
> 2 regular size pkg. (6 oz.) semi-sweet chocolate bits
> ½ jar chunky peanut butter

Crush the biscuits fairly fine. Melt the chocolate over hot water until just soft. Blend together the chocolate, crushed biscuits, and the peanut butter. Drop on wax paper and shape into nests. Makes 15. When hard, add jelly beans.

Mr. David Bainbridge
From a member of his mother's family

HOUSEHOLD HINTS

When serving foods from dishes, be careful to see that the rims of the dishes are perfectly clean. Foods left on rims or edges detract much, making foods look unappetizing.

In cleaning raisins pour boiling water over the raisins, a few at a time. When cool enough to handle, drain and rub each raisin between the thumb and finger till the seeds come out clean, then cut or chop the raisins.

A piece of brown wrapping paper soaked in vinegar, placed on the eyes and forehead, is good for a sick headache.

Satisfactory shoe trees can be made from old corset steels. Wrap each end with tissue-paper and insert in the shoes.

The cuffs of a man's discarded shirt, stitched together and bound, make good hot-dish holders. Run a tape through the buttonholes by which to hang up the holders.

Don't be afraid you are extravagant when you fill your refrigerator with ice. It is economy to keep the ice chest full, for when the ice gets low and the refrigerator warms, it takes twice as much ice to get it cool again.

The marble tops from old-fashioned bureaus and wash stands make excellent slabs for bread and pies.

When the kitchen chimney catches fire throw salt on the fire and the flames will be quickly extinguished. Salt may be used also to put out a fire in a gas stove oven.

If a housewife must keep a pan under her refrigerator to catch the melted ice, she may be glad to know how to keep this pan from rusting. By pouring melted paraffin over the bottom and sides of the pan when it is new, rust can be prevented, as the water does not touch the pan.

New uses for an electric fan:

1. You can send the overplus of heat from your tiny kitchen into your chilly dining room; or, if the odors are too pungent for this, you can blow these and the heat into the outer air.

2. You can cool a melon quickly without ice by wrapping it in wet cloths and placing it in the direct wind of the fan and moistening the cloth frequently.

3. If you open a window or door and place the fan properly, you can blow all the flies from the room -- also their less visible companions, the mosquitoes, and perhaps their quite invisible ones, the microbes.

This recipe traces its ancestry to the restaurant of the East Coast-based Jordan Marsh Department Store. It could be used as either a dessert of a side dish, especially with ham.

SCALLOPED PINEAPPLE

4 cups bread, cubed (8 slices -- do not
   cut off the crusts)
½ cup melted margarine
1 can (20 oz.) **crushed pineapple in juice**
2 cups sugar
3 eggs, beaten
1 cup milk

Mix all the ingredients together and put into a greased 2 qt. casserole. Bake at 325 degrees F. for 45-50 minutes or until brown on top.

Mrs. Tobi Van Dyke

RED PLUM PUFF PUDDING

1 doz. fresh red plums, halved* and pitted
1 cup sugar
½ cup water
2 Tbsp. Minute Tapioca
6 Tbsp. sugar
2 egg yolks, beaten until thick and lemon-colored
2 egg whites
⅛ tsp. salt
¼ tsp. cream of tartar
6 Tbsp. flour, sifted

Place the plums, 1 cup sugar, and the water in casserole. Sprinkle with tapioca and bake in a moderate oven (350 degrees) for 25 minutes. Add 6 Tbsp. sugar to the egg yolks. Beat the egg whites and salt until foamy. Add the cream of tartar and continue beating until stiff enough to hold up in peaks, but not dry. Fold in the egg yolks and then the flour gradually. Stir the plum mixture thoroughly and pour the batter over it. Reduce the oven temperature to 325 degrees and bake 25 minutes, or until the cake is done. Chill. Serve with whipped cream. Serves 8.
   *(Ed: Halved plums may be a little awkward to serve and eat, this can be remedied by cutting each plum into 4 or 6 sections. This dessert is also delicious served warm with milk or cream.)

Mrs. Helen E. Moore Spears

Cloche hats were still popular with ladies dining at "The Right Spot" lunch room in 1929.
Courtesy of Mr. Milton Kouroubetis

PICCALILLI RELISH

4 quarts chopped green tomatoes (about 32)
2 quarts chopped cabbage (about 1 large head)
2 cups sweet red peppers
1 cup chopped onions
½ cup salt

Sprinkle the salt over the vegetables. Let stand for 3-4 hours. Drain and press to remove liquid. Set aside.

Add to **4½ cups vinegar:**
   1½ cups brown sugar
   2 Tbsp. mustard seed
   1 Tbsp. celery seed
   1 Tbsp. prepared horseradish

Simmer for 15 minutes. Add the vegetables and heat to boiling. Pack in sterilized jars, leaving ⅛ inch headspace. Adjust caps. Makes 8 pints

Mrs. Charles (Wava) Apelgreen

GRANDMA'S PEANUT BUTTER PINWHEELS

1 Tbsp. real mashed potatoes
1 lb. box powdered sugar

Gradually add the powdered sugar to the mashed potatoes until dough-like. Roll out and spread with **peanut butter.** Roll up, slice, and refrigerate to harden.
   (1 Tbsp. of mashed potatoes doesn't sound like very much, but if you use more, you will have to increase the amount of powdered sugar to get the right consistency.)

Mrs. Dennis (Shirley) Hagye
From her Grandmother,
Mrs. Georgia Bowers

1930's

Jean Harlow comes to mind at the sight of this clinging white satin bias-cut gown. Multiple spaghetti straps end in back interest with a rhinestone pin holding loops of "spaghetti." The dress has self-covered buttons down the back leading to a large, soft inverted pleat. Circa 1930.

THE BOOM GOES BUST

A stunned America turned to face the 1930's. Plummeting stock prices and rising unemployment affected the lives of virtually every family in the United States. Bread lines, soup kitchens, and a growing legion of homeless people soon became familiar sights in cities from Maine to California. While politicians desperately chirped, "Prosperity is just around the corner," many people were forced to make drastic changes in the way they lived.

With so many people out of work, extravagance in fashion and entertaining seemed to be out of place. Servants became a luxury few could afford. Basic and often inexpensive clothing took the place of the elaborate creations of bygone days. Entertaining was generally done in the home with little of the stifling formality once dictated by polite society. Guests were treated to an evening of contract bridge, Mah-jongg, or Monopoly, all of which quickly became national crazes.

Families could no longer depend on the security of meat on the table at every meal. Macaroni and cheese, egg dishes, and vegetable sandwiches were nutritious alternatives when there was no money for a piece of beef. Expensive poultry was often replaced by a tempting combination of veal and pork appropriately named "City Chicken." Canned soups were used in a variety of ways; one of the most popular and creative of these was the tomato soup cake.

As prices fell so did the hem lines. Skirts became progressively longer until 1933. When President Franklin Roosevelt declared a bank holiday and the nation's economy was at its lowest ebb, ladies were wearing their skirts less than a foot off the floor.

Gone was the flat-chested, long-waisted flapper look of the 20's. When Mae West strutted her way through, "She Done Him Wrong," there was no doubt that once again the feminine figure was most definitely curved. The pouty, aggressive, immature child had grown into a new woman: competent; responsible; able to boost the sagging ego of the unemployed male.

Fortunately, times of great adversity also bring forth great innovations. The icebox was slowly giving way to mechanical refrigeration; freezer tray ice cream and gelatin salads gained instant popularity. Clarence Birdseye introduced packaged frozen fruits and vegetables in 1930, marking the beginning of a new era in food preparation. 1930 also saw the creation of a little cream-filled sponge cake with the spritely name, Twinkies.

The American work place was undergoing some major changes as well. Air conditioning in offices, theaters, and stores was making life more comfortable for employees and patrons. DuPont's new fiber, nylon, would revolutionize fabrics and hosiery; even the lowliest office girl could boast of legs as glamorous as those of Claudette Colbert or Greta Garbo. In 1931 and 1932 employers attempted to prevent further layoffs by shortening hours and redistributing labor; as a result of their efforts, the 5-day work week was born.

Suddenly the average worker had leisure time, and he decided to make the most of it. From Jean Harlow's slinky bias-cut evening dress to Marlene Dietrich's daring trouser suit, clothes were beginning to fit a more active life style. The rush to participate in miniature golf and bicycling required a more practical wardrobe, and casual clothes such as beach pajamas, sandals, shorts, and halter tops began to appear.

By 1935 the economy started to show signs of revival, and once again people had a little money for recreation and entertainment. Families were discovering the joy of travel. Motels slowly began to replace the faded tourist cabins. Deluxe train travel was still the way to go, but for the daring few, air passenger service was now available. Those who couldn't afford to travel flocked to the movie theatres, especially on bank night. From Walt Disney's *Snow White* to *Little Caesar, It Happened One Night* to *Gone With The Wind,* the 30's produced some of the most popular motion pictures ever made.

This was a time of memorable events and compelling personalities. Within a period of ten short years America saw the rise of Shirley Temple and the fall of John Dillinger. Radio listeners from coast to coast laughed along with Amos and Andy and danced to the mellow music of the King of Swing, Benny Goodman. Edward VIII gave up the English throne for a divorcee from Baltimore while Amelia Earhart gave up her life chasing a dream. The world cried with Charles Lindbergh on the death of his kidnapped son and marvelled at the birth of the Dionne Quintuplets. Sally Rand's fan dance created a sensation at the Chicago World's Fair, and the prodigal, demon rum, was welcomed back into the fold with the repeal of Prohibition. The decade which came in with a "Crash" was going out with a bang - - on September 1, 1939, Germany lit the fuse which touched off World War II.

1930 RECIPES

This recipe is very special to Mrs. Borough. It was used by her mother, Mrs. Nathaniel Holley of Tuscaloosa, Alabama.

TEA PUNCH

2 lbs. sugar
2 qts. water
Ungrated rind of Lemons
Boil for 5 minutes.
Add **2 tsp. almond extract**
2 tsp. vanilla
Juice of 6 lemons
Juice of 6 oranges
2 cups of strong tea (green)
1 qt. water
This makes about 5 quarts.

Mrs. Lester (Aileen) H. Borough
From her mother,
Mrs. Nathaniel Morgan (Rachel) Holley

DEPRESSION SOUP

4-5 slices of pork steak (cut into bite size pieces)
Fry with **1 large onion** (chopped) till well browned.
Add:
1 small can kidney beans (pour off the liquid)
1 large can (28 oz.) **tomato juice**
2 or 3 large potatoes (chopped), or more if desired
Cook till the potatoes and meat are tender.

Mrs. Eleanor Mays

MOM'S FRUIT DRESSING SALAD

1 can pineapple
4 Tbsp. flour
3 Tbsp. sugar
1 Tbsp. oleo or butter
2 eggs, beaten
1 cup whipping cream, whipped
Maraschino cherries
Small marshmallows

Combine the flour, sugar, and juice from the pineapple and maraschino cherries (add enough water to the combined juices to make 1 cup). Stir until smooth. Add the beaten eggs and butter; cook until the butter melts and the mixture thickens (stirring constantly). Cool. Fold the whipped cream into the mixture. Add the cherries, marshmallows, and pineapple. Chill. (Orange slices are also a nice addition. The amount of fruit you use is up to you.)

(If you wish to mold the salad, add 1 Tbsp. of gelatin, softened in a little water.)

Mrs. Walton (Carol) Collins
From her mother, Mrs. Hubert (Jeanne) Huebner

LENTIL SOUP

1 ham bone, small shank end of ham, several smoked ham hocks, or a small picnic ham
1 large onion, minced
3 qts. cold water
3 stalks celery (with tops), chopped fine
Several carrots, diced
1 can (28 oz.) **tomatoes**
Simmer 3-4 hours, then add:
1 cup lentils
Simmer about ½ hour, then add:
1 lb. potatoes, cubed
Simmer about ½ longer, than add:
SPAETZLE - (Mix together **1 cup flour, 1 tsp. salt, 1 egg, and ⅓ cup water.)**

Put the spaetzle on a board. Dip a knife into boiling soup and cut off small pieces of the dough dropping them into the boiling soup. Continue dipping the knife and cutting the dough into the soup. (Frozen or dried spaetzle may be used.)

Lastly add **¼ cup browned flour.** Brown the flour in a frying pan over low to medium heat; stir until brown, about the color of the lentils. Add in small amounts to the soup and stir in; it will not lump. **Salt** to taste.

Mrs. Margaret Whipkey

My mother made these rolls frequently when I was a child. Guests at our home always looked forward to Florence's Ice Box Rolls as an accompaniment to her "company meals". She would bake them in muffin tins which had a fluted base to make the rolls look very fancy. During my childhood, there was almost always a bowl of Ice Box Roll dough in the refrigerator, covered with a damp cloth, ready for family or unexpected guests.

FLORENCE'S ICE BOX ROLLS

2 cups boiling water
2 Tbsp. lard or butter
½ cup sugar
1 tsp. salt
Put in the boiling water. When lukewarm, add:
1 yeast cake, dissolved in ½ cup water
1 tsp. sugar
2 eggs, beaten
Enough flour to make as stiff as possible (about 8 cups)

Knead well and put in the ice box. Use as needed.
Make into small balls and place in muffin tins. Let rise at room temperature until double in bulk. Bake in a 350 degree oven for 20 minutes.

Mrs. Charles (Florence) Hurcomb
From her mother,
Mrs. Florence Gillmore Schiek

FROZEN SALAD

2 eggs, beaten
2 Tbsp. sugar
2 Tbsp. vinegar

Cook until thick. Cool slightly and pour over **¼ lb. marsh-mallows** cut into small pieces,* **4 slices of pineapple** cut up, and **1 small bottle of maraschino cherries** cut into fourths. Cool. Fold in **½ pt. cream whipped.** Freeze overnight. Serve on lettuce leaf.

*(Ed: ¼ lb. marshmallows equals approximately 2 cups miniature marshmallows.

Mr. David P. McLellan
From his mother,
Mrs. Agnes McLellan

The "family" was extremely important in the desperate years of the Depression. It was not uncommon for 3 generations to live together, giving children the wonderful opportunity to learn from both parents and grandparents.
Courtesy of St. Joseph County Extension Office.

CAULIFLOWER WITH SOUR CREAM

1 large head cauliflower
2 cups cooked ham, ground
1 egg, beaten slightly
1 cup thick sour cream
1 cup grated cheese

Break the cauliflower apart and cook it, uncovered, in a large amount of rapidly boiling salt water until barely tender (about 8 minutes). Drain and arrange alternate layers of vegetable and ham in a greased casserole. The top layer should be cauliflower. Mix the egg and sour cream and pour over the vegetable and ham. Sprinkle with cheese and heat in an oven (400 degrees F.) for 20 minutes.

Mrs. Edward Chambers

When the Lincoln Highway Inn was still in existence in Mishawaka, this salad dressing was the talk of the town. I was lucky to be able to persuade them to give the recipe to me.

LINCOLN HIGHWAY INN SALAD DRESSING

2 cups oil
½ cup vinegar
½ cup lemon juice
1 cup catsup
1 cup sugar
1 clove garlic, grated
Grated onion (size of an egg)

Mix ingredients together and refrigerate.

Mrs. Louis N. (Janice) Rugee

VOLCANO POTATOES

6 large potatoes
2 Tbsp. butter
1 tsp. salt
Dash of pepper
6 Tbsp. grated yellow cheese
½ cup rich milk
Dash of paprika

Pare, cook, and mash potatoes until smooth; add butter, salt, pepper, and hot milk; beat until light. Make into cones about 3 inches high and place on a platter that will stand the heat of the oven. In the top of each potato cone make a deep indentation. Mix the grated cheese with the paprika and fill each cone. Bake in a hot oven (450 degrees F.) until the cheese melts and browns slightly. Serves 6.

Mrs. Roy Allen

SCALLOPED SWEET POTATOES

6 sweet potatoes
6 slices pineapple
¾ cup pineapple juice
½ cup brown sugar
¼ cup butter

Slice the potatoes, and cut the pineapple into pieces. In a baking dish, alternate the potatoes and pineapple. Sprinkle the sugar on, and pour the pineapple juice over all. Dot with butter. Bake at the same temperature as chicken.*

*(Ed: Bake at 350 degrees for 60-70 minutes or until the potatoes are done. You might want to cover the dish with foil during baking. If your sweet potatoes are very large, only use 3 or 4 potatoes.)

Mrs. H. J. Rickert

This recipe was given to Mrs. Stoneburner by Mrs. Mary B. Taylor, about 1938. Mrs. Taylor was formerly the city clerk of South Bend during a part of the 1930's and a close friend of Mrs. Stoneburner's until her death.

BANANA NUT BREAD

1 cup sugar
½ cup shortening
2 eggs, unbeaten
2 cups all-purpose flour
1 tsp. baking soda
1 tsp. salt
½ cup chopped nutmeats
2 cups mashed ripe bananas

Cream shortening; add sugar, then eggs, one at a time. Beat this mixture well. Add the sifted dry ingredients to the above mixture alternately with the mashed bananas. Fold in the nutmeats. Bake in a loaf pan for about one hour in a 350 degree oven. (Test with a toothpick for doneness.)

Mrs. Glenn (Fannie M.) Stoneburner
From Mrs. Mary B. Taylor

PIES OF ONE CRUST

Brown the meringue by holding an electric hot plate over them as this saves heating the oven and browns the meringue quickly.

These waffles are wonderful for breakfast, brunch, or dessert. Because they can be frozen and quickly reheated in a toaster, they make a yummy after school snack. On a hot summer day, spoon some of your favorite ice cream between two waffles and you have a cool, refreshing treat.

PEACH WAFFLES

⅓ cup shortening
½ cup sugar
2 eggs
2 cups flour
3 tsp. baking powder
½ tsp. salt
1 cup milk
½ tsp. vanilla
½ tsp. lemon juice
1½ cups diced peaches

Blend the shortening with the sugar and eggs. Stir briskly. Mix and sift the dry ingredients. Add to the first mixture alternately with the milk. Add the vanilla, lemon juice, and diced peaches. Cook on a waffle iron. Sprinkle with powdered sugar and serve hot, or, if desired, serve with sliced fruit or whipped cream.

Mrs. Helene Sailer

''Here lies a poor woman who always was tired,
She lived in a house where help was not hired.
Her last words on earth were 'Dear Friends I am going
Where washing ain't done nor sweeping nor sewing,
But everything there is exact to my wishes
For where they don't eat, there's no washing of dishes,
I'll be where loud anthems will always be ringing,
But having no voice I'll be clear of the singing.
Don't mourn for me now, don't mourn for me never,
I'm going to do NOTHING for ever and ever.' ''

The Perfect Hostess - 1931.

Mrs. White's mother, served this chicken salad at her sewing club, her bridge club, and for afternoon teas.

CHICKEN AND WHITE GRAPE SALAD

4 cups diced cooked chicken
1 cup chopped celery
2 cups white seedless grapes
½ tsp. salt
½ tsp. freshly ground pepper
½ cup mayonnaise
½ cup sour cream
½ cup toasted almonds

Combine the chicken, celery, grapes, and seasonings. Add the mayonnaise and sour cream; toss to mix well. Mound the chilled salad on lettuce. Garnish with nut meats and pimento strips. Serves 6.

Mrs. Eugene G. (Annette) White
From her mother,
Mrs. George W. (Florence Burt) Ford

This unusual Alabama recipe is at least 50 years old. Mrs. Borough serves Smoked Eggs cut into wedges; they make a delicious addition to salads, sandwiches, etc.

SMOKED EGGS

¼ cup water
1 cup soy sauce
1 tsp. sugar
1 tsp. sesame oil
½ tsp. salt
½ tsp. liquid smoke
Pepper corns (black, green, or red), optional

Use 4-5 hard boiled eggs. Combine the above ingredients in a deep bowl. Add the eggs and marinate at room temperature for 3 hours. Turn frequently. Chill the eggs after marinating.

Mrs. Lester (Aileen) Borough

SCALLOPED CAULIFLOWER AND MUSHROOMS

1 large head cauliflower
2 Tbsp. butter
1 small onion, finely minced
3 Tbsp. flour
1 cup rich milk
1 cup canned mushrooms, sliced (or ½ lb. fresh mushrooms, sauteed)
¾ cup liquid from the mushrooms
1 tsp. salt
⅛ tsp. paprika
½ cup bread crumbs

Break cauliflower into flowerettes; cook in boiling water until tender. Drain and arrange in greased casserole. Melt butter in a saucepan, add onion and cook until tender. Then add flour, stirring constantly; when smooth, gradually add the milk and the liquid from the mushrooms. Cook until thickened. Add salt, paprika and mushroom slices. Pour this sauce over cauliflower and sprinkle the top with bread crumbs. Bake in a moderate oven until crumbs are brown, about 10 minutes.

Mrs. Roy Allen

RED CABBAGE - NORSE STYLE

6 cups (1½ quarts) finely sliced red cabbage
¼ cup butter
½ cup brown sugar
2 cups water
2 tsp. caraway seed
¾ cup vinegar
¾ tsp. salt

Combine all ingredients except the cabbage and bring to a boil. Drop in the cabbage and cook, covered, until tender, and the liquid is almost absorbed.

The Norwegian cook will advocate a 2 hour cooking period, but a shorter time will cook the cabbage and American palates will be better pleased. Serve with pork roast or roast fowl.

Maybelle Otterson

GOURMET SAUCE

¾ cup milk
1 8-oz. pkg. Philadelphia brand cream cheese, cubed
⅓ cup Parmesan cheese, grated

Heat the milk in a small saucepan over low heat. Add the cream cheese, stirring constantly, until melted and smooth. Blend in the Parmesan cheese. Serve over your favorite vegetable.

M.E. Parrott

CITY CHICKEN KABOBS

2 pork steaks, cut 1 inch thick
2 lbs. veal chuck shoulder roast
15-20 city chicken sticks
3 green peppers
6-8 small onions, 1 inch in diameter
Seasoning salt
Pepper
Garlic powder
Pepperidge Farm Stuffing, ground fine
½ cup milk
1 or 2 eggs

Cut the meat into pieces about 1 inch square. Cut the green pepper into 1 inch square pieces. Slice the ⅛ onion inch thick. Skewer pieces of pork, onion, veal and pepper until the stick is full. (This makes about 15 kabobs.) Season well with seasoning salt, pepper, and garlic powder. Combine the milk and eggs. Dip the kabobs into the milk-egg mixture, then roll in the ground stuffing. Pan fry until golden brown on all sides.

Place ½ cup of water and some chopped onion into a large racked baking dish. Place the kabobs on the rack, cover, and bake at 350 degrees for 1 hour and 15 minutes. Uncover and bake an additional 15 minutes, or until the meat is done.

Mrs. Mary Fischer
From Mr. John Lawecki

*M*achine oil stains, if obstinate, can be removed by touching the spots with chloroform.

SPANISH POT ROAST

2 lbs. shoulder beef
⅓ cup diced carrots
⅓ cup sliced onions
¼ cup fat
3 cups boiling water
1 green pepper, chopped
2 cups stewed tomatoes
3 Tbsp. flour
Salt and pepper

Cut the beef into medium sized pieces. Dust with salt and pepper and dredge with flour. Brown in heated fat, then place the onions and carrots over it. Add the boiling water and simmer slowly until the meat is tender. Remove the meat and add the tomatoes and green pepper to the gravy. Cook slowly for 10 minutes. Moisten the flour with cold water and stir into the sauce. Cook until thickened. Return the meat to the sauce and heat thoroughly. A little red pepper or a little tabasco sauce adds zest. Serve with plain boiled potatoes, cooked macaroni, or plain cooked rice, a vegetable salad, and spiced beets.

Mrs. Helene Sailer

1930 RECIPES

CHICKEN GUMBLEE

Take a **three or four pound chicken,** cut up as for frying; line a roasting pan with sliced bacon, put the chicken in the pan and sprinkle with a **cup of uncooked rice.** Add **one can or one-half pound fresh mushrooms** and a **No. 2 can of tomatoes;** cover with **slices of Bermuda onion** and **strips of green peppers.** Cook about 2½ hours, using a slow oven. Keep the dish covered for the first half of cooking time. Add seasoning to suit taste.*

*(Ed: ½-1 cup of chicken broth may be added during the baking time if more moisture is needed.)

Gladys Scoville

STUFFED BAKED TOMATOES

8 large firm tomatoes (reserve ½ cup tomato pulp)
1 cup soft bread crumbs
3 Tbsp. chopped green peppers
1 tsp. salt
4 Tbsp. butter
1½ cups diced cooked chicken
1 Tbsp. chopped onion
½ cup chopped celery
¼ tsp. paprika
1 egg, beaten

Wash the tomatoes and cut out the blossom ends. With a spoon, scoop out part of the pulp and seeds (reserve ½ cup of the pulp). Add the rest of the ingredients to the ½ cup of pulp; mix with a fork. Carefully stuff the tomato cases. Set in a baking pan and add ⅔ inch of water. Bake for 35 minutes in a moderately slow oven. Baste several times during baking.

Mrs. Helene Sailer

Children of all ages had to work to help their families make ends meet during the Depression. Fortunately there were fringe benefits.

Courtesy of St. Joseph County Extension Office.

BARBECUE SAUCE

1 medium onion, chopped
2 Tbsp. butter
2 Tbsp. vinegar
2 Tbsp. brown sugar
4 Tbsp. lemon juice
1 cup prepared catsup
½ cup chopped parsley (optional)
½ Tbsp. prepared mustard
½ cup water
3 Tbsp. Worcestershire sauce
¼ tsp. salt
Dash cayenne pepper

Brown the onions in butter. Add the remaining ingredients. Simmer for 30 minutes.

This recipe was always used with leftover pork roast for sandwiches. I use it with hamburger and with leftover beef, also.

Mrs. Arthur (Dagny) Diamond
From her mother,
Mrs. Marie Johnson Lenon

My father, Clyde Carr, was a barber in his own shop. His hours were long and the work hard. He went to the shop by 7:00 a.m. to clean up (when he no longer had a porter to do that work) and closed for many years at 9:00 at night.

On Christmas Eve, he always tried to close early, but if a late customer came in, he would try to take care of him. Mother tried to be flexible, so she always planned a Christmas Eve meal that could be warmed up if Daddy couldn't get away on time. Christmas Eve Spaghetti is still a tradition in our family.

ETTA CARR'S CHRISTMAS EVE SPAGHETTI

1 lb. hamburger
1 cup onion, chopped
1 green pepper, chopped
1 carrot, chopped
3 Tbsp. celery flakes
1 #2-can tomatoes
Salt and pepper to taste
½ tsp. chili powder
1 pkg. (½ lb.) **cooked elbow spaghetti**

Brown the hamburger and drain off the fat. Add the chopped onion, green pepper, carrot, and celery flakes. Cook till the onions appear to be clear. Add the can of tomatoes, salt, pepper, and chili powder. Add the cooked spaghetti. Cook on simmer for 15 minutes and serve or set aside to reheat later to serve. Sprinkle with Parmesan cheese when serving.

Mary Ellen Handwork
From her mother, Mrs. Etta Carr

THE smartest hostesses, noted for the originality of their teas, bridges and parties, have popularized open-face sandwiches. They are all the rage wherever women congregate for a social afternoon.

FASHION DECREES

THE OPEN-FACE SANDWICH

IN STUNNING NEW DESIGNS OF UTMOST SMARTNESS

CHICKEN AND DUMPLINGS

1 fat hen
1½ qts. water
Salt and pepper
7 Tbsp. flour
¾ cup water
Yellow food coloring

Take 1 fat hen and cook, whole or disjointed, in 1½ qts. of water, seasoned with salt. Cook for about 3 hours. When tender, lift out of the broth and cool. Cut the meat into serving size pieces and place in the oven to keep hot. Thicken the broth with the flour mixed with ¾ cup water. Blend until smooth with an egg beater. Season with salt and pepper. Add a few drops of yellow food coloring. Strain over the chicken. Reserve 4 cups of gravy in a flat stew pan for the dumplings.

DUMPLINGS:
    2 eggs
    Scant ⅔ cup milk
    1 Tbsp. oil or melted shortening
    1½ cups flour
    1 tsp. salt
    4 level tsp. baking powder
    2 Tbsp. chopped fresh parsley

Sift the dry ingredients into the liquid; stir briskly in a folding motion until blended. Drop the dumpling batter by the tablespoonful into the boiling gravy. Cover and cook gently for 10-15 minutes, or until done. (A few drops of yellow coloring may be added to the dumplings.) The secret of this recipe is that the gravy has to be thickened before the dumplings are dropped into it or you will not have dumplings. **NOTE:** For those who are not too fond of stewed chicken, I get frying chickens and fry them in the usual manner. Then I buy 4 cans of clear chicken broth and add a few drops of yellow food coloring; thicken it and proceed to make the dumplings according to the recipe. It never fails if you are sure to thicken the gravy, as it holds the dumplings up.

Mrs. Bernard Kamm

Water Lily Sandwich

ONE round slice whole wheat bread, spread with GOOD LUCK. Shape lettuce leaves on top of it, seasoning with mayonnaise. Cut petals by making narrow strips out of hard-cooked egg whites. Center of hard-cooked egg yolk mashed with GOOD LUCK and seasoned.

Good Luck Margarine Flyer.

Spring Sandwich

CUT circle of white bread, spread thick with GOOD LUCK, then with thin layer of mayonnaise. Place ring of thinly sliced radishes around outside edge. Slice of cucumber in center, surrounded by a ring of green pepper.

PORKY PIE

1½ lbs. pork shoulder
3 onions
4 Tbsp. Crisco
1½ cups hot water
3 Tbsp. flour
1 tsp. salt
1 Tbsp. sugar
⅛ tsp. pepper
1 tsp. paprika
3 tart apples

Put the pork and onions through a grinder; fry five minutes in Crisco. Add water, simmer 10 minutes and stir in the flour (mixed to a paste with a little cold water). Add seasonings and cook 3 minutes longer. Peel and core the apples and cut in thin slices; sprinkle with flour. Fill a baking dish with alternate layers of apple and meat, then cover with sweet potato biscuits made as follows:

1 cup flour
3 tsp. baking powder
½ tsp. salt

Mix the flour, baking powder, and salt; cut in **3 Tbsp. of Crisco.** Lightly mix in **1 cup finely mashed sweet potatoes.** Add **½ cup milk or water.** Roll out in ½-inch thickness on a lightly floured board. Cut with a biscuit cutter and place the biscuits on top of the meat mixture. Bake in a hot oven (425 degrees F.) for 40 minutes.

Mrs. H.J. Shreiner

SPANISH CAKE

1 cup sugar
½ cup butter
1 cup flour
1 tsp. baking powder
½ cup milk
1 tsp. cinnamon
¾ cup chopped nuts
2 eggs

Cream the butter and sugar. Add the eggs, beaten with the milk. Sift the flour, baking powder, and cinnamon; add. Mix in the nuts. Bake in a moderate oven.* Cover with your favorite frosting. Good served with whipped cream.

*(Ed: Bake in an 8 x 8-inch square pan for about 30 minutes at 350 degrees. Be sure to <u>grease</u> the baking dish. This is a firm cake, almost like a coffecake in texture.)

Mrs. Eugene G. (Annette) White
From her mother,
Mrs. George W. (Florence Burt) Ford

In the 1930's, young ladies were still taught to preside at a formal tea. Here two future hostesses demonstrate their expertise to their mothers and siblings at Central High School.

Courtesy of South Bend Community School Corporation.

Fortunately, in my day, brides were routinely given a pressure cooker. I have cooked many quick meals in mine, mostly this stew. If you do not have a pressure cooker, add enough water to cover the meat and simmer 1½ hours, or until the meat is tender. Then add the vegetables and cook until done. A crock pot may also be used.

LAKE TAHOE STEW

1½ lbs. chuck beef stew meat, cut up
2 Tbsp. cooking oil or shortening
1 onion, sliced
1 clove of garlic, peeled
½ tsp. allspice
¼ tsp. red pepper flakes
Salt and black pepper
1 bay leaf
2 Tbsp. lemon juice
2 Tbsp. Worcestershire sauce
½ cup dry red wine
4-6 peeled potatoes, halved
4-6 whole carrots
½ cup water

Brown the meat on all sides thoroughly in the hot oil. Drain the fat. Add the sliced onion and clove of garlic; stir. Add the spices, lemon juice, Worcestershire, and wine. Add the vegetables and water; cook 20 minutes in a pressure cooker or as suggested. Serve with crusty French bread and a stout red wine.

Mrs. A.T. (Betty) Lynch

I do not remember any birthday cake except this one. My mother used to put the cake on a footed cake plate with the icing piled high. It is an excellent, moist chocolate cake. I have tried others, but none are as good -- and the memories are better.

DEVIL'S FOOD CAKE

1 cup sugar
2 eggs, separated
½ cup shortening
1 cup sour cream
1 tsp. soda
1½ cup flour
2 squares baking chocolate, melted
1 tsp. vanilla
1 cup nut meats, chopped

Cream the shortening (I prefer butter), with the sugar. Add the beaten egg yolks. Add soda to the sour cream and blend. Combine the sour cream mixture alternately with the flour, beginning and ending with the flour. Add the flavoring, melted chocolate, and nuts. Fold in the egg whites which have been beaten fluffy but not dry.

Fill two greased 8-inch cake pans. Bake about 35 minutes at 350 degrees. Frost with Seven Minute Icing.

Mrs. Arthur (Dagny) Diamond
From her mother,
Mrs. Marie Johnson Lenon

Mrs. Dorothy Konold was the society editor for the **South Bend News Times** *the 1930's. Her column was called, "The Social Panorama."*

DUMP CAKE

1. 1½ cup flour
   1½ cup sugar
   2 pinches salt
   3 tsp. baking powder
   Sift together 2 times in a large bowl.

2. **3 eggs broken** in a measuring cup. Add **7½ Tbsp. melted butter** and then enough **milk** to make 1½ cups full of this liquid measure.

3. Beat 1. and 2. together 3-5 minutes. Pour into a square pan and bake at 375 degrees about 20-25 minutes.

MOM'S EASY FROSTING:
   2 cups powdered sugar, creamed with **4 Tbsp. soft butter** and **2 squares of melted chocolate** (or cocoa). Add **1 tsp. vanilla** and enough cream to make the frosting easy to spread.

Mrs. John (Jane) Olcott
From her mother,
Mrs. Dorothy Konold

CHOCOLATE ANGEL FOOD CAKE

1¼ cups sugar
¼ cup cocoa
¼ tsp. salt
1 tsp. vanilla
¾ cup cake flour
1¼ cups egg whites
1 tsp. cream of tartar
½ tsp. almond extract

Sift the sugar and flour before measuring, and 4 times after. Add the salt to the egg whites and beat until foamy. Sift in the cream of tartar and beat until stiff but not dry. Add the flavoring and beat until mixed. Add the sugar and flour, (to which the cocoa has been added) to the egg whites a little at a time through a sifter. Mix by cutting and folding gently. Turn into an unbuttered 9½-inch cake pan, tube style. Bake at 325 degrees for 1 hour.

NOTE: Use a rotary egg beater until the eggs are foamy, then beat with a wire whisk until stiff.

Mrs. Joseph McKown

DUTCH APPLE CAKE

2 cups sifted flour
3 tsp. baking powder
2 Tbsp. sugar
½ tsp. salt
¼ cup shortening
1 tsp. cinnamon
1 egg, well beaten
3 Tbsp. shortening
1 Tbsp. butter
¾ cup brown sugar, firmly packed
1 Tbsp. top milk*
¾ cup milk
2 cups apples, sliced thin
Cinnamon, to taste

Sift the flour with the baking powder, sugar, and salt. Cut in ¼ cup shortening until the mixture is as fine as corn meal. Combine the beaten egg and milk and add to the flour mixture, mixing until a soft dough is formed.

Melt the 3 Tbsp. shortening and butter together. Add the brown sugar, cinnamon, and milk; mix well. Pour into an 8 x 8-inch pan (greased). Press the apple slices onto the mixture in circles. Spread the dough over the apples. Bake in a moderate oven (350 degrees F.) for 50-60 minutes. Serve upside down with whipped cream.

*(Ed: In the days before homogenization, milk separated with the cream rising to the top, hence the name "top" milk. Today, half & half or whipping cream could be used.)

Mrs. Helene Sailer

RAISIN AND NUT FILLING

3 cups sugar
1 cup water
3 egg whites, beaten stiff
¼ cup dried figs
¼ cup dried apricots
¼ tsp. cream of tartar
1 tsp. orange flavoring
1 tsp. vanilla
⅛ tsp. salt
½ cup chopped raisins
¼ cup maraschino cherries, chopped
½ cup chopped nuts

Combine the water, sugar, salt, and cream of tartar. Boil to the soft ball stage (236 degrees F.). Pour slowly over the beaten egg whites, beating constantly. Add the flavorings. Continue beating the mixture until it is cool enough to spread. Pour half into a bowl. Add the fruits and nuts. Spread the fruit mixture between the layers of a cake and cover the top and sides with the remainder of the icing.

This makes enough frosting and filling for a large 3 layer cake. This delicious filling would be good anytime, but it would be especially good during the holiday season. If you can't find figs, dates or any other dried fruit would work equally well.

Mrs. Helene Sailer

ANGEL SUPREME

1 Angel food cake
6 eggs, separated
1½ cups sugar
½ cup lemon juice
½ tsp. lemon rind
1 envelope Knox gelatin

Mix ¾ cups sugar with the lemon juice, lemon rind, and the beaten egg yolks. Cook until the mixture coats a spoon. Mix the gelatin in ¼ **cup cold water** and add to the mixture. Cool.

Add the remaining sugar to the beaten egg whites. Add the cooled lemon mixture.

Tear up the cake into small pieces and place half in an angel cake tin (oiled). Pour the lemon mixture over the cake. Top with the remainder of the cake pieces.

Let set for 3-4 hours (at least) in the refrigerator.*

*(Ed: Mrs. Carol Collins recognized this recipe as one her Aunt Mae [Mary Dooley O'Brien] served to visiting relatives. She added to the richness of the dessert by serving it with ice cream on the top.)

Miss M. Geraldine Hatt
From her cousin,
Mrs. Fern Ware Small

GRAHAM CRACKER PIE

CRUST:
1½ cups crushed graham crackers (about 15)
½ cup melted butter
½ cup sugar
1/16 tsp. salt

Roll the crumbs very fine. Melt the butter; add the crumbs, sugar, and salt. Save ½ cup crumbs for the top of the pie. Place the remainder in a pie plate, pat and firm into the shape of a crust.

CUSTARD:
2 cups milk
2 egg yolks
1 Tbsp. cornstarch
½ cup sugar
½ tsp. vanilla
1/16 tsp. salt

Beat the egg yolks; add the milk, a little at a time, only until mixed. In a separate dish, mix the cornstarch with a little of this mixture, then combine with the sugar and salt. Add to the egg yolks. Add the vanilla and cook, stirring constantly, until thick. Pour into the graham cracker crust.

TOPPING:
2 egg whites
2 Tbsp. powdered sugar

Beat the egg whites till stiff. Add the powdered sugar. Put over the custard, being sure to touch the crumbs on the side. Sprinkle the reserved crumbs on top of the meringue and bake in a slow oven (300 degrees) about 20 minutes or until browned. Cool.

Mrs. Walton (Carol) Collins
From her mother,
Mrs. Hubert (Jeanne) Huebner

APRICOT CANDIES

¾ cup dried apricots
½ cup nut meats
¾ cup fresh coconut
1 Tbsp. lemon juice
1 tsp. grated lemon rind
1 tsp. grated orange rind

Wash the apricots; drain and put through a food chopper with the nut meats. Add the coconut, lemon juice, grated lemon and orange rinds. Mix and knead well. Roll out on a sugared board to one-quarter inch thickness. Cut into squares and roll in powdered sugar.

Mrs. H.M. Geleske

One of the best parts of baking is licking the bowl.
Courtesy of the St. Joseph County Extension Office.

PINEAPPLE REFRIGERATOR CAKE

1 cup butter
2¾ cups powdered sugar
4 eggs, separated
1½ cups grated pineapple, drained
30 to 35 lady fingers
1 tsp. lemon extract
1 cup candied cherries, chopped
2 cups whipping cream, whipped

Cream the butter till soft; add the sugar and continue creaming until fluffy. Beat the egg yolks until lemon colored. Beat them into the butter and sugar mixture. Fold in the flavoring, then the stiffly beaten egg whites. Split the lady fingers and place ⅓ of them flat side down over the bottom of a torte pan. Cover the lady fingers with ⅓ of the sugar mixture. Place over this half of the pineapple and cherries* which have been mixed together. Spread over this half of the whipped cream, a second layer of lady fingers, and ⅓ of the sugar mixture, followed by the remaining fruit and whipped cream. Top with a third layer of lady fingers and the remainder of the sugar mixture. Let the cake stand in the refrigerator at least 12 hours. To serve, remove the sides of the torte pan. Top the cake with fresh whipped cream and a sprinkling of chopped candied cherries. Cut in wedges and serve.
*(Ed: Candied cherries may be difficult to find during certain seasons; maraschino cherries may be substituted. If you don't want to grate your own fresh pineapple, use canned crushed pineapple.)

Misses Mary and Thaddessa Taylor

My mother never measured anything when she cooked. One day, however, when we were both older, she came to my home and as she cooked by pinches and dabs, I measured everything. I had to figure out the oven temperature and time of baking for myself.

SLAP JACK PIE

1 homemade, unbaked pie shell (in a large pie plate)

¾-1 cup brown sugar and
3½ Tbsp. flour, blended together.
Put in an unbaked pie shell. Pour in about 2-3 Tbsp. Karo dark syrup. (Kinda swirl it around as you pour it on.) Add several chunks of butter. Pour 1-1½ cups of milk on top of that. Sprinkle with cinnamon. Bake same as for a custard pie.*
*(Ed: Bake at 400 degrees for about 35 minutes or until the filling sets up.)

Mrs. Thomas (Jean) Gast
From her mother,
Mrs. Marion Wills Mower

UPSIDE DOWN APRICOT GINGERBREAD

3 Tbsp. butter
¼ cup brown sugar
1 tsp. vinegar
1 16-oz. can apricot halves, drained
¼ cup walnut halves and pieces

In the bottom of a heavy 10-inch skillet or baking pan, melt the butter and brown sugar; add vinegar and stir. Turn off the heat.
Arrange the drained apricot halves and nuts in the pan.
Pour the mixed uncooked gingerbread* on top of the apricots. Bake for 30 minutes at 375 degrees. Immediately invert the baked gingerbread onto a serving plate.
*(Ed: Use the recipe for Hot Water Gingerbread - 1870's.)

Mrs. A.T. (Betty) Lynch

PINEAPPLE TOPPING FOR GINGERBREAD

1 small pkg. (3 oz.) cream cheese
1 Tbsp. sugar
½ cup crushed pineapple, drained
½ cup whipping cream, whipped

Cream the cheese until smooth. Add the sugar and beat till smooth. Fold in the pineapple and whipped cream. Spoon over cooled gingerbread.

Mrs. A.T. (Betty) Lynch

1930 RECIPES

Radio filled many hours for people during the 1930's. In a time when money was scarce, it provided music, news, comedy, and drama. It also gave women the chance to keep up-to-date on the latest cooking innovations. Miss Taylor copied down this recipe for ice box cookies during one of her favorite radio broadcasts and placed it in her recipe file.

ICE BOX BUTTERSCOTCH COOKIES

2 eggs
2 cups brown sugar
¾ cup butter, melted
1 tsp. vanilla
1 cup chopped nuts
3½ cups cake flour
6 tsp. baking powder
½ tsp. salt

Beat the eggs; add the sugar and blend. After melting, cool the butter and add along with the other ingredients. Make into a roll and place in the ice box for 24 hours.*
*(Ed: Bake in a 400 degree oven for about 8-10 minutes.)

Misses Mary and Thaddessa Taylor

Electric refrigerators offered women the luxury of a tiny freezer compartment. Suddenly, ice cream could be made in freezer trays instead of using the old-fashioned ice cream makers which required endless cranking. Today, blenders and food processors make the job even easier.

FRESH PEACH ICE CREAM

2 cups peach pulp
¾ cup sugar
Juice of 1 lemon
Pinch of salt
½ pint cream
2 eggs, separated
2 Tbsp. sugar
½ tsp. almond flavor

Select soft peaches and mash them thoroughly. Add the sugar and lemon juice and dissolve. When the sugar is thoroughly dissolved, pour into a tray and freeze 45 minutes to 1 hour. Beat the egg whites, adding 2 Tbsp. sugar. Then add the beaten egg yolks and mix. Whip the cream to a thick custard consistency. (Do not over whip.) Combine with the beaten egg. Add the frozen peach pulp and mix lightly. Return to the chilling unit to freeze.

Mrs. Arthur DeWispelaere

Mr. Stickley used a special gadget of his own creation to crack the outer shells of the black walnuts, Then, to get rid of most of the stain, he ran the nuts through his wife's washing machine (there is no record of Mrs. Stickley's reaction to this). These cookies had to be good to deserve such dedicated ingenuity.

OATMEAL BLACK WALNUT COOKIES

½ pkg. brown sugar*
½ cup Crisco or margarine
1 egg
1 tsp. vanilla
½ tsp. almond extract
Beat thoroughly.
1 cup buttermilk
½ tsp. soda

Add the soda to the buttermilk. Add this mixture to the other ingredients and beat again.
1 cup oatmeal
Stir in and let stand about 5-10 minutes so that the oatmeal absorbs some of the liquid.
Add enough **flour** plus ¼ **tsp. baking powder** and **salt** to make the dough a bit stiffer than cake consistency.

Add to the above:
Raisins, Black walnuts, and Dates
Drop by spoonfuls. Flatten out with a spoon and sprinkle with sugar. Bake at 375 degrees till brown.
*(Ed: Many of the ingredients are given in specific quantities, but some are left to personal taste. Try using 1¼ cup packed brown sugar, 1¾-2 cups flour, 1 cup raisins, 1-1½ cup nuts, and ½-1 cup dates, chopped. After baking for 12-15 minutes, let them cool before packing in an airtight container; the flavor improves with age. Try sprinkling colored sugar on the cookies for parties or during the holiday season.)

Miss M. Geraldine Hatt
From Mrs. Lloyd (Odell) Stickley

In 1938, Bonnie Doon's opened a new drive-in restaurant in South Bend at the corner of LaSalle and Lafayette. Carhops posed for a photograph even before the restaurant's sign was in place.

Courtesy of Maureen and Howard Muldoon, Bonnie Doon Ice Cream Corp.

DATE PUDDING

Put **2 tsp. soda** over **1 pkg. (8 oz.) chopped dates.** Pour **1 cup boiling water** over the dates and soda and let cool.

Cream **1 cup sugar, 1 egg,** and **2 Tbsp. butter.** When the date mixture has cooled, combine with the sugar mixture. Sift **1 cup flour, 1 tsp. cinnamon, 1 tsp. cloves,** and **1 tsp. nutmeg** into the mixture. Add **½ cup nuts** and stir.

Pour into a 7 x 10-inch baking dish. Bake for 35-40 minutes in a 350 degree oven.

When serving, top with sauce and whipped cream.

SAUCE:
  1 Tbsp butter
  1 Tbsp. flour
  1 cup cold water
  1½ cups brown sugar

Mix the above ingredients and cook over medium high heat until the mixture boils. Remove from the heat and add **1 tsp. vanilla.**

Mrs. Robert (Claralu) Blake
From her mother-in-law,
Mrs. Earl (Daphne) Blake

"It isn't the MENU that matters it's the MEN YOU sit next to."

In 1937, we lived in Milwaukee; it was there that I created my recipe for Chocolate Torte. It is so good that I entered the recipe in the South Bend Tribune's Chocoholic Contest in 1983 and was one of the 12 finalists.

CHOCOLATE TORTE

Cut a **large angel food cake** into 1½ inch. pieces or squares. Put them into a large mixing bowl and cover. Melt **1 envelope Knox gelatin** in **¼ cup cold water;** let stand for 1 minute. Melt **2 squares bitter chocolate** in **¾ cup boiling water.** Add the gelatin to this chocolate mixture and let cool. Beat **3 egg whites** very stiff and fold in **1 cup sugar.** Beat **3 egg yolks** slightly and add to the chocolate mixture. When cool, fold the chocolate mixture in the stiffly beaten egg whites. Pour over the cake and toss lightly. Pour into a torte pan and chill 24 hours. Remove from the pan to a large plate. Frost with **whipped cream.**

Mrs. Pauline Stigall
President of the South Bend
Garden Club (1985)

This is a very good soft cookie from my aunt. These cookies were a great part of my childhood.

OLD-FASHIONED ORANGE COOKIES

  2 eggs
  1 cup solid shortening
  2 cups sugar
  1 cup less 2 Tbsp. milk
  ½ cup + 2 Tbsp. orange juice concentrate
  4½ cups flour
  2 tsp. baking powder
  1 tsp. salt
  ½ tsp. baking soda

Beat the shortening, sugar, and eggs. Add the dry and liquid ingredients alternately. Bake on greased and floured cookie sheets for approximately 8-10 minutes in a 350 degree oven. Use 1 rounded teaspoon of batter per cookie.

ICING:
  3 Tbsp. soft butter
  1 box (1 lb.) confectioners sugar
  Concentrated orange juice (to spreading consistency)

Mrs. Patrick (Sharon) Deneen
From her aunt,
Mrs. John Drew

RANGER COOKIES

  2 cups flour
  ½ tsp. baking powder
  1 tsp. soda
  1 tsp. salt
  1½ cups shortening
  2 cups brown sugar
  2 eggs, well beaten
  2 tsp. vanilla
  1½ cups quick cooking oats
  1 cup dates, cut fine
  1 cup nuts
  2 cups corn flakes

Sift the flour, baking powder, soda, and salt. Cream the shortening and sugar. Add the well beaten eggs and vanilla. Add the flour mixture and mix well. Stir in the oats, dates, and nuts. Last of all, lightly stir in the corn flakes. Drop by teaspoonfuls on ungreased cookie sheets. Bake in a 375 degree oven for 10-12 minutes.

OPTIONAL: Add 1 cup chocolate chips. You may sprinkle the tops of the cookies with granulated sugar.

Yields approximately 6 dozen.

Mrs. Robert (Claralu) Blake
From her mother-in-law,
Mrs. Earl (Daphne) Blake

HOUSEHOLD HINTS

On baking day, when the bread dough is placed in pans to raise, set the pans in the oven, heat your electric iron, place in oven, close the door, and you have just enough heat to cause the bread to rise nicely, free from draughts.

When cake has been stowed away in the larder for some time and becomes dry and hard, try the following plan: Soak it for a minute in cold milk and rebake it in a rather cool oven. It will taste almost like new again. Stale bread may be treated in the same way.

For shortening, buy some good beef fat and put it through the meat chopper. Place it in an enamel saucepan and cook until well tried out, stirring occasionally. After slightly cooling, pour the grease into a crock. If salt is added and it is kept closely covered in a cool place it will keep indefinitely.

Use lukewarm water for washing silk hose and dry in the house. Never expose to the sun in drying as the thread is likely to break in the sun and air.

Gummed reinforcement seals for note books will stop that run you find in your stocking just after you reach the office or school. The sticker may come off but the mucilage will prevent the run from going farther.

Rub corn meal on hands before hanging out clothes to prevent chapped hands.

Fresh grass stains can be removed by soaking in alcohol. If stain is old, rub with molasses and allow to stand several hours before washing.

Coffee grounds make a good sweeping compound for the basement floor. Save all your used grounds by depositing them in a strainer near the drain in the basement.

Freezing of clothes on the line during cold weather is prevented by using a little salt in the last rinsing water.

If you wash your phonograph records with soap and water and rinse well with clear water then dry well, they will sound clearer.

If you place candles in the refrigerator for a few days before using, they will last longer and the wax is less likely to drip.

If you wish to know if your telephone has rung during your absence, put a piece of paper and a piece of carbon paper between the clapper and the bell. A mark will be made on the paper if the bell has rung.

You will find adhesive tape a great help in mending breaks in taffeta dresses. If you are careful joining the edges of the break, it will defy detection.

To clean white fox furs, put one pound ground rice into a large bowl. Put the soiled fur into the rice and rub thoroughly. After this process, shake the fur thoroughly to shake out the rice. This is an excellent cleaning method.

CHILI SAUCE

4 qts. red, ripe chopped tomatoes (about 24)
2 cups chopped onions
2 cups chopped red sweet peppers (about 4)
1 chopped red hot pepper
1 cup sugar
3 Tbsp. salt
3 Tbsp. mixed pickling spices
1 Tbsp. mustard seed
1 Tbsp. celery seed
2½ cups vinegar

Combine the tomatoes, onion, peppers, sugar, and salt. Cook gently for 45 minutes.

Tie the spices in cheesecloth. Add to the tomato mixture and cook another 45 minutes. Stir frequently to prevent sticking.

Add the vinegar and cook slowly till thickened. Pour into sterilized jars, leaving ⅛ inch head space. Adjust the caps and seal. Makes 6 pints.

NOTE: Today I use my family recipe for Chili Sauce to make a quick and easy hors d'oeuvre. I mix 1 cup of Chili Sauce with 1 cup of grape jelly. Add cut up hot dogs or homemade meat balls (your favorite recipe) and simmer for 1 hour.

Mrs. Charles (Wava) Apelgreen

GINGER COOKIES

¾ cup oleo
1 cup white sugar
1 egg
5 Tbsp. molasses (Brer-Rabbit)
2½ cups flour
2 tsp. soda
1 tsp. baking powder
1 tsp. cloves
1 tsp. ginger
Salt (pinch)
Walnuts (if desired)

Chill after mixing. Shape into balls. Roll in sugar and bake at 350 degrees for about 10 minutes.

Mrs. Thomas (Jean) Gast
From her mother,
Mrs. Marion Wills Mower

RHUBARB AND RED RASPBERRY PRESERVES

2 cups rhubarb, diced
2 cups red raspberries
2 cups sugar

Blanch rhubarb by pouring boiling water over it. Let stand only a few seconds; then pour water off. Put all on the fire, and let boil. Cook 2 minutes. Remove from the fire and let stand 4 minutes.

Then add **2 more cups of sugar** and let boil 2 more minutes. Take off and let cool, stirring a little while cooking. Can. 3 quarts of berries makes 12 pints. Very good.

Mrs. Frank Coppes

My mother made this Orange Marmalade every winter when the oranges were plentiful. It gave off a marvelous aroma as it cooked, and the color and taste were delicious.

ORANGE MARMALADE

4 oranges
2 lemons

Grind fine. (Mother used a food chopper.) Measure. Add 3 times as much water. Let stand over night. On the second day, boil 10 minutes. Let stand over night. On the third day, do the same as the second. On the fourth day, boil 10 minutes. Add cup for cup of **sugar,** and boil about 15 minutes more. Pour into sterilized jelly glasses and cap with melted paraffin.

Mrs. Charles (Florence) Hurcomb
From her mother,
Mrs. Florence Gillmore Schiek

Crisp, firm ice-box cookies were very popular in the 1930's. These are quite a contrast to the moist, chewy cookies which seem to appeal to the taste buds of the 1980's.

RELIABLE COOKIE RECIPE

½ cup shortening
¼ cup peanut butter
1 cup brown sugar
1 egg
2 cups flour
1 tsp. soda
½ tsp. cinnamon
⅛ tsp. cloves
⅛ tsp. nutmeg
½ cup salted peanuts, chopped fine

Cream the shortening thoroughly. Blend in the peanut butter and sugar. Add the egg and beat well. Mix and sift the soda and spices with the flour; slowly add to the egg mixture. Add peanuts. Form into rolls and wrap in wax paper; let stand in the refrigerator several hours. Slice thin. Place on a baking sheet. Bake in 375 degree oven for 8-10 minutes.

Lucy Green

If your guests complain about your servants, send your guests away—you can get other guests, but you cannot get other servants.

BLACK WALNUT CARAMEL FUDGE

3 cups granulated sugar
1 cup milk
1 tsp. vanilla
½-1 cup black walnut meats or 1 tsp. walnut flavoring

Put 2 cups of sugar and 1 cup of milk in a pan and let come to a boil. In a metal skillet put the other cup of sugar and let it melt. Stir it all the time until it is amber colored and perfectly smooth. Pour this hot caramel into the pan of boiling sugar and milk. Cook to 236 degrees or until a small portion dropped in cold water will form a soft ball. Remove from the fire; allow to cool slightly. Then add the vanilla and nuts. Stir until it begins to thicken. Pour into a greased pan.* Cut in squares.

*(Ed: An 8 x 8-inch pan may be used.)

Mrs. E. W. Thompson

James
Lewis
Casaday
Collection

1940's

This black crepe dress is intricately pleated and draped in a most flattering style. It features a V-neckline and three-quarter length sleeves, which are tucked from shoulder to hem. The bodice is pleated with diagonal pleats overlapping one another to form a V-shape. The skirt is draped sarong-style. Circa 1940.

HOME FRONT WARRIORS

By 1941, the world was totally engulfed by the flames of war. Fueled by an insatiable lust for conquest, the Fascist powers rolled relentlessly onward, swallowing huge chunks of territory and enslaving millions of people. For a time, it seemed as though America could continue to wrap herself in the tenuous shield of neutrality until December 7th, when that illusion was shattered by Japanese bombs at Pearl Harbor.

Suddenly uniforms appeared everywhere. As in World War I, women were asked to step in and fill the jobs vacated by men who were being called into the service. These dungaree clad ladies, who would soon be immortalized as "Rosy the Riveter," won the grudging respect of their male co-workers and the gratitude of the nation.

With over 3 million women entering the work force for the first time, there seemed to be little time for domestic chores. Tasks which housewives had previously taken for granted now became true tests of feminine ingenuity. (It's hardly surprising that convenience foods made their debut during the war years.) To save fuel, patriotic ladies often prepared oven meals where the main dish, vegetable, and dessert were all baked at the same time. Food rationing began in May 1942; careful planning was now required to insure that healthful, appetizing meals were served without exhausting the family's supply of ration stamps. People were encouraged to help feed themselves by planting Victory Gardens. Since tin was in short supply, home canning boomed as women sought to preserve the summer's harvest. In the early years of the war, victory was far from certain. Every person was expected to do his part to defeat the enemy -- that meant no hoarding, no waste, and no complaining.

The needs of the military were blurring the lines between trash and treasure. There's an old cliche that money can't buy happiness; during World War II, it couldn't buy much else either. Many consumer goods were unavailable because of wartime shortages and rationing (except, of course, on the Black Market). It was terribly frustrating for people who had just been through the Depression to finally have a healthy paycheck and virtually nothing to buy except war bonds. Conversely, the waste fat which housewives returned to their grocer was used to make explosives. Also, ladies donated their old nylon stockings, which were used to make gun powder bags for naval guns. Scrap metal, tin cans, and old toothpaste tubes were all carefully collected and recycled.

Feeding allied servicemen around the world was a massive undertaking. Powdered eggs, non-fat dried milk, and other dehydrated foods were developed to meet the pressing need to preserve perishables. By 1944, families at home were able to benefit from this technology when a variety of boxed mixes began to appear for gingerbread, pancakes, pudding, and muffins. Although the canned meat, Spam, was introduced by Hormel in 1937, it was during the war that its notoriety reached legendary proportions. In years to come, housewives would also benefit from the discovery of Melamine or "Melmac" which was made into unbreakable dishes for the Navy.

Wartime fashions matched the no nonsense tenor of the times. The uniform of the home front warrior was man tailored and patriotically plain. Knee-length skirts (straight or frugally pleated) were paired with simple, unadorned jackets which were so severely padded at the shoulders that they resembled the deck of an air craft carrier. Silk or nylon stockings were virtually unattainable so sun tan creams and simulated seams drawn up the back of bare legs were visible signs of support for the war effort.

Women were cautioned not to waste fabric with nonessential items such as sashes and hoods. To conserve material, it even became popular to wear 2-piece bathing suits; coincidentally, this also provided some sensational pin-up pictures for boy friends and husbands overseas. Magazines offered tips on restyling old clothing or turning unrationed blankets and sheets into fashionable coats and dresses.

The postwar world burst upon the scene with a jubilant celebration on August 15, 1945, V-J Day. Once again people could afford the luxury of planning for the future. As the government began the monumental task of demobilization, women were expected to surrender their jobs to discharged servicemen and return to the traditional role of wife and mother. Many women welcomed the chance to put harsh wartime realities behind them and embrace a more sheltered way of life. Designer Christian Dior anticipated this mood when he introduced his first collection in 1947. He wanted to give women a flower-like appearance by dressing them in tightly fitted bodices and long, billowing skirts which accentuated and enhanced a woman's natural curves. The initial criticism of Dior's youthful, feminine designs was short lived as ladies soon rushed out to buy the "New Look."

The last half of the decade began in a rush of rose-colored optimism. After four years of trial and triumph, no obstacle seemed insurmountable -- this was a time to live again. Factories couldn't retool fast enough to meet the staggering demand for new consumer goods; women wanted streamlined kitchens with all the modern appliances while men lined up to buy new suits and snappy cars. As people actively went about the task of rebuilding their lives, it soon became apparent that for many Americans these truly were "The Best Years of Our Lives."

This is a recipe given to my father by some of his Canadian fishing companions. The best part of it, besides the taste, is the fact that everyone thinks there is wine in it. In fact, it is nothing but lowly beer.

CANADIAN CHEESE SOUP

Cook together in butter for 5 minutes:
½ cup diced celery
½ cup diced carrots
1 tsp. minced onion
Blend in **3 Tbsp. flour** and **½ tsp. salt**. Add **2 cups chicken broth** and cook slowly until the vegetables are cooked tender. Add **2 cups milk** and **½ lb. diced sharp American cheese.** Just before serving, add **½ cup beer.** Top with salted whipped cream and parsley.
About 4 servings.

Mrs. Louis N. (Janice) Rugee
From her father,
Mortimer P. Reed

AUNT MARGARET'S PEA SALAD

1 can (16 oz.) **peas, drained**
½-¾ cup celery, chopped
1 onion, chopped
3 (or more) **hard boiled eggs**
1 cup American cheese
Miracle Whip

Combine all the ingredients and mix well in a non-metal bowl. Chill thoroughly.
(Fresh peas or frozen, uncooked and drained peas may also be used. You might also want to substitute mild cheddar for the American cheese and a homemade creamy dressing for the Miracle Whip.)

Jerry and Sheri Wiener
From Aunt Margaret Van Allen

CRANBERRY CREAM SALAD

1 pkg. (3 oz.) **cherry gelatin**
3 Tbsp. sugar
1 cup boiling water
1 cup whole cranberry sauce
⅓ cup chopped celery
⅓ cup chopped walnuts
1 cup sour cream

Dissolve the gelatin and sugar in boiling water. Add the cranberry sauce. Chill until partly set; fold in the remaining ingredients. Turn into 1 large mold, or individual molds. Chill until firm. Serves 6.

Mrs. Glady Conant

PROPER CONDUCT WHEN DATING A MAN IN THE SERVICE

A young girl should not go alone to an army post or camp to visit a soldier unless he is her brother. On a visit to any other man she should be accompanied by another girl or a couple.

While at the post the girl should not attempt to bring her officer friends into intimate contact with enlisted men of her acquaintance. It is very embarrassing to both men and officers. They are like oil and water - they just don't mix.

Every girl should be insistent that her soldier-boy friend observe every rule of their camp and the army. She should make certain that they get back from leaves on time and that they violate no regulation because of her.

LENTIL SALAD

1 lb. lentils
½ medium sized red onion, chopped
    (you may use more, to taste)
1 or 2 ribs celery, chopped
½ green pepper, chopped
Chopped parsley

DRESSING:
    ½ cup olive oil
    2 Tbsp. wine vinegar
    Garlic, salt, and freshly ground pepper to taste

Rinse the lentils in a strainer, picking out any shriveled ones. Put the lentils in a large saucepan with 5 cups water; bring to a boil, cover, and simmer for 25 minutes. Time carefully so that the lentils are tender but not mushy. Drain and turn into a large casserole dish. Sprinkle with **3 Tbsp. olive oil.** Let them cool to room temperature. Add all the chopped vegetables.
Combine the dressing ingredients in a jar and mix thoroughly (or use a blender). Pour the dressing over the lentils and vegetables; toss gently. Cover and refrigerate several hours. Serve on lettuce and garnish with any of the following: sliced cucumbers; tomatoes; or hard boiled eggs.

Mrs. Kenneth (Amy) David

An important part of my family's holiday smorgasbord is Swedish Limpa Bread. We serve this sweet, flavorful rye bread with a jam made from lingonberries, which are native to Sweden and have a tangy flavor similar to that of the cranberry.

SWEDISH LIMPA BREAD

½ cup light brown sugar, packed
¼ cup light or dark molasses
¼ cup butter or margarine
1 Tbsp. salt
1 tsp. anise seed (caraway may be substituted)
2 Tbsp. grated orange peel
1 cup boiling water
½ cup warm water (105-115 degrees)
2 pkgs. active dry yeast
5 cups unsifted all-purpose flour
4 cups unsifted rye flour
Cornmeal
2 Tbsp. butter or margarine, melted

In a large bowl, combine the sugar, molasses, ¼ cup butter, salt, anise, and orange peel. Add 1 cup boiling water and stir until the sugar dissolves and the butter melts. Add **1 cup cold water.** Cool to lukewarm. Sprinkle the yeast over the ½ cup warm water in a measuring cup; stir until dissolved. Add the yeast to the molasses mixture and mix well. Gradually add 5 cups all-purpose flour and 1 cup rye flour; beat vigorously until smooth, and the dough leaves the side of the bowl. Gradually add 3 cups rye flour. (Mix the last of the flour in with your hand; the dough will be stiff.) Turn the dough onto a lightly floured surface and knead until smooth and elastic, about 10 minutes. Place in a lightly greased bowl, turning the dough to bring up the greased side. Cover with a towel and let rise in a warm place (85 degrees) which is free from drafts until double in bulk, about 1½ hours. Grease a large cookie sheet and sprinkle lightly with cornmeal. Punch down the dough and turn out onto a lightly floured surface. Cut the dough in half. Shape each half into an oval. On a lightly floured surface, roll each half with the palms of your hands into a loaf 12 inches long which tapers at the ends (torpedo shaped). Place the loaves on the prepared cookie sheet, 5 inches apart. With a sharp knife, make 4 diagonal slashes in the top of each loaf (¼ inch deep). Cover the loaves with a towel and let rise in a warm place, free from drafts, until double in bulk, 1-1¼ hours. Preheat the oven to 375 degrees; bake on the middle shelf of the oven for 35 minutes. (My oven always takes longer. The bread will be nicely brown and have a hollow sound when it is done. If in doubt, slice into a loaf; the center should not be doughy.) Cover with foil during the last 10 minutes of baking to prevent over browning, if necessary. Brush with butter. Makes 2 loaves.

Mrs. Karen Keller

ORANGE BREAD

Sift into a mixing bowl:
2¼ cups bread flour
2¼ tsp. baking powder
¼ tsp. soda
¾ tsp. salt
¾ cup sugar
Add:
¾ cup chopped pecans
2 Tbsp. melted butter
1 egg, beaten
¾ cup orange juice
1 Tbsp. grated orange peel

After the ingredients have been mixed together, place in a greased 5 x 9-inch pan. Bake for 60-70 minutes in a 350 degree oven. Cover with another pan for 20 minutes.

Mrs. George Omacht

GRANDMA SNYDER'S DINNER ROLLS

2 pkg. yeast
¼ cup warm water
1 cup scalded milk
¼ cup sugar
3 Tbsp. shortening
1 tsp. salt
1 egg
3½ cups flour

1. Soften yeast in the warm water.
2. Combine the milk, sugar, shortening, salt; cool to lukewarm.
3. Add 1¼ cups flour and beat well.
4. Add the egg and yeast.
5. Gradually add the rest of the flour to form a soft dough.
6. Knead on a floured surface 5-8 minutes.
7. Place in a greased bowl, turn and cover. Let rise in a warm place until doubled (about 1½-2 hours).
8. Turn out onto a greased surface and shape into a long fat rope. Using greased hands, pull off and shape into 24 balls. Place into a greased 13 x 9-inch pan. Let rise.
9. Bake in a hot oven 400 degrees, for 12-15 minutes.

Mrs. David (Christine) Bainbridge

MAMMA'S DRIED BEEF SPREAD

½ lb. grated sharp cheddar cheese
¼ lb. real dried beef, chopped
2 eggs, beaten
1 cup strained tomatoes (canned)

Mix the ingredients well. Cook till thickened; cool. Store in the refrigerator. This is a favorite with men.

Mrs. John N. (Muriel) Perkins

BLUEBERRY COFFEE CAKE

2 beaten eggs
4 Tbsp. melted shortening
1 cup sugar
2 cups sifted flour
1 cup milk
4 tsp. baking powder
1 tsp. salt
2-3 cups of blueberries

Combine the eggs, sugar, milk, and shortening. Add the flour which has been sifted with the baking powder and salt. Fold in the blueberries. Mix well and pour into a greased 9 x 13-inch pan. Sprinkle with a mixture of **½ cup brown sugar, 2 tsp. cinnamon, 2 Tbsp. flour, 2 Tbsp. melted butter,** and **1 cup broken nuts.** Bake for 20-25 minutes at 375 degrees F.

Mrs. Ronald (Pat) Olsen

CRANBERRY NUT BREAD

2 cups all-purpose flour, sifted
1 cup sugar
1½ tsp. baking powder
½ tsp. soda
½ tsp. salt
1 egg, slightly beaten
1 cup whole raw cranberries
1 cup chopped nuts

Put **2 Tbsp. melted butter,** the **grated rind and juice of 1 orange** and **boiling water** in a cup to make ¾ cup liquid. Let cool.

Sift flour, salt, soda, baking powder, and sugar together. Add the egg and the liquid in a cup. Mix only until the dry ingredients are blended and moistened. Fold in the nuts and cranberries. Pour the batter into a greased loaf pan. Bake at 325 degrees for 1 hour and 15 minutes or until done. Store for 24 hours. Refrigerate and keep that way.

Misses Mary and Thaddessa Taylor

Pity the poor Army cook! Whether at home or overseas, soldiers seemed duty bound to complain about the chow.
Fort Sill Recorder, January 14, 1944.

POTATO PANCAKES

4 lbs. potatoes
4 eggs
8 Tbsp. flour
2 tsp. salt
2 tsp. pepper
2 tsp. baking powder
1½ tsp. summer savory
8 Tbsp. milk

Grate the raw potatoes and onion. Let stand a few minutes, then drain off the excess water. Mix all the ingredients well. Fry in fat or oil until brown. (Fry with the lid on the skillet.) Serve hot with gravy or apple sauce.

Mr. Frank Sindlinger

Ratatouille is a vegetable stew from France. It can be eaten either hot from the oven or as a cold dish during the summer months.

RATATOUILLE

1 large onion, sliced
2 cloves garlic, chopped fine (optional)
1 large eggplant, peeled and cubed
3 small zucchini, sliced
2 Bell peppers, sliced
5 fresh tomatoes, peeled and cut into chunks
3 Tbsp. flour
½ cup olive oil
Grated Parmesan cheese

Heat the olive oil in a large skillet or Dutch oven. Saute the onions and garlic. Lightly flour the zucchini and eggplant; place in the skillet. Slice the green peppers and add. Cover and cook very slowly on a burner or in the oven for about 1-1½ hours. Add the tomatoes and cook gently until done. Serve with grated Parmesan cheese.

NOTE: Watch carefully. Sometimes when the vegetables are especially tender the cooking time is only about 50 minutes.

Mrs. Mary Fischer

MARJORAM RICE

Cook about **2 cups of rice;** drain.

In a skillet, saute about **2 Tbsp. chopped parsley** and **1 small can of mushrooms,** chopped in small pieces (fresh mushrooms may be used). Add **salt** and **pepper** to taste. Add the rice. Sprinkle **marjoram** on the rice to taste. Serve.

Mrs. Andrew (Magda) Eperjesi
From her mother-in-law,
Mrs. Elizabeth Eperjesi

CARROTS AND STRING BEANS AU GRATIN

3 cups cooked string beans
3 cups cooked carrots
5 Tbsp. shortening
1 small onion, minced
3 Tbsp. flour
2½ cups milk
1 tsp. salt
⅛ tsp. pepper
1 cup grated American cheese
2 eggs, beaten slightly
¾ cup soft bread crumbs

Prepare the string beans and carrots. Meanwhile, melt 3 Tbsp. shortening in a saucepan. Add the minced onion and cook until tender. Add the flour and stir until smooth. Add the milk, salt, pepper, and cheese; cook, stirring constantly, until the sauce is thickened. Remove the sauce from the heat and pour it over the eggs which have been beaten slightly.

Arrange the string beans, carrots, and sauce in alternate layers in a greased casserole. Top with buttered bread crumbs (having been mixed with 2 Tbsp. shortening or butter). Bake in a moderate oven (350 degrees) for 30 minutes.

Mrs. Helene Sailer

BAKED TOMATOES

6 medium sized fresh tomatoes
3 Tbsp. butter
2 Tbsp. flour
1 cup milk
1 tsp. salt
¼ tsp. paprika
1/16 tsp. sage
½ cup grated cheese
3 cups cooked macaroni
½ cup soft bread crumbs
4 hard cooked eggs
6 sprigs parsley

Scoop out the insides of the tomatoes. Make the stuffing as follows: Melt 2 tsp. butter; add the flour and stir in the milk gradually; add salt, paprika, and sage; cook 10 minutes, then take from the stove; add grated cheese and 1 cup of the macaroni. Fill the tomatoes with this mixture. Cover with bread crumbs, dot with the remaining butter, and bake until the tomatoes are cooked.* Surround the baked tomatoes with the remaining 2 cups cooked macaroni which have been sprinkled with melted butter and grated cheese, to taste. Garnish with slices of hard cooked eggs and parsley. (This stuffing may also be used to stuff green peppers.)

*(Ed: Bake at 350 degrees. This dish is good either hot or cold.)

Mrs. Helene Sailer

Mr. and Mrs. Louis N. Rugee spent many long hours working in their Victory Garden during World War II. This, however, was just the beginning for Mrs. Rugee who then had to can the vegetables she harvested.

During the war years, butternut squash was a dietary staple, much like potatoes. This recipe would do justice to the bounty from any Victory Garden.

BAKED BUTTERNUT SQUASH

1 large stemmed butternut squash
3 apples (cooking variety)
¼ cup water
8 Tbsp. brown sugar
8 pats of butter*
Cinnamon or nutmeg (your choice, to taste)

Cut the squash into slices about ¾ inch thick and peel (usually 8 slices). Place in and 8 x 14-inch Pyrex baking dish; pour the water into the bottom of the dish. Cover the squash with apples which have been sliced ⅛ inch thick. Sprinkle with cinnamon or nutmeg. Put 1 Tbsp. brown sugar on top of each slice of squash and top with a pat of butter. Cover the dish with foil and bake in a preheated oven at 350 degrees for 45 minutes. Remove the foil and continue to bake an additional 15 minutes, or until the squash tests done.

*(Ed: about ¼ cup butter, or to personal preference.)

Mrs. Mary Fischer
From Mr. John Lawecki

TURKEY SOUFFLE

2 Tbsp. butter or margarine
2 Tbsp. flour
1 cup milk
2 cups finely chopped turkey
2 Tbsp. finely chopped parsley
3 egg yolks
1 Tbsp. finely grated onion
1 tsp. salt
¼ tsp. pepper
½ tsp. paprika
3 egg whites
Fine bread crumbs

Melt the butter and stir in the flour. Gradually add the milk and stir until the mixture boils and thickens. Cook about 3 minutes longer, stirring occasionally. Add turkey, the slightly beaten egg yolks, and seasonings. Fold the stiffly beaten egg whites into the mixture. Top with crushed cereal or bread crumbs. Bake in a greased casserole in a moderate oven (350 degrees) for 40-50 minutes, or until delicately browned and firm in the center. Serves 4.

Serve with a sauce of your choice, if desired.

Misses Mary and Thaddessa Taylor

Mrs. Loney was a chef at a private club in Pennsylvania. Her recipe for Hamburger Sauce makes a tasty sandwich filling, very much like Sloppy Joes.

GRANDMA ALVIE'S HAMBURGER SAUCE

2 lbs. hamburger
3 medium onions, diced
2 Tbsp. chili powder
1½ tsp. cinnamon
1½ tsp. nutmeg
1 scant tsp. prepared mustard
½ tsp. oregano
¼ tsp. garlic powder
1 cup mashed carrots
1 cup mashed potatoes
2 qts. water
Salt and pepper

THICKENING:
3 Tbsp. cornstarch, blended with:
½ cup water

Brown the hamburger with the onions. Add the remaining ingredients and simmer for 4-5 hours. Finally thicken with the cornstarch mixture.

Mrs. W.F. (Deborah) Mayers
From her mother-in-law,
Mrs. Alva Loney

During World War II, American servicemen were stationed in many foreign countries around the world. When they returned home, they brought with them a taste for the exotic dishes they had enjoyed overseas. American cuisine was developing a decidedly international flavor thanks to the growing popularity of dishes such as curry from India, sukiyaki from Japan, and pizza from Italy.

HOMEMADE PIZZA

1 cup very warm water
1 pkg. active dry yeast
2 Tbsp. shortening
¼ tsp. salt
4 cups all-purpose flour
1 can (12 oz.) tomato sauce
¼ cup chopped onion (or onion to taste)
1 tsp. salt (optional)
1-1½ tsp. oregano (dried)
1 tsp. sweet basil (dried)
Dash of pepper

To make the crust, sprinkle the yeast over the water and stir until dissolved. Add the shortening, salt, and 2 cups of flour. Mix till smooth. Gradually add the remaining flour, mixing with the hands, till the dough is stiff enough to leave the sides of the bowl. Place the dough on a floured board and cover with the bowl to rest for 10 minutes. Knead for 8-10 minutes. Place in greased bowl in a warm place and cover with a towel. Let rise for about 1 hour or until double in bulk.

While the dough is rising, combine the remaining ingredients and adjust to taste. Simmer in a saucepan until the onion is tender.

When the dough is ready, punch it down with your fist and knead for a few minutes. Spread in a greased pizza pan. (If spread thinly, this recipe will make three 12 inch crusts.) Bake the crust for a few minutes at 450 degrees before adding the sauce to insure the crispness of the crust. After baking a few minutes, spread the sauce evenly over the crusts. Top with your favorite toppings and bake at 450 degrees for 20-25 minutes, or until the crust is golden and the topping bubbly.

Extra pizzas may be covered with foil or plastic wrap and frozen. There is no need to thaw them before baking.

TOPPING:
Mozzarella cheese - I use 1 lb. of cheese on each pizza. (I put the cheese on the pizza during the last 15 minutes of baking time.)
Hamburger, pork or Italian sausage - Brown and drain well
Mushrooms - fresh or canned
Green peppers, anchovies, pepperoni, ham, olives - whatever your heart desires.

Mrs. David (Margie) Canfield

STUFFED HAM SLICE

1 slice ham
2 tart apples, diced
¼ cup sugar
1 Tbsp. parsley
½ cup dry fine bread crumbs
¼ cup chopped celery
Salt and pepper

Mix the bread crumbs, celery, parsley and the diced apples which have been sweetened with the sugar. Season with salt and pepper. Spread this stuffing over the ham and roll up with the dressing inside. Tie with string or fasten with skewers. Place in a baking pan and pour about ½ **cup of water** over the ham roll. Cover and bake in a moderate oven (350 degrees F.) until done, about 45 minutes. Serves 2-3.

Mrs. Helene Sailer

CHICKEN PAPRIKAS AND DUMPLINGS

1 onion, chopped
4 Tbsp. shortening
1 Tbsp. paprika
¼ tsp. black pepper
1-2 tsp. salt
4-5 lb. chicken, disjointed
1½ cups water
½ pt. sour cream

Brown the onion in the shortening. Add the seasonings and chicken; brown for 10 minutes. Add the water and cover; let simmer slowly until tender (about 30 minutes). Remove the chicken Add the sour cream to the drippings in the pan and mix well. Add the dumplings and arrange the chicken on top. Heat through and serve.
NOTE: For more gravy, add ½ pt. sweet cream to the sour cream and thicken with flour.

DUMPLINGS:
3 eggs, beaten
3 cups flour
1 Tbsp. salt
½ cup water

Mix all the ingredients together and beat with a spoon. Drop the batter by teaspoonfuls into boiling salted water. Cook about 10 minutes; drain and rinse with cold water. Drain again and add to the Paprikas.

Sue Stratigos
From a friend with an
Hungarian mother-in-law

SALMON POTATO SCHOONERS

Scoop out **6 or 7 medium baked potatoes;** mash. Beat in **⅓ cup hot milk, 1 egg, ⅓ cup finely chopped onion** cooked until tender in **2 Tbsp. butter, 1 tsp. salt, ¼ tsp. paprika, dash of cayenne, 1½ cups flaked canned salmon,** and **1 tsp. lemon juice.** Stuff the mixture into the potato shells. Sprinkle with **buttered bread crumbs** and bake in a moderate oven (375 degrees F.) for 20 minutes.

Mrs. Helen Sailer

*Olive and Nut Sandwiches were a **very** popular item on The Philadelphia's menu. It was perfect for luncheons during the meat rationed years of World War II.*

OLIVE AND NUT SALAD SANDWICH

1 lb. crushed green olives
¼ lb. ground roasted cashews or your
    favorite nut meat

Combine olives and nuts.
Add **mayonnaise** until proper consistency of a salad mix. Serve on a dark bread as a sandwich for an interesting change of pace.

Mr. Ted Poledor
From The Philadelphia Recipe Book

Shortly after we were married, Mom gave me the recipe for Aunt Anna's Steak Rolls. This was a welcome addition to our beginning recipe collection. Economical, yet elegant, it makes a wonderful main dish for company when served by candlelight with a good tossed salad, mashed potatoes with butter, and a rose or red wine.

AUNT ANNA'S STEAK ROLLS

Saute **onion** until transparent. Flour **cubed steak** on both sides (season the **flour** with **Lawry's salt** and **garlic salt**). Place a small strip of **bacon** (partially cooked) and about 1 tsp. of the sauteed onion in the middle of each steak. Roll up and secure with toothpicks. Roll again in flour. Brown the steak rolls on all sides in **melted butter** over medium heat. Add a little water to the pan and loosen all the good browned particles. Place the steak rolls back in the pan with **canned mushrooms** (drained). Bake about 2½ hours in a slow oven (300-325 degrees). Do not cover with a lid.*

This recipe contains no measurements; these are adjusted according to the number of people you are serving and your personal taste in seasonings. I've found that adults eat an average of 1½-2 rolls each.

Steak Rolls are great for today's busy, working women. The completed Steak Rolls can be frozen and reheated another time. Spend one afternoon preparing them and enjoy two or three quick and delicious meals.

*(Ed: If your pan cannot be used safely in the oven, transfer the steak rolls to a casserole and bake. Be sure to baste the meat frequently during the baking time so that it doesn't dry out.)

*Jerry and Sheri Wiener
From Mrs. Wiener's Aunt Anna*

At Christmas time, our family always begins our smorgasbord with several kinds of fish such as smoked and pickled herring, smoked and fresh oysters, and perhaps some boiled shrimp with cocktail sauce. The appetizer course includes several varieties of cheese, rye or whole wheat crackers, and an extensive relish tray. The main course usually includes potato sausage, Swedish Meat Balls with Dill Sauce, potato salad, and plenty of Swedish Limpa bread. As a finale, we enjoy Swedish Rosettes (a light crispy cookie dusted with powdered sugar), Ebleskiver (a Danish pastry somewhat like a filled cake donut), and a Swedish Almond Tea Ring.

Don't forget to greet your guests at the door with steaming mugs of hot, spiced wine. The smorgasbord is a wonderful feast, perfect for the grandest of all holidays.

SWEDISH MEAT BALLS WITH DILL SAUCE

½ cup finely chopped onion
2 Tbsp. margarine
1 cup soft bread crumbs
⅔ cup milk
2 eggs, beaten
2 tsp. salt
½ tsp. allspice
½ tsp. pepper
2 lbs. lean ground beef

Saute the onion in the margarine until tender. Soak the bread crumbs in the milk for 5 minutes. Add the eggs and spices; mix well. Add the ground beef and onions; mix well. Shape into 1-inch balls. Fry in a large skillet over moderate heat, turning frequently to brown on all sides. (Makes about 5 doz.) Serve hot with Dill Sauce.

DILL SAUCE:
2 Tbsp. margarine
3 Tbsp. flour
½ tsp. salt
¼ tsp. dry mustard
1½ cups milk
½ pt. (1 cup) sour cream
1 tsp. dill weed (or more, to taste)

Melt the margarine in a small saucepan. Blend in the flour, salt, and dry mustard. Add the milk. Cook, stirring constantly, over moderate heat until thickened. Stir in the sour cream and dill weed. Serve immediately.

*Mrs. Karen Keller
From her mother,
Mrs. Christine Carlson*

WINNING THE WAR AT HOME

Food management, one of wartime's most important jobs, rests squarely on the shoulders of the American homemaker. Food will win the war and make the peace only if it is administered wisely by the meal planners, so that supplies will be adequate to meet the ever-increasing demands.

We have never been in a war like this one. We have never had to fight in all four corners of the earth at once. This is total war.

1. Each civilian man, woman, and child should have a ration book.

2. Watch your local paper for the dates your ration stamps become valid. Red are for meats and related items; blue are for processed foods.

3. Point values will be adjusted from month to month to take care of fluctuating supplies. Get out of that old food rut so that you are ready to meet big shifts in shortages and supplies.

4. It is the responsibility of every homemaker to provide variety and balance in her menus. It is important to keep our men, women, and children strong and healthy to continue the fight.

5. Help the dealer by shopping at hours when he is least busy. Shop in person and have your points and money ready. Buy as few times in a week as possible.

6. Plan your menus carefully. Figure the total number of points you will have to spend for your family each week. For an average family of 4, this amounts to 64 points for meats, fats, and cheese, and approximately 48 points for processed foods.

Use your points carefully so that you will not run out of stamps. You can take the stamps from more than 1 book belonging to your household if you need to.

7. Include at least 1 low point meat in every week's menus. Buy cuts with bone in, then use the bones for soup stock and the boned meat separately.

8. Waste during wartime is sabotage. Store your food carefully to prevent spoilage. Use the freezer compartment of your refrigerator to store fresh meat you can't use within a few days of purchase.

9. Cook meat just long enough to reach desired degree of doneness - avoid shrinkage.

10. Use meat extenders, such as noodles, rice, oatmeal, and vegetables which carry the flavor of the meat and yet increase the number of servings.

11. Use leftovers to give variety and interest in meals. Do not use leftover dishes on 2 successive days.

Meals Without Meat — 1943   69 Ration Recipes for Meat

This recipe from Girl Scout camp is still used by Mrs. Sipocz. With a salad and roll, it makes a quick and easy meal.

BLUSHING BUNNIES

¾ **lb. macaroni noodles**
1 **can tomato soup**
6 **slices of American cheese, melted**

Cook the macaroni according to package directions. Mix all ingredients and serve. This can be used as a main dish or a side dish with meat.

Miss Jenny Spiocz
From her mother,
Mrs. Josephine Sipocz

CHRISTMAS DINNER - 1945

Roast Young Tom Turkey
Giblet Dressing w/Onions
Cream Turkey Gravy
Snow Flake Mashed Potatoes
Early June Buttered Peas
Buttered Asparagus Tips
Home Made Pumpkin Pie (By Batja)
Country Hot Biscuits (By Batja)
U.S. Army Preserved Butter
R. and G. American Coffee

CHOW FORMATION!

558th Ordnance HM Company (TK) A.P.O. #72.

H.T. Staples
Mess Sgt.

CANDIED YAMS

2 **lbs. yams** (4 medium)
½ **cup** (1 stick) **butter**
¾ **cup firmly packed light brown sugar**
¼ **tsp. salt**
⅓ **cup water**

Cook the potatoes in the skins until tender but still firm (about 20-30 minutes). Pare and cut diagonally in halves or thirds.

In a skillet, melt the butter; add the sugar and salt. Stir until smooth. Add the water. Add the potatoes, turning to coat on all sides. Cover and cook over low heat for 20 minutes. Serves 8-10.

Mrs. Herb (Betty Ann) True

CHILI BEEF & SPAGHETTI

Saute **½ lb. ground beef** with **¼ cup chopped onion** in **2 Tbsp shortening or salad oil** until the beef is browned; stir frequently as it cooks. Add **1 8-oz. can tomato sauce,** plus **1 3-oz. can sliced mushrooms** (liquid and all). Season with **½ tsp. chili powder, ½ tsp. Worcestershire sauce, ½ tsp. salt,** and a **dash of pepper.** Simmer 10 minutes. Meanwhile, cook **4 oz. of spaghetti** in **2 quarts of rapidly boiling water** to which you have added **2 tsp. salt.** Cook until tender. Drain. Dot with **butter or margarine.** Serve with chili beef. Sprinkle with grated **Parmesan cheese.** Makes 2 generous servings.

Mrs. Eleanor Carr

SHRIMP LOUISIANA

- **1 Tbsp. butter**
- **1 Tbsp. flour**
- **1 whole onion, finely chopped**
- **1 green pepper, cut up**
- **A few springs of finely chopped parsley**
- **2 Tbsp. shallot tops** (or fresh green onions)
- **½ tsp. Worcestershire sauce**
- **1 can (28 oz.) tomatoes**
- **½ cup water**
- **1 shake cayenne pepper**
- **Salt and pepper to taste**
- **1 lb. fresh shrimp, cooked**

Saute the onion and green pepper in the butter. Add the flour, then the remaining ingredients. Cook slowly for 20 minutes. Serve over rice. Serves 4.

Mrs. John R. (Virginia) Lionberger

HOUSEHOLD HINTS

*W*hen fats are no longer usable for any cooking purposes they are ready for the salvage can. Clean a large tin can. Warm the fat and pour it through a cloth into the can. It makes no difference whether the fat is darkened in color. Keep it cool until at least one pound (2 cups) is collected, then take it to your meat dealer and he will buy it from you at the established price. In the war effort, fats are vital as a source of glycerine for explosives, drugs and medical supplies. It is estimated that just one pound of waste fat makes enough glycerine to fire four 37 mm. anti-aircraft shells.

*O*ne way in which sauces are proving especially adept is in masking the flavor of less popular but none the less nutritious and plentiful foods. In fact, no matter what your family's main food hate may be, you can disguise the outcast so beautifully, with a well seasoned sauce, that folks will consume it with enthusiasm.

*B*ecause of the sugar shortage, it is recommended that instead of making preserves, jams and jellies from ripe fruits, fruits be first canned and the homemaker preserve from the canned product as needed and as sugar is available. Preserves and jellies made in this manner will be found to be equal in quality to the product secured from fresh fruits.

*T*he most noticeable difference between a supper and dinner is in the main course of the meal. At a dinner it is always a roast, steak, or fowl. At a supper it is usually a plate of cold cuts, a salad, or perhaps some chafing dish specialty, Welsh rarebit, chicken a la king, or the like. If there is soup at supper it is served in two-handled cups, instead of the soup plates used at dinner. Bread-and-butter plates are always on the supper table and coffee is usually served in a man-size cup rather than the dinner demi-tasse.

*T*he hostess whose husband arrives home from the office and announces that he has brought a chum with him must appear to be very happy over the unexpected guest even though she is burning inwardly. She may take her husband to task later (the private conversations of husbands and wives are not in the realm of etiquette) but, in front of the guest, she must be pleasant. If she has plenty to eat in the house, she need not worry, but if she has only enough for two, she must feign loss of appetite unless there is an opportunity to send someone down to the corner grocery store.

The Home Economics room at Central High School provided a pleasant atmosphere for learning in the 1940's.

Courtesy of the South Bend Community School Corporation.

DATE CAKE

½ cup fat
1 cup light brown sugar
1 egg
⅔ cup chopped dates
1 cup buttermilk
2 cups flour
1 tsp. soda
2 tsp. cinnamon
1 tsp. cloves
½ tsp. nutmeg
¼ tsp. salt

Cream the fat and sugar. Add the rest of the ingredients. Beat 3 minutes. Pour into a loaf pan lined with wax paper. Bake at 350 degrees for 45 minutes to 1 hour, until done, cool and frost.

DELICIOUS FROSTING:
1 cup dark brown sugar
⅔ cup granulated sugar
⅔ cup water
2 Tbsp. butter
½ tsp. vanilla

Mix the sugars, water, and butter in a pan. Boil gently and stir frequently until the mixture reaches the soft ball stage (234-240 degrees F.). Set aside for 15 minutes. Add the vanilla and beat until creamy. Add a few drops of cream after you beat it for a while - say ¼ cup. Spread over the cooled cake.

Mrs. Lester (Aileen) H. Borough
From Neva Jackson Miller

FUDGY APPLESAUCE CAKE

⅓ cup soft butter or margarine
1 cup sugar
2 eggs
1 cup unsifted flour
⅓ cup cocoa
½ tsp. salt
1 tsp. cinnamon
½ tsp. soda
½ cup chopped walnuts
1 cup applesauce
¼ cup milk

Cream the butter and sugar until fluffy; beat in the eggs. Combine the dry ingredients and mix well. Combine the applesauce and milk; add alternately with the flour mixture. Stir only until well blended. Pour into a greased 9-inch square baking pan.

Bake in a 350 degree oven for 45-50 minutes or until the surface is firm when touched lightly. Serves 8-10 people.

Mrs. Charles (Mary) Taylor

GRANDMA ALVIE'S WAR CAKE

Boil together and cool:
1 cup brown sugar (or light molasses)
1¼ cup water
⅓ cup shortening
2 cups raisins
½ tsp. nutmeg
2 tsp. cinnamon
½ tsp. cloves
Add:
1 tsp. soda (dissolved in 2 tsp. water)
1 tsp. salt
2 cups flour
1 tsp. baking powder
1 cup dates, chopped (optional)
1 cup nuts, chopped (optional)

In a greased pan, bake for 50 minutes in a 325 degree oven (or until cake tests done).*

*(Ed: During the war years, these cakes were often baked in tube pans. A 13 x 9 x 2-inch pan would also work well.)

Mrs. W.F. (Deborah) Mayers
From her mother-in-law,
Mrs. Alva Loney

1940 RECIPES

When the chiffon cake was introduced in 1948, it was hailed as the first new cake in 100 years. The secret of this light, airy cake is the use of cooking oil instead of shortening.

APRICOT CHIFFON CAKE

**30-oz. can apricot halves
2¼ cups cake flour
1½ cups sugar
1 Tbsp. baking powder
1 tsp. salt
½ cup oil
5 egg yolks
2 tsp. grated lemon peel
1 cup egg whites (7-8 eggs)
½ tsp. cream of tartar**

Drain the apricots, reserving the syrup. Puree the apricots in a blender. Sift the flour, sugar, baking powder, and salt into a large mixing bowl. Make a "well" in the center. Add the oil, egg yolks, ⅔ cup reserved syrup, 1 cup apricot puree, and the lemon peel. Beat until smooth.

Beat the egg whites with the cream of tartar until stiff peaks form. Fold the yolk mixture into the egg whites. Pour into an ungreased tube pan (10-inch); bake at 325 degrees for 55 minutes. Increase to 350 degrees and bake 10 minutes longer or until tests done. Cool inverted.

(This recipe can be cut in half. Bake in a loaf pan at 325 degrees for 50-55 minutes till done.)

SAUCE (for half recipe):

Mix the remaining puree and syrup with about **1 tsp. cornstarch** and a scant **½ tsp. almond extract.** Cook until thickened and boiling. Add a generous **tsp. light rum,** to taste.

Cheryl Haas

A modern kitchen was every woman's dream. This display proudly graced the appliance section of Wyman's Department store.

Mr. Sindlinger served in the Army during World War II. After the war, he scaled down this "mess hall" recipe for his personal use. The icing makes enough to frost the top of the cake and between the layers. Cakes were frosted in this way during the war years to conserve sugar.

FRANK'S SPICE CAKE

Bake at 350 degrees - 2 layers*

Cream together:
    **1 cup sugar
    ½ cup shortening
    3 tsp. soda
    1 tsp. salt
    ¾ tsp. cinnamon
    ½ tsp. ginger
    ½ tsp. nutmeg
    1 tsp. baking powder**
Add:
    **2 eggs
    7 oz. evaporated milk
    4 oz. water
    2 cups flour
    ¼ cup molasses
    ¼ cup ground raisins (add last)**

ICING:
    **10 oz. powdered sugar
    4 oz. brown sugar
    3 oz. shortening
    1 egg
    4 oz. ground raisins
    Add evaporated milk as needed****

*(Ed: Bake in 2 9-inch layer pans for about 25 minutes.)
**(Remember 8 oz. = 1 cup. Today's cook would probably use butter or margarine instead of shortening in the icing. For extra flavor, 1 tsp. of vanilla might also be added.)

Mr. Frank Sindlinger

APPLE CRISP PUDDING

**4 cups apples, peeled and sliced
½ cup water
1 tsp. cinnamon
1 cup sugar
¾ cup flour
7 Tbsp. butter**

Butter a casserole. Add the apples; pour the water and cinnamon over them. Work the sugar, flour, and butter together with a pastry blender until crumbly. Spread over the apple mixture and bake uncovered at 400 degrees for 30 minutes.

Mrs. Wayne (Judy) Bartholomew

An elegant tea was served at the Women's Literary Club meeting held late in 1949. (L-R): Mrs. Walter McInerny, Mrs. Rollo Page, Mrs. Eugene Warner, Mrs. Hillier, Mrs. W. Hale Jackson, and Mrs. George M. Studebaker.

OATMEAL CAKE

1¼ cup boiling water
1 cup oatmeal

Pour boiling water over the oatmeal and let stand for 20 minutes.

Cream together:
1 cup brown sugar
½ cup oleo
1 cup white sugar

Add:
2 eggs

Stir in the oatmeal mixture. Add:
1⅓ cup flour
1 tsp. cinnamon
1 tsp. soda
½ tsp. salt
½ cup nuts

Bake in a greased 9 x 13-inch pan at 350 degrees for 30 minutes.

TOPPING:
1 cup brown sugar
¼ cup milk
1 cup coconut
6 Tbsp. butter
½ tsp. vanilla
¼-½ cup nuts

Melt the butter in a pan. Add the remaining ingredients and mix. Spread the mixture over the cake while warm; put under the broiler until lightly browned. (This only takes a minute or two; be sure that it doesn't burn.)

Mrs. Ervin (Doris) Purucker
From her mother,
Mrs. Charles (Mary) Taylor

Sally Day took a cookie recipe and converted it into a delicious cake. It makes two nice 8-inch layers. (Be sure you remember to grease and flour the cake pans.)

CHOCOLATE FUDGE RAISIN CAKE

Mix:
½ cup lard
1½ cup sugar
2 eggs
2 Tbsp. cocoa
1 tsp. vanilla

Add alternately:
2 cups flour
1 tsp. baking powder
1 tsp. soda
1 cup sour milk

Add:
½ cup raisins

Bake for 35 minutes at 350 degrees. Frost with a fudge frosting.

Sally Day

PEANUTTY APPLE UPSIDE-DOWN PIE

½ cup chopped cocktail peanuts
¼ cup packed brown sugar
2 Tbsp. margarine
1 Tbsp. water
1 Tbsp. light corn syrup
Pastry for 2-crust pie
4 cups sliced, pared cooking apples (5-6 medium apples)
1 Tbsp. lemon juice
⅓ cup sugar
1 Tbsp. flour
½ tsp. cinnamon
½ tsp. nutmeg
Whipped cream, optional

Sprinkle the peanuts over the bottom of a buttered 9-inch pie plate. In a saucepan, combine the brown sugar, margarine, water, and corn syrup; heat to boiling. Cook, stirring constantly, for 3 minutes. Pour over the peanuts.

Roll out half of the pastry; fit into the pie plate. Sprinkle the lemon juice over the apples while slicing. Mix the sugar, flour, and spices; add to the apples. Mix lightly. Turn into the pastry crust. Roll out the remaining pastry; fit it over the filling. Seal and flute the edges. Cut several slits in the top. Bake at 400 degrees for 35 minutes, or until done. Immediately invert onto a serving platter. Garnish with whipped cream, if desired.

Mrs. Glady Conant

FRESH STRAWBERRY PIE

1 baked and cooled 9-inch pie shell
1 small pkg. (3 oz.) cream cheese
1 qt. fresh strawberries
1 cup granulated sugar
3 Tbsp. cornstarch
1 cup whipping cream

Spread the cream cheese, which has been blended with a sufficient amount of cream to soften it, over the bottom of the baked pie shell. Wash the berries; hull and drain them well. Place half of the berries in the cream cheese coated pie shell. Slice the remaining berries and mash them slightly with a fork or spoon. Stir in the sugar and cornstarch. Let the berries sit for about 10 minutes; this will draw the juice. Bring the mixture slowly to a boil, stirring frequently so that it does not stick. Cook slowly for about 10 minutes; continue to stir. Cool. Spread over the uncooked berries in the pie shell. Place the pie in the refrigerator until very cold.

Top with whipped cream when ready to serve.

This pie is best served on the day it is prepared. The crust can become soggy if it is allowed to sit for too long.

Mrs. Ervin (Bertha) Purucker

CHERRY NUT TORTE

Grease a 9 x 15-inch pan.
   2 cups sugar
   2 eggs, well beaten
   2 cups flour
   2 Tbsp. melted butter
   2 tsp. soda
   2 tsp. cinnamon
   Pinch of salt
Mix well, then add:
   1 cup chopped nuts
   4 cups (2 cans) well drained sour cherries
      (save the juice)
Bake in a 350 degree oven for 1 hour

TO SERVE:
Make a red cherry sauce to pour over the Torte.
   2 cups cherry juice
   2 Tbsp. cornstarch
   1 cup sugar
Cook until thickened. Cool. If desired, top with whipped cream or ice cream.

This is my family's favorite dessert.

Mrs. John (Millie) Yoder

RICE PUDDING
(Rizogalo)

1 qt. milk, heated
½ cup sugar
2 eggs
⅓ cup long grained rice
½ cup water
1 tsp. vanilla
⅛ tsp. salt
1 stick cinnamon

In a heavy saucepan, parboil rice for 5 minutes in ½ cup salted water. Add the hot milk slowly and cook approximately 1 hour, stirring frequently. Add the sugar and cinnamon stick during the last 15 minutes. Remove the pan from the heat. Beat the eggs and stir a little of the hot mixture into the eggs. Pour the eggs into the rice mixture and replace the pan on low heat; stir until thickened. Add the vanilla. Mix and pour into individual serving dishes or a large serving bowl. Sprinkle with ground cinnamon and allow to cool. Serves 6.

Mrs. Ruby L. Stratigos

BEAUTIFUL JUNK!

Time was when a pile of ignominious scrap—
Old tires, tin cans, a discarded rat-trap—
Would gravely offend our sensitive eye
As it lay in a heap in an alley near by,
But a strange transformation has now taken place
An old stove, an iron bed, now has glamor and grace,
And proudly ensconced in our most public light,
We view it with pride, a right noble sight!

Beautiful junk!

We treasure each pan, old flat iron, old pump,
No more are they cast with disdain on the dump.
With princely mien, in the scrap drive they shine
And the clang that they make sends
*   a thrill down our spine.*
For we know they all go to be melted down,
Their destiny shaped, and their mission found.
And out of their chaos soon will arise
Tanks, guns, hand-grenades—planes
*   take to the skies!*

Beautiful junk!

So let us all join in the great drive for scrap,
For your piece of scrap may "scrap" a Jap!
And relinquish your hold on that old gate or fence,
It will help give the Axis a kick in the pants!
Hunt for that old discarded rusty plow-share,
White-elephant book-ends (you may have a pair).
They emerge from the cauldron at the end of their trip,
A rifle, a sub, or a proud battleship!

Beautiful junk!

Old keys, in disuse, with nothing to do,
Precious nickel and brass, (we all have a few)
Will put the "ax" in Axis if we'll all turn them in,
Girl Scout salvage jars keep them neat as a pin,
You'll find one located in your favorite drug-store,
Candy kitchen, bank, or lunchroom, or theater door,
We'll turn scrap into planes, tanks, and ships by the score.
Keep 'em flying, rolling, sailing—put more scrap in this war!

Beautiful junk!

By. Mrs. Wm. J. Fagaly

South Bend went wild as the movie, "Knute Rockne, All-American," premiered here on October 4, 1940. Among the Hollywood celebrities present were (crouching L-R) Charles Ruggles, Owen Davis, Bob Hope, Jimmy Fidler, Donald Crisp, Pat O'Brien, and Ronald Reagan. Mrs. Knute Rockne stands in front of the towering Franklin D. Roosevelt, Jr.

During the war years, patriotic women baked millions of cookies for servicemen on army posts and overseas. With rationing, women often used sugar substitutes; corn syrup, honey, and molasses were among the most popular. Date Peanut Butter Cookies travel well and would have received a rousing welcome from any soldier, sailor, or marine.

DATE PEANUT BUTTER COOKIES

½ cup shortening
¾ cup peanut butter
½ cup sugar
1 tsp. vanilla
½ cup corn syrup or honey
2 eggs, beaten
1 cup chopped dates (or prunes)
2 cups sifted enriched flour
2½ tsp. baking powder
½ tsp. salt
¼ cup milk

Cream the shortening, peanut butter, sugar, and vanilla. Beat until light and fluffy. Add the syrup and beat thoroughly. Add the eggs, then dates. Sift the flour, baking powder, and salt; add to the creamed mixture alternately with the milk. Blend well. Drop by teaspoonfuls onto greased baking sheets and bake at 350 degrees for 15 minutes.

Misses Mary and Thaddessa Taylor

FUDGE COOKIES

2 sq. unsweetened chocolate
1 cup milk
2 cups sugar
1 tsp. salt
1 tsp. margarine
1 tsp. vanilla
24 marshmallows, quartered
3 cups graham cracker crumbs
½ cup chopped nuts

Add the chocolate to the milk and cook over low heat, stirring constantly, until the mixture is smooth and blended. Add the sugar and salt; stir until the sugar is dissolved and it boils. Cook, without stirring, until a small amount of the mixture forms a soft ball in cold water. Remove from the heat. Add the margarine and vanilla without stirring. Cool to lukewarm, then beat until slightly thickened. Add the graham cracker crumbs, marshmallows, and nuts. Drop from a teaspoon onto wax paper and let stand until firm Makes 4 doz.

Mrs. Glady Conant

CHOCOLATE PEANUT SQUARES

1 cup shortening
½ cup white sugar
1½ cups brown sugar, packed
2 eggs, separated
1 Tbsp. cold water
1 tsp. vanilla
2 cups sifted flour
¼ tsp. salt
1 tsp. soda
1 7-oz. bar semisweet chocolate
1 cup chopped salted peanuts

Cream the shortening until light. Gradually beat in the white sugar and ½ cup of the brown. Beat until fluffy. Add the slightly beaten egg yolks, water, and vanilla. Blend thoroughly. Sift the dry ingredients together three times and add to the first mixture, stirring well. Spread evenly in 2 greased 8 x 12-inch pans, smoothing out the dough with a spatula. Sprinkle with the chocolate which has been cut into small pieces (or use the little chocolate drops especially made for cookies); gently press into the dough. Beat the egg whites until stiff. Gradually add the remaining brown sugar, continuing to beat thoroughly. Spread the meringue on top of the chocolate layer and sprinkle the peanuts over it (you might want to press the peanuts gently into the meringue). Bake in a moderate oven (375 degrees) for 25 minutes. Allow to stand until almost cool. Carefully cut with a sharp knife into 2-inch squares. Remove from the pan with a spatula. Leave the cakes exposed to the air overnight before serving.

Misses Mary and Thaddessa Taylor

1940 RECIPES

"He says Notre Dame men can eat anything"

The Doughboy symbolized the American soldier for many people until the early years of World War II, when everybody's favorite hero became G.I. Joe.

The Dome, 1940 -- Courtesy of the University of Notre Dame Archives.

FRUIT COOKIES

2 cups brown sugar
1 cup butter and lard or vegetable shortening, mixed
½ cup sour milk
3 eggs
½ lb. raisins
1 cup currants
1 cup dates
1 cup chopped candied fruit
1 heaping tsp. soda
½ tsp. salt
1 cup nutmeats
¼ tsp. each of cloves and allspice
1 tsp. cinnamon
⅛ tsp. nutmeg
3 cups flour

Cream the shortening; add the sugar and beat well. Add the eggs one at a time. Sprinkle some of the flour on the fruit and nuts. Sift the flour with the soda, salt, and spices. Add the dry ingredients to the egg mixture alternately with the milk. Stir in the fruit. Drop by teaspoonfuls onto greased cookie sheets. Bake at 350 degrees for 12-15 minutes. This makes about 6 dozen.

I like to mix the fruits and nuts with ½ cup of wine (any kind) the night before; cover well. More fruit and nuts may be added if desired.

Mrs. Harvey (Margaret) Rostiser

When you drain vegetables, collect all the liquids and pour them into a covered jar. Store in the refrigerator and use them for making soups and sauces.

BOILED COOKIES

2 cups sugar
4 Tbsp. cocoa
¼ lb. margarine (1 stick)
½ cup milk
Mix together and boil for 1 minute.
Add:
3 cups quick oats
1 cup coconut
1 tsp. vanilla
Pinch of salt
Mix well and drop by the teaspoonful onto wax paper.

Mrs. Charles (Mary) Taylor

A recent survey made in one of our large cities indicates that undissolved sugar left in the bottom of coffee and tea cups by lackadaisical stirrers totals 2,500,000 lbs. annually. So enroll your family in the spoon-stirring club. Urge them to use less sugar in coffee and tea, and to stir it well. Sugar left unstirred in the bottom of the cup doesn't sweeten the drink and is a waste!

Our family always makes at least one batch of these cookies for Christmas. The recipe came from my father's aunt, Mrs. Roscoe Wilson, or as the family called her, Aunt Phronie.

DREAM BARS

1 cup flour
½ cup butter
½ cup brown sugar

Mix with the fingers to a crumbly mass and pat into a greased shallow pan. Bake 10 minutes in a 375 degree oven. Do not overbake. Remove from the oven and pour over it a mixture made of the following:

1 cup brown sugar
2 Tbsp. flour
2 eggs
½ tsp. salt
1 cup nut meats, chopped fine
¼ tsp. vanilla

Return to the oven and bake 20 minutes longer. Remove from the oven and sprinkle with powdered sugar. Cut into bars.

An 8-inch square baking dish works well.

Diane Barts
From her great-aunt,
Mrs. Roscoe (Leona) Wilson

Mrs. Rostiser's "Scrapbook Recipes" appeared in the **South Bend Tribune** *for nearly 50 years. Each week she contributed one recipe, publishing the favorite dishes of local ladies as well as her own. Connie's Fudge was one of the most popular of her many excellent recipes; the Tribune still receives requests for it around the holidays.*

CONNIE'S FUDGE

In a large bowl put:
> **One 9¾ oz. plain milk chocolate bar**
> **Two 6 oz. packages chocolate bits**
> **Two squares baking chocolate, cut fine**
> **Two cups broken nut meats**
> **One pint jar marshmallow creme**
> **One tablespoon vanilla**

In a heavy pan:
> **One large can evaporated milk**
> **Four and one-half cups sugar**
> **One stick butter** (¼ pound)
> **One stick margarine** (¼ pound)

Bring the second mixture to a full rolling boil (be sure) and boil for six minutes. Pour over the first mixture and stir till all is well melted and blended. Pour into greased pans to set. Makes about four pounds.

Mrs. Harvey (Margaret) Rostiser

When I was born, my Mom was staying with Uncle Emery and Aunt Mary on their farm in Ohio while Daddy was "off to war." Through the years, special times and memories were visits to their farm - - feeding the animals, the taste of the water from the pump, homemade ice cream, and all the jars of canned food in the cellar. These frozen cucumbers are a delightful change of pace from regular pickles, and they are wonderfully cool and crisp on a hot summer day.

AUNT MARY'S FROZEN CUCUMBERS

> **2 qts. small cucumbers, sliced** (unpeeled)
> **2 scant Tbsp. salt**
> **2 onions, sliced**

Mix together and let set for 2 hours. Drain.

SYRUP:
> **1½ cups sugar**
> **½ cup vinegar**
> **1 tsp. celery seed** (I use about ½ tsp.)

Bring to a boil and let stand until cold.

Put the drained cucumbers in containers, cover with syrup and freeze. Fill the containers only ¾ full as the syrup has a tendency to ooze out of the lids if they are filled too full.

Jerry and Sheri Wiener
From Mrs. Wiener's Aunt Mary

PEANUT BUTTER CANDY

Sift a **1 lb. box of powdered sugar** into a bowl and set aside. Turn a burner on low heat. Place **2 sticks (1 cup) margarine** and **8 oz. peanut butter** (crunchy or smooth) in a pan and melt. Add the powdered sugar and mix well.

Butter a large pan (9½ x 11½ x 1-inch). Use the finger tips to pat the candy firmly into the pan. Cool about half an hour. Melt **6 oz. (1 cup) semisweet chocolate chips or a 6-8 oz. Hershey Chocolate bar.** Pour the chocolate over the peanut butter mixture. When completely cooled, cut into squares.

Mrs. Harrison (Lola) Lyons
From her mother-in-law,
Mrs. Ida Bainbridge

Life on the Notre Dame campus changed during the war years. For example, food in the dining hall was now served on cafeteria trays instead of family-style on tables set with china and silver. Courtesy of the University of Notre Dame Archives.

TOFFEE CRUNCH COOKIES

> **1½ cups sifted flour**
> **½ tsp. soda**
> **½ tsp. salt**
> **½ cup butter or margarine**
> **¾ cup brown sugar**
> **⅓ cup pecans, chopped**
> **1 egg**
> **1 tsp. vanilla**
> **1 cup finely chopped English toffee candy bars**

Combine the flour, soda, and salt; sift. Cream the butter and sugar; add the egg and vanilla. Mix until smooth and creamy. Stir in the dry ingredients. Blend in the chopped candy bars and pecans. Drop with a tablespoon 2 inches apart on a greased cookie sheet. Bake at 350 degrees for 12 or 15 minutes. Remove from the baking sheet and cool.

Mrs. Alexis (Mary Clarke) Coquillard

Mrs.
George Earl
Carroll

1950's

This glamorous black
glass-beaded and sequined
evening gown was worn by
Mrs. George Earl Carroll. It
has a sleeveless bodice and low
rounded neckline. Bugle beads form
a zig-zag line down the front of the gown,
with a side slit to complete the look. Circa 1950.

THE RACE FOR SPACE

By 1950 the century was preparing to settle into a comfortable period of middle age. Unlike the decade of social upheaval following World War I, America was now flourishing in an atmosphere of cozy prosperity. Home builders strained to keep pace with the galloping birthrate as people feverishly worked to acquire the modern conveniences of the Jet Age. Even the growing conflict in Korea seemed unable to divert most families from their single-minded pursuit of the "American Dream."

A boxie little cyclops called television was dramatically changing the way we perceived our world. By combining the best features of radio and motion pictures, this marvelous medium allowed people to obtain the latest information about food, fashion, news, and sports without leaving their homes. Ralph Kramden, Uncle Miltie, Sky King, and the Mouseketeers became as familiar to most folks as the neighbors next door.

Families were still eating Sunday dinner at home, but the demands of post-war life were steadily bringing about a change in eating habits. Housewives were clamoring for more convenience foods, and soon brownies, rolls, and angel food cake could all be made from mixes. Busy people with no culinary pretentions and cast iron taste buds eagerly stocked huge home freezers with "TV dinners." Nutritionists shuddered as the healthy meals of the 1940's were replaced by pizzas, cheeseburgers, and submarine sandwiches. Snacking became a national obsession elevating "chips 'n dip" to the very heights of fashionable fodder.

Now that homes were being designed with counters joining dining room to kitchen, housewives were no longer isolated from the rest of the house. Pretty pastel colors, ruffled curtains, and cupboards agleam with the latest electric can openers, blenders, and hand mixers, all combined to make the kitchen a warm inviting place for family and friends alike.

People were finding alternatives to the traditional meal around the dining room table. Outdoor barbecues were an extremely popular way to entertain. Hostesses were no longer tied to the cumbersome routine of the formal dinner; now smart meals were often served buffet style. Every family had their favorite television shows; when conflicts arose at mealtime, mom was increasingly forced to take a deep breath and bring out the TV trays. Restaurants were attracting more people for that special meal, but it wasn't until 1955 that the (sesame) seeds of a revolution were planted -- the first McDonald's opened for business and "fast food" began to take America by storm.

Beneath the order and stability of the 50's lurked a penchant for extremes. Cars grew to be 8-cylinder leviathans with leering chrome grills and huge tail fins. The foot tapping beat of the Big Bands were being drowned out by the brash sounds of Rock 'N Roll. The driving beat of Buddy Holly may have turned music upside down, but it took Elvis Presley's gyrating hips to make Rock a sensation. Even politics was not exempt as Senator Joseph McCarthy took inspiration for his crusade against communism from the Salem witchcraft trials.

It seemed as though moderation was generally not to be found in the world of fashion, either. For the first time couturiers gave women a choice of two totally divergent looks; Dior's sophisticated flower-like full skirts were still fashionable, but so, too, was a skirt whose petals had definitely been plucked. Generous kick pleats were needed to enable women to walk in these pencil-slim creations. (Nevertheless, they proved to be incredibly effective when worn by ladies dancing to the seductive Latin rhythms of the rhumba, mambo, and the cha cha cha.) Unquestionably a certain fashionable bravado was needed to wear skin-tight toreador pants, baby doll pajamas, or shoes with pointed toes and 4-inch stiletto heels.

By 1957 there was a new look to the "New Look." Dior introduced a shorter, loose fitting chemise which bore the rather unglamorous title, the sack dress. Although viewed with some skepticism at first the style soon became popular as comfort triumphed over elegance.

Although the golden days of Hollywood were drawing to a close, women still wanted to look like the "stars." Some ladies tried to capture Audrey Hepburn's youthful innocence by wearing capri pants, turtleneck sweaters, and flat shoes. Still others rushed out to buy padded bras which hopefully would give them curves rivaling those of Marilyn Monroe and Jane Russell. Ava Gardner in a mink coat sent cash registers ringing, and words can't describe what Brigitte Bardot did for the bikini.

When the Russians sent Sputnik I into orbit on October 4, 1957, they challenged America to the greatest race of all times -- the race for space. At first this nation was caught off guard, awed by the magnitude of the accomplishment. Soon, however, the scientific community, which had provided us with everything from a vaccine for polio to drip-dry clothing, proved equal to the task. On April 9, 1959, all eyes were focused on 7 men, the team ready to lead the way to the moon and beyond. During the next decade, the Astronauts became a source of intense national pride at a time when America desperately needed heroes.

During the 1950's, neighborhood groceries were being replaced by modern supermarkets which were able to offer an abundance of fresh produce and seafood year round. Families could even enjoy such exotic treats as artichokes, papayas, mangoes, and Alaskan King crab.

HOT CRABMEAT APPETIZERS

1 onion, minced
1 Tbsp. butter
1 Tbsp. flour
½ tsp. salt
Dash of pepper
¼ pt. cream
½ lb. crabmeat (Alaskan)
¼ cup grated American cheese
¼ cup butter, softened
Dash of Worcestershire sauce
Toast rounds or small baking shells

Cook the onion in 1 Tbsp. butter until golden brown. Add the flour, salt, and pepper. Add the cream and cook until thick. Add the crabmeat and cook until hot (but do not boil). Spread on toast rounds or put in small baking shells.

Mix the American cheese with ¼ cup butter. Add the Worcestershire sauce and spread on the crabmeat mixture. Brown.

Mrs. Ralph S. Sollitt

During the 1950's, every kid wanted to be a cowboy. Westerns were a television mainstay, popularizing such six-gun heroes as Roy Rogers, Wild Bill Hickok, and the Maverick Brothers. What could have been a more appropriate lunch for a little buckaroo than Chuck Wagon Soup.

CHUCK WAGON SOUP

2 Tbsp. fat
1 cup onions, chopped
½ cup green pepper, chopped
1 clove garlic, minced
1 qt. water
¾ cup elbow macaroni
2 cups potatoes, diced
No. 2 can tomato juice
17 oz. can chili con carne, <u>without beans</u>
½ cup minced salami, bologna, or hamburger

Cook the fat, onion, green pepper, and garlic together in a large, heavy kettle until yellowed. Add the remaining ingredients. Cover and simmer for 45 minutes to 1 hour. Add salt and pepper, if desired. If too thick, add more water. Yields 4 large servings.

Mrs. Walton (Carol) Collins

INDIAN CHICKEN BALLS
(Canapes)

4 oz. softened cream cheese
2 Tbsp. mayonnaise
1 cup chopped, cooked chicken or 2 cans
    (5 oz.)drained chicken
1 cup sliced blanched almonds
1 Tbsp. chopped chutney
1 Tbsp. curry powder*
½ tsp. salt
½ cup flaked coconut (optional)

Beat the cheese and mayonnaise until blended. Add the rest of the ingredients except the coconut. Shape into 36 balls and chill 1 hour. Roll in coconut, if desired. Chill 3-4 hours before serving. Serve dispersed with purple grapes, if desired. About 60 calories each.
*Use 1 tsp. curry powder if you like a milder flavor.

Mrs. John (Jane) Olcott

Welcome to the St. Joseph County 4-H Fair, August 2, 1950.
Courtesy of the St. Joseph County Extension Office.

SENATE BEAN SOUP

Wash and soak overnight in a large kettle **1 lb. dried navy beans,** in **water** to cover. Next morning add enough water to make 5 qts. Add a **smoked ham bone** with some meat on it (a sizeable ham hock may be used). Simmer for 1 hour or so, or until the beans begin to mush. Add **3 medium potatoes** which have been cooked and mashed, **1 cup each chopped onion and chopped celery,** and **2 good-sized cloves of minced garlic.** Simmer for 1 hour, stirring frequently. Remove the bone; cut up the meat and return it to the soup. Season to taste with **salt** and **pepper**. Makes about 4½ qts. (This can be frozen.)

Mrs. Mary Jo Hruska

SNAILS WITH HERB BUTTER

1 can (18 count) **extra large snails**
½ cup (¼ lb.) **butter or margarine, softened**
2 small cloves garlic, minced or pressed
2 tsp. chopped chives or green onion tops
1 Tbsp. minced parsley
18 clean, dry snail shells (real or artificial)
6-8 Tbsp. grated Parmesan cheese

Drain the snails and rinse; drain thoroughly on paper towels. Stir together the butter, garlic, chives, and parsley until well blended. Put a small bit of the seasoned butter mixture in each shell and then tuck in a snail. Seal it with the remaining butter mixture, dividing the butter evenly between the snails. Press the buttered surface firmly into the grated cheese. Place the shells, cheese side up, in snail pans or individual baking pans. Bake uncovered in a 500 degree oven for 5 minutes or until the cheese is lightly browned and the butter is bubbly. Serve hot. If desired, serve on sliced French bread or rolls. Makes 18 appetizers.

Mr. John Charles Bryant

EGG DIP

6 hard boiled eggs, finely chopped
½ cup chopped parsley
1 bunch green onions, chopped
¼-½ tsp. salt
1 tsp. dill (adjust to taste)
⅔ cup mayonnaise

Mix the seasonings together; then add the eggs, parsley, and mayonnaise. Served chilled.

Mrs. John (Jane) Olcott

CREAM OF MUSHROOM SOUP

1 lb. fresh mushrooms, coarsely cut
2 Tbsp. butter
2 cups water
¼ cup finely chopped onion
2 beef bouillon cubes
8 oz. heavy cream
Salt and pepper to taste
½ cup dry white wine

Saute the onions in butter until transparent; add the mushrooms and saute another 3-4 minutes. Do not brown. Add the water, bouillon cubes, and wine. Salt and pepper to taste. Add the heavy cream. Stir constantly until just heated through (do not boil). To serve, sprinkle with a little Parmesan cheese or parsley.

Mrs. Paul (Mary Yena) Rohleder

CLAM DIP

1 pkg. (8 oz.) **cream cheese, softened**
1 Tbsp. mayonnaise
1 8-oz. can minced clams, drained
¼ tsp. Worcestershire sauce
2 tsp. onion, grated
2 tsp. parsley, chopped
1½ tsp. lemon juice
¼ tsp. salt
3 drops tobasco sauce (optional)

Mix together all ingredients. Serve chilled. It's best to make the dip a day ahead so that the flavors have a chance to blend.

Mr. Ervin Purucker

SHRIMP DIP

1 large pkg. (8 oz.) **cream cheese**
⅓ cup mayonnaise
3 Tbsp. chili sauce
2 tsp. lemon juice
½ tsp. onion juice
½ tsp. Worcestershire
½ lb. cooked shrimp (or an 8-oz. can)

Mix all ingredients together and serve·chilled.

Mrs. John (Jane) Olcott

It was great fun to be a kid in the 1950's, especially at Leeper Park.

Courtesy of the South Bend - Mishawaka Area Chamber of Commerce.

Every fall, Mrs. Rohleder makes a large kettle of her Leek and Potato Soup and freezes it. Using the different variations, she can always have a dish of hot soup ready to warm a cold winter's evening.

LEEK AND POTATO SOUP

1. Saute **3 large leeks** (cleaned well and cross cut) in **2 Tbsp. butter or olive oil** until transparent; set aside.
2. Peel and cube **10 lbs. of good quality white potatoes.** Place the potatoes in a large, heavy pan, cover with water and cook until fork tender, but not mushy. Skim off the foam while cooking. **Salt and pepper** to taste.
3. Add the leeks.
4. Add **1 stick of butter** or good (not soft) margarine.
5. Add **½ gal whole milk.**
6. Add **1 pt. heavy cream.**
7. Heat to boiling, being careful not to burn the soup.
8. Spoon the soup into 1 qt. freezer containers and freeze. (If the soup is to be served without freezing, allow to sit in the refrigerator over night and then reheat.)
9. When ready to serve, thaw and reheat.

VARIATIONS:
A. Add 1 can cream-style corn. Sprinkle with crisp bacon when served.
B. Add 1 can clams or 2 fillets of white fish, cut into 1 inch cubes (or add both). Heat until the fish is flaky. Sprinkle with parsley when served.
C. Thaw and put the soup into a blender; mix until smooth. Heat or serve cold with a slice of lemon.

Mrs. Paul (Mary Yena) Rohleder

CORN CHOWDER

2-3 slices bacon
1 small onion, chopped
3 cups corn
2 medium potatoes, cooked and diced
4 cups milk
2 Tbsp. flour
1 tsp. salt
¼ tsp. pepper
1 Tbsp. butter

Dice the bacon and fry till brown. Add the onion and saute until golden. Add the corn, potatoes, milk, and seasonings. Bring to a boil. Thicken with flour (which has been blended with a little potato water or milk). Cook about 2 minutes. **NOTE:** Using the potato water, cooked down, makes it richer. Dice the potatoes quite small and cook in water (not too much) till soft. Add the other ingredients. Measurements of ingredients do not have to be exact; they may be adjusted to taste.

Mrs. Walton (Carol) Collins

Streamlined Jet Age furnishings transformed the home in the 1950's.

The green, red, and white layers of this salad make it a perfect addition to any party menu, especially during the Christmas season.

PARTY FRUIT MOLD

1 3-oz. pkg. cherry gelatin
¾ cup boiling water
2 l-lb. cans pears, drained (save the juice)
Maraschino cherries
1 3-oz. pkg. lemon gelatin
¾ cup boiling water
¾ cup cold water
1 8-oz. pkg. cream cheese, softened
½ tsp. salt
1 Tbsp. cream
1 cup whipping cream, whipped
1 3-oz. pkg. lime gelatin
¾ cup boiling water
1 #2 can crushed pineapple, drained (save the juice)

Dissolve the cherry gelatin in boiling water. Add ¾ cup pear juice. Chill until partially set. Pour a layer about ½ inch thick into the bottom of a 2-quart mold (a 13 x 9-inch dish also works well) and chill until almost firm. Put a cherry in the center of each pear and place cherry-side down in the mold. Pour remaining cherry gelatin on top and chill until firm.

Dissolve the lemon gelatin in boiling water and add the cold water. Chill until partially thickened. Beat the cream cheese, salt, and cream with an electric mixer until light and fluffy. Beat in the lemon gelatin. Fold in the whipped cream. Pour over the first layer and chill until firm.

Dissolve the lime gelatin in boiling water. Add ¾ cup pineapple juice. Chill until partially thickened. Fold in the crushed pineapple. Pour over the second layer. Chill overnight.

(Be sure to start far enough ahead so that each layer has a chance to set before adding the next layer.)

Mrs. Ervin (Bertha) Purucker

*During the 1950's, **The Loft** was one of South Bend's most popular restaurants. Owners, Andrew Callas, Dan Metros, Spiro Metros, and William Metros, always provided their guests with fine food in an atmosphere of warmth and elegance. The community was saddened when The Loft closed in the fall of 1981.*

PEPPER POT SOUP

3 46-oz. cans College Inn chicken broth or enriched chicken broth
4 cups chopped celery
2 cups diced onions
4 16-oz. cans peeled tomatoes, crushed
5 bay leaves
1 tsp. sugar, heaping
1 tsp. pepper, heaping
1 tsp. chicken bouillon
4 cups diced green pepper

DUMPLINGS:
4 eggs
¾ cup milk
¼ tsp. nutmeg
¼ tsp. pepper
1½ - 2 cups flour

Blend all ingredients together into a thick and smooth batter. Use the amount of flour needed for a consistency that would drop from a spoon.

ROUX:
½ cup margarine
¾ cup flour

Melt margarine and stir in flour making a thick Roux. Cook until slightly browned.

Place first 8 ingredients in a large stock pot and mix well. Partially cover pot and cook approximately 1½ hours until celery is tender.

Add green peppers and bring soup to a boil. Drop dumplings from a wet teaspoon into the hot soup. When dumplings are finished, reduce heat to simmer.

Pour ½ of the hot soup broth into the hot thick roux, stirring constantly until thoroughly blended. Revert this mixture into soup and stir well for 5 minutes to thicken. Season to taste, especially with pepper.

THE LOFT RESTAURANT
112 West Colfax Avenue
South Bend, Indiana 46601

OXTAIL SOUP

2 lbs. oxtails, more or less -- cut by butcher
2 Tbsp. oil
Brown oxtail pieces well.
Water, stock, or canned beef consomme, or a mixture of these - enough to cover oxtails
1 12-oz. can of beer
1 tsp. pepper
Salt to taste

Simmer 3-4 hours or until the meat is tender or cook 1 hour in a pressure cooker. If this is done the day before, the broth can be chilled and any fat removed from the top.

PEEL AND CHOP:
1 large onion
2-3 carrots
2-3 stalks of celery
Other **vegetables** such as the solid hearts of celery, Chinese cabbage, broccoli stems, or sweet red peppers may be used. Steam vegetables only till just tender.

TO OXTAILS AND BROTH ADD:
½ cup rolled oats
1 tsp. thyme

Simmer 5 minutes.
Add the vegetables; taste to correct the seasoning. Garnish with parsley or chives. Serves 4.
(If thyme is added during cooking, it loses its distinctive flavor. By leaving vegetables in large pieces and simmering stock until it is reduced to half, this can be served as a stew. Accompany with a good whole-grain bread.)

Mrs. Joel (Lou Ann) Bullard

MARY'S CRABMEAT AND MACARONI SALAD

1 lb. crabmeat, cooked and shredded
(you may use canned - drained)
½ cup frozen peas, rinsed and drained (not cooked)
1 cup small shell macaroni, cooked
¼ cup diced celery
¼ cup chopped shallots
½-¾ cup mayonnaise
Salt and pepper to taste
1 tsp. lite soy sauce
Several good dashes of Tabasco sauce

Mix the ingredients and serve over shredded lettuce. (Place the peas in a colander; drain the macaroni over them to thaw.) Finely shred carrots and serve them on the plate beside the salad - do not mix. Top the carrots with a few raisins. Top the crab salad with ripe olive sections or parsley. Serve with Melba toast and a cup of soup.

Mrs. Paul (Mary Yena) Rohleder

CUCUMBER RING MOLD

1 envelope unflavored gelatin
¼ cup fresh lemon juice
2 Tbsp. cold water
½ cup boiling water
2 Tbsp. sugar
¾ tsp. salt
2 cups chopped cucumbers
1 8-oz. pkg. cream cheese
1 cup salad dressing or mayonnaise
¼ cup minced onion
¼ cup minced parsley

Soften the gelatin in the lemon juice and cold water; dissolve in boiling water, and add sugar and salt. Peel the cucumbers, cut them in half, and scrape out the seeds. Chop them finely, then drain. Add the softened cream cheese, the salad dressing, onion, and parsley to the chopped cucumbers; mix well. Stir in the gelatin mixture and pour into a 6½ cup ring mold. Chill several hours or until firm. Serves 8.

Mrs. Glenn (Fannie M.) Stoneburner

SPINACH AND APPLE SALAD

Thoroughly wash and dry **8-10 cups fresh spinach.** Remove the stems and tear into pieces.

Wash, but do not peel, **6 tart red apples** (Jonathan or Winesap). Core and chop into large, bite-size chunks.

Toss with a dressing made of:
1 cup mayonnaise
1 cup sour cream
2 Tbsp. sugar
Serves 8.

Mrs. Patrick (Sharon) Deneen
From her friend,
Sue Sheehan

CORNED BEEF SALAD

1 pkg. (3 oz.) lemon Jello
1½ cups hot water
1 can corned beef (flaked finely)
1 cup chopped celery
Onion salt (½-¾ tsp. works well)
½ cup green pepper, chopped
2 boiled eggs, chopped
1 cup Miracle Whip

Dissolve the Jello in the boiling hot water. Add the other ingredients and refrigerate overnight. To serve, cut into squares and garnish with radishes, olives, and lettuce.

Miss M. Geraldine Hatt
From Mrs. David Condit

Mrs. Barts often serves this salad at family gatherings. It can easily serve a dozen people, and the delicate pink color looks lovely in her Mother's crystal bowl. It works equally well with fresh or frozen strawberries.

SPRINGTIME SALAD

1 pkg. (3 oz.) strawberry jello
1 cup hot water
1 cup sliced fresh strawberries (can use frozen strawberries)
1 cup diced marshmallows (about 12)
½ cup chopped nuts
¾ cup canned pineapple chunks, drained
1 cup undiluted Carnation milk (condensed milk)
2 Tbsp. lemon juice

Dissolve the jello in hot water. Cool until syrupy (15-20 minutes), then add the nuts, berries, marshmallows, and pineapple. Chill the Carnation Milk in a refrigerator (freezer) tray until icy crystals form (15-20 minutes). Whip the milk until stiff, about 1 minute. Add the lemon juice and whip until very thick. Fold the fruit mixture into the whipped milk. Chill 1 or 2 hours.

Mrs. Roger (Louise) Barts

STRAWBERRY SOUR CREAM SALAD

1 large pkg. (6 oz.) strawberry jello
1½ cups boiling water
1 can (20 oz.) crushed pineapple
2 boxes (10 oz.) frozen strawberries
2 mashed bananas
1 pt. sour cream

Mix all the ingredients together except the sour cream (add the strawberries while still frozen). Pour half of the mixture into a dish and let set. After it is set, spread the sour cream over the jello, then pour the rest of the mixture over that and let set. This makes a great Christmas salad.

Mrs. Robert (Helen) Veith

LEMON BREAD

¾ cup sugar
6 Tbsp. shortening
Grated rind of 1 lemon
2 eggs
1½ cups flour
½ tsp. salt
1 tsp. baking powder
½ cup milk

Beat the eggs well. Add the sugar, shortening, and lemon rind. Sift the dry ingredients. Add alternately with the milk. Bake in a greased 9-inch loaf pan at 325 degrees for 35-45 minutes.

MIX:
¼ cup sugar
Juice of 1 lemon
Pour over the hot bread. Let cool in the pan.

Mrs. Joel (Lou Ann) Bullard

BLUEBERRY COFFEE CAKE

¾ cup sugar
¼ cup margarine
1 egg
1 tsp. vanilla
¾ cup milk
1¾ cups plus 2 Tbsp. flour
3 tsp. baking powder
½ tsp. salt
1½ cups blueberries (fresh)
2 Tbsp. sugar

TOPPING:
2 Tbsp. sugar mixed with
½ tsp. cinnamon

Rinse and drain the blueberries. Cream the sugar, shortening, egg, and vanilla. Add the milk and blend well. Spoon the flour into a dry measuring cup. Level off and pour the measured flour onto a square of waxed paper. Add the baking powder and salt to the flour and stir to blend. Add the blended dry ingredients to the creamed mixture, stirring only until all the flour is moistened. Spread half of the batter in the bottom of a greased 9-inch square pan. Spread the blueberries over the batter and sprinkle with 2 Tbsp. sugar. Cover the blueberries with the remaining batter and sprinkle with the topping. Bake at 375 degrees for 35-40 minutes. The cake should be lightly browned and will spring back when touched in the center.

Mrs. Karen Keller
From her mother,
Mrs. Christine Carlson

PECAN (OR WALNUT) BUNS

1 cake yeast
½ cup lukewarm milk
¼ cup sugar
½ tsp. salt
1 egg, beaten
¼ cup shortening
2¼-2½ cups flour
12 Tbsp. butter
1 cup brown sugar
Nuts

Mix together the milk, sugar, and salt. Crumble the yeast into the mixture and stir until dissolved. Stir in the beaten egg and shortening. Mix in the flour, first with a spoon and then by hand, using only enough to make the dough easy to handle. Turn out onto a lightly floured board and knead until smooth and elastic. Place in a greased bowl, turning once. Cover and let rise until double (1-2 hours). Punch down, pull edges to the center, and turn over in the bowl. Let rise again until double (30-45 minutes). Place on a lightly floured board; divide in half (for easier handling) and leave while you fix the sugar mixture.

In the bottom of an 8-inch cake pan, melt **6 Tbsp. butter.** Mix in **½ cup brown sugar,** spreading as evenly as possible. Press in nuts. Repeat with the second pan. Roll out half of the yeast dough into a rectangle (6 x 10-inches). Brush with melted butter and sprinkle with **brown sugar or a sugar/cinnamon mixture.** Roll up along the wide side of the rectangle and cut into 8-10 slices. Place, cut side up, on top of the sugar mixture in the cake pans. Repeat with the second half of the dough.

Let rise until double and almost fills the pans. Bake at 400 degrees for 20-25 minutes. Invert on a plate immediately and cool.

Mrs. John (Lola Mae) Philippsen

STRAWBERRY BREAD

3 cups flour
1 tsp. baking powder
1 tsp. salt
3 tsp. cinnamon
2 cups sugar
2 pkg. (10 oz.) **frozen strawberries, thawed**
4 eggs, beaten
1¼ cups oil
1¼ cups chopped pecans

Make a well in the center of the dry ingredients and add the strawberries. Mix the eggs, oil, and pecans and pour into the dry ingredients. Stir until moistened. Pour the mixture into greased loaf pans. Bake at 350 degrees for 1 hour. Yields 2 loaves.

Mrs. Glady Conant

ONE-STEP SUPPER ROLLS

1 cup dairy sour cream
1 egg
**2 cups Pillsbury Hungry Jack Buttermilk Pancake
and Waffle Mix**
Poppy seeds or sesame seeds, if desired.

In a large mixing bowl, combine the sour cream and egg. Add the pancake mix (measure by lightly spooning into the cup and leveling off). Blend until the dry ingredients are well moistened. Drop by tablespoons onto a greased cookie sheet. Sprinkle with poppy seeds or sesame seeds, if desired. Bake at 375 degrees for 12-18 minutes, until lightly browned. Serve warm.

To reheat, wrap loosely in foil and bake at 350 degrees for about 10 minutes.

These rolls are also good when baked as directed in 12 greased muffin cups.

(Pillsbury Extra Light or Sweet Cream Pancake and Waffle Mix may be used for the buttermilk pancake mix.)

Mrs. Mary Fischer
From Brother Peter
(Kitchen of Holy Cross House)

Don't wipe the silver with the napkin. It is unthinkable in a private house. If you're obliged to eat in a dirty restaurant, wipe the silver unobtrusively under the table's edge.

ORANGE PEEL BREAD

PREPARE THE ORANGE PEEL:
Scrape off the white and mince the yellow. (The peel from a medium orange should equal about ½ cup.) Cover the peel with water and cook until tender. Add **½ cup sugar** and boil until thick as honey. Let cool.

Put in a bowl:
1 Tbsp. soft butter
¼ cup sugar
1 egg yolk
1 cup milk (or ¾ cup milk and ¼ cup
frozen concentrated orange juice)

Sift and add:
2 cups flour
2 tsp. baking powder
Dash of salt

Beat well. Add the peel and syrup. Bake in a 9-inch loaf pan for 45 minutes at 325 degrees.

This tangy bread is very good toasted.

NOTE: Orange marmalade, gently melted, may be substituted for the prepared orange peel.

Mrs. Joel (Lou Ann) Bullard

KOLACH

6 cups (or more) **flour**
½ lb. plus ½ stick butter
Dash of salt
12 level Tbsp. sugar
12 egg yolks, beaten
1 cup milk (warm)
1 cake (1 oz.) **yeast or 2 pkg. dry yeast**
2 Tbsp. vanilla

FILLING:
1½ lbs. ground walnuts
2 cups granulated sugar
12 egg whites
1 tsp. cinnamon

Mix the flour, butter, salt, and sugar. Set aside. Dissolve the yeast in the warm milk; pour over the egg yolks. Mix, then add the vanilla. Combine thoroughly with the flour mixture. Form into a ball and place in a greased bowl. Cover with plastic wrap and let set overnight in the refrigerator.

Make the filling by beating the egg whites till stiff. Add the sugar and cinnamon, then fold in the ground nuts. Store in the refrigerator overnight, also.

Next day, remove the dough from the refrigerator and form into 4 balls. Roll one of the balls out to about ¼ inch thick. Spread one quarter of the filling mixture on the dough. Roll loosely like a jelly roll. Put on a cookie sheet (2 rolls to each cookie sheet). Roll out and fill the remaining 3 balls of dough. Cover the rolls with dish towels and let the dough rest for 1 hour in a warm oven. Remove from the oven and brush with milk. Return to a 350 degree oven and bake for 30-35 minutes.

Mrs. Marianne Wilcox

Because they are made the night before, Cheese Souffle Sandwiches are an easy do-ahead dish for the busy hostess or career woman. They suit anyone's tastes because you add your own fillings. Be sure to serve them immediately, however, because they deflate like a real souffle.

CHEESE SOUFFLE SANDWICHES

8 slices bread (for 4 sandwiches)
Fill with **ham, crab, cheddar cheese, chicken or anything else you desire** in your sandwich.
4 eggs, beaten
2 cups milk

Combine milk and eggs and pour over the sandwiches. Let stand over night. Bake in a 350 degree oven for 40 minutes. Serves 4. (Be sure to grease your baking dish, especially if you are using cheese.)

Mrs. John R. (Virginia) Lionberger, Jr.

CAULIFLOWER AND CURRY SAUCE

1 head of cauliflower
Boiling water
Salt

CURRY SAUCE:
    2 Tbsp. butter, melted
    4 Tbsp. finely chopped onion
    ½ tsp. salt
    1 tsp. curry powder
    2 Tbsp. flour
    ¼ cup chopped almonds
    Watercress

Wash the cauliflower and place the unbroken head in boiling water (to which 1 tsp. salt has been added). Cook until tender, 15-20 minutes. Drain, saving 1 cup of the water for the sauce.

Melt the 2 Tbsp. butter in a saucepan; add the onion and cook slowly until tender. Stir in the salt, curry powder, and flour, blending well with the onion. Slowly add the cup of cauliflower water, stirring constantly. Cook over low heat for about 5 minutes. Pour over the cauliflower. Sprinkle the almonds over the top. Garnish with watercress and serve.

Mrs. James M. Wilson

MAGDA'S CAULIFLOWER

Take **1 box frozen cauliflower or 1 fresh head of cauliflower,** separated into flowerets. Cook until tender; drain.

Saute ¾ **cup bread crumbs** in **1 stick of margarine;** make sure not to burn the crumbs, just make them nice and brown. Put the crumbs on the cauliflower and add ½ **cup sour cream.** Toss together and serve.

Mrs. Andrew (Magda) Eperjesi

CELERY CASSEROLE

Cook **4 cups of celery** (cut in 1 inch pieces) for 8 minutes until tender, but still crisp.

Drain and place in a 1 quart casserole. Add:
    1 5 oz. can water chestnuts, drained and sliced
    1 can condensed cream of chicken soup
    1 pimiento, sliced
    ¼ **cup toasted slivered almonds**
Sprinkle over the mixture in the casserole:
    ½ **cup toasted bread crumbs**
    2 Tbsp. melted butter
Bake at 350 degrees for 35 minutes. Serves 6-8.

Mrs. Mary Fischer
From her friend,
Barbara O'Brien

Mrs. Gast received this recipe from her niece, Mary Lou (Carey) Chavis. She got it from her mother-in-law who is a Cherokee Indian (from the Carolinas). It is a delicious cross between cornbread and a souffle and makes an excellent vegetable side dish.

CORN SPOON BREAD

2 slightly beaten eggs
1 can (reg. size) cream style corn
1 can (reg. size) corn, drained
1 pkg. corn muffin mix (8½ oz. size)
1 cup sour cream
½ cup melted oleo
1 cup (4 oz.) shredded Swiss cheese

Combine all ingredients except the cheese. Grease an 11 x 7-inch baking dish. Bake at 350 degrees for 35 minutes, then sprinkle the cheese on top and bake 10 minutes more. Double the recipe to fill a 13 x 9-inch pan.

Mrs. Thomas (Jean) Gast

ZUCCHINI PROVENCAL

2 Tbsp. butter or margarine
½ cup chopped onion
1 clove garlic, minced
4 zucchini, unpeeled and sliced
2 tomatoes, peeled and chopped
1 tsp. salt
⅛ tsp. pepper
¼ tsp. oregano

In a skillet, melt the butter. Add the onion and garlic. Cook until tender. Add the zucchini and the remaining ingredients. Mix well and cook over a moderately low heat for 10 or 15 minutes, until the zucchini is crisp and tender. Serves 4.

Mrs. Glady Conant

MUSHROOM CASSEROLE

1 lb. mushrooms (fresh), cooked in a little **butter** only until you smell them.

Add ½ **cup celery** (diced), ½ **cup diced onion,** and ½ **cup mayonnaise.** Mix the above with the mushrooms. Put **3 slices of diced buttered bread** in the bottom of a 9 x 9-inch casserole. Add the mushrooms mixture on top and then **3 more slices of diced buttered bread** on top of that.

Beat **2 eggs;** add **1 cup of milk** and pour over the bread mixture in the casserole.

Let stand for at least 1 hour or overnight.

Spread **1 can of mushroom soup** (undiluted) over the top and bake in a 325-350 degree oven for 45 minutes to 1 hour.

Mrs. John W. (Pauline) Stigall

1950 RECIPES

In 1954, I gave birth to my first baby out in Colorado Springs (Phil was stationed at Fort Carson). Since by mother was too ill, my teenage brother volunteered to come and help me with the baby. Talk about the blind leading the blind! We were stranded without a car and nothing to do but wash diapers, sterilize bottles, clean house, etc. We started experimenting with recipes, and this is one of the results. I still make them, and people always ask for the recipe.

DEVILED EGGS

12 hard boiled eggs
Heaping ½ cup mayonnaise
½ tsp. salt
Pepper
1 tsp. curry powder
1 tsp. mustard
½ cup (heaping) **finely minced onion**

Combine the egg yolks with the remaining ingredients and fill the egg whites. Sprinkle with **paprika.**

Mrs. Philip (Patricia) Potts

BROCCOLI & CORN CASSEROLE

1 16-oz. can of cream style corn
1 10-oz. pkg. chopped broccoli, cooked and drained
1 beaten egg
12 saltine crackers, crushed
1 Tbsp. minced onion
2 Tbsp. melted margarine
½ tsp. salt
Pepper to taste

Combine all ingredients and bake at 350 degrees for 35-40 minutes. (Double the recipe to serve 10.)

Mrs. G. Toms (Margie) Yarger
From her mother

These Candied Sweet Potatoes are delicious. At Thanksgiving, I make them in a pan on top of the stove because my oven is always too full.

CANDIED SWEET POTATOES

Slice **6 pared, cooked sweet potatoes.** (I use canned sweet potatoes.) Place in a greased casserole. Add a syrup made of **1 cup brown sugar, ¼ cup water, ¼ cup oleo or butter, and ½ tsp. salt.**
Bake at 350 degrees for 45 minutes, basting occasionally.*
*(Ed: Remember when using a glass baking dish, it is advisable to lower the temperature or shorten the baking time.)

Mrs. Robert (Helen) Veith

BAKED BEANS

2 lbs. Great Northern or Navy beans
Sort and wash the beans thoroughly. Put the beans in a large kettle, cover with **boiling water** and boil for 2 minutes. Remove from the heat, cover, and let the beans soak overnight. Next day, drain the beans and discard the water. Put the beans back into the kettle and add:

3 qts. cold water
2 tsp. salt

Cover and simmer for 1 hour. (Skim off the foam.) Drain the beans and save the liquid.

SAUCE:
1 lb. bacon, sliced
2 medium onions, chopped
1½ cups firmly packed brown sugar
2 cups ketchup
2 Tbsp. dry mustard
1 Tbsp. salt

Dice 4 strips of bacon and put in a skillet or saucepan. Add the onions and cook over medium heat until the bacon is crisp and the onions are transparent. Add the ketchup, mustard, salt, and brown sugar. Bring the sauce to the boiling point.
Butter a 4 qt. casserole or bean pot. Put in ⅓ of the beans, ⅓ of the sauce, and ⅓ of the bacon strips (which have been cut in half). Repeat the layering ending with the bacon. If necessary, add 1 cup reserved bean liquid. Cover and bake at 275 degrees for 5-6 hours. Check every hour to make sure that the beans have not baked dry. Add some of the reserved bean liquid as needed.
The beans are even better warmed up on the second day.

Mrs. Roger (Louise) Barts

SOUR CREAM FILLED POTATOES

4 large baking potatoes
¼ cup butter or margarine, softened
¾ cup sour cream
¾ tsp. salt (or less)
¼ tsp. pepper
¼ tsp. paprika

Scrub the potatoes in cold water and let dry. Bake in a 350 degree oven till soft.
Cut the potatoes in half lengthwise. Scoop out the pulp and put through a ricer. Beat in the butter, sour cream, salt, and pepper. Pile the potato mixture back into only 6 shells. Ruffle with a fork and sprinkle with paprika. Bake in a hot oven (425 degrees) for 15 minutes until heated through. Serves 6.

Mrs. Andrew (Magda) Eperjesi

This has been the dressing recipe used in the Lamon family at Thanksgiving and Christmas for years. It is very convenient because it can be frozen before cooking.

DRESSING FOR TURKEY OR HEN

Brown in **½ cup oleo:**
 ½ cup chopped onions
 3 cups celery leaves and stalk
Add a total of **10 cups bread crumbs** (5 cups cornbread and 5 cups white bread)
Moisten the bread with **2 cans of chicken broth.** Add:
 ½ tsp. thyme
 2 tsp. sage
 1 tsp. salt
 ½ tsp. pepper
 1 tsp. vinegar

Place in a well greased pan and bake for 1 hour at 350 degrees.

Mrs. Lester (Beth) Lamon
From her mother-in-law,
Mrs. H.F. Lamon
of Maryville, Tennessee

When you're peeling fruit and the juice has a tendency to run down your arm, or when water runs down your arm while doing housework, put an old rubber bottle ring on your arm.

FANCY FILLETS

 1 pkg. frozen fish fillets (1½-2 lbs.)
 1 10-oz. can frozen shrimp soup (canned soup may be used)
 2 Tbsp. milk
 1 tsp. lemon juice
 ¼ tsp. prepared mustard
 ½ lb. fresh mushrooms, or 1 can stems and pieces, drained (I slice the fresh mushrooms.)

GARNISH:
 8 medium shrimp (optional)
 1 Tbsp. chopped chives

Defrost the fish and soup. Preheat the oven to 350 degrees. Saute the mushrooms in the margarine until just brown. Grease a shallow baking dish; arrange the fillets flat in the bottom. Mix the soup, milk, juice, mustard, and mushrooms; pour over the fish and dot with margarine. Bake for 30 minutes or until the fish flakes easily.

Meanwhile, cook, shell, and devein the shrimp. Garnish the fish with the shrimp and chopped chives. Serves 4-6.

Mary Jo Hruska

South Bend Tribune, December 16, 1954.

Jenny is a high school student who has been spending some of her afternoons working as an intern at the Museum. As a favor to those members of the Sipocz family who don't like green peppers, Jenny's mother always makes part of the stuffing into meatballs, thereby keeping everyone happy.

HUNGARIAN STUFFED PEPPERS

 2 cans tomato soup
 ½ can water
 1 tsp. Worcestershire sauce
 1 tsp. garlic salt
 Pepper to taste
Mix and put into a large kettle.

 1½ lbs. hamburger
 1 cup cooked rice
 1 egg
 4 cored green peppers, washed and cleaned
 Pepper and salt (pinch of each)

Mix the hamburger, rice, egg, salt and pepper; stuff into the green peppers. Put the peppers into the sauce. Cover the kettle, bring to a simmer, and cook for 1 hour. Serve with mashed potatoes.

Miss Jenny Sipocz
From her mother,
Mrs. Josephine Sipocz

When I prepare this dish, I always make a triple batch: I bake a double batch in a 9 x 13-inch pan for evening dinners or meetings; and a single batch in a 9 x 9-inch pan to serve the family before the guests arrive. The only complaint I get from family and friends is that the recipe never seems to make enough.

MEAT 'N BISCUIT SQUARES

1 lb. ground lean pork, veal, or beef
½ cup chopped onion
1 cup crumbled Bleu cheese (grated American or Swiss cheese may also be used)
1 egg
¼ tsp. Tabasco sauce (optional)
1½ tsp. salt
2 Tbsp. chopped parsley
Rich Biscuit Dough (see following recipe)
1 egg yolk, beaten

Heat the oven to 400 degrees. Cook the meat and onion slowly, but do not brown. Stir while cooking to break up the meat. Take from the heat. Cool. Then mix with the cheese, egg, Tabasco sauce, salt, and parsley.

Divide the biscuit dough in half. Roll or pat each half into a 9-inch square. Put half the dough into a 9 x 9 x 1¾-inch square pan. Spread with the meat mixture; cover with the other square of biscuit dough. Brush with the egg yolk.

Bake about 30 minutes. Serve hot in squares with tomato or mushroom sauce made from **1 can of soup** and **½ cup of milk**.

RICH BISCUIT DOUGH:
2 cups sifted flour
3 tsp. baking powder
1 tsp. salt
½ cup shortening or salad oil
1 egg
½ cup milk

Sift the flour, baking powder, and salt into a bowl. Cut in the shortening. Stir in the egg and milk. Round up on a lightly floured board. Knead lightly about 15 times.

Mrs. Charles (Florence) Hurcomb

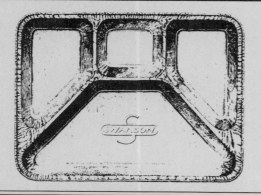

MARINATED LAMB KABOBS OR CHOPS

For **2 lbs. of lamb:**
¼ cup lime juice
¼ cup dry wine (red or white)
1 tsp. dry mustard
Several drops of Tabasco (if desired)
2-3 cloves of garlic (if desired)

Blend the marinade ingredients together. Place the lamb in the marinade and refrigerate. (The longer the meat marinates, the stronger the flavor will be; 4 hours are necessary for a moderate flavoring.) Grill the lamb outdoors over coals or indoors in your broiler until pink. (Well done lamb becomes tough.)

If grilled as kabobs, you may use par-boiled onions, green pepper, and raw tomato quarters on the skewers.

Garnish with lime wedges or ripe olives.

Mrs. Joel (Lou Ann) Bullard

SAUERBRATEN

4 lbs. beef*
1 Tbsp. salt
12 whole cloves
6 bay leaves
1 large onion, sliced
6 or 8 whole peppercorns
6 or 8 whole allspice
10 whole coriander
10 whole mustard seeds
1 cup cider vinegar
1 cup water
2 Tbsp. brown sugar
6 or 8 ginger snaps, broken

Mix all the ingredients except the beef and ginger snaps. Soak the meat in the marinade 1-2 days, turning occasionally.

When ready to cook, take the meat out of the liquid and drain. Brown the meat in a little fat or oil (use a large pot). Pour the liquid over it, including the seasonings and onion. When it is cooking, add the ginger snaps which have been broken into pieces. Let simmer for 2-3 hours, or until tender.

Remove the meat from the pot and strain the juice. Return the juice to the pot. Bring the juice to a boil and slowly add a mixture of **1 cup water** and **¾ cup browned flour** to thicken the gravy. Stir constantly.

Serve the sliced meat with potato pancakes or Kartoffel Klosse (potato dumplings); pour the gravy over all.

NOTE: To brown the flour, place it in a heavy skillet over low heat and stir constantly until the flour browns.

*(Ed: It is best to use a boneless pot roast of beef - rump, chuck, or round.)

Mr. Frank Sindlinger

> *If a baby's dress has lace or ribbon trim, place it in a mesh bag before laundering. Remove from the dryer while slightly damp. Iron immediately or enclose in a plastic bag to store in the refrigerator until ready to iron.*

ASPARAGUS WITH SOUR CREAM

4 lbs. asparagus, cleaned
Water with 2 tsp. salt added
6 egg yolks, slightly beaten
1 cup sour cream
½ tsp. salt
⅛ tsp. white pepper
1 Tbsp. lemon juice
2 Tbsp. chopped chives

Cook the asparagus in water until done.

In a saucepan, mix the egg yolks with the sour cream, salt, and pepper. Cook over low heat, stirring constantly with a wire whisk, for 2-4 minutes until heated through. Remove from the heat; add the lemon juice and chives. (Makes 1½ cups.)

To serve, pour the sauce over the asparagus or serve the sauce separately in a sauce boat.

Mrs. Glady Conant

Beef Stroganoff derived its name from one of the leading merchant families of St. Petersburg in the long ago days of the czars. Its delicious flavor (and the ready availability of commerical sour cream in the 1950's) has made this dish one of Russia's most welcome imports.

GROUND BEEF STROGANOFF

1 lb. ground beef
½ cup onion, chopped
2 Tbsp. flour
2 tsp. salt
¼ tsp. pepper
1 can (8 oz.) mushrooms, undrained
1 can (10½ oz.) cream of chicken soup, undiluted
1 cup sour cream
2 Tbsp. parsley
Cooked noodles

Brown the meat and onion. Pour off any grease. Add the flour, salt, pepper, and mushrooms. Cook for 5 minutes over medium heat, covered. Add the soup and simmer uncovered for 10 minutes. Stir in the sour cream and noodles (adjust the quantity to personal taste). Sprinkle parsley over all.

If desired, the noodles may be served separately from the Stroganoff; this would allow each guest to spoon on the amount of Stroganoff he prefers.

Mrs. Patrick (Sharon) Deneen

MEATBALLS IN SAUCE

1 lb. ham, ground
½ lb. pork, ground
3 eggs
1 cup cracker or bread crumbs
½ cup milk
Salt and pepper to taste
1 cup brown sugar
3 Tbsp. dry mustard
1 cup wine vinegar

Mix together the first 6 ingredients until well blended. Roll into small balls about 1½ inches in diameter. Place the balls into a shallow baking pan. Mix the brown sugar, mustard, and wine vinegar in a saucepan and heat until it comes to a boil. Pour the sauce over the meatballs and bake in a 350 degree oven for about 1¼ hours. Serve immediately.

Mr. John Charles Bryant

TUESDAY NIGHT TV AND RADIO PROGRAMS
All Times Listed Are Central Standard Time.

TIME P.M.	WSBT-TV Channel 34	WNDU-TV Channel 46	WSJV-TV Channel 52	WSBT-960 CBS	WNDU-1490 ABC	WJVA-1580 MUTUAL
5:00	Popeye Theatre		Looney Tune	Dinner Winner 960 Serenade	Polka Parade Crosiar's Corner	Lax Wax
5:15		My Little Margie			It Happened Today	
5:30	Sports	Take Ten	3 Star Special	News	. . . Mel Allen	. . . Sports Time— News
5:45						
6:00	News-Weather	Annie Oakley		Boland-Sports Lowell Thomas	Your Gov. Musicale	Sign Off
6:15	Doug Edwards		John Daly			
6:30	Name That Tune	Jonathan - Winters News	Conflict	Bing Crosby Edward R. Mur.	Tunesmith	
6:45						
7:00	Phil Silvers	$100,000 Big Sur. —Rep. Comm.		Robert Q. Lewis	News—Tunesmith	
7:15						
7:30	Hoosiers for Hand-ley	Hoosiers for Hand-ley	Dick Powell	Suspense	Bishop Fulton Sheen	
7:45						
8:00		Susie	Broken Arrow	News—Son Jeep Johnny Dollar	Ted Pfister—News Weather	
8:15	Red Skelton	Circle Theatre	Dupont Theatre	Campaign '56	Great Bands	
8:30				U.N. Report—News		
8:45						
9:00	$64,000 Question		UAW Citizenship Elk. Co. Dem.	Notebook — New Amer.—Amos And.	Tunesmith	
9:15		Dem. Comm.	Night Owl Theater	Treasury Show		
9:30	Trust Your Wife?	Highway Patrol			News— Tunesmith	
9:45						
10:00	Press Conference	Charades	Eddie Rickenbaker	CBS News—Local Sports—Orchestra	John Vandercook —Tunesmith	
10:15						
10:30	Weather-News	Weather. Deadline		Dance Orchestra	News—Tune-smith	
10:45	Spts—Nightwatch	Spts Lamp The.				
11:00				News—Club 960	News, Weather — Music	
11:15	Scores, Weather					
11:30					News, Weather	
11:45						

WEDNESDAY TV AND RADIO PROGRAMS

A.M.						
6:00				Market-Ramblers Meditations	News—Out of Sack	
6:15				News—Rise Shine First Edition	News—Out of Sack	
6:30	RFD 34	Farm News				
6:45						
7:00	Good Morn—News	Today—Wickard Senator		News Roundup Rise-Shine	News, Weather Out of Sack	Going Forward
7:15	Good Morning	Today Today Our Town				Roundup Sports Top Nine
7:30				News Desk	News, Weather	
7:45						
8:00	Capt. Kangaroo News	Today — Medita-tions		Top Tune—Rise Tangle Tunes	Breakfast Club	Rob. F. Hurleigh Coffeetime
8:15	Capt. Kangaroo	Today Today Our Town		Page 1—Rise Shine Devotions		Going Forward
8:30						
8:45						
9:00	Homemaker's Time	Ding Dong School		Arthur Godfrey Sunny Melodies	My True Story	Prayertime News—Youth for
9:15	Arthur Godfrey	Bandstand		Arthur Godfrey	When Girl Marries Whispering Streets	Christ Tabernacle
9:30						
9:45						
10:00	Arthur Godfrey	Home — Window in Home		Arthur Godfrey	Showcase Jack Parr	News—Going For-ward
10:15	Strike It Rich	Home		Timely Topics Howard Miller	School of Air Faith for Today	Queen for a Day
10:30						
10:45						
11:00	Valiant Lady	Tic Tac Dough		Wendy Warren Backstage Wife	Mrs. Riley's Shop-per's Guide	Gabriel Heatter
11:15	Love of Life		The Pastor	Helen Trent	Out to Lunch	
11:30	Search for Tomor-row	It Could Be You	RFD 52	Our Gal Sunday	News, Weather	News, Trading Post
11:45	The Guiding Light					
P.M.						
12:00	News—Intermis-sion	Mother's Movies	Video Treats	Luncheon Club	Paul Harvey Farm Fare—Kaye	News—World Thought for Day
12:15	As World Turns		Mother's Matinee		Out to Lunch	Going Forward
12:30						
12:45						
1:00	City Detective			Harlan Hogan 2nd Mrs. Burton	News — Women Only	News—Going For-ward
1:15	Afternoon Show	Tennessee Ernie		Strike It Rich Ma Perkins	News, Weather Women Only	News—Bob Por-ter
1:30						
1:45						
2:00	Big Payoff	Matinee Theatre	Film Festival	House Party	News, Weather Women Only	Going Forward
2:15	Musical Memo			Nora Drake	News, Weather Women Only	News—Bob Porter
2:30	House Party	Dem. Comm.		Young Dr. Malone		
2:45						
3:00	Brighter Day	Queen for a Day		Road of Life Pat Buttram	News, Weater Matinee	Bob Porter
3:15	Secret Storm			Pet Tune—Songs	News, Weather	Eye Opener
3:30	Edge of Night	Modern Romances	Circle 52 Ranch	Harlan Hogan	Matinee	
3:45						
4:00	Kaleidoscope 105	Comedy Time	Mickey Mouse Club	Record Shop	News, Weather— Rumpus Room	Polka Time
4:15		Little Rascals			Kuntry Kapers Weather	
4:30						
4:45						
5:00	Popeye Theatre		Looney Tune The-ater	Dinner Winner 960 Serenade	Polka Parade Crosiar's Corner	Lax Wax
5:15		My Little Margie			It Happend Today	
5:30		Take Ten			Mel Allen	Sports Time—News
5:45	Boland—Sports			News		

South Bend Tribune, October 30, 1956.

CHICKEN LOAF WITH MUSHROOM SAUCE

2 cups chopped chicken, well packed (cooked)
3 Tbsp. margarine or chicken fat
1 onion (size of an egg), **chopped**
¾ cup chopped celery
1 qt. (about 6 slices) **day-old bread**
⅛ tsp. pepper
½ tsp. poultry seasoning
1 tsp. salt
½ tsp. M.S.G.
1 egg
½ cup chicken broth

MUSHROOM SAUCE:
4 tsp. margarine
1 cup sliced mushrooms
2 Tbsp. flour
1½ cups milk
½ tsp. salt
⅛ tsp. pepper

Put the chicken into a 3 qt. mixing bowl. Saute the onion and celery in the fat until soft. Tear the bread into bite-size pieces and add to the chicken. Sprinkle the next 4 ingredients over the bread. Beat the egg; stir into the broth and pour over the bread. Mix thoroughly. Turn the mixture into a greased loaf pan and bake 35 minutes at 350 degrees. Let set for at least 15 minutes before serving. Serve with Mushroom Sauce.

MUSHROOM SAUCE:

Heat the margarine; add mushrooms and cook 3 minutes until they are juicy. Remove the mushrooms from the skillet and stir in the flour. Gradually add milk and cook, stirring until thickened and smooth. Stir in the seasonings and add the mushrooms. Serve hot over the chicken loaf. Serves 4.

Mrs. Glenn (Fannie Mae) Stoneburner

THICK OVEN STEW

Grease a roaster pan (or spray with Pam).
Put in: Cut up **beef** (raw); **onions; carrots; celery;** and **potatoes** (no need to peel the potatoes).

Add: **1 can mushroom soup**
 1 can tomato soup
 1 pkg. dry onion soup mix
 1½ cups water

Cover and bake at 300 degrees for 2 hours.
The quantity of meat and vegetables used is left up to the cook.

Mrs. Charles (Wava) Apelgreen

For a very special meal, Mrs. Barts makes her Stuffed Cabbage Rolls. The anise gives them a wonderful flavor. The time spent in making them is amply rewarded by the compliments you receive.

STUFFED CABBAGE ROLLS

Large head of cabbage (about 21-24 large leaves)
Place the cabbage leaves in boiling water until they are pliable. Drain. Cut out the thick veins so the leaves will roll more easily.

MEAT FILLING:
3 lbs. ground beef
3 medium onions, cut fine
1 cup Minute Rice
2 tsp. sweet basil
Salt and pepper to taste
1 clove garlic, minced
Few dashes nutmeg
4-5 eggs
Mix together.

SAUCE:
2 cans (6 oz.) **tomato sauce** (or use 1 large 15-oz. can)
2 cloves garlic, minced
1 round tsp. anise seed
2 Tbsp. brown sugar

Simmer the sauce ingredients 10-15 minutes. (I usually double the sauce recipe.)
Put about 1 heaping Tbsp. of the meat mixture onto a cabbage leaf; roll up folding in the edges. Place the rolls in a casserole. Pour the sauce over the rolls. Cover the casserole and bake in a 350 degree oven for 1½-2 hours.

Mrs. Roger (Louise) Barts

OVEN STEW

In a deep pot with a lid, place:
2 lbs. beef stew meat or oxtail joints
1 lb. carrots, cut into 1-inch chunks
2 onions, cut in wedges
3 celery stalks, cut in 1-inch chunks
½ cup catsup
4 Tbsp. tapioca
1 Tbsp. Lawry seasoned salt

Cover and bake at 250 degrees for 5-6 hours. ½ hour before serving, add:
5 potatoes, cut up
1½ lb. pkg. frozen green beans

Cook until the vegetables test done. Serves 4-6.

Mrs. Jean Savarese

My Mother duplicated this recipe after enjoying it in a restaurant in Washington, D.C. It quickly became a part of my family's most loved menu:

Shrimp Swimming in Butter
Tossed Mixed Green Salad
Salt Rising Bread to dip in the Shrimp Butter
Champagne
Rocky Road and Pralines 'N Cream Ice Cream
Coffee

Over the years, the table service has become more elegant, but no matter how the trimmings have changed, the menu is always the same -- and always delicious.

SHRIMP SWIMMING IN BUTTER

4 lbs. shrimp (fresh)
1½-2 (12 oz.) **bottles of beer**
¾-1 cup butter

BEER SEASONINGS:
½ tsp. Lawry's salt
½ tsp. garlic salt
¼ tsp. lemon pepper
3 bay leaves

BUTTER SEASONINGS:
2 tsp. lemon juice
½ tsp. garlic salt
¼ tsp. Lawry's salt
¼ tsp. lemon pepper

Peel, devein, and clean the shrimp. Put the shrimp in a non-metal pan and add the beer to cover along with the Beer Seasonings. Bring to a boil over medium heat. Simmer just until the shrimp are no longer raw, but still are a little under-done (about 2-3 minutes). Drain immediately and run under cold water for 30 seconds. Remove the bay leaves. Set aside.

In a wok or large frying pan, melt the butter over medium heat until browned (do not burn). Add the Butter Seasonings and stir 2-3 minutes. Add the shrimp and just heat through, stirring until the shrimp are well coated, 1-2 minutes.

Spoon into individual, warmed casseroles or bowls, making sure that all servings have plenty of butter. Serve while sizzling, placing the casseroles on larger plates that have room for both the casseroles and slices of salt-rising bread. Serves 4-6.

NOTE: Using frozen shrimp or margarine is fine, but it does affect the final flavor. The seasonings may also be adjusted according to personal taste.

Jerry and Sheri Wiener
From Mrs. Wiener's mother,
Mrs. Harold (Jo) Scott

To determine if dress or fabric colors run before buying, see if the color comes off on a white hankerchief.

Mrs. Lionberger served Shrimp Delight for her Christmas open house. It became a delicious tradition which her friends eagerly anticipated each year.

SHRIMP DELIGHT

1 can frozen shrimp soup*
2 large pkg. (8 oz.) **cream cheese**
½-1 tsp. curry powder
1 can (small) **ripe olives, chopped**
3 tsp. fresh lemon juice
1 clove garlic
Worcestershire sauce
1 small can shrimp

Mix together all the ingredients. Heat in a 350 degree oven for 20 minutes. Serve in a chafing dish with crackers. Good!!

*(Ed: If you can't find frozen shrimp soup, canned shrimp soup is available.)

Mrs. John R. (Virginia) Lionberger

Consumer spending rose sharply during the prosperous 1950's. Appliances were especially popular purchases.

BAKED PORK CHOPS

Brown **pork chops.** Mix **one can of milk** with **one can of mushroom soup.**

Cut out squares of aluminum foil. Cut up **one raw potato** (as many as you want to eat), **carrots** and **onion; salt and pepper** all. Put one pork chop onto one square of aluminum foil; lay potatoes, carrots, and onions on top. Spoon 4 Tbsp. of the soup mixture over the top of the vegetables. Put another pork chop on top of this and spoon 2 more Tbsp. of soup over the top.

Seal up well and bake in a 325-350 degree oven for 1½ hours.

(If you just want one pork chop per package, put the potatoes, carrots, and onions in first with the pork chop on the top.)

Mrs. Robert (Helen) Veith

CHICKEN WITH WINE

1 frying chicken, cut up*
2 Tbsp. flour
1 tsp. garlic salt
½ tsp. rosemary
¼ tsp. seasoned pepper
6 Tbsp. butter, melted
¾ cup dry white wine
1 cup sliced fresh mushrooms
¼ cup sliced green onions
2 Tbsp. butter
2 Tbsp. minced parsley

Dredge the chicken in seasoned flour. Brown the chicken on all sides in melted butter. Add the wine. Cover the pan and cook on low heat for 25 minutes. Saute the onions and mushrooms in the remaining butter. Add to the chicken, then cover the pan and cook about 15 minutes longer, or until the chicken is tender. Before serving, sprinkle parsley over the chicken. Serves 4.

*(Ed: This recipe works equally well with the skin removed from the chicken before browning.)

Mrs. Glady Conant

To remove paraffin from jams and jellies more easily, place a string or thread across the glass before pouring the paraffin in.

MARINATED BRISKET

1 brisket
1 or 2 onions, sliced

MARINADE:
⅓ cup barbecue sauce
½ cup port wine
2 Tbsp. soy sauce
1 tsp. brown sugar
Garlic powder, to taste
Lawry's seasoned salt, to taste

Mix the marinade ingredients together.
Slice the onions and put in the bottom of a roasting pan. Place the brisket on top of the onions. Pour the marinade over the meat, turning the meat a few times. Marinate overnight in the refrigerator.
Cover the pan with foil and place in the oven. Bake until almost tender at 325 degrees*. Remove from the oven and drain off the gravy. Chill and drain off the fat. Add 1 can of drained mushrooms to the gravy. Slice the meat. Pour gravy over the meat and reheat in the oven.

*(Ed: Bake for about 4 hours for a 4 lb. brisket. Fresh mushrooms are also very good.)

Mrs. Marlene Abrams

IF YOUR RECIPE CALLS FOR:	YOU MAY USE:
3 8x1½-inch round pans	2 9x9x2-inch square pans
2 9x1½-inch round pans	2 8x8x2-inch square pans or 1 13x9x2-inch rectangular baking dish
1 9x9x3-inch loaf pan	1 9x9x2-inch square pan

BARBEQUE SAUCE
(To Can)

2 qts. tomatoes
10 onions, medium size
3 green peppers, diced
1 cup sugar
2½ cups vinegar
2 Tbsp. salt
1 Tbsp. cinnamon
1 Tbsp. Allspice
1 Tbsp. nutmeg
½ Tbsp. cloves

Chop the tomatoes and onions. Mix together with the peppers, sugar, and vinegar; cook until tender. Add the spices last and boil for 10 minutes. Can in sterilized jars.*

*(Ed: If you're using a pressure cooker, can in the jars at 10 lbs. of pressure for 10 minutes.)

Mrs. Walton (Carol) Collins

CONEY ISLAND HOT DOG SAUCE

2 Tbsp. shortening
½ lb. ground beef
1 onion, chopped fine
1 can (6 oz.) tomato paste
1½ cups water (2 tomato paste cans full)
3 Tbsp. vinegar
¼ cup pickle relish
1 tsp. salt
1 Tbsp. chili powder
1 Tbsp. prepared mustard
¼ tsp. black pepper
Dash of cayenne pepper

Heat the oil in a saucepan. Brown the meat and onion, breaking up the meat in fine pieces. Stir in the tomato paste, water, vinegar, pickle relish, and salt. Simmer 25 minutes. Blend in the chili powder, mustard, pepper, and cayenne pepper. Simmer 5 minutes longer. Spread on hot dogs and enjoy.

Mrs. Stephen (Susan) Weaver
From her mother,
Mrs. Eleanor Carr

Children love these moist, flavorful cupcakes. They are perfect for picnics or cookouts because there is no gooey frosting to mess up little fingers.

NUT TOPPED BANANA CUPCAKES

BATTER:
   2¼ cups sifted cake flour
   2½ tsp. baking powder
   ½ tsp. baking soda
   ½ tsp. salt
   1 cup sugar
   ½ cup shortening
   2 eggs
   1 tsp. vanilla
   1 cup mashed banana
   ¼ cup sour milk or buttermilk

TOPPING:
   2 Tbsp. melted butter or margarine
   4 Tbsp. brown sugar
   ½ cup finely chopped pecans

Sift together the flour, baking powder, soda and salt. Cream the shortening; add the sugar gradually and continue beating until light and fluffy. Add the eggs, one at a time, beating well after each addition. Stir in vanilla. Add the flour mixture alternately with the bananas combined with the milk, blending until smooth. Pour into well-greased cupcake pans and bake in a moderate oven, 375 degrees, about 25 minutes or until done.

For the topping: Mix the butter, sugar, and nuts. When the cupcakes are removed from the oven, press the nut mixture onto the top of each cupcake. Return to the oven and bake 2-3 minutes longer.

Mrs. Roger (Louise) Barts

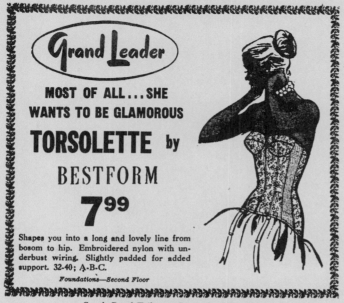

South Bend Tribune, December 18, 1955.

To substitute dry milk for whole milk in baking, sift into the flour 1 Tbsp. dry milk for each ¼ cup milk the recipe calls for. Add water as you would milk.

My mother used this recipe when she entertained her Bridge club in the late 1950's. The pretty red color makes this a perfect cake to serve on many special occasions, especially Christmas, Valentine's Day, and the 4th of July.

RED DEVIL'S FOOD CAKE

Mix and set aside:
   1 oz. water
   1 oz. red food coloring*
   3 Tbsp. Nestle's Quik

Measure the following:
   ½ cup shortening
   1½ cups granulated sugar
   2 eggs
   2¼ cups flour
   1 cup buttermilk
   1 tsp. vinegar
   1 tsp. baking soda

Beat the shortening till creamy, then cream in the sugar. Beat the eggs in with a spoon, one at a time. Add the food coloring mixture and mix well (using an electric mixer) for about 10 minutes.

Add the buttermilk alternately with the flour. Remove the bowl from the mixer and add the soda (dissolved in the vinegar) by hand. Mix well and pour into 2 greased and floured 8-inch pans. Bake at 350 degrees for 25-35 minutes.

WHITE FROSTING::
   ¼ lb. butter
   ½ cup shortening
   3 Tbsp. flour
   1 cup granulated sugar
   ⅔ cup milk
   1 tsp. vanilla

Cream together the butter, shortening, and sugar. Add the flour, 1 tablespoon at a time. Then add the ⅔ cup of milk slowly, with the mixer on low speed. Add the vanilla and mix. Turn the electric mixer on high speed and beat for 12 minutes. Frost the cake only after it has completely cooled.
*Most grocery stores sell red food coloring in 1 oz. bottles.

Mrs. David (Stephanie) LaDow
From her mother

Rinse raisins thoroughly in hot water and drain before adding them to muffins; they'll taste plump and juicy and won't withdraw any moisture from the batter.

1950 RECIPES

Robertson's Department Store celebrated its Golden Anniversary in 1954.

HOT FUDGE SAUCE

¼ cup cocoa
½ cup sugar
½ cup water
6 large marshmallows

Cook the cocoa, sugar, and water slowly to the soft ball stage. Remove from the heat and stir in the marshmallows. Serve hot over ice cream.

Mrs. Walton (Carol) Collins

FRESH APPLE CAKE

3 cups diced fresh apples (with peel)
3 cups flour
1½ cups sugar
1 tsp. soda
1 tsp. vanilla
½ tsp. salt
2 eggs
1½ cups Mazola oil
½ cup black walnuts, ground

Mix and bake in a 350 degree oven for 45 minutes. Do not over bake. Use a 9 x 12-inch pan.

This cake will keep for weeks, if it's kept covered with foil in the refrigerator. It's good plain or with a topping. The black walnuts make the flavor.

Mary Haag

This was a favorite of my father-in-law, Earl Blake. Men love this moist, delicious chocolate cake.

MIRACLE WHIP CAKE

1 cup sugar
1 cup Miracle Whip salad dressing
2 cups flour
⅓ cup cocoa
½ tsp. salt
2 tsp. soda
2 tsp. vanilla
1 cup hot water

Cream the salad dressing and sugar together. Add the dry ingredients. Lastly, add the hot water. Beat well. Pour into a greased and lightly floured 9 x 13-inch pan. Bake for 30 minutes at 350 degrees. Frost when cool with your favorite frosting.

Mrs. Robert (Claralu) Blake
From her mother-in-law.
Mrs. Earl (Daphne) Blake

COOKIE PIE CRUST

1 cup flour
1 stick margarine, melted (½ cup)
2 Tbsp. sugar

Mix well and press into a 9-inch pie pan. Bake about 15 minutes in a 350 degree oven. Cool and add your favorite pie filling. Makes 1 crust.

Mrs. Charles (Florence) Hurcomb

What a difference 50 years makes! Robertson's window displays showed quite a contrast in fashions from 1904 to 1954.

THIRD ANNUAL

Front Page Dinner

OCTOBER 27, 1953

"WHAT WE SEE FOR 83!"

OUTER SPACE ITEMS

1953 Banquet - Ladies of the South Bend Press Club.

The Menu

Saturnian Rings Fruit en Tasse

Venusian Highland Relishes

Roast Rib of Martian Dessert Ox
Jet Metal Wrapped Moon Pomme'
Plutonian Legumes

Hearts of Phobos Salat, Mercurian Dressing
Asteroid Ice with Rigelesian Wafers

Space Bread   Butter from Deimos

Mercurian Roast Coffee

This is the quickest, easiest, most delicious cake I bake. I use a butter cream frosting, and it seems ideal.

3 MINUTE BANANA CAKE

2 cups sifted cake flour
1 tsp. baking soda
½ tsp. salt
¼ cup milk
2 eggs
⅓ cup shortening
1 cup mashed bananas (3 medium)
¼ cup vinegar (cider)
1 tsp. vanilla
1½ cups sugar

Have ingredients at room temperature. Sift the flour, baking soda, and salt together. Combine the vinegar, milk, and vanilla. Beat the eggs and sugar together for 1 minute. Add the flour mixture, shortening, ½ of the liquid and ½ of the bananas. Stir to dampen the flour. Beat vigorously for 1 minute. Add the remaining liquid and banana. Beat 1 minute. Turn into 2 well-greased 8-inch layer pans. Bake in a moderately hot oven (375 degrees) for 25-30 minutes.

Mrs. Arthur (Dagny) Diamond

CHERRY TARTS

1½ cups graham cracker crumbs
¾ cup sugar
⅓ cup butter, melted

FILLING:
1 pkg. (8-oz.) cream cheese
½ cup sugar
2 eggs
1 tsp. vanilla

TOPPING:
1 cup sugar
½ tsp. cinnamon
2 Tbsp. cornstarch
1 can (1 lb.) tart cherries, drained*
Water
1 Tbsp. butter
Red vegetable coloring, if desired
1 cup heavy cream, whipped

Mix the crumbs, sugar, and butter; press into the bottom and sides of 12 small tart pans (about 4 inches in diameter). To prepare the filling: Beat the cream cheese until light and fluffy. Add the sugar, eggs, and vanilla; beat until smooth. Pour into the pie shells. Bake at 375 degrees for 20 minutes. Cool. To prepare the topping: Mix the sugar, cinnamon, and cornstarch. Add enough water to the cherry juice to make 1 cup. Add to the sugar and cook, stirring constantly, until thick. Add the butter and a drop or 2 of coloring, if desired. Cool. Add the cherries and chill thoroughly. Spoon over the cheese layer; top with whipped cream. Chill until serving time.

*(Fresh or frozen tart cherries may also be used. Instead of tarts, this also works well as a 10-inch pie.)

Mrs. Roger (Louise) Barts

This tasty cake is a favorite of Mrs. Philippsen's son, Eric.

MASHED POTATO TORTE

1 cup butter
2 cups sugar
½ cup milk
4 eggs, beaten separately
1 cup peeled, cooked, and grated potatoes
2½ cups flour
½ tsp. cloves
½ tsp. cinnamon
½ tsp. allspice
2 tsp. baking powder
1 bar German sweet chocolate, grated
¼ cup nuts, finely chopped
Grated rind of 1 lemon

Cream together the butter and sugar until fluffy. Add the milk, egg yolks, and potatoes. Sift together the flour, spices, and baking powder; add with the remaining ingredients to the sugar mixture. Fold in the beaten egg whites. Grease and flour two 9-inch cake pans. Bake at 350 degrees for 45 minutes. Frost with milk chocolate frosting.

Mrs. John (Lola Mae) Philippsen

This recipe is a favorite from my childhood. It is the cake that I asked my mother to bake every year for my birthday. It really is GREAT, with a wonderful chocolate flavor.

REALLY GREAT CHOCOLATE FUDGE CAKE

Grease and flour two 9-inch layer pans.
Preheat the oven to 350 degrees.
Cream together ¼ **cup butter** with 1½ **cups sugar.** Blend in **2 egg yolks** (save the whites) and **4 squares of melted unsweetened chocolate.**
Sift together 1⅞ **cups flour, 2 tsp. baking powder** and **1 tsp. salt.** Stir into the batter alternately with ½ **cup milk** and **1 tsp. vanilla.**
Make a meringue with the **2 egg whites,** beaten until stiff peaks form and ½ **cup sugar.** Fold the meringue into the batter.
Bake at 350 degrees for 30-40 minutes. A toothpick inserted into the center of the cake should come out clean. This cake takes some work, but it's worth it!

Mrs. Karen Keller
From her mother,
Mrs. Christine Carlson

A tablespoon of vinegar added to the soap and water in which jeans are washed will keep them soft, lint-free, and easier to iron.

FANNIE'S CREAM CHEESE POUND CAKE

1 8-oz. pkg. Philadelphia cream cheese
3 cups sugar
1 lb. butter (or ½ lb. each butter and margarine)
3 cups flour
6 eggs

Cream the cream cheese, sugar, and butter until fluffy. Add 1 cup flour and 2 eggs. Beat well and repeat twice. Bake at 350 degrees in an angel food pan for 80-90 minutes, or until done. (Place a large pan of water in the bottom of the oven while baking.)

Fannie Taylor

Mary Rose Blank and Elsie Rupel ready a project for the 1953 4-H Fair.   *Courtesy of the St. Joseph County Extension Office.*

TIPSY PARSON CAKE

1 Angel food loaf cake
1 pkg. French vanilla instant pudding (mixed with 2 scant cups of milk)
⅓ cup cream sherry
½ pt. whipping cream (unsweetened)

Cut the cake lengthwise into 3 layers. Pour the wine into a small juice glass. Using a turkey baster, baste the first layer (which has been placed on a flat cake plate) lightly with wine. Spread one-third of the vanilla pudding over the first layer. Add the second layer of cake and baste with wine. Spread with one-third of the pudding. Add the third layer and baste with the remaining wine. Spread on the rest of the pudding.
Whip the cream (do not add sugar). Spread the whipped cream over all four sides and the top. Use toothpicks at each corner to hold the cake in place. Refrigerate over night.
When ready to serve, cut into 8 slices. This can be frozen if made ahead of time.

Mrs. Della Mann

This is one of my daughters' favorite cakes; it's always in demand on their birthdays. Start the frosting as soon as the cake goes into the oven so that you can put it together warm. Watch out, though, or you may have a fight to see who gets to lick out the frosting pan.

MALLO-NUT FUDGE CAKE

3 oz. chocolate, cut very fine
¾ cup boiling water
1¾ cups sifted cake flour
1½ cups sugar
¾ tsp. salt
½ tsp. baking powder
¾ tsp. soda
½ cup shortening
⅓ cup thick sour milk
1 tsp. vanilla
2 eggs, unbeaten
18 marshmallows, cut in half
½ cup nuts, cut (broken)

Put the chocolate in a mixing bowl. Pour boiling water over the chocolate and stir until melted. Cool. Sift the flour, sugar, salt, baking powder, and soda into the chocolate mixture. Drop in the shortening. Beat 200 strokes (2 minutes on mixer at low speed). Scrape the bowl and spoon. Add the sour milk, vanilla, and eggs; beat 200 strokes (2 minutes on mixer at low speed). Bake in 2 square 8 x 8 x 2-inch greased pans in a moderate oven (350 degrees F.) for 30-40 minutes. While the cake is warm, press the marshmallows onto one layer, turned bottom-side up. Spread the Minute-Boil Fudge Frosting; put other layer on top. Add the nuts to the remaining frosting and spread on top of the cake. Decorate each corner with a quartered marshmallow.

MINUTE-BOIL FUDGE FROSTING
3 oz. chocolate, finely cut
2¼ cups sugar
10½ Tbsp. milk
3 Tbsp. shortening
3 Tbsp. butter
1½ Tbsp. corn syrup
⅛ tsp. salt
1½ tsp. vanilla

Place the chocolate, sugar, milk, shortening, butter, corn syrup, and salt in a saucepan. Bring slowly to a full rolling boil, stirring constantly; boil briskly for 3 minutes. (On a rainy or very humid day, boil the mixture 5 minutes.) Cool to lukewarm. Add the vanilla and beat until thick enough to spread. If frosting becomes too thick, add a little cream or soften over hot water.

Mrs. Roger (Louise) Barts

Fruitcakes have long been a part of holiday feasting and gift giving. Mrs. Bowers makes Jubilee Fruitcake for her family every Christmas.

JUBILEE FRUITCAKE

2 cups shortening (part butter)
1 cup brown sugar
1 cup white sugar
4 eggs
2 cups applesauce
2 tsp. soda
4 cups flour
1 cup small gum drops
1 cup raisins
1 cup dates
1 cup nut meats
1 tsp. cinnamon
1 tsp. cloves
1 tsp. nutmeg

Cream the shortening and sugar together. Add the unbeaten eggs one at a time and beat. Mix in the applesauce. Add the sifted flour, soda, and spices. Mix the raisins, dates, nuts, and gum drops with flour and add to the batter. Bake in a 10 inch tube pan for 1½ hours at 350 degrees. Put a small pan of water in the oven to keep the cake from getting too dry.

Mrs. Maxine Bowers

GINGERSNAP LEMON PIE

1 pkg. lemon pudding mix
⅓ cup sugar
2 cups water
2 egg yolks, unbeaten
2 egg whites, unbeaten
4 Tbsp. sugar
Gingersnap crust

Combine the pudding mix, sugar, and ¼ cup water in a saucepan. Add the egg yolks and blend well. Add the remaining 1¾ cups water. Cook and stir over medium heat until the mixture comes to a full boil and is thickened (about 5 minutes). Remove from the heat.

Beat the egg whites until foamy. Add 4 Tbsp. sugar (2 Tbsp. at a time) and beat until soft peaks form. Gently fold into the hot filling. Pour into the gingersnap crust. Spread with whipped cream and sprinkle gingersnap crumbs on top.

GINGERSNAP CRUST:
Combine 1¼ cups fine gingersnap crumbs and 3 Tbsp. sugar. Add ¼ cup melted butter and mix well. Press the crumbs into a pie pan. Bake at 375 degrees for 5-8 minutes. Cool before filling.

Mrs. Walton (Carol) Collins

PRIZE LEMON MERINGUE PIE

Baked 9-inch pie shell
1½ cups sugar
7 Tbsp. cornstarch
½ tsp. salt
1½ cups hot water
3 eggs, separated
½ cup lemon juice
Grated peel of 1 lemon
2 Tbsp. butter
1 tsp. lemon juice (for meringue)
6 Tbsp. sugar

Mix the sugar, cornstarch, and salt in a saucepan. Add hot water gradually and cook over direct heat, stirring constantly 6-8 minutes or until thick and clear. Remove from the heat and stir about ¼ cup of the hot mixture into the beaten egg yolks. Pour the mixture back into the pan and stir while cooking 6 minutes over low heat. Remove from the heat and add the lemon juice, peel, and butter. Cool.

Fill the pie shell. Beat the egg whites with the lemon juice until stiff. Gradually beat in the sugar until the meringue holds high, glossy peaks. Spread on the pie from the crust in. Bake at 400 degrees about 8 minutes. Cool.

Mrs. Eleanor Carr

PECAN PIE

1 9-inch pastry crust
3 eggs (medium)
⅔ cup sugar
½ tsp. salt
⅓ cup butter
1 cup corn syrup (dark Karo)
¼ cup finely grated pecans
1 cup pecan halves

Heat the oven to 375 degrees.

Beat the eggs, sugar, salt, butter, and syrup until blended. Stir in the pecan halves. Sprinkle and pat ¼ cup grated pecans into the bottom of the pastry lined pie pan. Pour the syrup-pecan mixture into the pie shell. Bake until set (40-50 minutes). Let stand 15 minutes before slicing. Serve with a teaspoonful of **heavy cream (whipped).** Refrigerate leftovers.

For variation, melt 2 squares (1 oz. each) unsweetened chocolate with the butter, then beat in remaining ingredients.

This pie is very rich; servings should be smaller than regular pie wedges. The recipe works better when a glass pie plate is used.

Mrs. Paul (Mary Yena) Rohleder

FRESH APPLE COBBLER

10-12 fresh apples, peeled and sliced into a 9 x 13-inch pan. Sprinkle with **¾ cup sugar.** Add 2 inches of **water** and set in the oven at 350 degrees to get hot. Then remove from the oven and drop the following dough by teaspoonfuls over the apples: **1 stick oleo,** softened and **1 scant cup sugar.** Cream together and add **1 egg, 1 cup flour,** and **1 tsp. baking powder.**

Bake for 1 hour at 350 degrees or until golden brown. Eat warm.

Mary Haag

APPLE CRISP

6 medium apples, peeled
1 cup brown sugar
¾ cup flour
1 cup oatmeal
½ cup plus 2 Tbsp. margarine

After peeling, thinly slice the apples into a lightly greased pan; pat down. Mix the brown sugar, flour, and oatmeal. Mix in the butter with the fingers. Pat on top of the apples. Bake in a 350 degree oven for about 1 hour.

Miss M. Geraldine Hatt
From Mrs. George (Dora) Olson

APPLE SLICES

3 lbs. tart cooking apples
1 cup water
1¼ cups sugar
1 tsp. cinnamon
¼ tsp. salt
2 Tbsp. cornstarch
¼ cup cold water

CRUST:
2 cups flour
½ tsp. baking powder
½ tsp. salt
¾ cup lard or Crisco
1 tsp. lemon juice
2 egg yolks, beaten
½ cup water

Pare and core the apples, then cut into eighths. In a large saucepan, bring the water, sugar, cinnamon, and salt to the boiling point. Add the apples and cook slowly for 10 minutes. Blend the cornstarch and ¼ cup cold water; add to the hot mixture. Cook for 5 minutes longer, stirring gently.

Cut the shortening into the sifted flour, baking powder, and salt, as for pie crust. Mix the lemon juice, egg yolks, and water together and sprinkle over the flour mixture; blend the liquid in lightly. Divide the dough into 2 parts. (More dough will be required for the bottom crust than the top crust.) Roll the first crust to fit the bottom and sides of a shallow pan, about 9 x 13-inches.

Fill the bottom crust with the apple mixture. Roll the remaining dough to fit the top and seal the edges. Cut a design for steam vents into the top crust. Bake in a hot oven (450 degrees) for 20 minutes, then reduce the heat to 350 degrees and bake for 30 minutes longer.

Ice with a thin confectioner's sugar icing or sprinkle with confectioner's sugar. Cut into 12 pieces and serve.

Mrs. Eleanor Carr

BUTTERFINGERS

l lb. butter
6 cups flour
2 tsp. vanilla
2 cups chopped nuts
8 Tbsp. sugar or 1 cup sugar (powdered)

Cream the butter thoroughly, then add the sugar gradually. Add a little flour at a time; add vanilla. Add nuts. Form into "fingers" and bake at 350 degrees for 10 minutes. Roll in sifted **powdered sugar.** This makes 4 dozen.

Mrs. Lester (Aileen) Borough
From her mother,
Mrs. N.M. (Rachel) Holley

CANTALOUPE FRASCATI

Cut sweet, ripe **cantaloupes** into halves and remove the seeds. Fill each half with **½ cup raspberries or strawberries.** Sprinkle with **1 Tbsp. sugar** and a little **sherry.** Cover with wax paper and chill for 1 hour. Cover with the following meringue:

3 egg whites
¼ tsp. salt
6 Tbsp. sugar

Beat the egg whites with the salt until frothy. Add the sugar, 1 tablespoon at a time, and continue beating until stiff and glossy. Spoon the meringue lightly onto each half and bake in a 400 degree oven until lightly browned, about 5 minutes.

Mrs. James Lee Wilson

HOT FUDGE PUDDING CAKE

1 cup sifted flour
2 tsp. baking powder
¼ tsp. salt
¾ cup sugar
2 Tbsp. cocoa
½ cup milk
2 Tbsp. melted shortening
1 cup chopped nuts
1 cup brown sugar, packed
¼ cup cocoa
1¾ cups hot water

Sift the flour with the dry ingredients into a bowl. Stir in the milk and melted shortening. Blend in the nuts. Spread in a square pan (9 x 9-inch). Sprinkle on the brown sugar and ¼ cup cocoa. Pour hot water over the entire batter. Bake for 45 minutes in a 350 degree oven. During baking, the cake mixture rises to the top and the chocolate sauce settles to the bottom.

Mrs. Charles (Mary) Taylor

MRS. CARROLL'S COOKIES

1 lb. butter or oleo
1 cup powdered sugar
1 tsp. vanilla
4 cups plain flour

Mix the butter and powdered sugar. Add the vanilla and flour. Beat all together. Make little balls and flatten with a glass (flour the bottom of the glass). Bake on ungreased cookie sheets for 10 minutes at 350 degrees.

Mrs. George Earl (Florence Vaughan) Carroll

My mother's recipe makes the best moist, chocolatey brownies I've ever had. They are a cake type brownie which disappear almost as soon as they are made.

DELUXE BROWNIES

½ cup margarine
1 cup sugar
4 well beaten eggs
1 cup flour
1 cup nuts (optional)
1 can (1 lb.) chocolate syrup

Cream the margarine and sugar together. Add the eggs, then the flour. Finally add the syrup and nuts. Bake in a greased 9 x 13-inch pan at 350 degrees for 25 minutes. Cool, then frost with the following:

FROSTING:
1 cup sugar
6 Tbsp. margarine
⅓ cup milk
½ cup chocolate chips
Boil the sugar, margarine, and milk, then beat in the chocolate chips. Remove from the heat; stir until the chips are melted. Spread on the brownies.

Mrs. Karen Keller
From her mother,
Mrs. Christine Carlson

These Fruit Squares are a favorite of Mrs. Cira. This is the recipe she takes to her club parties.

FRUIT SQUARES

½ cup shortening (I now use butter-flavor Crisco)
½ cup margarine
1½ cups sugar
Cream well. Add:
4 eggs, one at a time
Beat well. Add:
2 cups flour
1 Tbsp. lemon juice or lemon extract
1 tsp. vanilla

Mix well and beat until light and fluffy. Spread in a jelly roll pan or a 1-inch deep cookie sheet. With a knife, divide the dough into 20-24 squares. Spoon 1 Tbsp. fruit pie filling onto each square.

Bake in a 350 degree oven for 40 minutes. Cool. Sprinkle with powdered sugar. Cut into squares keeping the fruit in the middle of each square. Serve. Good luck and enjoy.

Mrs. Rose Cira

This is a family recipe from Mrs. Borough's home in Tuscaloosa, Alabama.

SOUTHERN PECAN BARS

¼ cup margarine
⅓ cup packed brown sugar
1 cup flour
¼ tsp. baking powder
¼ cup broken pecan pieces
2 eggs
¾ cup dark brown syrup
¼ cup brown sugar
2 Tbsp. flour
½ tsp. salt
1 tsp. vanilla
¾ cup chopped pecans

Cream the margarine and ⅓ cup of brown sugar. Add the flour, baking powder, and ¼ cup pecan pieces. Pat in the bottom of a well-greased 9 x 9-inch pan. Bake at 350 degrees for 10 minutes.

While this is baking, beat the eggs until foamy. Add the syrup, ¼ cup brown sugar, 2 Tbsp. flour, salt, and vanilla. Mix and pour over the baked crust.

Sprinkle ¾ cup pecans over the top. Bake at 350 degrees for 20 minutes for chewy bars. (For crunchier bars bake 25-30 minutes.)

Mrs. Lester (Aileen) Borough

Keep beverages cold at a backyard barbecue by filling a small wheelbarrow or child's wagon with ice. Stick the bottles into the ice. The wagon can be moved easily to different groups of people around the lawn and then back to the house for refills.

LIME DESSERT

2 cups chocolate cookie crumbs
⅓ cup melted butter or margarine
Combine and put in the bottom of a 9 x 13-inch pan.
1 pkg. (3 oz.) lime jello
1¾ cups boiling water
¼ cup lime juice
2 tsp. lemon juice
1 cup sugar
1 large can Carnation milk, chilled

Dissolve the jello in the boiling water. Add the lime juice, lemon juice, and sugar. Chill until partially set and whip.

Whip the Carnation milk (which has been chilled) and add to the jello. Pour the mixture over the cookie crumbs and shave some semi-sweet chocolate over the top. Chill in the refrigerator until ready to serve. Serves 16.

Mrs. Ronald (Pat) Olsen
From Mrs. Ann Lundburg

BONNIE DOON ICE CREAM CORPORATION

BONNIE DOON BANANA BOAT

Peel a **banana** and cut lengthwise. Place in the bottom of a glass dish. Add **one scoop of Bonnie Doon vanilla ice cream** in the middle. Place **one scoop of Bonnie Doon chocolate ice cream** on one side and **one scoop of Bonnie Doon strawberry ice cream** on the other side. Pour **strawberry sauce** over the scoop of chocolate ice cream, **pineapple sauce** over the strawberry ice cream, and **chopped nuts, whipped cream** and a **cherry** over the vanilla ice cream. Enjoy!

KIEFLIES

1½ lbs. sifted flour
1 doz. egg yolks
1 lb. butter
½ lemon (1 tsp. juice)
Pinch of salt
2 tsp. vanilla
½ pt. sour cream

Mix the butter, yolks, salt, and lemon juice together first. Add the flour alternately with the vanilla and sour cream. Refrigerate for 24 hours. Rolled into 144 balls, a little smaller than golf balls. Flatten like pancakes and roll thin. Place a little filling on each rolled out piece of dough. Roll up and pinch the edges together; shape like a crescent. Bake in 350 degree oven for 10 minutes, or until lightly brown. Sprinkle with powdered sugar, if desired.

FILLING:
1 doz. egg whites, beaten stiff
1 box (1 lb.) powdered sugar
2 lbs. nuts
1 Tbsp. vanilla
1½ tsp. orange juice
1½ Tbsp. lemon juice
Mix all ingredients together.

Miss Jenny Sipocz
From her aunt

The Bonnie Doon Ice Cream Corporation was founded by Herman and Andrew Muldoon in 1938. The company has continued to make ice cream in Mishawaka for half a century.

DIAGONAL BAR COOKIES

⅔ cup sugar
¾ cup margarine
1 unbeaten egg
2 tsp. vanilla
2 cups flour
½ tsp. baking powder
⅓ cup red jelly or jam

Cream the sugar and margarine together. Add the egg and vanilla and mix well. Stir in the flour and baking powder and mix until smooth. Divide the dough into 4 parts; shape each into a roll 13 inches long and ¾ inches thick. Place 4 inches apart on a baking sheet. Make a depression about ⅓ inch deep lengthwise down the center of each roll with a knife handle. Fill the depressions with jelly. Bake in a 350 degree oven for 15-20 minutes until light brown. While warm, cut diagonally into bars. Makes about 5 dozen cookies.

Doris Roberts

Business was booming in 1950 at the Bonnie Doon Drive-in on Lincoln Way West in South Bend.

Courtesy of Howard & Maureen Muldoon, Bonnie Doon Ice Cream Corp.

South Bend Tribune, October 28, 1956.

LEMON BARS

1 cup butter
2 cups flour
½ cup powdered sugar
Cream together. Press into a greased 9 x 13-inch pan and bake for 20 minutes at 350 degrees.

4 eggs, beaten
2 cups sugar
1 tsp. baking powder
6 Tbsp. lemon juice
4 Tbsp. flour
Combine the ingredients and spread over the baked crust. Bake at 350 degrees for 20-25 minutes. Sprinkle with powdered sugar. This is our best cookie recipe.

Mrs. John (Millie) Yoder

My children loved to make this candy. When the soda is added, it foams and boils in a most spectacular fashion. It really does "melt in your mouth."

OLD-FASHIONED SPONGE CANDY

Bring to a boil in a large pan:
1 cup dark corn syrup
1 cup sugar
Boil to the hard crack stage.
Add **4 tsp. baking soda** and stir rapidly.
Pour into a well buttered 9-inch square pan.

Mrs. Charles (Florence) Hurcomb

MERINGUE HEATH TORTE

6 3-oz. Heath bars, freeze and crush
2 cups whipped cream
Fold the candy into the whipped cream.

FOR THE MERINGUE:
6 egg whites
2 cups sugar
2 tsp. vanilla
½ tsp. cream of tartar
Dash of salt

Beat the egg whites on high. Gradually add the sugar when the egg whites are stiff; then add the flavorings.

On brown paper or foil, draw two circles (9-inches in diameter). Spread the meringue inside the circles. Bake in 275 degree oven for 1 hour until the meringue dries out.

Carefully remove the meringues from the paper or foil. Place one layer on a plate and spread with half of the whipped cream mixture. Top with the other meringue layer and the remaining whipped cream mixture. Decorate with some additional crushed Heath bars, if desired.

Mrs. G. Toms (Margie) Yarger
From her mother-in-law

Mrs. Purucker tried many cut-out cookie recipes, but this was her favorite. These crisp, delicate cookies will stay fresh for weeks in an air-tight container, but they probably won't be around long enough for freshness to become a problem.

HOLIDAY SUGAR ROLL-OUTS

1½ cups sifted confectioner's sugar
1 cup margarine
1 egg
1 tsp. vanilla
½ tsp. almond flavoring
2¼ cups flour, sifted
1 tsp. soda
1 tsp. cream of tartar

Cream the sugar and margarine. Add the egg and flavorings. Stir in the dry ingredients. Refrigerate 2-3 hours. Roll dough very thin (⅛ - 3/16 inches). Cut out cookies and place them on lightly greased cookie sheets. Decorate with colored sugar. Bake in a 375 degree oven for 7-8 minutes until delicately brown.

This dough is very rich and must be handled with care when it is rolled out. Be sure that your rolling pin and board are floured.

If you use cookie cutters of different sizes, place the smaller cookies on one sheet and the larger cookies on another. If small and large cookies are mixed on one sheet, the little ones will burn before the larger ones have baked.

Mrs. Ervin (Bertha) Purucker

This wonderful recipe has served two generations and is working on a third. When I was a girl, my Mom constantly received requests for this recipe, and now I get requests, too! Mother used these cookies as her gifts to special friends. She would wrap the cookies in Saran wrap and give them to people to hang on their Christmas trees. Many of her friends kept them for years and considered them among their favorite ornaments. (Mother left a collection of 350 cookie cutters.)

LIFE-LIKE COOKIE DOUGH

½ cup butter or shortening
½ cup sugar
½ tsp. soda dissolved in 2 Tbsp. milk
½ tsp. vanilla
1 egg, beaten
1 pinch of salt
2½ cups flour

Cream the butter and sugar. Add the soda and milk. Add the vanilla and egg; mix in the salt and flour.

Roll out the dough flat. Cut out with cookie cutters. Bake in a 350 degree oven for 10 minutes.

ICING:
4 Tbsp. butter
5 cups confectioner's sugar
¼ tsp. salt
2 unbeaten egg whites
About 2 Tbsp. cream (Pet Milk)

Mix all ingredients together. The icing may be tinted; it may also be thinned and used as a glaze.

Linda Haines Dillard
From her mother,
Una (Spence) Haines

BREAD & BUTTER PICKLES

4 qts. sliced pickles (unpeeled pickles or cucumbers)
4 medium onions, sliced
2 green peppers, diced (or 1 red and 1 green mango peppers)
⅓ cup salt, sprinkled on top (non-iodide)
2 garlic cloves, diced

Soak the above ingredients in water, cooled with 2 trays of ice cubes, for 2 or 3 hours until the ice melts. Drain. Place in a pan and add the following mixture; **3 cups vinegar; 1½ tsp. tumeric; 2 tsp. mustard seed; 1½ tsp. celery seed;** and **5 cups sugar.** Bring to a boil over medium heat. Put in hot jars and seal. Chill and they are ready to eat.
NOTE: Use regular white vinegar - 5%.

Mr. Philip Potts

BUTTER CREAMS

½ cup butter
1 tsp. vanilla extract
1 tsp. salt
⅔ cup (half a 15 oz. can) sweetened condensed milk
6 cups (about 1½ lbs.) sifted confectioner's sugar

In a medium-size bowl, cream together the butter, vanilla, and salt. Blend in the sweetened condensed milk until smooth. Gradually add the sugar. Blend well after each addition until the mixture becomes very stiff. Turn the mixture from the bowl onto a clean board. Carefully knead in all the sugar. (The mixture should be smooth, not sticky.) Cut the mixture into pieces so that when molded they will be the size of a marble or slightly smaller. With the palms of your hands, mold each piece into a ball. Place the pieces onto a wax-lined cookie sheet. Place in the refrigerator to chill for several hours or overnight (they may be frozen). Dip the balls into the Dipping Chocolate. Makes 2 lbs. of fondant.

DIPPING CHOCOLATE:
8 squares (½ lb.) semi-sweet chocolate
⅓ slab household paraffin wax

Place the chocolate and wax into the top of a double boiler. Place over hot water and heat over medium heat. (Never melt paraffin over direct heat.) Stir with a wire whisk until the chocolate is melted and well blended. Remove the double boiler from the heat. (Enough for 2 lbs. of fondant.)

It is easier and more fun when two people do the dipping. One person should insert a double pronged fork into the bottom of a butter cream ball and carefully dip it into the chocolate. Also, try using kitchen tongs and decide which method you prefer. The second person should be constantly stirring the chocolate, remaining watchful that it doesn't begin to cool and thicken (Keep the chocolate over a very low heat.)

Mrs. Marge Campbell

BUCK EYES

¼ cup butter or margarine (at room temperature)
1 lb. confectioner's sugar
2 cups crunchy peanut butter
3 cups rice cereal
12 oz. pkg. chocolate chips
⅓ stick paraffin wax

Mix the first 4 ingredients together thoroughly and form into small balls. Using a double boiler, melt the chocolate chips and paraffin wax together over hot water. Roll the balls into the chocolate mixture and place on waxed paper to cool. Makes about 4 doz. balls.

Mrs. Charles (Florence) Hurcomb

Mrs. Thomas Clarke

1960's

This mini-skirted black silk bombazine dress has a wide band of chinchilla fur around the hemline of the skirt. Black self-covered buttons stretch from neck to waist. A rhinestone belt around the slightly dropped waist completes this simple yet elegant look. This dress was worn by Mrs. Thomas Clarke. Circa 1973.

ANYTHING A GO-GOES

After 10 years of comparative tranquility, America was looking for new leadership, someone young and vital who could harness the growing enthusiasm of the children of the postwar "Baby Boom." From the time of his election, President John F. Kennedy seemed able to touch the conscience of the nation. He asked each individual to make a commitment to bring an end to suffering and injustice in the world. Unfortunately, with the assassination of Kennedy and Civil Rights leader, Dr. Martin Luther King, people were left without a rallying point. Suddenly we became a generation in search of a cause, and like lightening to a rod, segregation and the war in Vietnam drew much of people's collective frustration and rage.

For some, it seemed better to "drop out" of society than live in a world which refused to conform to their ideals. These Hippies or "flower children" sent up the chant, "Make love not war," unleashing a sexual revolution which quickly shook the American family clear down to its grass roots. Marriage, while nice, was no longer considered a must; divorce was on the rise, and the birth rate was sluggish at best.

Women were suddenly free to pursue careers outside the home, and since men were no longer the sole bread winners, the traditional husband/wife roles began to blur. Ladies, too, wanted to dress for success; during the next decade, the tailored suit surged back into the fashion spotlight. Working men and women both began to rely on crock pots and microwave ovens to put fast, yet nourishing meals on the table.

Technology was turning the American home into a labor-saving showcase. In 1960, DuPont introduced a non-stick coating for cookware called Teflon. Irons and ovens were now "self-cleaning," refrigerators were "frost-free," and clothes were permanent press. Gadgets were being invented to handle even the most basic tasks; after all, what home would be complete without a trash compactor and an electric toothbrush.

Americans no longer wanted to think of themselves as faceless figures in a great melting pot; each ethnic group worked diligently to establish its own identity. Restaurants quickly fell into step and were soon offering everything from "Soul Food" to tacos and linguini. Some ethnic delicacies required special equipment such as the Oriental wok, and certainly no up-to-date hostess would be without Switzerland's gift to America, the fondue pot. As a growing interest in French Haute Cuisine developed, people gravitated to the word "gourmet" as if it guaranteed an instant rise in social status. The heritage of our early pioneers was not totally forgotten; a "back to nature" movement sprang up which advocated casting off modern conveniences and returning to the simpler world of home-baked bread and hand-loomed fabrics.

It was inevitable that the social upheaval which characterized the 1960's would have a significant impact on the world of fashion. The early years of the decade were dominated by the sophisticated styles popularized by First Lady, Jacqueline Kennedy. This elegant look was soon replaced, however, by the "little girl" styles of British designer Mary Quant. Childlike innocence quickly gave way to sex and seduction as skirts grew perilously short, culminating finally in the eye-popping micromini. Although women could not bend, sit, or walk in a breeze while wearing these skirts, the mini did bring about the decline of the girdle and the debut of pantyhose.

As the end of the decade neared, an attempt by fashion designers to force a major change in hemlines backfired dramatically; women resoundingly rejected the midi skirt and set out to chart their own fashion course. Pant legs grew wider forming huge bell bottoms which were balanced by jackets with mammoth lapels, long tunic vests, and death-defying platform shoes. Ladies paraded through the late 60's and early 70's in a flurry of halter tops, hot pants, and go-go boots. When given freedom of choice, women often proved incapable of picking clothes which were either practical or flattering.

Like the fiery launch of a Redstone rocket, a new group of personalities burst onto the world scene. An English rock group with the unlikely name, the Beatles, quickly began to dominate popular music, starting a craze for "mod" clothes and longer hair. Charlie Brown, Snoopy, and the Peanuts Gang livened up the comic strips with the homespun wit of cartoonist, Charles Schultz. Of course, few people could hope to equal the adulation lavished on the astronauts of Projects Mercury, Gemini, and Apollo.

To some people, the 1960's were a time of miracles (man first set foot on the surface of the moon and the lowly New York Mets finally won the World Series); to others, however, the real miracle lay in the fact that somehow, amidst the chaos, civilization had managed to survive at all. America has found herself in many difficult situations in the quarter of a century since 1960: strikes, riots, the end of an undeclared war, and the resignation of a President. In psychedelic flashes, we have been buffeted by beehive hairdos and love beads, disco and designer label clothing --- and we have prevailed; there can be no more eloquent testimony to the resilience of the human spirit.

1960 RECIPES

WARM DRIED BEEF DIP

8 oz. creamed cheese
2 Tbsp. milk
¾ cup dried beef, chopped
1 Tbsp. minced onion
2 Tbsp. chopped green pepper
¼ tsp. seasoned pepper
½ cup sour cream
¼ cup sliced almonds

Blend the cream cheese and milk. Mix in all the other ingredients. Put in a casserole and warm in the oven at 350 degrees for 15 minutes, or until hot.

Mrs. Stephen (Susan) Weaver
From her mother,
Mrs. Eleanor Carr

ARTICHOKE DIP

½ cup (or more) chopped artichoke hearts
½ cup Parmesan cheese
½ cup mayonnaise

Mix the ingredients together thoroughly. Place in an oven-proof bowl. Bake at 350 degrees for 15 minutes. Serve with crackers.

Mrs. Claude (Mary) Renshaw

MEXICAN PARTY DIP

Spread on a large serving platter:
1 (8 oz.) can bean dip

Add in layers:
1 cup guacamole
2 cups sour cream

Sprinkle with:
Dry taco seasoning
2 Tbsp. chopped onions
2 Tbsp. chopped green chilies
½ cup chopped tomatoes
Salt and pepper

Top with:
1 cup shredded Monterey Jack or Colby cheese
Sliced black or green olives

Chill: Serve with taco chips.

Mrs. Michael (Sharon) Love
From her sister,
Mrs. Mark (Teresa) Hildebrand

HOT CRAB MEAT DIP

Combine:
1 8-oz. pkg. softened cream cheese
1 Tbsp. milk
1 6½-oz. can flaked crab meat
½ tsp. cream style horseradish
2 Tbsp. finely chopped onion
¼ tsp. salt and pepper

Blend together all ingredients with a mixer. Then add ½ cup toasted almonds. Bake at 375 degrees for 15 minutes. Serve hot in a chafing dish with crackers.

Mrs. John (Jane) Olcott

CONBOY'S WONDER DIP

1 pt. sour cream
1 pt. mayonnaise
3 Tbsp. onion flakes
3 Tbsp. parsley flakes*
2 Tbsp. dill seed
2 Tbsp. Beau Monde (Spice Island)

Mix the ingredients together in a blender; the dip should be the consistency of sour cream. Chill. The dip keeps well in the refrigerator for 2-3 weeks. Great for "veggies" or chips.
*(Ed: Fresh parsley may be substituted for the parsley flakes, and if dill seed can not be found, use dill weed.)

Mrs. John N. (Muriel) Perkins
From her neighbor,
Mrs. James Conboy

SALMON CHEESEBALL

1 1-lb. can red salmon, drained (remove skin and bones)*
1 (8-oz.) pkg. cream cheese
1 Tbsp. lemon juice
2 tsp. grated onion
1 tsp. horseradish
¼ tsp. salt
¼ tsp. liquid smoke
Parsley, fresh or dried
Pecans or walnuts

Soften the cream cheese and combine it with all the other ingredients except the parsley and nuts. Mix well. Chill several hours. Combine the parsley and nuts; coat the shaped salmon. Chill well.
*Use red salmon only. Pink salmon is less expensive, but it gives a flat taste.

Mrs. Eric (Faye) Philippsen

ZESTY SHRIMP AND ARTICHOKE HEARTS

1 15-oz. can artichoke hearts
25 medium-size shrimp, cooked and cleaned
1 egg yolk
¾ cup oil
¼ cup red wine vinegar
2 Tbsp. Dijon mustard
2 Tbsp. fresh chopped parsley
2 Tbsp. chopped chives
1 Tbsp. minced shallots or green onions
Salt and pepper to taste

1. Cut the artichokes and shrimp into bite-size pieces.
2. Combine the egg yolk, oil, vinegar, and mustard in a bowl; beat well.
3. Gently stir in the artichokes and shrimp. Add the other ingredients.
4. Marinate in the refrigerator for at least 2 hours, stirring occasionally.
5. Before serving, drain off the marinade. Serve with toothpicks or on melba toast rounds. Serves 8.

Mrs. John (Virginia) Lionberger, Jr.

BACON-WRAPPED WATER CHESTNUTS

24 pieces water chestnuts (canned)
2 Tbsp. light brown sugar
8 strips bacon

Drain the canned water chestnuts until very dry. Mix with the brown sugar. Cut each bacon strip into three sections. Wrap the bacon around a water chestnut and attach both ends with a tooth pick. Roast the wrapped water chestnuts in a hot oven (425 degrees) for 15 minutes or until the bacon is golden brown. Serve hot.

Jeannie Tiniti

CHILI

3 lbs. hamburger
3 Tbsp. chili powder
3 tsp. salt
1½ tsp. sugar
1½ cup onion, chopped
3 cans (15 oz.) tomato sauce
1½ cups water
1 or 2 cans kidney beans
Garlic to taste

Brown the meat and onion. Pour off the grease. Add the remaining ingredients and cook for 1 hour over low heat.

Mrs. Patrick (Sharon) Deneen

Busy Christmas shoppers hurry across Michigan Street — 1972.

PIQUANT COCKTAIL MEAT BALLS

2 lbs. ground beef round
1 cup packaged corn flake crumbs
⅓ cup dried parsley flakes (you may also use fresh parsley)
2 eggs
2 Tbsp. soy sauce
¼ tsp. pepper
½ tsp. garlic powder
⅓ cup catsup
2 Tbsp. instant minced onion (fresh minced onion may also be used)
1 can (1 lb.) jellied cranberry sauce
1 bottle (12 oz.) chili sauce
2 Tbsp. firmly packed brown sugar
1 Tbsp. lemon juice

Preheat the oven to 350 degrees.
In a large bowl, combine the ground beef, corn flake crumbs, parsley flakes, eggs, soy sauce, pepper, garlic powder, catsup, and minced onion; blend well. Form into small meat balls, about the size of walnuts. Arrange the meat balls in a 15½ x 10½ x 1-inch pan.
In a medium-size saucepan, combine the cranberry sauce, chili sauce, brown sugar, and lemon juice. Cook over moderate heat, stirring occasionally, until the mixture is smooth and the cranberry sauce is melted. Pour over the meat balls.
Bake, uncovered, for 30 minutes. Serve in a chafing dish with toothpicks. Makes about 60 meatballs.

These meat balls are also an excellent choice for luncheons, picnics, or family gatherings.

Mrs. Harrison (Lola) Lyons

1960 RECIPES

Mrs. Mullins, the Executive Director of the Northern Indiana Historical Society, enjoys entertaining, but her responsibilities seem to leave her very little time to cook. Sweet & Sour Sausage Balls are easy to prepare and make an excellent addition to any buffet table. Mr. and Mrs. Mullins serve these tangy meatballs in an elegant chafing dish for their Christmas Open House.

SWEET & SOUR SAUSAGE BALLS

2 lbs. hamburger
2 lbs. Italian sausage*
4 eggs, slightly beaten
1½ cups soft bread crumbs
Fresh parsley and garlic salt to taste

Mix and shape into balls about 1 inch in diameter. Bake at 350 degrees until done; drain. Makes 150 balls.

SAUCE:
3 cups catsup
¾ cup brown sugar
½ cup white vinegar
½ cup soy sauce

Combine the sauce ingredients. Pour over the meatballs and cook for 30 minutes. Stir occasionally.

If made ahead, freeze the meatballs in the sauce. Reheat in a 350 degree oven until heated through.

*If you desire, you may use 4 lbs. of sausage instead of half sausage and half hamburger.

Mrs. James (Kathleen Stiso) Mullins

PERFECT EGGNOG

Combine in a <u>large</u> punch bowl:
2 qts. milk
4 cups sugar
Add:
12 beaten egg yolks
Slowly add:
1 cup brandy
2 cups rum
3 cups bourbon*
To this, fold in:
12 egg whites, beaten stiff
3 cartons (½ pint) whipped cream (sweetened with
3 tsp. sugar)

Sprinkle with **freshly grated nutmeg** and chill overnight.

*If you want to make Rudolph's nose glow a little brighter this holiday season, double the brandy, rum, and bourbon.

Mrs. Michael (Sharon) Love
From her sister,
Mrs. Mark (Teresa) Hildebrand

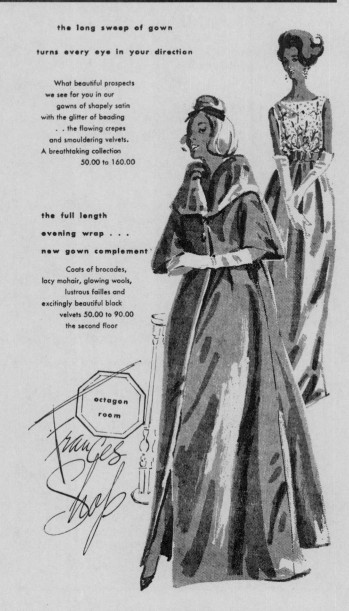

The South Bend Tribune, November 17, 1963

IRISH CREAM LIQUEUR

¼ Tbsp. coconut extract
1 8-oz. can Eagle Brand milk
1 pt. whipped cream
2 Tbsp. chocolate syrup
1½ cups cheap brandy

Mix together. Will keep 4-5 weeks in the refrigerator. Very rich.

Mrs. John (Jane) Olcott

INTER-CONTINENTAL PATE

3 Tbsp. unsalted butter
2 small white onions, chopped
1 Tbsp. dried rosemary, crumbled
1½ tsp. salt
1½ tsp. freshly ground white pepper
1½ tsp. ground thyme
½ tsp. dried basil, crumbled
½ tsp. nutmeg
1 lb. 3 oz. chicken livers, washed, trimmed,
    and patted dry
1¾ cups (3½ sticks) unsalted butter,
    at room temperature
1½ hard cooked eggs
2 Tbsp. Cognac
2 Tbsp. dry Sherry
1 Tbsp. chopped fresh parsley

Preheat the oven to 400 degrees F.
Melt 3 Tbsp. butter in a large ovenproof skillet over medium heat. Add the onion, rosemary, salt, pepper, thyme, basil, and nutmeg; saute until the onion is soft, about 10 minutes.
Add the chicken livers to the skillet and saute until browned, about 5 minutes. Transfer the skillet to the oven and bake until the livers are cooked through, about 5-8 minutes. Remove from the oven and let cool completely.
Mix 1¾ cups butter in a food processor until light and fluffy. Add the liver mixture, egg, Cognac, Sherry, and parsley; puree until smooth. Transfer to serving dishes or crocks. Chill until firm about 2 hours or overnight. Makes about 4½ cups.
Serve with French bread and thinly sliced dill pickle.

Mrs. John C. (Jan) Frieden

CLAM CHOWDER

2 cups potatoes, pared and cubed
½ cup onion, chopped
½ cup celery, chopped
1 cup water
1 tsp. salt
Dash of pepper

Cook the above until the potatoes are done, about 10 minutes. Mash a little and add:
1 cup milk
1 can Manhattan style clam chowder
1 (7½ oz.) can minced clams and juice
½ cup wine
½ cup whipping cream

Heat until warm. You may put parsley on top for garnish.

Mrs. A.J. (Sarah) Paul

TOMATO CELERY SOUP

1 small chopped onion
2 Tbsp. butter
1 10½-oz. can tomato soup
1 tsp. minced parsley
⅛ tsp. pepper
½ cup finely chopped celery
1 Tbsp. lemon juice
1 tsp. sugar
¼ tsp. salt
1 soup can water

Saute the onion and celery in butter; do not brown. Add the tomato soup, water, parsley, lemon juice, sugar, salt, and pepper. Simmer for 5 minutes (the celery will remain crisp). Top with unsweetened whipped cream and parsley.

Mrs. Stephen (Sharon) Gumz

Gold-colored, sparkle-plastic or jeweled eyeglass frames are correct for evening wear. The latter should not be so ornate that they steal the show from your other jewelry.

To give hair height, it should be teased only at the roots, close to the scalp. Leave the ends, which are more easily damaged, smooth.

In 1984, Mr. Casaday very generously donated a large portion of his historic costume collection to the Northern Indiana Historical Society. He has been a major influence on theatrical life in Northern Indiana for half a century.

BROCCOLI SOUP

1 10-oz. pkg. chopped broccoli
6 cups water
¾ cup chopped onion
2 tsp. salt
2 chicken bouillon cubes
8 oz. pkg. American cheese (2 cups)
2 cups milk

THICKENING:
¼ cup butter, melted
¼ cup flour
½ cup cold water

Cook the broccoli, onion, salt, and chicken bouillon cubes together in the 6 cups of water until the broccoli is tender. (Do not drain.) Add the milk and heat through. Mix together the thickening ingredients and add to the soup. Stir well. Run the soup through a blender. Add the cheese and cook until melted.

Mr. James Lewis Casaday

1960 RECIPES

My daughter needed a lavender punch to serve at a bridal shower. She hit upon this recipe which is good tasting as well as pretty.

LAVENDER & OLD LACE PUNCH

2 cups water
6 inches of cinnamon stick
¼ tsp. cloves
Boil, cool, and strain. Add:
4 cans frozen grape juice, undiluted
½ cup lime juice

Pour all the ingredients over ice in a punch bowl. Just before serving add **2 quarts of ginger ale.**

Mrs. Charles (Wava) Apelgreen
From her daughter,
Mrs. Sue Leber

VEGETABLE BEEF SOUP

Soup bones, about 1 lb.
3 lbs. beef, cut into pieces
6 cups water
2 cups tomato juice
2 large onions
1 Tbsp. salt
2 tsp. Worcestershire sauce
½ tsp. chili powder
2 bay leaves
1 cup celery, diced
1 cup carrots, diced
1 cup potatoes, diced
1 cup cabbage, diced

Brown the beef in a small amount of oil. Add the bones, water, tomato juice, onion, and seasonings; cover and simmer for 2 hours. Add the vegetables (more water and/or tomato juice may have to be added before cooking the vegetables). Cover and simmer until done. This recipe can be doubled or tripled with ease.

Mrs. David (Margie) Canfield

ORANGE SHERBET SALAD

1 pkg. (6 oz.) orange jello
2 cups boiling water
1 pt. (16 oz.) orange sherbet
1 large can Mandarin oranges

Dissolve the jello in the boiling water. Add the sherbet and stir. Add the Mandarin oranges. Refrigerate.
Whipped cream and nuts on the top make it good.

Mrs. John R. (Virginia) Lionberger, Jr.

This wonderful, hearty soup comes from the Stanley Clark School's "Old Fashioned Day" lunch. The bean mixture makes a terrific gift giving idea; drop 2 cups of beans into a pretty calico bag and include a copy of the recipe.

CALICO BEAN SOUP

BEAN MIXTURE - one pkg. each:
Yellow split peas
Green split peas
Blackeye peas
Black beans
Red kidney beans
Navy beans
Pinto beans
Great Northern beans
Baby lima beans
Large lima beans
Pearled barley
Combine and store for future use.

TO MAKE THE SOUP:
Wash **2 cups of beans** thoroughly. Place in a large kettle. Cover with water. Add **2 Tbsp. salt** and soak overnight. Next day, add **2 quarts of water**, a **small bay leaf, 1 lb. of ham**, and a **ham bone**. Simmer 2½-3 hours.

ADD:
1 finely cut or shredded potato
1 cup finely cut celery
1 large chopped onion
1 large grated carrot
1 8-oz. can Spanish style tomato sauce
1 16-oz. can tomatoes
1 large pod red pepper (optional)
Salt and pepper
¼ tsp. thyme
1 Tbsp. sugar
Juice of 1 lemon

Simmer another 60 minutes. Make 8 servings.

Mrs. John C. (Jan) Frieden

SAN FRANCISCO SALAD

2 qts. mixed salad greens (at least half spinach)
1 can (11 oz.) **Mandarin oranges, drained**
1 cup sliced fresh mushrooms
½ cup **Wish-Bone Italian Dressing**
1 can **Durkee's French Fried Onions**

In a salad bowl, arrange the salad greens, oranges, and mushrooms. Chill. Just before serving, toss with the Italian dressing and onions. Makes 6-8 servings.

Mrs. Walton (Carol) Collins

POTATO SOUP WITH RIVALS

5 medium potatoes, peeled and diced
1 small onion, chopped
1 clove garlic, finely chopped
¾ cup flour
1 egg
2 cups milk
1 large can evaporated milk
2 Tbsp. butter
3 tsp. salt
½ tsp. pepper
Chopped parsley, to taste

Cook the potatoes with just enough water to cover. Add the onion and garlic.

Mix the flour and egg together with the fingers until the mixture is crumbly.

Add the milk to the cooked potatoes (do not drain the water off of the potatoes). Add the butter, salt, and pepper. Roll the rival mixture (blend of flour and egg) in your hand and allow small pieces to crumble off into the soup. Simmer until done, about 10 minutes. If the soup is too thick, add more milk.

Garnish with parsley.

Mrs. David (Margie) Canfield

MOLDED GAZPACHO ASPIC

2 envelopes unflavored gelatin
3 cups tomato juice (or half tomato juice and half Snap-E-Tom)
¼ cup wine vinegar
1 clove garlic, crushed
¼ tsp. pepper
Dash of cayenne
¼ cup chopped cucumber
¼ cup chopped pimiento
2 large tomatoes, chopped
½ cup chopped onions
¼ cup chopped green pepper

Soften the gelatin in 1 cup cold tomato juice, then heat until it simmers. Add the rest of the juice, the vinegar, garlic, pepper, and cayenne. Cool in the refrigerator until slightly thickened. Add the remaining ingredients. Pour into a 6 cup mold. (A lightly oiled Bundt pan makes a pretty mold.)

DRESSING:
Mix together:
  ¼ cup sour cream
  ¼ cup mayonnaise
  ½ tsp. salt
  1 tsp. horseradish

Mrs. John C. (Jan) Frieden
From her Gourmet Lunch Group

CHERRY SALAD SUPREME

1 pkg. (3 oz.) raspberry flavored gelatin
1 can (21 oz.) cherry pie filling
1 pkg. (3 oz.) lemon flavored gelatin
1 pkg. (3 oz.) cream cheese
⅓ cup mayonnaise or salad dressing
1 can (8¾ oz.) crushed pineapple - (1 cup)
½ cup whipping cream
1 cup miniature marshmallows

Dissolve the raspberry gelatin in **1 cup boiling water;** stir in the pie filling. Turn into a 9 x 9 x 2-inch baking dish and chill until set. Dissolve the lemon gelatin in **1 cup boiling water.** Beat together the cream cheese and mayonnaise. Gradually add the lemon gelatin. Stir in the undrained pineapple. Whip ½ cup whipping cream; fold into the lemon mixture with 1 cup miniature marshmallows. Spread atop the cherry layer and top with **2 Tbsp. chopped nuts.** Chill until set. Makes 12 servings.

The sweetness of the bottom layer is balanced by the tartness of the top.

Cheryl Haas

TO RESTORE OLD LINENS OR REMOVE DIFFICULT STAINS
(FOR WHITE FABRIC ONLY)

Mix together 2 gallons warm water, 1 cup automatic dishwasher detergent and 1 cup liquid bleach. Soak item (s) until desired whiteness is attained. Launder as usual, then add ½ cup white vinegar to the final rinse.

Mrs. J. Bruce (Sue) Wagner

FRUIT SALAD

1 lb. white grapes
1 large can chunky pineapple, drain and save the juice for the dressing (cut the chunks into smaller pieces)
¼ lb. walnuts
30 small marshmallows
Sliced bananas
Mandarin oranges

DRESSING:
  2 whole eggs, well beaten
  1 Tbsp. flour
  1 Tbsp. vinegar
  A little salt
  Reserved pineapple juice
  Sugar to taste
  Lump of butter

Cook the dressing ingredients until thick. Cool. Add to the fruit and blend. Chill and serve. (Add the walnuts right before serving or they will darken the color of the salad.)

Mrs. Rose Cira

CREAMY ZUCCHINI SOUP

4 cups chicken broth
6 medium zucchini, diced
13 oz. heavy cream or 1 can (13 oz.) **evaporated milk**
1 tsp. onion salt
1 tsp. celery salt
¼ tsp. thyme
Salt and pepper to taste
Sprigs of fresh parsley (for garnish with each serving)

Combine the chicken broth and zucchini in a large saucepan. Cover and cook over medium heat for about 15 minutes, or until zucchini is tender. Cool. Pour in small quantities into a blender jar and puree. Return to the saucepan. Add the cream or milk, onion salt, celery salt, thyme, salt and pepper. Heat to steaming and add additional seasonings, if desired. Garnish and serve. (DO NOT BOIL; this would cause the soup to curdle.)

Mrs. Glenn (Fannie Mae) Stoneburner

CRANBERRY FLUFF

2 cups raw cranberries, ground
3 cups tiny marshmallows
¾ cup sugar

Combine the above ingredients using the juice and all from the cranberries. Chill overnight. The next day add to the above:
2 cups diced, unpared tart apples
½ cup seedless green grapes
½ cup broken walnuts
¼ tsp. salt
1 cup cream, whipped

Fold all together and chill. This can be used as a dessert or salad. Serves 16.

Mrs. Daniel W. Fowler

SPAGHETTI SALAD

1 lb. spaghetti (cooked, drained, and cooled)
1 large bottle Wish-bone Italian salad dressing
½ jar Supreme Salad Seasonings
1 red onion
1 green pepper
2 tomatoes, diced
1 avocado

Marinate the spaghetti in Italian salad dressing, salad seasoning, onion, and green pepper overnight. Just before serving, add the tomatoes and avocado.

Mrs. Walton (Carol) Collins

TOMATO SOUP ASPIC

2 Tbsp. unflavored gelatin
½ cup cold water
1 can tomato soup
3 3-oz. pkgs. cream cheese
1 cup chopped celery
½ cup chopped green pepper
½ cup chopped stuffed olives
1 heaping Tbsp. grated onion
2 Tbsp. lemon juice
1 cup mayonnaise
1 Tbsp. Worcestershire sauce
1 or 2 tsp. Tabasco (to taste)
Salt to taste

Soften the gelatin in cold water. Heat the soup in a double boiler, then add the cream cheese. Whip with a rotary egg beater until smooth. Add the gelatin. Stir until dissolved. Cool, then add the other ingredients. Pour into an oiled mold or utility dish. Chill until firm. Serves 8-12.

Mrs. Lester C. (Beth) Lamon

CAROLINA COLESLAW

1 large cabbage (about 3 lbs.), **trimmed, quartered, and cored**
1 medium sweet green pepper, cored, seeded, and minced (for color ½ green pepper and ½ sweet red pepper may be used)
1 medium sweet onion (Bermuda or Spanish), **peeled and chopped fine**

DRESSING:
1 cup sugar
1 tsp. salt
1 tsp. dry mustard
1 tsp. celery seed
1 cup cider vinegar
⅔ cup vegetable oil

With a sharp knife, slice each cabbage quarter very fine. Combine with the green pepper and onion in a large bowl and toss to mix.

Mix the sugar, salt, mustard, and celery seed in a small saucepan. Add the vinegar and oil and let come to a boil over moderate heat, stirring until the sugar dissolves. Pour over the cabbage and toss well to mix. Cool to room temperature. Cover and refrigerate until ready to serve.

I have kept this coleslaw for 2 months in the refrigerator, and it was still good and crisp.

Mrs. Patrick (Sharon) Deneen

TAFFY APPLE SALAD

Bowl I:
>   **1 large can** (20 oz.) **pineapple chunks** (drain
>   and retain the juice)
>   **2 cups miniature marshmallows**
Mix and cover; refrigerate overnight.

Bowl II:
>   **Pineapple juice** (from the pineapple chunks)
>   **1 Tbsp. flour**
>   **1½ Tbsp. white vinegar**
>   **½ cup sugar**
>   **1 egg, beaten well**
Mix together. Cook till thick and refrigerate overnight.

Mix together in a large bowl:
>   **3 cups diced apples** (do not peel)
>   **1 (8 oz.) container Cool Whip**
>   **1½ cup Spanish peanuts** (use salted or
>   unsalted, to taste)

Add the contents of Bowls I and II to the apple mixture.
Mix and refrigerate at least 6 hours. Serves 12-15.

Mrs. A.J. (Sarah) Paul

---

*If a dress absolutely requires a slip (otherwise why wear
one?) get a bra-slip. Think in terms of eliminating extra
layers, cutting down the bulk of your undergarments and
freeing as much skin as possible.*

FROZEN COLESLAW

1 medium cabbage, shredded
1 tsp. salt
1 carrot, grated
1 green pepper, chopped

Mix the salt with the cabbage. Let stand for 1 hour and
then squeeze out the excess moisture. Add the carrot and
green pepper. While the cabbage is standing, make the
dressing.

DRESSING:
>   **1 cup vinegar**
>   **¼ cup water**
>   **1 tsp. mustard seed**
>   **1 tsp. celery seed**
>   **2 cups sugar**

Boil the dressing ingredients for 1 minute; cool. Pour the
dressing over the slaw mixture. Cover and freeze in pint
containers.

Mrs. Charles (Wava) Apelgreen

BEST-EVER MACARONI SALAD

4 cups cooked elbow macaroni
½ cup cut-up scallions (tops included)
6 sliced radishes
2 Tbsp. minced parsley
1 cup mayonnaise
4 chopped hard boiled eggs
2 Tbsp. vinegar
2 tsp. prepared mustard
½ tsp. celery seed
1½-2 tsp. salt
⅛ tsp. pepper

Combine all ingredients and chill.

Mrs. Patrick (Sharon) Deneen

---

*My sister-in-law presented her Broccoli Salad for the first
time a few years ago at our family's Christmas gathering.
Besides being a very attractive dish, the blend of flavors is
fantastic, especially for us broccoli lovers.*

BROCCOLI SALAD

1 lb. fresh broccoli, washed and chopped
1 small red onion, chopped
1 cup sunflower seeds
½ lb. bacon, fried crisp and chopped
½ cup raisins
Layer in a bowl. Cover and refrigerate.

SAUCE:
>   **1 cup mayonnaise**
>   **¼ cup sugar**
>   **1 tsp. salt**
>   **1 Tbsp. vinegar**
Mix. Add to vegetables when ready to serve.

Jerry and Sheri Wiener
From Gae Wiener

FIRE AND ICE SALAD

2 large sweet Spanish onions, sliced in rings
6 large firm, ripe tomatoes, peeled & cut into wedges
1 green pepper, cut into strips
¾ cup cider vinegar
¼ cup water
1½ tsp. celery salt
1½ tsp. mustard seed
½ tsp. salt
2 Tbsp. sugar
¼ tsp. coarsely ground pepper

Place the prepared vegetables in a shallow bowl. Mix the remaining ingredients in a saucepan. Bring to a boil and boil hard for 1 minute. Pour while hot over the vegetables. Chill for several hours. Serve.

Mrs. Stephen (Susan) Weaver
From her mother,
Mrs. Eleanor Carr

TACO TOSSED SALAD

SALAD:
1 medium head lettuce, washed, drained, and chilled
1 medium bunch Romaine lettuce, washed, drained, and chilled
1 small bunch green onions, chopped with tops and all
2 medium tomatoes, cut into wedges (slice thinly)
1 thinly sliced ripe avocado (optional)
Tear lettuce into bite-sized pieces; put into a large bowl (or clean dish pan). Set aside or place in the refrigerator.

SALAD DRESSING:
1 lb. lean ground beef
½ cup finely chopped onion (not green onions)
1 envelope taco seasoning
1 small can (8 oz.) tomato sauce
Brown the meat, breaking apart any large clumps. Add the onions and cook until they "wilt." Add the seasoning and tomato sauce and set aside to cool.

EXTRAS:
1 cup shredded cheddar cheese
2 cups crushed corn chips
1 can kidney beans, drained and chilled
Remove the lettuce from the refrigerator and add the chopped green onions and the thinly sliced tomato wedges. (If avocado is used, add it now.) Add the corn chips and kidney beans. Toss the salad with your fingers; be gentle. Finally add the cooled meat mixture and toss again lightly. Transfer the salad to a serving dish and top with the shredded cheese. Serves 4-6.

Cheryl Haas

BROCCOLI MARINADE

1 lb. fresh mushrooms, sliced
1-1½ bunches broccoli (flowerets only)
2 chopped green onions

DRESSING:
1 tsp. salt
½ cup sugar
1 tsp. paprika
1 tsp. celery seed
1 Tbsp. onion powder
¾ cup oil, plus ¼ cup wine vinegar

Let the dressing stand for 1 hour before putting it on the salad. Do not let the dressing stand on the vegetables for more than an hour before serving or the vegetables become soggy. 8-10 servings.

Mrs. Herb (Betty Ann) True

SPINACH SALAD

1 lb. fresh spinach
12 strips bacon
2 cloves garlic
10 slices stale French bread, cubed
½ cup chopped pecans

Shred the spinach. Fry the bacon until crisp; drain and chop it. Use the bacon grease (to which the garlic has been added) to fry the bread cubes. After frying, place the croutons on a paper towel to drain. Toss the spinach, pecans, and bacon with the dressing and top with the croutons.

DRESSING:
1 cup virgin olive oil
⅓ cup raspberry vinegar
1 Tbsp. Dijon mustard
1 Tbsp. peanut butter (smooth)
2 garlic cloves, crushed
¼ tsp. salt
1 tsp. sugar
Freshly ground pepper

Blend together.

Mrs. David (Stephanie) LaDow

REFRIGERATOR ROLLS

CREAM:
    ½ cup sugar
    ½ cup butter

ADD:
    2 eggs
    1½ tsp. salt
    1 cup cold water
    1 cup scalded milk
    2 pkg. yeast in ¼ cup warm water

Stir in **3 cups unsifted flour.** Beat hard as you add **3 more cups unsifted flour.** Cover in the same bowl. Put in the refrigerator.

When ready to use, punch down and let the dough rest for 5 minutes. Shape as desired. (Mrs. Purucker makes cloverleaf rolls.) Place in well-greased cupcake pans. Let them rise until doubled, about 2 hours. Bake at 400 degrees for 10-12 minutes.

Mrs. Ervin (Doris) Purucker

HILARY'S COFFEECAKE

    ¼ cup sugar
    1 tsp. cinnamon
    2 cups flour
    1 cup sugar
    1½ tsp. baking powder
    1 tsp. soda
    1¼ tsp. salt
    1 tsp. vanilla
    ½ cup margarine
    2 eggs
    1 pt. sour cream
    ¼ cup chopped nuts
    6 Heath bars (coarsely crushed)
    ¼ cup butter, melted

Grease and flour a bundt pan. Combine ¼ cup sugar and the cinnamon. Set aside.

In a large bowl combine the remaining ingredients, except for the nuts, candy, and ¼ cup butter. Blend at low speed until the ingredients are moistened, then at medium speed for 3 minutes.

Spoon half of the batter into the pan. Sprinkle with 2 Tbsp. of the cinnamon-sugar mixture, then with half of the nuts and crushed candy bars. Cover with the remaining batter. Pour ¼ cup melted butter over the batter, then sprinkle with the remaining candy and nuts, and the cinnamon-sugar mixture.

Bake at 325 degrees until the top springs back and the sides are loosened from the pan (45 to 60 minutes -- nearer 60 minutes, really). Cool for 15 minutes and sprinkle with powdered sugar, if desired. Reheat and serve the second day.

Mrs. A.J. (Sarah) Paul

Judging begins on the Union Township entries for the 1962 St. Joseph County 4-H Fair. (L to R): Mrs. Esther Singer, Mrs. Hazel Burnett, Beverly Geyer, Becky Beach, and Judy Howell.

Courtesy of the St. Joseph County Extension Office.

Mrs. White has fond childhood memories of this coffee cake. It was passed down to her by her mother who acquired the recipe from a close friend in her bridge club.

STREUSEL COFFEE CAKE

    1 cup margarine
    2 cups sugar
    2 eggs
    1 cup sour cream
    1 tsp. vanilla
    2¼ cups sifted flour
    1 tsp. baking powder
    ¼ tsp. salt

Cream together the margarine and sugar. Add the eggs. Fold in the sour cream, vanilla, flour, baking powder, and salt. Pour half the batter into a greased tube pan. Top with half the streusel mixture. Add the rest of the batter and sprinkle with the remaining streusel mixture. Bake in a 350 degree oven for 1 hour or until done.

STREUSEL MIXTURE:
    Mix together:
    ½ cup brown sugar
    2 Tbsp. flour
    2 tsp. cinnamon
    2 Tbsp. melted margarine
    ½ cup chopped nuts

Mrs. Daniel E. (Nancy) White

1960 RECIPES

GREEN TOSSED SALAD

1 head romaine, torn in pieces
1 head Boston bibb lettuce
1 tomato, chopped
1 can hearts of palm, drained and halved
1 can artichoke hearts, drained and halved

LEMON MUSTARD DRESSING:
  6 Tbsp. oil
  2½ Tbsp. fresh lemon juice
  1 tsp. sugar
  1 tsp. salt
  ½ tsp. freshly ground pepper
  ½ tsp. Dijon mustard
  1 small garlic clove, crushed

Combine all the dressing ingredients in a bowl and whisk well.

Combine the lettuce and tomato in a large salad bowl and toss. Add the hearts of palm and artichokes; toss again. Just before serving, pour the dressing over the salad and toss well.

Mrs. David (Stephanie) LaDow

SWEET BANANA BREAD

2 pkg. active dry yeast
5½ to 6 cups sifted all-purpose flour
¾ cup milk
½ cup butter or margarine
½ cup sugar
1 tsp. salt
2 eggs
2 ripe bananas, mashed (1 cup)

Combine the yeast and 2 cups of the flour. Heat together the milk, butter, sugar, and salt till just warm, stirring occasionally to melt the butter. Add this mixture to the dry ingredients. Add the eggs and banana. Beat for 30 seconds at low speed of the electric mixer, scraping the sides of the bowl. Beat for 3 minutes at high speed. By hand, stir in enough of the remaining flour to make a moderately stiff dough. Turn out onto a lightly floured surface. Knead until smooth, 5-8 minutes. Place in a lightly greased bowl, turning once. Cover and let rise until double, about 1 hour. Punch down. Cover and let rest for 10 minutes.

Divide the dough in half. Shape into 2 round loaves; place on greased baking sheets. Make vertical cuts about ⅛-inch deep around each loaf at ¾-inch intervals. Slightly beat **1 egg white** with **1 tsp. water.** Brush over the entire surface of the loaves. Let rise again until double, 30-45 minutes. Bake in a 400 degree oven for 30 minutes.

You may need to bake the loaves slightly longer (5 to 10 minutes). For a softer crust, cover the bread with a dish towel while the bread cools.

Cheryl Haas

WILTED LETTUCE SALAD

4 cups head lettuce, in bite-size pieces
2 cups fresh young spinach
4 Tbsp. sliced green onion
2 hard boiled eggs
12 strips of bacon, crumbled
     (reserve ¼ cup bacon drippings)
¼ cup vinegar
1 Tbsp. water
½ tsp. salt
1 tsp. sugar
1 avocado

Combine the lettuce and spinach in a salad bowl. Add the onion. Slice the hard boiled eggs and add along with the crumbled bacon.

Add the vinegar, water, salt and sugar to the ¼ cup of bacon drippings. Bring to a boil and pour over the salad. Slice the avocado and add to the salad. Toss gently and serve.

Mrs. Philip (Patricia) Potts

GLAZED ORANGE ROLLS

1 cup milk
3 Tbsp. butter
½ cup sugar
½ tsp. salt
1 pkg. yeast
3 eggs
4½ cups flour
6 Tbsp. butter, softened
½ cup sugar
1½ tsp. shredded orange peel
2 cups sifted confectioner's sugar
3 - 4 Tbsp. orange juice

Scald the milk; place in a bowl with 3 Tbsp. butter, ½ cup sugar, and salt. Cool to lukewarm. Add the yeast. Let stand for 3 minutes. Add the eggs and 1 cup flour; beat well. Add enough flour to make a moderately stiff dough, beating well. Turn out onto a floured surface; knead till smooth and satiny, about 10 minutes. Place in a greased bowl, turning to coat the surface. Cover. Let rise till double, about 2 hours. Divide the dough in half; roll each to 12 x 8-inches. Stir together the softened butter, ½ cup sugar, and orange peel; spread over the dough. Roll up, starting with the long side; seal seams. Slice each into 18 rolls. Place in greased (2½ inch) muffin pans (or use three 9-inch round pans.) Let rise till double, about 1½ hours. Bake at 375 degrees for 15 minutes. Combine the confectioner's sugar and enough orange juice to make of glaze consistency. Drizzle over the warm rolls.

Cheryl Haas

JEAN GAST'S SPECIAL CHICKEN SALAD

3 cups chicken, cut into large cubes (I use 6 large chicken breast halves baked in butter)
½ cup blanched and toasted almonds
½ cup green seedless grapes, sliced in half
¾ cup chopped celery

DRESSING:
½ tsp. salt
¾ cup Miracle Whip
1½ tsp. vinegar
Scant ½ tsp. sugar

Mix the ingredients for the dressing and toss with the first four ingredients.

VARIATIONS:
⅔ cup candied dills
3 hard cooked eggs
½ cup pineapple tidbits

Sometimes I use pineapple and grapes together. I personally don't like the candied dills and hard cooked eggs in the salad quite as well.

Mrs. Thomas (Jean) Gast

CRAB MEAT SALAD

1 cup crab meat
½ cup sliced water chestnuts
1 cup celery, sliced
½ cup slivered almonds
3 Tbsp. mayonnaise
Lemon juice
½ tsp. curry powder
Salt and pepper

Toss all ingredients together and serve on a bed of crisp lettuce with a side dish of sliced fresh strawberries. Serves 4.

Mrs. Claude (Mary) Renshaw

HONEY-ORANGE DRESSING
(For Fruit)

2 Tbsp. honey
2 Tbsp. orange juice
1 cup sour cream
Grated orange rind

Blend the honey and orange juice; gently fold into the sour cream. Chill. Garnish with orange rind.

Mrs. Walton (Carol) Collins

WESTERN STYLE DRESSING

1 cup Wesson oil
1 tsp. salt
1 clove garlic, minced
½ cup sugar
¼-½ cup vinegar
1 tsp. pepper
1 tsp. paprika
½ tsp. dry mustard
1 medium onion, grated
1 tsp. Worcestershire sauce
1 can tomato soup

Put all the ingredients into a quart jar and shake well. Keep refrigerated.
(It is best to try ¼ cup vinegar first. Taste and add more if you wish.)

Mrs. Melvena Whitaker

OLIVE OIL DRESSING

⅓ cup olive oil
1 Tbsp. cider vinegar
1 Tbsp. lemon juice
¼ tsp. dry mustard
¼ tsp. salt
¼ tsp. pepper
1 clove garlic, crushed (or ½ tsp. garlic powder)

Blend all the ingredients in a blender or shake vigorously. Let sit, the longer the better.

Mrs. John N. (Muriel) Perkins
From her daughter,
Mrs. John Luttrell

BRAN MUFFINS

MIX TOGETHER:
1 15-oz. box Raisin Bran flakes
5 cups flour
3 cups sugar
5 tsp. soda
ADD:
1 qt. buttermilk
4 eggs, beaten
1 cup melted shortening or oil

Bake in muffin cups at 375 degrees for 15-20 minutes. Makes 4 dozen muffins. (The batter may be kept in the refrigerator for several weeks and baked as needed.)

Mrs. Frank (Maureen) Sindlinger

BUTTERMILK SWEET ROLLS

2 pkgs. dry yeast
½ cup warm water
1¼ cups buttermilk
2 eggs
5½ - 6 cups flour
½ cup butter or margarine, softened
½ cup sugar
2 tsp. baking powder
2 tsp. salt

Dissolve the yeast in warm water in a bowl. Add the buttermilk, eggs, 2½ cups flour, the margarine or butter, sugar, baking powder, and salt. Blend for 30 seconds on low speed, scraping the bowl. Beat for 2 minutes on medium speed. Stir in the remaining flour to make the dough easy to handle.

Turn onto a well-floured board; knead for 5 minutes or about 200 turns. Roll the dough out to about ¼ inch thickness. Spread softened **butter** onto the dough. Spread **⅓ cup sugar** and **2 tsp. cinnamon** onto the dough. Sprinkle with a little water.

Roll like a jelly roll and cut into 1-inch pieces. Place into prepared pans:

In a 13 x 9 x 2-inch pan, melt **½ cup margarine.** Add **1 cup brown sugar, 4 Tbsp. corn syrup,** and **1 tsp. maple flavoring,** then mix. Add **1 cup chopped nuts** and spread the mixture evenly over the pan.

In an 8 x 8 or 9 x 9-inch pan do the same: **¼ cup margarine, ½ cup brown sugar, 2 Tbsp. corn syrup,** and **½ tsp. maple flavoring.** Add **½ cup chopped nuts;** spread the mixture evenly over the pan.

Let the dough rise for 1 hour, covered. Bake at 375 degrees for about 25 - 35 minutes. (You may want to let them rise a little longer than called for; the longer they rise, the fluffier they are.)

Mrs. Eric (Faye) Philippsen
From her friend,
Mrs. Paul (Ellen) Cahill

These muffins may take some time to prepare, but they are well worth the effort. Mrs. Haas acquired the recipe for Virginia Orange Blossoms from a steward after they were served at a tea for naval wives in San Diego.

VIRGINIA ORANGE BLOSSOMS

Make the coating before making the muffins.

COATING:
Mix **2¾ cups sugar** and the **grated rind and juice from 2 oranges and 2 lemons.** Stir frequently while making the muffins.

MUFFINS:
To **3 well-beaten egg yolks** gradually add **1⅓ cups sugar,**

then **½ cup cold water** and **1 tsp. vanilla.** Sift together 3 times: **1½ cup sifted cake flour, ½ tsp. salt,** and **1½ tsp. baking powder.** Fold the dry ingredients into the egg mixture. Fold in the **stiffly beaten whites of 3 eggs.** Fill greased tiny muffin tins half full and bake at 400 degrees for 15 minutes till delicately brown. Remove from the pans and dip in the coating while still warm. Let stand on wire racks to drain over night. Makes about 50 tiny tea muffins (about 1¼ inch in diameter).

These may be made 2 days before needed since the crystallized coating keeps the sponge cake fresh.

Cheryl Haas

PEANUT BRITTLE COFFEECAKE

2 cups Bisquick mix
1 cup finely crushed peanut brittle (about 5 oz.)
¼ cup packed brown sugar
¼ tsp. cinnamon
¼ tsp. nutmeg
2 Tbsp. margarine
⅔ cup buttermilk or soured milk
1 slightly beaten egg
1 tsp. vanilla

In a bowl, combine the Bisquick, peanut brittle, brown sugar, cinnamon, and nutmeg. Cut in the margarine until crumbly. Set aside ⅓ of the mixture. Add the buttermilk, egg, and vanilla to the remaining mixture; mix well. Spread in a greased 9-inch round cake pan. Sprinkle the top with the reserved crumbs. Bake in a 350 degree oven for 35 to 45 minutes, or until done. Cool in the pan on a rack. Yields 6 - 8 servings.

Mrs. Maxine Bowers

BAKING POWDER BISCUITS

2 cups flour
3 tsp. baking powder
½ tsp. salt
6 Tbsp. butter
¾ cup milk (approx.)

Sift the dry ingredients into a bowl. Cut in the butter until it's the size of peas. Stir in the milk. Place on a floured board and knead 3 or 4 times. Press out with your hands (make the dough about 1 inch thick). Cut with a biscuit cutter or glass. Bake on a baking sheet in a 450 degree oven for 12 minutes.

Mrs. Stephen (Sharon) Gumz

Otis R. Bowen and his wife, Beth, occupied a special place in Hoosier hearts during his two terms as governor of Indiana from 1973-1981. He was, without doubt, one of the most popular governors in the State's 171 year history.

BETH BOWEN'S BLUEBERRY MUFFINS

1½ cups flour
½ cup sugar
3 tsp. baking powder
½ tsp. salt
Mix together:
1 egg, well beaten
½ cup milk

Stir the egg mixture into the dry ingredients. Just before completely blended, add ¼ cup melted shortening. Add 1 cup fresh or frozen blueberries. Pour into baking cups (paper) or greased muffin tins. Bake at 400 degrees for 20-25 minutes. Makes 12 muffins.

Mrs. Stephen (Sharon) Gumz

OVERNIGHT CASSEROLE

10 slices bread, buttered
3 cups grated cheese (1¼ lbs.)
2 good cups milk
4 eggs
1 tsp. salt
Scant tsp. dry mustard

Butter a very large casserole. Sprinkle with some of the cheese and some of the bread pulled apart into fine pieces. Alternate layers of cheese and bread with the cheese on the top and bottom. Mix the remaining ingredients and pour over the cheese-bread layers. Let stand in the refrigerator over night. Before baking, allow the casserole to warm to room temperature. Bake in a 350 degree oven for 1 hour.

Mrs. Mary Jo Hruska

BRAN MUFFINS

Pour 1 cup boiling water over 1 cup All-Bran; let stand.
½ cup margarine
1 cup sugar
Cream the margarine and sugar; add 2 beaten eggs.
Add the cooled bran along with 2 cups of buttermilk.
2½ cups sifted flour
2½ tsp. soda
½ tsp. salt
Add 2 cups of All-Bran. Fold in. Bake the muffins in a 400 degree oven for 20 minutes.

Mrs. Ervin (Doris) Purucker

ZUCCHINI BREAD

3 eggs
2 cups sugar
1 cup vegetable oil
2 cups raw zucchini, peeled and grated
3 tsp. vanilla
3 cups flour
1 tsp. salt
1 tsp. baking soda
½ tsp. baking powder
3 tsp. cinnamon
1 cup coarsely chopped walnuts

Beat the eggs until light and foamy. Add the sugar, oil, zucchini, and vanilla; mix lightly, but well. Combine the flour, salt, baking soda, baking powder, and cinnamon. Add to the egg-zucchini mixture. Stir until well blended; add the walnuts and pour into two greased 9 x 5 x 3-inch loaf pans. Bake for 1 hour at 350 degrees. Makes 2 loaves.

Mrs. Ronald (Georgianne) Compton

CREAMED MUSHROOMS, PEAS, AND WATER CHESTNUTS

2 Tbsp. each butter and flour
½ tsp. salt
⅛ tsp. nutmeg.
Dash of pepper
1 can (3 oz.) mushroom crowns, undrained
Half & Half or milk
1 pkg. (10 oz.) frozen peas, cooked and drained
1 can (5 oz.) water chestnuts, drained and halved

Melt the butter in a saucepan. Stir in flour, salt, nutmeg, and pepper. Drain the broth from the mushrooms; add enough Half and Half or milk to make 1 cup. Gradually add to the flour mixture. Cook, stirring constantly, until thickened. Add the mushrooms, peas, and water chestnuts. Heat through.

Cheryl Haas

1960 RECIPES

Swiss farmers served fondue to make use of their leftover cheese and stale bread. Today, fondue parties fit perfectly into America's more casual style of entertaining. Just keep in mind, however, that the first one to lose his bread in the fondue pot must buy the wine for the next party.

SWISS CHEESE FONDUE

1 lb. Emmenthaler cheese (large holes)
½ lb. Gruyere cheese (medium holes)
¼ lb. Tilsiter cheese (small holes)
1½ cups Rhine wine
1 Tbsp. cornstarch
Dash of pepper
Freshly grated nutmeg, to taste
1 oz. Kirsch
Bread cubes (Beef stick cubes also work well)

Place the cheese in a ceramic fondue pot. (Do not use a metal pot. A heavy metal pan may be used if it holds and conducts heat evenly. Use a heat defuser for the top of the stove.) Add the wine. Cook over medium heat, stirring constantly, until the mixture becomes creamy and thick (bubbling). Add the cornstarch, pepper, and nutmeg. Lastly, add the kirsch. Put the fondue pot on its burner and set it on the table, ready to serve. With fondue forks, dip the bread cubes into the cheese mixture. Serves 4.
(Important: Use only imported cheese.)

Mrs. Margaret Lamb

Don't be put off because of the onions. This delicious cheesey casserole would be a perfect side dish with chicken or charcoal-grilled steaks.

ONION CASSEROLE

5 large white onions, sliced and sauteed until tender
1 cup cubed cheddar or Monterey Jack cheese
5 slices buttered toast, cut into cubes.

Mix the above ingredients and put into a buttered casserole. Add the following sauce:
¼ cup flour
¼ cup butter
2 cups milk
¼ tsp. salt

Make a white sauce by melting the butter in a pan. Add the flour and stir. Slowly add the milk, stirring constantly. Bring to a boil to thicken. Add the salt. Add a little of the white sauce to **2 beaten eggs;** blend the egg mixture into the white sauce and mix well. Pour this sauce over the onions, cheese and toast. Bake for 45 minutes at 350 degrees.

Mrs. Arthur (Emma) Schlorch

POTATO CHEESE BAKE

8 medium potatoes
½ cup minced onion
1 cup Miracle Whip (mayonnaise)
Salt and pepper to taste
Velveeta cheese

Boil the potatoes in the jackets; when done, peel and dice. Place in a 9 x 13-inch baking pan. Mix in the onion. Add the salt and pepper. Spread the Miracle Whip over the potatoes and toss. Top with a layer of cheese. Bake in a 350 degree oven until the cheese melts and browns slightly.

Mrs. David (Christine) Bainbridge

You can't beat this yummy souffle for brunch, luncheon, or a simple supper. Because it's more substantial than most souffles, you don't have to worry about it taking a dive at an inopportune moment, and any leftovers can be frozen for future use.

CHEESE SOUFFLE

¾ lb. (12 oz.) **Monterey Jack cheese, shredded**
1 cup Bisquick
½ cup milk
4 eggs, beaten
¾ stick of butter, melted
3 Tbsp. cottage cheese
Salt and pepper

Mix the ingredients and pour into a buttered 3-qt. souffle dish. Bake in a 350 degree oven for 45 minutes.

Mrs. Michael (Sharon) Love

CORN PUDDING

2 cups corn
2 Tbsp. flour
1 tsp. salt
3 Tbsp. butter
3 whole eggs
2 Tbsp. sugar
1¾ cups milk

Blend the butter, sugar, flour, and salt. Add the eggs, beating well. Stir in the corn and milk. Pour the ingredients into a buttered casserole and bake for 45 minutes at 325 degrees. Stir once half way through the baking time. When done, the pudding will be golden brown and a silver knife inserted will come out clean.
This can be prepared ahead of baking and kept in a jar in the refrigerator. Just shake well and pour into a baking dish.

Mrs. Stephen (Sharon) Gumz

The Farmer's Market has been a South Bend landmark since the early days of the community when farmers brought their produce into town and sold it from the backs of their wagons.

TACO PIE

2 lbs. ground beef
1 cup chopped onion
2 env. Taco seasoning
1 4-oz. can green chilies, drained
2 cups shredded Monterey Jack cheese
3 cups milk
1½ cups Bisquick
6 eggs, slightly beaten

Grease a 9 x 13-inch pan or Pyrex dish. Brown the ground beef and onion; drain the fat. Add the Taco seasoning and mix. Press the meat mixture evenly into the pan. Add the chilies and sprinkle the cheese evenly over all.

Mix the milk, Bisquick, and eggs. Pour this mixture over the meat and cheese (this will be very runny). Bake for 40 minutes in a 400 degree oven (375 degrees for a Pyrex dish) or until a knife comes out clean. Let stand to cool somewhat and then cut into squares. Serve in the center of a plate; people can then add their own toppings.

TOPPING:
Shredded lettuce, chopped tomatoes, onions, black or green olives, avocado or guacamole, hot sauce, shredded cheddar cheese, kidney beans, drained and washed, **sour cream,** and **crushed Doritos or nachos.**

Really load on the toppings.

Mrs. Patrick (Sharon) Deneen

ZUCCHINI & TOMATO CASSEROLE

4 medium zucchini, washed and quartered
3 medium tomatoes, peeled and cut into wedges
    lengthwise
1 medium white onion, sliced
½ cup cracker crumbs
1 cup grated sharp cheese
1 tsp. salt
Pepper, oregano, savory
¼ cup butter
½ Tbsp. brown sugar

Alternate layers of zucchini, tomatoes, and onion in a buttered casserole, sprinkling each layer with crumbs, cheese, and seasonings to taste. Dot each layer with butter. Sprinkle the brown sugar over the tomato layers. The top layer should be cheese. Cover and bake in a 350 degree oven for 60 minutes. Uncover and bake 15 minutes longer.

Mrs. Herb (Betty Ann) True

SOUR CREAM NOODLE CASSEROLE

1 8-oz. pkg. medium noodles
1 lb. ground beef
2 Tbsp. butter
1 tsp. salt
½ tsp. pepper
¼ tsp. garlic salt
1 8-oz. can tomato sauce
1 cup creamed style cottage cheese
1 cup sour cream
½ cup chopped onions
¾ cup shredded sharp cheddar cheese

Cook the noodles in boiling salted water according to package directions. Rinse and drain. In a skillet, brown the meat in butter. Add the salt, pepper, and garlic salt, then the tomato sauce. Simmer for 5 minutes.

Combine the cottage cheese, sour cream, chopped onions, and noodles. Pour into a 2-qt. casserole; top with the meat mixture. Sprinkle the shredded cheese on top. Bake at 350 degrees for 25-30 minutes. Serves 6.

This dish can be frozen. It is best made the day before.

Mrs. Lester (Beth) Lamon
From Mrs. Frank H. Luton of Nashville, Tenn.

CREAMED SPINACH

Cook **1 box (10 oz.) frozen spinach** with **4 - 5 strips of bacon.** When tender, cut up or run through a food chopper. Return to the pan and add **½ cup whipping cream or sour cream, ½ tsp. nutmeg, salt and pepper.** Simmer until the flavors mingle and the liquid cooks down.

(Chopped frozen spinach and chopped bacon may also be used at the beginning.)

Jerry and Sheri Wiener

My family always asks me to make my Sweet Potato Casserole for Thanksgiving dinner. Many people comment that this dish tastes almost like a dessert; people who don't usually like sweet potatoes always seem to like this casserole. People ask to take the leftovers home with them.

SWEET POTATO CASSEROLE

3 cups mashed sweet potatoes
1 stick butter or margarine (½ cup)
1 tsp. vanilla
1 cup sugar
2 eggs, beaten

Mix the ingredients together with an electric mixer on low speed until well blended. Pour into a greased rectangular baking pan.

TOPPING:
⅓ cup flour
⅓ cup butter or margarine
1 cup brown sugar
⅓ cup milk
1 cup chopped nuts

Mix the topping ingredients together with an electric mixer on low speed until well blended. Spread evenly on top of the potato mixture. Bake at 325 degrees for 30 - 40 minutes or until set in the center.

Mrs. Karen Keller

VARIATION:

BUTTERNUT SQUASH CASSEROLE

Substitute **3 lbs. of butternut squash** (peeled, cooked, and mashed) for the sweet potatoes. Mix the **⅓ cup milk** with the squash, **sugar, eggs, vanilla,** and **margarine.** Make a topping of **1 cup light brown sugar, ⅓ cup flour, 1 cup chopped pecans,** and **⅓ cup margarine.** Bake at 350 degrees for 80 - 90 minutes. (Cover with foil if the squash begins to get too brown on top.) Serves 6 - 8.

Jennifer Warlick

BROCCOLI SOUFFLE

2 pkgs. frozen broccoli
4 Tbsp. margarine
¼ cup chopped onion
2 Tbsp. flour
¼ cup water
8 ounces Cheese Whiz
3 eggs, well beaten

TOPPING:
¼ cup melted oleo
¾ cup Italian bread crumbs

Thaw and drain the broccoli. Brown the onions in margarine. Add the flour and stir. Remove from the heat, add water and stir. Heat until thick. Remove from the heat, add cheese and stir. Butter a 2 qt. casserole and fill with the broccoli mixture. Fold in the eggs. Spread on the topping. Bake uncovered at 350 degrees for 45 minutes.

Mrs. Robert (Helen) Veith

TOMATO CASSEROLE

2 (15 oz.) **cans stewed tomatoes**
½ cup dark brown sugar
1 cup Croutettes stuffing cubes
1 Tbsp. Worcestershire sauce (or more to taste)
Salt and pepper to taste
3 Tbsp. butter

Mix 1 can drained tomatoes and 1 can undrained tomatoes with the rest of the ingredients, except the butter. Place in a 2 quart buttered baking dish. Dot with butter and bake at 350 degrees for 45-60 minutes.

Mrs. Donald (Elie) Olson

TURNIPS WITH ONIONS

6-8 small white turnips
3 medium onions, sliced
¼ cup butter
Salt
Black pepper

Peel and cut the turnips into ½ inch slices. Cook in boiling, salted water for 10-15 minutes, or until just tender. Drain. Cook the onions in butter over medium heat until lightly browned. Add to the turnips.

Mrs. Eveline O'Neal
From her daughter,
Brenda O'Neal

BROCCOLI CASSEROLE

2 pkg. frozen broccoli (whole or cut)
1 can cream of mushroom soup (undiluted)
½ cup mayonnaise
1 Tbsp. lemon juice
½ cup sharp cheese, grated
1 jar (2 oz.) **pimento, chopped**
1 cup crushed cheese crackers
½ cup toasted almonds or pecans

Arrange the cooked broccoli in an oblong casserole. Mix the soup, mayonnaise, and lemon juice; spoon over the broccoli. Top with the crushed crackers, cheese, pimento, and nuts. Bake at 350 degrees for 20 minutes. Serves 8.

Mrs. Ronald (Pat) Olsen
From her daughter-in-law,
Mrs. Ronald (Karla) Olsen, Jr.

GREEN RICE

2 cups Minute Rice (4 cups cooked)
1(8 oz.) jar Cheese Whiz
1 stick butter (½ cup)
¾ cup celery, chopped
¾ cup onion, chopped
1 lb. broccoli, cooked
2 cans mushroom soup

Cook the rice following package directions. Pour the Cheese Whiz over the hot rice.

Saute the onions and celery in the butter and combine with the rice. Add the cooked broccoli. Stir in the mushroom soup. Bake in a 350 degree oven for 1 hour.

Mrs. Stephen (Sharon) Gumz

SWEET POTATO AND CELERY STUFFING

4 cups cooked, mashed sweet potatoes
5-6 stalks of celery, chopped
2 Tbsp. oil
1 onion, chopped
2 cups fresh white bread crumbs

Heat the oil and fry the onion and celery until soft. Stir the celery mixture into the sweet potatoes; add the bread crumbs. Season with **sage** and plenty of **salt** and **pepper.***

*(Ed: if you wish to bake the stuffing outside the turkey or chicken, grease a large casserole and bake for about 1 hour at 375 degrees.)

Mrs. Eveline O'Neal
From her daughter-in-law,
Janice Odom

CORNED BEEF CASSEROLE

1 pkg. (8 oz.) **elbow macaroni**
1 can (12 oz.) **corned beef, chopped**
¼ lb. cubed yellow cheese (5-6 slices of American cheese works just as well)
1 can (10½ oz.) **cream of chicken soup** (I like to use cream of celery soup - it's not quite so rich.)
1 soup can of milk
½ cup chopped onions (optional)
¾ cup buttered bread crumbs

Cook the macaroni in salted water according to package directions, drain and rinse. Combine the remaining ingredients except the bread crumbs. Alternate the soup mixture with layers of macaroni in a greased 2 qt. casserole. Top with the bread crumbs. Bake in a 375 degree oven for about 45 minutes. Serves 4-6.

Mrs. Lee (Jill) Brummett

VEGETABLE MEDLEY

2 10-oz. pkgs. frozen mixed vegetables
½ cup finely chopped celery
2 cans (10¾ oz.) **condensed cream of celery soup**
½ tsp. seasoned salt
1 pkg. toasted onion soup mix
½ cup water
2 Tbsp. melted butter

Combine all the ingredients except the vegetables in a crock pot. Stir well. Add the frozen mixed vegetables and cook on low for 4-6 hours, or on high for 2 hours. Stir well before serving.

This may also be made on top of the stove. Cook over low heat and stir frequently to prevent sticking. Serves 6.

Mrs. Karen Keller
From her sister-in-law,
Freda Carlson

MIXED VEGETABLE DISH

2 boxes mixed vegetables (frozen) - cook in a little salted water and drain.

Mix the vegetables with **1 can of mushroom soup** and put into an 8 x 11½-inch greased casserole.

Cover with **sliced Velveeta cheese.** Pull apart slices of **soft bread** (crumbs made from about 3 slices of bread works well) and put the crumbs on top of the cheese layer.

Pour **1 stick of melted butter** over all.

Bake in a 350 degree oven for 20 minutes.

Mrs. Margaret W. Wilder

Protesters gathered outside the St. Joseph County Courthouse in the early 70's to voice their opinion of the latest efforts to end the war in Vietnam.

BUCKEYE CORNED BEEF

3½ lb. corned beef brisket
2 bay leaves
6 peppercorns
Cold water to cover

Rinse the corned beef and place in a large pot; cover with water. Slowly bring this to a boil. After 5 minutes, skim and add the bay leaves and peppercorns. Cover the pot and simmer for about 3-4 hours until tender. Remove the meat from the water. Trim off any fat and stud with **whole cloves.**

SAUCE:
5 Tbsp. catsup
2 Tbsp. oil
1 Tbsp. prepared mustard
⅓ cup brown sugar
3 Tbsp. cider vinegar

Mix all the ingredients together in a small pan. Cook for about 5 minutes. Spread the sauce over the brisket and bake at 350 degrees for about 30 minutes.

Mrs. Bipin (Linda) Doshi

RICE DELICIOUS

1 stick oleo (½ cup)
1 medium can water chestnuts
1 4-oz. can mushrooms
1 can onion soup
1 cup Uncle Ben's raw rice

Slice the water chestnuts and mushrooms, saving the liquid; saute in the oleo. Combine the sauteed vegetables, onion soup, rice, and **1 soup can of water** (use the liquid from the nuts and mushrooms). Put in a covered casserole. Bake at 300 degrees for 1 hour.

Mrs. Thomas (Jean) Gast

This recipe is the first thing I ever cooked for my husband. When I can't think of the name of it, I call it "Imitation Beef Wellington" because really that's what it is. It's easy, but looks like you fussed over it.

CONTINENTAL STEAK ROLLS
With Sour Cream Sauce

1 lb. round steak or 4 4-oz. minute steaks (I prefer the minute steaks)*
¼ cup flour
¼ tsp. salt
⅛ tsp. pepper
2 Tbsp. butter
3 Tbsp. finely chopped onion
3 Tbsp. finely chopped mushrooms (use fresh mushrooms)
1 can crescent dinner rolls

Cut the steak into 4 pieces (if using round steak). Coat with a mixture of flour, salt, and pepper. Brown in butter. Remove from the pan. Saute the mushrooms and onions in the same pan. Divide the mixture into quarters and place on one end of the browned meat. Fold the other end over. Unroll the crescent dough leaving 2 triangles joined to form a rectangle (there will be 4). Press the perforations together to seal. Place the prepared meat in the center of each rectangle. Fold up the sides of the dough and seal tightly in the center. Place seam side down on a cookie sheet and bake at 400 degrees for 10-12 minutes. Serve with Sour Cream Sauce. Makes 4 servings.
*(Ed: When using round steak, it may be necessary to pound the meat to flatten it.)

SOUR CREAM SAUCE:
1 cup dairy sour cream
1 Tbsp. butter
½ tsp. chopped chives
¼ tsp. salt

Heat, but do not boil. Serve hot.

Mrs. Karen Keller

CALICO BEANS

½ lb. bacon, diced
1 lb. hamburger
¾ cup brown sugar*
1 tsp. salt
1 tsp. dry mustard
1 Tbsp. vinegar
½ cup catsup
1 onion, diced
1 can (15 oz.) butter beans
1 can (15 oz.) red beans
2 cans (16 oz.) pork and beans, partially
   drained

Fry the bacon until crisp; remove from the pan. In the bacon fat, brown the hamburger and onion. Drain. Mix with the remaining ingredients and bake in an ungreased casserole for 40 minutes in a 350 degree oven.

*(Ed: For diabetics, omit the brown sugar and substitute 3 tsp. Sweet 'N Low brown sugar substitute. This makes a fine side dish [somewhat like baked beans] or a main dish. You might want to omit some of the brown sugar if you wish to serve it as an entree.)

Mrs. John (Millie) Yoder

CAROLINE'S BAKED RICE CASSEROLE

Saute:
   2 Tbsp. butter
   3 tsp. chopped onion
   2 cups chopped celery

Mix together in a 1½ or 2 qt. casserole:
   1 can (10¾ oz.) cream of mushroom soup
   1 can (10¾ oz.) cream of chicken soup
   1 can beef consomme
   ¾ cup regular rice
   1 tsp. poultry seasoning
   Salt to taste
   1 can (4 oz.) chopped mushrooms with juice

Add the onions and celery to the mixture in the casserole. Bake covered for 30 minutes in a 350 degree oven.
Add:
   1 cup slivered almonds (browned in butter)

Bake uncovered for 15 minutes longer. Let stand for 10-15 minutes to thicken before serving. Serves 6-8. This is good with any chicken recipe.

Mrs. John N. (Muriel) Perkins

KARABAKH LOBY
(Russian Beans)

1 lb. string beans, ends removed
4 Tbsp. butter
2 cups chopped onion
1 medium green pepper, chopped
3 medium tomatoes, peeled, seeded, and chopped
1 heaping Tbsp. sweet basil
1 egg
1 cup sour cream
1 tsp. salt
Freshly ground black pepper

Bring 3 quarts of salted water to a boil. Add the beans; bring to a boil and cook over low heat, uncovered, for 8-10 minutes or until the beans are tender but still firm. Drain the beans and pour cold water over them; set aside.

Melt the butter in a large skillet; add the onions and green pepper. Cook until tender, but not brown. Stir in the tomatoes and basil. Boil rapidly for 1-2 minutes until most of the juices have evaporated. Stir in the green beans and simmer until heated through.

Beat together the egg, sour cream, salt and pepper. Stir into the vegetable mixture; heat and transfer to a serving bowl.

(Canned green beans may be used. Do not boil them, just add them to the melted butter and proceed with the recipe. This is also excellent without the sour cream and egg mixture.)

Mrs. David (Margie) Canfield

PIZZA CASSEROLE

1 lb. sausage
1 lb. ground pork
1 green pepper, diced
1 medium onion, diced

Saute the above and then add:

2 15-oz. cans pizza sauce
½ tsp. oregano
¼ tsp. Italian seasoning
Garlic salt to taste.

Simmer for 10-15 minutes.

Cook and drain 7-oz. of macaroni. Mix 1 beaten egg with ¾ cup milk and add to the macaroni; mix well.

In a 9 x 13-inch dish, put ⅓ of the meat mixture. Layer with the macaroni mixture, 1 cup shredded mozzarella cheese, 6 slices of American cheese, and the remaining meat mixture. Top with Parmesan cheese and bake at 350 degrees for 30 minutes (uncovered).

Mrs. Patrick (Sharon) Deneen

1960 RECIPES

ROUND STEAK CASSEROLE

1 round steak
1 can cream of mushroom soup
1 can French fried onion rings
1 can mushrooms, drained

Trim as much fat as possible from the round steak and remove the bone. Cut the round steak into slices, squares, or chunks. Place the meat into a casserole dish. Add the soup, onion rings, and mushrooms. Mix to coat the meat. Cover and bake for 1 hour in a 350 degree oven.

This will make its own gravy. Serve over rice or noodles or with potatoes.

Mrs. David (Christine) Bainbridge

SWISS BLISS

2 lbs. chuck steak, cut 1½ inches thick
1 can (1 lb.) tomatoes, drained (save the juice)
1 envelope onion soup mix
1 can (4 oz.) sliced mushrooms, drained
½ cup green pepper, diced
1 Tbsp. steak sauce
1 Tbsp. chopped parsley

Cut the steak into serving size pieces and arrange in a 3 qt. casserole.

Drain the tomatoes, reserving the juice, and arrange over the steak.

Sprinkle the soup mix, mushrooms, and green pepper over the tomatoes.

Combine the reserved tomato juice with the remaining ingredients and pour over all.

Cover and bake for 2 hours at 350 degrees.

Mrs. Charles (Wava) Apelgreen

FAMILY ROUND STEAK DINNER

Cut **round steak** into 4-6 pieces. Pound the meat on both sides. Combine **½ cup flour, 1 tsp. salt,** and **¼ tsp. pepper;** coat the steaks. Brown a **clove of garlic** in **2 Tbsp. of hot fat;** remove the garlic and brown the steaks. Place the browned steak in a casserole and sprinkle lightly with **basil.** Add **¼ cup water.** Cover and bake at 350 degrees for 1 hour.

Top the meat with a layer of **sliced onions** and a layer of **1-inch thick potato slices.** Sprinkle with **salt, pepper,** and **seasoning salt.**

Stir **1 Tbsp. flour** into the hot fat in which the steak was browned. Add bouillon, made by dissolving **1 bouillon cube** in **1 cup of hot water.** Cook, stirring until thickened. Pour over the steak and vegetables. Cover and bake at 350 degrees for 1 hour.

Mrs. Eleanor Carr

SWEDISH MEATBALLS
With Red Sauce

1½ lbs. hamburger
1 cup bread crumbs
1½ tsp. salt
2 eggs
4 Tbsp. onions chopped
2 Tbsp. melted butter
¼ tsp. pepper
⅛ tsp. nutmeg
1 Tbsp. flour
½ cup cream
1 Tbsp. brown sugar

Combine all the above ingredients. Mix well and form into bite-size balls. Brown them in a 375 degree oven for about 30 minutes (an ungreased 15½ x 10½ x 1-inch jelly roll pan or cookie sheet works well for this).

RED SAUCE:
3 small cans (8 oz.) tomato sauce
¾ cup brown sugar
3 Tbsp. cider vinegar
½ stick butter
½ cup onion, chopped

Brown the onions in the butter. Add the other ingredients and simmer for 20 minutes. Put in the meatballs and serve warm.

Mrs. Bipin (Linda) Doshi

SCALLOPED EGGPLANT OR ZUCCHINI

1 medium eggplant or zucchini
3 tomatoes, peeled and chopped
1 small onion, chopped
1 small green pepper, chopped
1 Tbsp. brown sugar
1 tsp. salt
3 Tbsp. butter
¼ cup flour
1 cup fine bread crumbs
2 Tbsp. butter

Pare the eggplant (or zucchini) and cut into cubes. Cook in boiling salted water for 7 minutes. Mix the tomatoes, onion, green pepper, brown sugar, and salt. Melt the 3 Tbsp. butter in a heavy pan; blend in the flour. Add the vegetable mixture. Cook 5 minutes, stirring constantly. Place the eggplant (or zucchini) in a buttered baking dish; pour the tomato mixture on top. Sprinkle with bread crumbs and dot with the 2 Tbsp. butter. Bake for 20-30 minutes at 350 degrees. Serves 6.

Mrs. A.J. (Sarah) Paul

SHIRLEY'S LIMA BEANS

2 pkgs. (10 oz.) **frozen baby limas**
1½ lbs. **fresh mushrooms**
1 **onion, chopped fine**
½ cup **cream** (or Half and Half)
10 stalks **celery, cut into ½ inch pieces**
½ lb. **butter or margarine**
2 Tbsp. **flour**
½ tsp. **salt**
Pepper
Jigger of sherry

Cook the beans according to package directions. Saute the onions, and celery in the butter; add the mushrooms. Cook till tender. Sprinkle in the flour, salt, and pepper; blend well. Remove the pan from the stove and stir in the cream. Add the beans. Mix and put in a casserole. Just before warming, drizzle with sherry.

Mrs. Philip (Patricia) Potts

GOOD & SIMPLE CHICKEN

2 **fresh** (not frozen) **fryers, about 3 lbs. each**

Clean the chickens and pat dry inside and out with paper toweling. Let the chickens stand until room temperature. Pat again to remove any moisture.

Pre-heat your oven to 450 degrees. Take a small amount of oil and rub it all over the outside of the birds. **Salt** and **pepper** the birds inside and out. Put the chickens in a shallow roasting pan and roast at 450 degrees for 1 hour to 1 hour and 15 minutes. When done, remove from the oven and let the chickens set for 10-20 minutes before carving.

The chickens will have a very crisp skin and the leftovers are great for sandwiches.

Mrs. David (Stephanie) LaDow

This recipe came directly from Los Angeles via a good friend who served it when we visited there about ten years ago.

CALIFORNIA CHICKEN

2 **chicken breasts**
2 **legs and thighs** (joined together)
½ cup **melted butter or margarine**
½ cup **honey**
¼ cup **prepared mustard**
1 tsp. **curry powder**
Salt to taste

Bone and skin the chicken. Mix the other ingredients until smooth; pour this mixture over the chicken and bake in a glass baking dish for 1-1½ hours in a 350 degree oven. Baste frequently.

Mrs. Glenn (Fannie M.) Stoneburner

Hong Kong Steak is a favorite of the more affluent Oriental families everywhere. It requires a bit of bottled Oyster Sauce, a popular sauce in the East. If you haven't already done so, buy a bottle and start enjoying this rare treat. It's available in Chinatown and Oriental stores; it keeps almost forever.

HONG KONG STEAK

4 **filet mignon steaks, thick-cut**
4 strips **bacon**
1 Tbsp. **sweet butter**
1 clove **garlic, smashed**
3 **green onions, chopped fine**
1 Tbsp. **soy sauce**
2 Tbsp. **Oyster Sauce**
1 tsp. **MSG** (Accent)
3 Tbsp. **Sake** (Japanese Rice wine) **or sherry**
1 tsp. **powdered ginger**
1 **chicken bouillon cube**
½ cup **boiling water**
1 tsp. **cornstarch**
1½ tsp. **sugar**

Put the bacon around the outside of the steaks; fasten with toothpicks. Set aside on a broiler pan. Saute the onions and garlic in the butter for 2 minutes. Stir in the soy sauce, Oyster Sauce, sugar, MSG, sake or sherry, ginger, bouillon cube, and water. Blend well. Stir in the cornstarch, a little at a time, to blend. Cover and simmer for 5 minutes, until the sauce thickens. Broil the steaks to the desired doneness. Slice each steak into 3 pieces and place on 4 servings dishes. Spoon the sauce over the steaks and serve hot. Serves 4.

M.E. Parrott

This elegant poultry dish was served at the 1981 Renshaw family reunion in Sarasota, Florida.

TIA'S YUMMY CHICKEN MARSALA

¼ cup (½ stick) **butter**
2 cloves **garlic**
2 cups **fresh mushrooms**

Saute the mushrooms and garlic until soft (separately).

4 **chicken breasts,** skinned and boned (cut into cutlets).

Dredge the cutlets in **four, salt,** and **pepper.** Brown in butter (after sauteeing the garlic and mushrooms).

Mix all together, adding **Marsala, Madeira,** or **Sherry** wine (sweet) to taste (½-1 cup) Serves 4.

Mrs. Claude (Mary) Renshaw
From her sister-in-law,
Christina Renshaw

SAUSAGE CASSEROLE

1 lb. sausage
3 ribs celery
1 small green pepper
1 medium-size onion
1 pkg. dehydrated chicken noodle soup
1 small can mushrooms
½ cup uncooked rice

Cook the sausage until done. (Break it into small pieces as it cooks.) Remove the sausage from the pan and drain. Cook the vegetables in the sausage drippings. Mix the sausage and vegetables with the rice. Add the package of noodle soup and the mushrooms. Add **2½ cups of hot water** and mix well. Pour into a 2-qt. casserole and bake at 350 degrees for 40 minutes. Serves 6.

Mrs. Lester (Beth) Lamon
From her mother,
Mrs. Kenneth Luton
of Knoxville, Tennessee

PORK CUTLETS & SOUR CREAM SAUCE

1 pork tenderloin, sliced about ½ inch thick
Salt and pepper to taste
1 tsp. sweet or medium paprika
2 Tbsp. butter
2 Tbsp. oil
¼ cup finely chopped onion
½ cup dry white wine
½ cup chicken broth
½-¾ cup sour cream

Pound the meat. Sprinkle with salt, pepper, and paprika. Saute in the butter and oil until browned and cooked. Transfer the meat to a platter. Pour off the excess fat and add the onions to the skillet. Cook until wilted. Add the wine and deglaze the pan. Add the chicken broth and simmer for 5 minutes. Remove the sauce from the heat and add the sour cream. Put through a fine sieve and pour over the meat.

Mrs. David (Stephanie) LaDow

OPEN-FACE SHRIMP SANDWICHES

1 can (5 oz.) small shrimp, drained and rinsed
1 cup celery, sliced
¼ cup mayonnaise
Salt and pepper
Softened butter
3 English muffins, split
3 slices mozzarella cheese, cut in triangles
6 tomato slices

Mix the first 3 ingredients and season with salt and pepper. Butter the English muffins and spread with the shrimp mixture. Put a cheese triangle on each and put under the broiler until the cheese melts. Top each with a tomato slice and serve. Makes 6.

Mrs. Mary Jo Hruska

HOT CHICKEN SALAD

2 cups cooked chicken, cubed
2 cups celery, thinly sliced
1 cup toasted bread cubes (or stuffing mix)
1 cup mayonnaise
½ cup toasted chopped almonds
2 Tbsp. lemon juice
2 tsp. grated onion
½ tsp. salt

½ cup shredded cheddar cheese
1 cup toasted bread cubes

Heat the oven to 450 degrees. Combine all the ingredients except the cheese and 1 cup bread cubes. Pour the mixture into a baking dish and sprinkle with the cheese and the remaining bread cubes. Bake for 10-15 minutes or until bubbly. This is a great luncheon dish.

Mrs. Mary Fischer
From a friend in Niles, Michigan

BAKED BONELESS CHICKEN IN SAUCE

Chicken breasts, boned
Ham, thinly sliced
Bacon strips
1 cup sour cream
1 can (10¾ oz.) cream of mushroom soup (or cream of chicken)
Sherry to taste
Worcestershire sauce, to taste
Pepper
Slivered almonds

Bone the chicken breasts. Take several slices of ham (3 or 4) and lay the chicken on top of them. Wrap strips of bacon around the chicken and ham. Place in a casserole dish. Blend together the sour cream, soup, sherry, and Worcestershire sauce. Pour over the chicken. Sprinkle with pepper and slivered almonds. Bake in a 325 degree oven for 2 hour (or a 300 degree oven for 3 hours).

Quantities are flexible and can be adjusted to the number of people to be served. There is plenty of sauce for 4 or 5 whole chicken breasts.

Mrs. Claude (Mary) Renshaw
From her sister-in-law, Chris Lumianski

As a new bride, I was always looking for recipes to serve for 2. (This was originally for 1.) Over the years, I have expanded the original recipe to accommodate our growing family. It was and still is a great favorite - a good "last minute preparation" recipe that has a great "worked all day on it" flavor.

CHICKEN & RICE

4-5 Tbsp. margarine or butter
1 clove garlic (optional)
1 large onion, chopped coarsely

Saute the onions and garlic in the butter. Remove the garlic and discard. Set the onions aside in a bowl.

4-6 pieces of chicken, skinned
Salt and pepper
⅓ cup cornstarch (approximately)

Dust the chicken with a mixture of salt, pepper and cornstarch. Place the chicken in the pan where the onions were sauteed and brown a few minutes on each side. Remove the chicken to the bowl with the onions.

½-¾ cup dry white wine
¾-1 cup raw rice

Add the wine and rice to the pan and cook a few minutes, scraping up the drippings.

1 can condensed tomato soup
1 cup water

Add the soup and water to the pan; stir in. Return the onions and chicken to the pan. Spoon some of the sauce on top of the chicken. Cover and simmer for about 30 minutes or until the chicken is tender and the rice is cooked. Stir occasionally to prevent sticking. Add some more water as needed (about 1-1½ cups more may be desired). Serves 4.

Mrs. Robert P. (Karen) Curtis

Dale Redmon, my roommate at Michigan State University, was in the Navy before coming to college. His duties aboard ship included being a cook's mate in the galley. The one dish he remembered how to cook in civilian life was Chicken & Rice, which he made every other night until I cried "uncle."

CHICKEN & RICE

¾ cup regular rice
1 can (10¾-oz.) cream of chicken soup
1 envelope Lipton's dry onion soup
1½ cup water

Mix all ingredients together. Place **chicken breasts** on top of this mixture and bake at 350 degrees until the chicken is tender, about 1½ hours. The rice should be thick and creamy.

Mr. Claude Renshaw

This recipe has a bit of fruit (tomatoes are fruit, you know), dairy products, starch, and meat -- all 4 food groups are rolled into one wonderful meal. It's not too spicy and is quite filling. However, the best thing about this recipe is that it is usually my husband, Richard, who makes it. This is especially popular at our church carry-in dinners.

MONTEREY CHICKEN

½ cup cottage cheese
1 pkg. (3 oz.) cream cheese
½ cup sour cream
1 tsp. salt
⅛ tsp. garlic powder
4 oz. green chilies, diced
3 cups cooked chicken, cut up (chicken breasts are best)
3 cups cooked rice (cook in chicken broth)
1 cup grated Monterey Jack cheese
2 fresh tomatoes, coarsely chopped
¾ cup corn chips, coarsely crumbled

Blend the cottage cheese, cream cheese, and sour cream until smooth. Add the remaining ingredients, except the corn chips. Pour into a shallow 2-quart baking dish. Sprinkle on the corn chips. Bake in a 350 degree oven for 25-30 minutes. Yields six generous servings.

Rev. Mary H. Kendzora
St. Paul's Memorial United
Methodist Church

CHICKEN IN LEMON CREME

4 boned chicken breasts

Roll the breasts in a mixture of **flour, salt** and **pepper.** Brown in **1 stick of margarine** (½ cup). Transfer from the skillet to a Pyrex baking dish.

SAUCE:
In a small saucepan combine:
2 Tbsp. lemon juice
2 Tbsp. Sherry
Salt, pepper, and nutmeg to taste

Bring to a boil. Pour the sauce into a blender.
ADD:
1 cup heavy cream
Whip up in the blender. Pour the sauce over the chicken.

Sprinkle **Parmesan cheese** over the top (use a lot of cheese). Bake in a preheated 350 degree oven for 30 minutes, leaving the casserole uncovered.

Mrs. Claude (Mary) Renshaw
From her friend,
Jean Singer

CHICKEN ENCHILADAS

SHELLS:

In a skillet with ¼ **inch oil,** lightly fry **corn tortillas** (about 2 doz.) for 1 minute on each side. Drain on paper towels. Store in a crockpot on low.

FILLING:

Cook **6 chicken breasts** on top of the stove in boiling water, or covered in the oven (for 1 hour). Shred the chicken after removing the skin and bones.

MIX:

2 pkgs. (8 oz. each) **cream cheese**
2 (8 oz.) **cartons sour cream**
2 Tbsp. **liquid taco sauce**
½ cup **minced onions**
2 cans **chopped mild green chilies**
Salt and pepper

Add the shredded chicken to the cream cheese mixture. Put 2 Tbsp. of the chicken mixture onto each cooked tortilla shell. Roll and place in a Pyrex baking dish. Sprinkle with **shredded Monterey Jack cheese.** Bake in a 325 degree oven for 40-45 minutes (or microwave for 15-20 minutes on medium high heat -- cover with wax paper). Serve. Yields 2 dozen enchiladas.

Mrs. Michael (Sharon) Love
From her sister,
Mrs. Mark (Teresa) Hildebrand

SAUSAGE STRATA

6 slices **bread**
1 lb. **sausage**
1 tsp. **mustard**
1 cup (¼ lb.) **shredded Swiss cheese**
3 **eggs,** slightly beaten
1¼ cups **milk**
¾ cup **light cream**
½ tsp. **salt**
Pepper
Nutmeg
1 tsp. **Worcestershire sauce**

Trim the crusts from the bread. Fit the bread into the bottom of a baking dish (10 x 6 x 1½-inch).

Brown the sausage; drain all fat. Stir in the mustard. Spoon the sausage evenly over the bread. Sprinkle with the cheese.

Combine the remaining ingredients and pour over the cheese. Bake at 350 degrees for 30-35 minutes until puffed and set. Trim with parsley and serve immediately. Serves 6.

Mrs. James (Kathleen Stiso) Mullins

In the early years of the 20th century, a chef created a new dish to honor one of Italy's most famous coloratura sopranos, Madame Luisa Tetrazzini. The diva's fame has dimmed with the passing years, but Chicken Tetrazzini remains as popular as ever. This variation of the old recipe would be a great way to use leftover turkey following the Thanksgiving holiday.

TURKEY TETRAZZINI

8 oz. **spaghetti, cut in 2-inch pieces**
¾ cup **canned mushrooms, sliced** (reserve the liquid)
4 Tbsp. **butter**
3 Tbsp. **chopped onion** (or dried onion flakes)
½ tsp. **celery salt**
¼ tsp. **marjoram**
½ tsp. **rosemary, crushed**
1 can **cream of chicken soup**
1 tall can (12 oz.) **evaporated milk**
2 Tbsp. **chopped red pimento**
2-2½ cups **turkey** (or chicken)
⅓ cup **shredded sharp Cheddar cheese**
¼ cup **Parmesan cheese**

Prepare the leftover turkey or chicken by cutting into small pieces, ½ to 1-inch long. Cook the spaghetti; drain and rinse with hot water. Drain the mushrooms, saving the liquid. Melt the butter in a saucepan and saute the onion (omit this step if using dried onion flakes). Add the seasoning and the mushroom liquid to the melted butter. Blend in the soup and stir until smooth. Gradually add the evaporated milk, stirring constantly until smooth and thickened. Heat, but do not allow the sauce to boil.

In a buttered 2 quart casserole, mix the cooked spaghetti, sliced mushrooms, pimento, and turkey. Pour the sauce over the mixture and mix well. Top with the Cheddar and Parmesan cheese. Bake in a preheated 350 degree oven for about 30 minutes or until lightly browned on top.

A green salad and hot garlic bread are excellent with this. Serves 8.

Dr. Lillian Holdeman

This is one of my husband's favorite dishes. It's quick, easy, and can expand to feed anywhere from 2 to 20. The sauce is also delicious when used with chicken.

BAKED FISH

Mix equal portions of **mayonnaise** and **sour cream.** Add chopped **purple onion** (about ½ cup for each 1 cup of mayonnaise and 1 cup of sour cream). Pour over the fish which has been placed in a baking dish. Bake at 350 degrees until fish flakes done. Just before the fish is done, sprinkle with **grated cheddar cheese** and return to the oven until the cheese melts.

Mrs. J. Oliver Cunningham

Tippecanoe Place, the home of Clement Studebaker, as it looked at the turn of the century---

SHRIMP CREOLE PLUS RICE

¼ cup butter
1 cup chopped onion
1 cup diced celery
2 Tbsp. flour
1 tsp. salt
1 tsp. sugar
Dash of cayenne
1 tsp. paprika
½ small bay leaf
4 drops Tabasco sauce
½ cup diced green pepper
1 large can (28 oz.) tomatoes
2 cups cooked shrimp

Melt the butter in a frying pan. Add the onion and celery and cook slowly until tender, but not brown. Add the flour and seasonings; stir until blended. Stir in the green pepper and tomatoes. Cook 10 minutes over low heat, stirring occasionally. Add the shrimp and heat. Serve in a casserole lined with Cheese Rice.

CHEESE RICE:
3 cups water
1 Tbsp. butter
1 tsp. salt
1½ cups uncooked rice
½ lb. (2 cups) shredded American cheese
2 Tbsp. chopped onion
1 tsp. prepared mustard

Bring water to boiling point. Add the butter, salt, and rice. Bring to boil again, reduce heat to low, and cook covered until tender (20-25 minutes).
Stir the cheese, onion, and mustard into the hot rice.
Line a 2 qt. casserole with the rice and fill the center with the Shrimp Creole.

Mrs. Lester C. (Beth) Lamon

SEAFOOD THERMIDOR

1 lb. fresh or frozen cod fillets
1 small onion, quartered
1 lemon slice
1 can condensed cream of shrimp soup
3 Tbsp. flour
¼ cup milk
¼ cup dry white wine
¼ cup (1 oz.) mozzarella cheese, shredded
2 Tbsp. snipped parsley
½ cup soft bread crumbs
2 Tbsp. grated Parmesan cheese
2 tsp. butter or margarine
½ tsp. paprika

Thaw the frozen fish; skin, if necessary. Cut the fish into bite-size pieces. Place the fish, onion, and lemon into a greased skillet. Add water to cover. Bring to a boil and reduce the heat to simmer; cover and cook 5-6 minutes, or until the fish flakes easily.

In a small saucepan, blend the soup and flour; gradually stir in the milk and wine. Cook until thickened and bubbly, stirring often. Add the mozzarella and parsley.

Carefully drain the fish well, removing the onion and lemon; fold into the sauce. Put the mixture into a medium casserole (an 8 x 8-inch dish also works well) and top with the following: combine the bread crumbs; Parmesan cheese; butter or margarine; and paprika.

Heat in a hot oven of 400 degrees until the topping is browned, or put it under the broiler for the same results.

This is very good served with rice or on toast. To make the dish extra special, some small shrimp might be added to the sauce. Serves 4-6.

Mrs. Glenn (Fannie Mae) Stoneburner

Today Tippecanoe Place has been converted into a lovely restaurant. The enclosed porch is the perfect place for a relaxing luncheon.

Mrs. Renshaw serves this recipe every year during the Lenten season. It's a quick and easy meal for family or guests.

SALMON KEDGEREE

1 can (7¾ oz.) salmon
Milk
3 hard cooked eggs
1½ cups chopped onion
¼ cup butter
2 cups hot cooked rice
¼ cup snipped parsley
Salt and pepper, to taste
Sprigs of parsley for garnish

Drain and flake the salmon, reserving the salmon liquid. Add enough milk to the salmon liquid to measure ⅓ cup. Slice the eggs in halves and remove the yolks. Chop the egg yolks and cut the egg whites into strips. Saute the onion in 2 Tbsp. butter.

In a saucepan, combine all the ingredients except the egg yolks, adding salt and pepper to taste. Heat gently, stirring occasionally, until heated through. Mound the mixture on a heated serving platter. Sprinkle with the chopped egg yolks and garnish with additional sprigs of parsley. Serves 4.

Mrs. Claude (Mary) Renshaw

Our next door neighbors in Arlington, Virginia, had the last name "Bright." When we adopted their recipe, we gave it their name. It's great for picnics and informal lunches. Because the sandwiches can be frozen, they're perfect for busy people.

"BRIGHT" BURGERS

1½ lbs. hamburger
1 medium onion, chopped
½ green pepper, chopped
1 rib celery, chopped
½ tsp. salt
1 can tomato soup
1 Tbsp. prepared mustard
5 Tbsp. green tomato relish or 2-3 Tbsp. pickle relish
15-20 slices cheese
15-20 small (or 12 large) hamburger buns

Cook together the hamburger, onion, green pepper, and celery. Add the salt, soup, mustard, and relish and stir together. At this point the hamburger mixture can be frozen, or the sandwiches may be assembled, wrapped in foil and frozen.

To assemble the sandwiches, spread the meat sauce on the hamburger buns, top with a slice of cheese, and wrap individually in foil. Heat in the oven until the cheese melts. Yield: 15-20 sandwiches.

Mrs. Robert P. (Karen) Curtis

CRABMEAT AND BROCCOLI CASSEROLE

1 bunch fresh broccoli or 1 pkg. frozen broccoli
½ lb. fresh crabmeat or 1 pkg. frozen crabmeat
  (flaked and the membranes removed)
½ pint sour cream
¼ cup chili sauce
1 small onion, chopped finely
1 cup grated cheese (sharp cheddar)
2 Tbsp. fresh lemon juice
1 Tbsp. grated lemon peel
Salt and pepper

Cook the broccoli until tender; break into small pieces. Mix with the crabmeat, sour cream, chili sauce, onion, cheese, lemon juice, lemon peel, salt and pepper. Put into a small, shallow, buttered casserole. Bake in a 350 degree oven for about 20 minutes or until the cheese is melted and the top is browned. Serves 4.

(This dish can be made early in the day, or the day before and refrigerated.)

Mrs. Judd (Mary Lou) Leighton

SEAFOOD NEWBURG

2 Tbsp. butter or margarine
1 pt. scallops (if large, cut in half)
1 Tbsp. lemon juice
½ tsp. salt
Dash of cayenne, if desired
1½-2 cups cooked crabmeat
1 lb. shrimp, cooked and deveined

NEWBURG SAUCE:
⅓ cup butter or margarine
¼ cup flour
½ tsp. salt
¼ tsp. paprika
1½ cups light cream
¾ cup fish stock
3 egg yolks
¼ cup dry sherry

2 Tbsp. butter or margarine
½ lb. mushrooms, washed and thickly sliced

In a medium skillet, saute the scallops in 2 Tbsp. hot butter or margarine for about 5 minutes (stirring). Add the lemon juice, ½ tsp. salt, cayenne, and the cooked crabmeat and shrimp; toss to mix well. Remove from the heat.

Make the Newburg Sauce: Melt ⅓ cup butter or margarine in a medium saucepan. Remove from the heat and stir in the flour, salt, and paprika until thoroughly blended. Gradually stir in the cream and the fish stock. (Use the broth from cooking the crab and shrimp, or use bottled clam juice for the fish stock.) Cook the sauce over medium heat, stirring constantly, until the mixture thickens and comes to a boil. Boil for 1 minute. Remove the sauce from the heat.

In a medium bowl, beat the egg yolks well. Stir in about ½ cup of the hot sauce, then stir the egg yolk mixture into the sauce in the saucepan. Add the sherry. Cook over low heat, stirring constantly, until heated through. Do not boil.

Saute the mushrooms in 2 Tbsp. of hot butter for several minutes, stirring until they're golden and tender. Drain off the liquid and save (if the Newburg Sauce becomes too thick, use the mushroom liquid to thin it).

Combine the Seafood Newburg Sauce with the seafood mixture and the sauteed mushrooms. Keep warm until ready to serve.

Turn the Seafood Newburg into a chafing dish or warmed serving dish. Serve with rice or slices of toasted bread.

Diane Barts

TO COOK SHRIMP

Rinse the **shrimp** and remove the shells. Devein by slitting down the back of each shrimp with a sharp knife; lift our the sand vein.

In a large pan, combine **1 qt. water, 1 lemon slice, a sprig of parsley, 1 Tbsp. salt, ½ bay leaf,** and several **whole black peppers.** Cover the pan and bring to a boil over medium heat; simmer for 10 minutes.

Add the shrimp. Once again bring the mixture to a boil. Reduce the heat and simmer, covered, until the shrimp are tender, about 3-5 minutes. Drain.

CRAB SUPPER PIE

1 cup (4 oz) **shredded Swiss cheese**
1 unbaked 9-inch pastry shell
7½-8 oz. crabmeat, drained and flaked
2 green onions, sliced (with tops)
3 beaten eggs
1 cup light cream
½ tsp. salt
½ tsp. grated lemon peel
¼ tsp. dry mustard
Dash of mace
½ cup sliced almonds

Sprinkle the cheese over the bottom of the pastry shell. Top with the crabmeat and sprinkle with green onion. Combine the eggs, cream, salt, lemon peel, dry mustard, and mace. Pour over the crabmeat. Top with sliced almonds. Bake in a slow oven (325 degrees) for about 40-45 minutes or till set. Remove from the oven and let stand 10 minutes before serving. Serves 4.

(I sometimes add extra crabmeat or sliced mushrooms. If the mushrooms are canned, be sure to drain them.)

Cheryl Haas

ENGLISH MUFFINS A LA SCALLOPS AU GRATIN

1 lb. scallops, (thaw, if frozen)
1 cup chicken broth
¼ cup butter or margarine
¼ cup onion, chopped
¼ cup green pepper, chopped
1 pimiento, chopped (canned works well)
3 Tbsp. flour
¼ tsp. dry mustard
¾ tsp. salt
Few grains of pepper
¾ cup tomato juice
¾ cup grated cheddar cheese
⅓ cup milk
6 English muffins (split, toasted, and buttered)

In a pan, combine the scallops and chicken broth. Bring to a boil; reduce heat and simmer about 5 minutes until the scallops are opaque throughout. Drain the scallops and set aside, saving the broth for soup.

In a skillet, melt the butter. Add the onion and green pepper; saute for 5 minutes. Blend in the flour and seasonings. Add the tomato juice gradually and cook, stirring until thickened. Add the cheese and pimiento and mix. Pour in the milk and cook stirring constantly. Fold in the scallops and heat to boiling. Spoon the mixture onto 6 toasted and buttered English muffin halves. Serve the remaining 6 toasted and buttered English muffin halves in a basket. Serves 6.

Mrs. Claude (Mary) Renshaw

1960 RECIPES

TO HELP A BOY KEEP HIS SHIRTTAIL TUCKED IN

Just sew some lace on the hem of the shirt. That will teach him to keep it tucked in.

STUFFED FILLET OF SOLE IN CHEESE SAUCE

12 fillets of sole (8 to 10 oz.)

DRESSING:
- **1 small bag** (8 oz.) **Pepperidge Farm Dressing, minus ½ cup**
- **2 cans small shrimp, cut up**
- **1 stick butter** (½ cup)
- **2 eggs, jumbo**
- **1 15-oz. can chicken broth**
- **4 Tbsp. onion, finely chopped**
- **3 generous dashes celery salt**

SAUCE:
- **8 Tbsp. flour**
- **8 Tbsp. butter** (½ cup)
- **4 cups milk**
- **1 tsp. salt**
- **2 dashes pepper**
- **2 cups sharp cheddar cheese, grated**
- **2 generous pinches curry powder**

Spray a 9 x 13-inch Pyrex dish with Pam cooking spray and set aside. Rinse the fillets in water and dry thoroughly.

DRESSING:

Melt the butter in the chicken broth (in a sauce pan). Beat the eggs and add to the dry dressing along with the onion, celery salt, shrimp, and all but ¾ cup of the butter and chicken broth mixture. Mix the dressing gently. Place 3 generous Tbsp. of dressing on the skin side of each fillets; roll up and place in the casserole dish, seam side down.

SAUCE:

Melt the butter in a large frying pan. When melted and bubbly, remove from the heat and add the flour, mixing well. Add the milk, little by little, returning to medium heat after 1 cup has been added. Add the salt and pepper. Allow the sauce to thicken to medium consistency. Add the cheddar cheese and stir until well mixed. Take off the heat and stir in the curry powder.

Pour the sauce over the fillets and bake in a 325 degree oven for 35 minutes.

To serve, place the stuffed fillets on a plate and spoon some of the sauce over them. Garnish with fresh parsley flowerets. Serves 8 generously.

Mrs. Donald (Elie) Olson

MOM G'S SPAGHETTI DELUXE
(For 14-16)

- **4 cans** (No. 2½) **tomato puree**
- **6 large cloves garlic, minced**
- **2 cans** (6 oz.) **tomato paste**
- **½ tsp. ground oregano**
- **2 jumbo onions, sliced and sauteed**
- **2 jumbo green peppers, cut julienne and sauteed**
- **½ cup sugar** (or more to taste)
- **3-4 lbs. Italian hot or sweet sausage links, cut into 3 inch pieces**
- **Pork chops** (1 per guest)
- **Meatballs** (recipe follows)
- **Salt and pepper to taste**
- **2 lbs. vermicelli** (prepared according to package directions)

TO MAKE THE SAUCE: Saute the onions and green peppers until browned. Pour into a large kettle (8-10 qts.). Add the tomato puree, tomate paste, minced garlic, and oregano. Simmer over low heat, covered.

Saute the pork chops, sausage, and meat balls until lightly browned. (I make the meatballs the night before.) Add the meat to the sauce. Sprinkle with salt and pepper to taste; add the sugar. Simmer together for 4 hours, covered at all times. Stir often. If necessary, adjust the seasoning by adding more salt, pepper, or sugar until the desired flavor is achieved. (The finished sauce is fairly thick.)

Cook the spaghetti in salted water with 2 Tbsp. olive oil added to keep the pasta from sticking together. Cook according to package directions. Drain the pasta and place in a serving bowl with enough sauce to further keep it from sticking. Cover with foil and place in a warm oven until the rest of the meal is ready to be served.

Serve with salad greens, Italian dressing, and buttery garlic basil bread.

MEATBALLS ITALIAN:
- **3 lbs. ground round**
- **3 jumbo eggs**
- **1½ cups** (or more) **Contadina Italian seasoned bread crumbs**
- **2 envelopes Lipton's onion soup mix**
- **¼ cup parsley** (dried or fresh)
- **2 Tbsp. Worcestershire sauce**
- **½ cup whole milk** (or enough to moisten the meat mixture)
- **Salt and pepper to taste**

Mix together all the meatball ingredients. Add enough milk to make the mixture moist enough to roll into 1½-inch balls, but not too moist. (If too much liquid is added, the meatballs will not hold together during the 4 hour cooking time.) Makes about 30 meatballs.

Mrs. Donald (Elie) Olson

SKILLET ZUCCHINI

1 lb. ground beef
¼ cup chopped onion
1 Tbsp. flour
1 cup tomato sauce
¾ cup water
¼ cup chopped green pepper
1 tsp. oregano
½ tsp. chili powder
½ tsp. salt
3 cups zucchini, thinly sliced
1 cup Parmesan cheese

Brown the beef and onion. Sprinkle the flour over the meat; stir. Add the tomato sauce, water, green pepper, oregano, chili powder, and salt; mix. Season the zucchini with salt and pepper. Arrange over the meat. Cover and simmer until the zucchini is tender, about 15 minutes. Top with cheese. Serves 6.

Mrs. Ronald (Georgianne) Compton

SPAGHETTI SAUCE

12 oz. tomato paste
30 oz. tomato sauce
24 oz. water
1 tsp. oregano
1 tsp. sugar
1 tsp. red wine vinegar
½ tsp. pepper
1 tsp. garlic powder (adjust to taste)
2 tsp. parsley flakes
2 tsp. Parmesan cheese

Combine the ingredients and simmer at least 1 hour. This can be frozen or canned.

Mrs. Walton (Carol) Collins

MARINATING SAUCE FOR PORK CHOPS

Clove of garlic
1 scallion or onion
½ cup water
½ cup ketchup
½ cup soy sauce
½ cup sugar or honey
½ cup salad oil
¼ cup vinegar
2 Tbsp. horseradish
½ cup wine
Salt and pepper to taste

Mix the ingredients in a pan. Bring to a boil and cool. Marinate the pork chops overnight. (Use 10-12 chops.)

Mrs. A.J. (Sarah) Paul

PASTA DOUGH

2 cups semolina flour (white flour works)
2 eggs, slightly beaten
1 tsp. olive oil
¾ tsp. salt
2-4 Tbsp. warm water

Mound the flour in a large bowl or on a cutting board. Make a well in the center and add the eggs, olive oil, salt, and 2 Tbsp. warm water.

Using a fork or the fingers, combine all ingredients until the dough forms a ball. If the mixture is still too dry to hold together, add the remaining water.

Lightly flour a cutting board and knead the dough for 8-10 minutes, until it is smooth and elastic. Cover the dough with a bowl or with plastic wrap and let it rest 30-60 minutes. Roll out. Cut by hand or by noodle machine. Dry on paper towels or a pasta stand about 2-4 hours.

Mrs. Brian (Carolyn Rohleder) Straup

The South Bend Tribune, August 9, 1974.

This recipe was a 4-H Club winner. Mrs. Hruska serves it with a tossed salad, garlic bread, and spumoni ice cream. If you don't want to make meatballs, the meat mixture may be added to the sauce instead.

ITALIAN SPAGHETTI AND MEATBALLS

TO MAKE MEATBALLS:

Combine **1 small clove of garlic** (chopped), **2 Tbsp. Parmesan cheese, 3 slices toast** (crumbled), **1 egg, 1 tsp. salt, ¼ tsp. pepper** to **one pound of hamburger.** Form into balls and brown. Put into the following sauce and simmer -- the longer the better.

SAUCE:

Brown **¼ cup onions, ¼ cup chopped celery,** and a **small clove of garlic** in **2 Tbsp. oil.** Add **2 cans tomato paste, 1 No. 2½ can whole tomatoes, 1½ tsp. salt, 1 tsp. granulated sugar, ¼ tsp. nutmeg, ½ tsp. oregano, ⅛ tsp. pepper, ¼ cup chopped parsley,** and **¼ cup Parmesan cheese.** Mushrooms may be added.

Mrs. Mary Jo Hruska

SPINACH RICOTTA TART

½ pkg. pie crust mix or use your own recipe for a
   1-crust pie
2 pkgs. (10 oz.) frozen chopped spinach
1 small onion, minced
3 Tbsp. butter or margarine
½ tsp. salt
¼ tsp. nutmeg
Black pepper
15 oz. ricotta cheese
1 cup light cream
½ cup grated Parmesan cheese
3 eggs, slightly beaten

Prepare the crust for a 1-crust pie. Line a 9-inch pie plate with the pastry; flute the edge, making a high rim to hold the filling. Prick the bottom and sides of the crust. Cover with wax paper and add a layer of rice or dried beans to keep the crust from puffing up during baking. Bake at 400 degrees for 5 minutes. Remove the rice and wax paper to let the pastry brown and bake 6-8 minutes longer. Cool on a wire rack.

Cook the spinach. Drain <u>very</u> well. Saute the onion in butter. Add the spinach, salt, nutmeg, and pepper. Combine the ricotta cheese, cream, Parmesan cheese, and eggs; mix well. Stir in the spinach mixture.

Pour into the baked pastry shell. Bake at 350 degrees for 50 minutes, or until the custard is set and the top is lightly browned.

Jennifer Warlick

BARBEQUE SAUCE

64 oz. ketchup
24 oz. chili sauce
⅔ cup prepared mustard
2 Tbsp. dry mustard
3 cups brown sugar
4 Tbsp. freshly ground pepper
3 cups wine vinegar
24 oz. beer
2 cups lemon juice
1 cup thick steak sauce
Few drops of Tabasco
½ cup Worcestershire
2 Tbsp. soy sauce
4 Tbsp. salad oil
2 small cloves garlic, minced or pressed

Mix all the ingredients and simmer 2 hours.

Makes 2 gallons. Try freezing the leftovers for future cookouts.

Mrs. John (Jane) Olcott

PASTITIO
(Pasticcio)

7 oz. ziti macaroni
¾ lb. ground beef
1 small onion, chopped
15 oz. can tomato sauce
1 tsp. salt
1½ cup (6 oz.) grated Kasseri cheese
⅛ tsp. ground cinnamon
1¼ cups milk
3 Tbsp. margarine
2 eggs, beaten
⅛ tsp. ground nutmeg

Cook the macaroni; drain. Cook and stir the beef and onion in a 10-inch skillet until light brown; drain. Stir in tomato sauce and salt. Spread half of the macaroni in a greased square baking dish (8 x 8 x 2-inch) and cover with the beef mixture. Mix ½ cup of the cheese and the cinnamon; sprinkle over the beef. Cover with the remaining macaroni.

Cook and stir the milk and margarine in a 2-qt. saucepan until the margarine is melted. Remove from the heat. Stir at least half of the milk mixture gradually into the beaten eggs and then blend into the milk mixture in the saucepan. Pour over the macaroni. Sprinkle with the remaining 1 cup cheese. Cook uncovered in a 325 degree oven until brown and the center is set, about 50 minutes. Sprinkle with nutmeg. Garnish with parsley, if desired.

Mrs. Holly Grant

GOURMET PIZZA

Cheese Pastry: see below
2 lbs. mild Italian sausage
2 cans (8 oz.) tomato sauce
1 tsp. each: oregano and crumbled sweet basil
1 clove garlic, minced
4 medium tomatoes, thinly sliced
Green pepper strips
½ lb. small fresh mushrooms, thickly sliced
4 cups (16 oz.) grated mozzarella cheese
2 Tbsp. grated Parmesan cheese

Divide the Cheese Pastry dough in half. On a lightly floured surface, roll each half into a 13-inch circle. Transfer each to a 12-inch pizza pan, buttered and dusted with Parmesan cheese; crimp the edges. Partially bake in a preheated 425 degree oven for 9 minutes. Remove to wire racks to cool.

Break the sausage into bits in a skillet; lightly brown, stirring occasionally. For the sauce: mix together the tomato sauce, oregano, basil, and garlic. Assemble each pizza as follows:

Evenly distribute ¼ of the sausage over the bottom, sprinkle with 1 cup mozzarella cheese, top with a layer of tomato slices, add another ¼ of the sausage, and pour ½ the sauce over the top. Arrange the pepper strips in spoke fashion to divide the pizza into 8 wedges. Arrange the mushroom slices around the outside edge. Brush with melted butter. Over each pizza sprinkle 1 cup mozzarella cheese and 1 Tbsp. Parmesan cheese. Bake at 425 degrees for 10-20 minutes or until done.

CHEESE PASTRY:

Combine **2⅔ cups flour, ⅓ cup grated Parmesan cheese, 2½ tsp. baking powder,** and **1 tsp. salt.** Cut in **¼ cup each butter and lard** until crumbly. Gradually add about **¾ cup milk,** mixing lightly with a fork until the mixture leaves the sides of the bowl. Knead in the bowl 10 times or until smooth.

The crust tastes like cheese crackers. You may use one jelly roll pan instead of 2 round pizza pans, if you desire.

Cheryl Haas

COCONUT-PINEAPPLE CUPCAKES

1 cup shredded coconut
¼ cup water

Combine the coconut and water. Let stand while making the cake batter.

2½ cups sifted flour
3 tsp. baking powder
1 cup sugar
1 tsp. salt
2 eggs
½ cup shortening
1 cup crushed pineapple, undrained
1 tsp. vanilla

Sift the flour, baking powder, and salt together 3 times. Cream the shortening; add the sugar gradually. Beat until light and fluffy. Add the eggs one at a time, beating well after each addition. Add the sifted dry ingredients alternately with the pineapple. Add the vanilla and the coconut mixture. Turn into muffin pans lined with paper cups. Fill ½ full. Bake at 350 degrees for 25-30 minutes.

BUTTER CREAM ICING:
½ cup butter or margarine
2 Tbsp. warm milk
½ tsp. vanilla
2 cups sifted confectioner's sugar

Cream the butter thoroughly. Add the milk and vanilla. Blend in the confectioner's sugar. Makes 18 cupcakes.

Mrs. Eleanor Carr

RAW APPLE CAKE

2 cups apples, chopped (with or without the peel)
1 cup sugar
1 egg
½ cup salad oil
1½ cups sifted flour
1 tsp. soda
½ tsp. allspice
1 tsp. cinnamon
¼ tsp. salt
1 cup chopped nuts

Pour the sugar over the apples and let stand for 20 minutes. Add the beaten egg and oil. Combine the dry ingredients and sift over the apples. Stir till the mixture is well blended. Add the nuts. Bake in a 9-inch square pan (greased) for 1 hour at 350 degrees.

Mrs. Frank (Maureen) Sindlinger

I received this recipe from a friend in the Junior League of New Orleans. Orange Jezebel Sauce keeps forever in the refrigerator, and with a little ribbon and lace, makes an excellent gift idea. It is good when used with cream cheese and crackers, as a condiment, or as a dip with egg rolls or won ton.

ORANGE JEZEBEL SAUCE

2 10-oz. jars apple jelly
2 12-oz. jars apricot jam
3½ Tbsp. dry mustard
4 Tbsp. horseradish
Grated zest of 2 large oranges

Blend all the ingredients in a food processor for just a few seconds on and off. Stir in:
1 Tbsp. poppy seed
Pour into small jars. Store in the refrigerator.

Mrs. John C. (Jan) Frieden

BANANA SPLIT CAKE

2 cups Graham cracker crumbs
¼ lb. butter (½ cup), melted
Mix and place in a 9 x 11-inch pan.

2 cups powdered sugar
¼ lb. butter
2 eggs
Mix and beat for 15 minutes.

1 tsp. vanilla
Dash of salt
Add and beat some more. Pour over the Graham cracker crust.

1 can (20 oz.) **crushed pineapple, drained**
5 bananas, sliced
Arrange over the beaten mixture. Cover with **Cool Whip.** Sprinkle with **pecans** and **Maraschino cherries.** Refrigerate.

Mrs. Melvena Whitaker

CHAMPIONSHIP CHEESECAKE

CRUST:
Mix **2 cups Graham cracker crumbs** with **1 stick of melted butter** and **½ cup sugar.** Press into the bottom of a 9 x 13-inch pan.

FILLING:
Mix **3 pkgs.** (8 oz.) **cream cheese,** softened and **1 cup sugar.**

Beat till fluffy and add **1½ tsp. vanilla.** Add **5 eggs,** one at a time.
Pour onto the crust mixture slowly. Bake at 275 degrees for 1 hour. Remove from the oven (leave the oven on). Cool for just 5 minutes. Top with Sour Cream Topping and bake for 5 additional minutes. Refrigerate before serving. Serves 12-14.

SOUR CREAM TOPPING:
Mix **1 pt. sour cream, ¾ cup sugar,** and **1 tsp. vanilla.**

Mrs. Michael (Sharon) Love

CHERRY NUT PUDDING CAKE

¼ cup oleo
¾ cup sugar
1 egg
1½ cups flour
½ tsp. salt
2 tsp. baking powder
½ cup milk
1 lb. can tart red cooking cherries, drained
1 tsp. almond extract
½ cup chopped nuts

Cream the oleo and sugar. Add the egg and beat. Sift the dry ingredients and add alternately with the milk. Fold in the cherries, flavoring, and nuts. Place in an 8-inch pan. Bake in a 350 degree oven for 50 minutes. Sprinkle with **powdered sugar.**

Mrs. A.J. (Sarah) Paul

OVEN-BAKED APPLE PANCAKES

4 eggs, well beaten
1 cup milk
¼ tsp. salt
1 cup flour
3 tart medium apples (Do not use canned or frozen apples.)
1 Tbsp. cinnamon
½ cup sugar

Mix the beaten eggs, milk, salt, and flour until smooth. Let the batter rest.
Peel, core, and cut the apples into ¼-inch wedges. Combine the sugar and cinnamon; sprinkle over the apples. (Adjust the sugar to the tartness of the apples.) Toss to mix.
Using **2 Tbsp. of butter per pan,** butter two 9-inch pie pans. Divide the apples between the 2 pans. Stir the batter and pour half over each pan of apples. Bake in a preheated 375 degree oven for 30 - 40 minutes or until the pancakes are golden brown, puffed, and set. Serve hot,

Mrs. David (Christine) Bainbridge

LEMON MARBLE POUND CAKE

1¼ cups sugar
1 cup butter
½ cup milk
1 tsp. lemon peel
1 Tbsp. lemon juice
2¼ cups sifted cake flour
1 tsp. baking powder
3 eggs

Mix together and set aside:
2 Tbsp. boiling water
1 Tbsp. sugar
1 square unsweetened chocolate

In a large mixing bowl, cream the butter and sugar until light and fluffy (8-10 minutes at medium speed). Beat in the milk, lemon peel and juice. Sift the flour and baking powder; add to the creamed mixture. Beat until smooth (2 minutes). Add the eggs, one at a time, beating one minute after each. Beat one minute more, scraping the sides.

Add the chocolate mixture to one half of the batter. In a greased 9 x 5 x 3-inch loaf pan alternate spoonfuls of light and dark batter. Run a spatula through to marble. Bake at 325 degrees for 1 hour and 20 minutes. Cool 10 minutes before removing from the pan.

Cheryl Haas

BAKED DOUBLE CHOCOLATE CHEESE CAKE

3 8-oz. pkgs. cream cheese
1 14-oz. can sweetened condensed milk
8 1-oz. squares semi-sweet chocolate, melted
4 eggs
2 tsp. vanilla extract
1 tsp. flour
1 cup mini chocolate chips
Crust for a 9-inch pie

Preheat the oven to 300 degrees.
Line the bottom and half way up the sides of a 9-inch springform pan with the pie crust.

In a large bowl, beat the cheese until fluffy. Add the sweetened condensed milk and beat until smooth. Add the remaining ingredients except for the mini chips. Mix well. Toss half of the chips with the flour and fold into the mixture. Pour into the prepared pan. Sprinkle the remaining chips over the top. Bake for 1 hour or until the cake springs back when lightly touched. Cool to room temperature. Remove the sides of the springform pan. Serve. Refrigerate any leftovers.

Mrs. W.F. (Deborah) Mayers

---

*T*o clean your range more efficiently, remove drip pans, burners and oven racks. Place them into a large garbage bag and add 2 cups of ammonia. Tie the garbage bag and allow to sit overnight. The next day remove the range parts and wash. They will look brand new!

Mrs. James (Marilyn Everly) Parent

TRIPLE CHOCOLATE CHEESECAKE

CRUST:
¼ lb. lightly salted butter (1 stick)
2 cups chocolate wafer cookie crumbs, very finely ground
¼ cup sugar

FILLING:
2 lbs. (4 8-oz. pkgs.) cream cheese
1¼ cups sugar
1 Tbsp. rum
1½ tsp. vanilla extract
3½ oz. German sweet chocolate, (melted over simmering water in the top of a double boiler)
Pinch of salt
4 large eggs
¼-½ cup chocolate chips (mini-chips work well)

TOPPING:
2 cups sour cream
½ cup sugar
1 tsp. almond extract

Melt the butter for the crust over a very low heat. Combine with the crumbs and sugar until well blended. Press the mixture over the bottom and up the sides of an ungreased 10-inch springform pan. There should be enough to coat the entire pan.

In a mixer, combine the cream cheese and sugar; beat for 2 minutes or until soft. Add the rum, vanilla, melted chocolate, and salt; blend thoroughly. Add the eggs, one at a time, keeping the mixer on the lowest speed. Mix just until each egg has been incorporated into the batter. Stir in the chocolate chips. Pour the filling into the crust and bake in a preheated 350 degree oven for 40 minutes. (Put a cookie sheet under the springform pan; some butter from the crust might seep out and cause your oven to smoke.) Remove the cheesecake from the oven and let stand on the counter top for 10 minutes while you prepare the topping.

Combine the sour cream, sugar, and almond extract with a rubber spatula in a bowl. Spread evenly over the top of the baked cheesecake. If desired, you may sprinkle a few chocolate chips over the top for garnish. Return to a 350 degree oven for 10 minutes. Remove from the oven and place in the refrigerator to cool immediately. This prevents cracks from forming in the cheesecake.

This does not freeze well.

Mrs. Patrick (Sharon) Deneen

The ladies of the Greek Orthodox Church are renowned for their baking.

Shown at a Good Samaritan bake sale are (L to R): Mrs. Antonis, Mrs. Vasilakis, Mrs. Rorres, and Georgia Babuses.

Courtesy of Mr. Milton Kouroubetis.

APPLE WALNUT PAN CAKE

1 can apple pie filling
2 cups sifted flour
1 cup sugar
1½ tsp. soda
1 tsp. salt
2 eggs, beaten
1 tsp. vanilla
⅔ cup vegetable oil
¾ cup chopped walnuts

Spread the pie filling in the bottom of a greased 9 x 13-inch pan. Add the flour, sugar, soda, and salt (sift in). Combine the eggs, vanilla, oil, and ½ cup walnuts; mix well. Pour over the ingredients in the pan and stir only until well blended (do not over mix). Smooth the batter evenly in the pan. Bake for 40-50 minutes at 350 degrees. Remove the cake from the oven and while hot, puncture the top all over with a fork. Pour the hot topping over the cake and sprinkle with the remaining ¼ cup nuts.

TOPPING:
1 cup sugar
½ cup sour cream
½ tsp. soda

Combine the sugar, sour cream and soda in a saucepan. Cook over moderate heat, stirring constantly until the mixture comes to a boil. Remove from the heat and pour over the cake.

NOTE: This recipe may be made with a different flavor of pie filling. Pecans may be substituted for walnuts.

Mrs. Karen Keller

PINA COLADA PUDDING CAKE

⅓ cup white rum (80 proof)
1 four serving pkg. vanilla instant pudding
1 pkg. white cake mix (2 layer size)
4 eggs
¾ cup water
¼ cup oil
1 cup flaked coconut

Blend all the ingredients except the coconut in a large mixer bowl. Beat for 4 minutes at medium speed. Add the coconut; mix well. Pour into 2 greased and floured 9-inch cake pans. Bake at 350 degrees for 25-30 minutes. Cool in the pan for 15 minutes. Remove from the pans and cool on racks. Fill and frost with Pina Colada Frosting. Chill. Refrigerate any leftover cake.

PINA COLADA FROSTING:
8 oz. crushed pineapple, undrained
1 four serving pkg. vanilla instant pudding
⅓ cup white rum (80 proof)
9 oz. whipped topping (thawed)

Combine the pineapple (with the juice), the pudding mix, and the rum in a bowl. Beat until well blended. Fold in the whipped topping.

(1 cup of coconut may be sprinkled over the cake once it is frosted.)

Mrs. James (Kathleen Stiso) Mullins

TEXAS CAKE

Sift together **2 cups sugar** and **2 cups flour** and put into a bowl.

In a saucepan, melt **2 sticks of oleo** (1 cup), **¼ cup cocoa**, and **1 cup water.** Stir well and bring to a boil. Pour over the sugar and flour while hot and mix well.

Add **½ cup buttermilk** (or sour cream) and **1 tsp. soda** dissolved in the buttermilk. Add **2 beaten eggs, ½ tsp. vanilla, ½ tsp. cinnamon,** and **½ tsp. salt.** Pour into a greased cookie sheet (or jelly roll pan) and bake for 25 minutes in a 350 degree oven.

FROSTING:
Bring to a boil:
1 stick oleo
6 Tbsp. milk
4 Tbsp. cocoa

Add **1 (1-lb.) box of powdered sugar, 1 tsp. vanilla** and mix well. Add **1 cup chopped nuts.** Pour frosting over the cake.

Mrs. Ervin (Doris) Purucker

PINA COLADA CHEESECAKE

CRUST:
   1 stick lightly salted butter
   2 cups vanilla wafer crumbs, very finely ground
   ¼ cup sugar

FILLING:
   2 lbs. cream cheese (four 8-oz. pkgs.)
   1½ cups sugar
   2 tsp. pineapple extract*
   2 round slices candied pineapple, sliced into thin slivers
      and soaked in 3 Tbsp. dark rum for 1 hour
   1 Tbsp. rum (in which pineapple was soaked)
   Pinch of salt
   4 large eggs

TOPPING:
   2 cups sour cream
   ¼ cup sugar
   1 tsp. coconut extract
   ½ cup grated fresh coconut

For the crust, melt the butter over very low heat. Combine with sugar and crumbs until well blended. Press the mixture over the bottom and up the sides of an ungreased 10-inch springform pan.

To make the filling, combine the cream cheese and sugar; beat for 2 minutes or until soft. Add the pineapple extract, pineapple slivers, and rum; blend thoroughly. Add the eggs, one at a time, keeping the mixer on the lowest speed in order to prevent too much air from destroying the proper consistency of the batter. Mix just until each egg has been incorporated into the batter. Pour the filling into the crust and bake in a preheated 350 degree oven for 45 minutes. (If the ingredients were not at room temperature, add 5 minutes to the baking time.) Remove from the oven and let stand on the counter top while you prepare the topping (this is essential).

Combine the sour cream, sugar, and coconut extract. Spread evenly over the top of the baked filling. Sprinkle with the grated coconut and return to the 350 degree oven for 10 minutes. Remove from the oven and immediately place in the refrigerator. This prevents cracks from forming in the cheesecake.

   *(Ed: If you are unable to find pineapple extract, ¼ cup pineapple juice may be substituted.)

Cheryl Haas

YUM YUM CAKE

1. **One yellow cake mix** - Follow the directions on the box.
2. Grease a heavy medium deep cookie sheet and spread the cake mix onto it.
3. Bake for 20 minutes at 350 degrees, or until done.
4. Cool the cake for a least 1 hour.

5. Mix together **1 5½-oz. box of vanilla instant pudding, 2 cups of milk,** and **1 8-oz. pkg. of cream cheese,** softened.
6. Beat the pudding-cream cheese mixture until creamy. Spread onto the cooled cake.
7. Spread **1 giant size container of Cool Whip** carefully over the cream cheese mixture.
8. Sprinkle **one large can of well-drained pineapple** (crushed) over the Cool Whip.
9. Sprinkle **1 small can of coconut** over the cake.
10. Sprinkle **1 cup of chopped walnuts** over the cake.
11. Arrange **15-20 maraschino cherries,** cut in half, over the top of the entire cake and sprinkle with more coconut.

Mrs. Thomas (Jean) Gast

TURTLE CAKE

   1 14-oz. pkg. carmels
   ⅔ cup butter or margarine
   ½ cup evaporated milk
   1 pkg. German chocolate cake mix
   1 cup chocolate chips
   1 cup pecans

Melt the carmels in the milk and butter. Make the cake mix according to the directions on the box. Pour half of the cake mix into a greased 13 x 9-inch pan. Bake 10-15 minutes in a 350 degree oven until the center puffs. Pour the carmel mixture over the cake. Top with the chocolate chips and nuts. Pour the remaining cake batter over the top and bake in a 350 degree oven for 25-30 minutes until a toothpick comes out clean. Cool before cutting.

Mrs. A.J. (Sarah) Paul

ARKANSAS CAKE

   2 sticks of margarine (1 cup)
   5 eggs
   2 cups sugar
   2 cups flour
   1 tsp. almond flavoring
   1 tsp. vanilla flavoring

Blend the softened margarine and sugar. Add the eggs one at a time; beat well after each addition. Add the flavoring and then the flour. Bake in a well greased and floured mini Bundt pan.* Bake at 325 degrees for 1 hour and 15 minutes. Let cool for 15 minutes and then remove the cake from the pan. When cool, dust with **powdered sugar.**

This cake is like a pound cake with a crisp coating.

   *(Ed: A regular Bundt pan may be used; reduce the baking time to 1 hour.)

Mrs. Ronald (Nancy) Eversole

I pull this recipe out every June during strawberry season. It is the best fresh strawberry pie I've ever had.

GREAT FRESH STRAWBERRY PIE

1½ cups flour
2 Tbsp. sugar
2 Tbsp. cold milk
½ tsp. salt
½ cup Mazola corn oil

(Do not use any other kind of oil because, for some reason, it will not work.)

Blend the ingredients together and pat by hand into a 9-inch pie pan. Bake in a 450 degree oven for about 10 minutes; the crust will be starting to brown. Cool the crust, then fill.
(This crust is super easy and very flaky. The taste is slightly sweet. It can be used for other one-crust pie recipes, and is especially good when the filling is slightly tart.)

FILLING:
Clean and drain **1 quart of fresh, ripe strawberries**
Cook together:
1 cup sugar
2 well-rounded Tbsp. cornstarch
2 Tbsp. white Karo syrup
1 cup water
2 Tbsp. strawberry jello

In a saucepan, blend together the sugar and cornstarch. Slowly mix in the syrup and water, stirring well so that there are no lumps. Cook until the mixture is thick and clear. Remove from the heat and add 2 Tbsp. strawberry jello dry mix. Stir until the jello is dissolved. Immediately add the strawberries to the hot filling and stir in. When the filling has begun to cool, pour into the crust. Refrigerate.

Mrs. Karen Keller

TRIED & TRUE PECAN PIE

½ cup sugar
¾ cup white corn syrup
½ stick margarine (¼ cup)
3 eggs, slightly beaten
1 tsp. vanilla
1 cup whole or broken pecans
Dash of salt
1 10-inch pie shell, unbaked

In a medium sized pan, mix the sugar, syrup, and margarine. Bring to a boil, and boil for 3 minutes. Pour slowly over the very lightly beaten eggs. Add the vanilla, pecans, and salt. Pour into the pie shell. Bake at 350 degrees for 40-45 minutes or until firm in the center. Serves 8.

Karen Ripy

APPLE DUMPLINGS

6 apples, peeled and sliced

DOUGH:
2 cups flour
1 tsp. salt
2 tsp. baking powder
¾ cup shortening
½ cup milk

SYRUP:
2 cups sugar
2 cups water
¼ cup butter
½ tsp. cinnamon
½ tsp. nutmeg

Cook together the sugar, water, cinnamon, nutmeg, and butter for the syrup. Prepare the dough (as for pie crust). Roll out the dough and cut into 6 squares. Fill each with sliced apples. Fold the corners together and pinch the edges to seal. Place in a baking dish and pour the syrup over the dumplings before baking. Bake for 35 minutes or until the apples are done at 375 degrees.
NOTE: Be sure to stir the syrup occasionally so that it won't burn. When I'm in a hurry, I divide the dough in half and roll each half to fit into a 13 x 9-inch pan. Place the apples on top of the bottom crust and cover with the remaining dough. After cutting slits in the top crust, pour the syrup over all and bake.

Mrs. A.J. (Sarah) Paul

Over the years, America has fallen in love with many things from movie actresses to sports cars. These romances come and go, but one special passion always seems to endure -- the Chocolate Chip Cookie. Ruth Wakefield, owner of the Toll House Inn of Whitman, Massachusetts, had no idea what she was starting when she dropped those first bits of chopped chocolate into her cookie dough in the early 1940's. Her basic recipe has been adapted into many forms since then; Chocolate Nut Pie is one of these.

CHOCOLATE NUT PIE

Mix:
½ cup flour
1 cup sugar
2 eggs, slightly beaten
1 stick oleo, melted (then cooled)
Fold in **1 cup chocolate chips** and **1 cup walnut pieces.** Add **1 tsp. vanilla.**
Pour into an unbaked 9-inch pie shell. Bake at 350 degrees for 30-40 minutes. Test with a toothpick.

Mrs. A.J. (Sarah) Paul

DIABETIC APPLE CRISP

Preheat the oven to 375 degrees. Butter an 8 x 8 or 9 x 9-inch baking dish.

6 apples (cored, peeled, quartered, and sliced)
1 tsp. Sweet 'N Low brown sugar substitute
½ tsp. cinnamon
¼ tsp. nutmeg
2 tsp. lemon juice

Combine the above and put into the buttered baking dish.
BLEND:
¾ cup flour
⅛ tsp. salt
¾ stick margarine (6 Tbsp.)

When crumbly, spread the flour mixture over the apples.
Make a syrup (or use a purchased imitation brown sugar syrup) of:
½ cup water
2 tsp. cornstach

Cook until thick, then add:
2 tsp. Sweet 'N Low brown sugar substitute

Pour over the other ingredients and bake in a 375 degree oven for 45 minutes.
This is my own concoction. It tastes great; we eat it with milk poured over it.

Mrs. John (Millie) Yoder

SUGAR-FREE CHERRY FILLING
(For Pies or Tarts)

This fills a 9-inch pie pan (use a **double crust unbaked pie shell**).

2 cans (16 oz.) **sour cherries,** drained (save the liquid)

Using **1⅓ cups cherry liquid,** add:
3½ Tbsp. cornstarch
15 packets of Equal
½ tsp. salt
¼ tsp. almond extract
1 Tbsp. margarine

Cook the cherry liquid mixture until thickened and clear, stirring constantly. Add the cherries. Pour into the crust. Put the top crust on and seal the edges.
Preheat the oven to 425 degrees. Place the pie on a cookie sheet (place on the center shelf of the oven). Bake at 425 degrees for 15 minutes. Lower the oven temperature to 350 degrees and bake for 30 minutes longer.

Mrs. John (Millie) Yoder

TILLIE'S APPLE SLICES

CRUST:
2½ cups flour
¼ cup sugar
1 tsp. baking powder
½ tsp. salt
¾ cup shortening
1 egg, beaten
¼ cup water
2 tsp. lemon juice

FILLING:
10-12 apples, sliced
1 cup sugar
¼ cup flour
½ tsp. cinnamon
½ tsp. nutmeg
Dots of butter

Preheat the oven to 400 degrees.
CRUST: Cut the shortening into the dry ingredients. Work in the beaten egg, lemon juice, and water which has been combined. Divide into top and bottom crust (use a 13 x 9-inch pan).
FILLING: Toss the sliced apples with the sugar and spices. Place the mixture on the bottom crust. Dot with butter. Add the top crust and prick with a fork. Bake 20 minutes at 400 degrees, then reduce the oven temperature to 350 degrees and bake until done, about 35 minutes.
Drizzle with **¾ cup powdered sugar** mixed with enough **water** to make a glaze (while the pie is still warm). Serves 12.

Mrs. Stephen (Sharon) Gumz

BUTTERSCOTCH PIE

1 Tbsp. gelatin
¼ cup cold water
1 cup milk, scalded
3 egg yolks, well beaten
1 cup brown sugar
¼ tsp. salt
1 tsp. vanilla
3 egg whites, beaten stiff
1 cup whipping cream, whipped
1 9-inch pie shell, baked

Soften the gelatin in the cold water. Scald the milk. Beat the egg yolks until frothy and light. Mix the yolks, sugar, salt, and milk in the upper part of a double boiler. Cook over boiling water, stirring constantly, until the mixture is slightly thickened. Add the gelatin and stir until dissolved. Chill until partly thickened. Fold in the vanilla, egg whites, and whipped cream. Turn into the pie shell and chill. Garnish with whipped cream, if desired.

Mrs. Walton (Carol) Collins

COFFEE-TOFFEE PIE

PASTRY SHELL:
- ½ pkg. (10 oz. size) **piecrust mix**
- ¼ cup **brown sugar, firmly packed**
- ¾ cup **finely chopped walnuts**
- 1 sq. **unsweetened chocolate, grated**
- 1 tsp. **vanilla extract**

Preheat the oven to 375 degrees.

Make the pastry shell: In a medium bowl, combine the piecrust mix with the brown sugar, walnuts, and grated chocolate. Add 1 Tbsp. water and the vanilla; using a fork, mix until well blended. Turn into a 9-inch well greased pie plate; press firmly against the bottom and side of the plate. Bake for 15 minutes. Cool on a wire rack.

FILLING:
- ½ cup **soft butter**
- ¾ cup **granulated sugar**
- 1 sq. **unsweetened chocolate, melted and cooled**
- 2 tsp. **instant coffee**
- 2 **eggs**

In a small (but not too small) bowl beat the butter until creamy with a portable electric mixer at medium speed.

Gradually add the granulated sugar, beating until light. Blend in the melted chocolate and the instant coffee.

Add 1 egg and beat for 5 minutes. Add the remaining egg and beat for 5 minutes longer.

Pour into the baked pie shell. Refrigerate, covered, overnight.

COFFEE TOPPING:
- 2 cups **heavy cream**
- 2 Tbsp. **instant coffee**
- ½ cup **confectioner's sugar**
- **Chocolate curls**

In a large bowl, combine the cream with the 2 Tbsp. instant coffee and the confectioner's sugar. Refrigerate for 1 hour.

With a portable electric mixer, beat the cream mixture until stiff. Decorate the pie with the Coffee Topping and garnish with chocolate curls. Refrigerate for 2 hours before serving.

Mrs. Claude (Mary) Renshaw
From her sister-in-law,
Mary Ann Lumianski

MILE HIGH STRAWBERRY PIE

- 1 cup **sugar**
- 2 **egg whites**
- 1 pkg. (10 oz.) **frozen strawberries, partially thawed**
- 1 tsp. **vanilla**
- 1 Tbsp. **lemon juice**
- **Pinch of salt**
- 1 cup **heavy or whipping cream, whipped***
- 1 **9-inch pastry shell or crumb crust, baked**

Combine the sugar, egg whites, strawberries, vanilla, lemon juice, and salt in a large mixer bowl. Beat the mixture at high speed for 15 minutes until thick, fluffy and voluminous. Fold in whipped cream and pile the mixture into the baked pie shell. Freeze several hours. After the pie is frozen, wrap the pie well in foil or plastic wrap. (May be frozen for up to 3 weeks.) To serve, remove from the freezer; slice and serve immediately. Makes one 9-inch pie. Serves 8.

*I have used frozen whipped topping in place of the whipped cream and it works just as well.

Be sure that you use a sharp knife to cut the pie because the crust is frozen, too.

Mrs. Eleaner Carr

OLD FASHIONED BREAD PUDDING

- 2 **eggs**
- 2¼ cups **milk**
- 1 tsp. **vanilla**
- ½ tsp. **ground cinnamon**
- ¼ tsp. **salt**
- 2 cups **dry bread cubes**
- ½ cup **brown sugar**
- ½ cup **raisins**

Slightly beat the eggs. Add the milk and spices. Stir in the bread cubes, allowing them to stand for a few minutes to absorb some of the liquid. Add the brown sugar and raisins, mixing well. Pour into a generously buttered 8-inch casserole. Set the casserole in a pan of hot water and bake in a 350 degree oven for 45 minutes or until a knife inserted in the center comes out clean. Serve with lemon or vanilla sauce. Serves 4.

Mrs. A.J. (Sarah) Paul

Motorists lined up at gas pumps as the OPEC oil embargo created a gasoline shortage in 1973.

From the Portland Oregonian
Reprinted in the South Bend Tribune,
October 21, 1973.

Mrs. Bamber bakes her Apple Slices when she wants to treat the employees of the Superette, her family's grocery store. She finds that it is easier to serve than a regular pie because it can be cut into squares instead of wedges. Most varieties of apples will work in the dessert; however, if Mrs. Bamber thinks the apples are too sweet, she sprinkles a little lemon juice over them to improve their flavor.

APPLE SLICES

12 cups sliced apples

SUGAR MIXTURE:
1½ cups sugar
4 Tbsp. cornstarch
1 tsp. flour
2 tsp. cinnamon

CRUST:
4 cups flour
1⅓ cups lard
2 tsp. salt
8-12 Tbsp. water

In a medium bowl, put the sugar, cornstarch, flour, and cinnamon; mix together. For the crust, combine the flour and salt. Cut in the lard with a pastry blender until the particles are the size of small peas. Add the water a tablespoon at a time. Toss and mix gently with a fork after each addition of water. Add only enough water to hold the dough together (too much water will make the dough sticky and tough -- too little water causes the edges to crack and the pastry will tear easily). Roll out half of the dough to fit a 15½ x 10½ x 1-inch cookie sheet. Sprinkle the crust with a little of the sugar mixture and cover with half of the apples. Add more of the sugar mixture, then top with the remaining apples, and finally the rest of the sugar mixture. Dot with oleo. Roll out the remaining dough and cover the pie; seal the edges and make slits in the top crust. Bake in a 425 degree oven for 15 minutes. Turn down the oven to 375 degrees and continue to bake for 30-40 minutes more. After the pie has cooled, mix **1 cup confectioner's sugar** and enough **milk** to make a heavy paste and dribble it over the top crust.

Mrs. John Bamber

OVEN CHART

Very slow oven	-	250 to 275 degrees
Slow oven	-	300 to 325 degrees
Moderate oven	-	350 to 375 degrees
Hot oven	-	400 to 425 degrees
Very hot oven	-	450 to 550 degrees

CHOCOLATE MOUSSE

In a food processor or blender, finely process **1 (12-oz) pkg. chocolate chips** (semi-sweet morsels). Add **6 egg yolks,** one at a time, and **2 Tbsp. Kahlua.**

In a saucepan over medium heat, cook **½ cup sugar** and **⅔ cup water** till clear (no more than 3 minutes). DO NOT BOIL. Pour slowly into the chocolate mixture and mix thoroughly.

In a separate bowl, whip **3 (½ pt.) cartons whipping cream,** sweetened with **3 Tbsp. confectioner's sugar** and **1 tsp. vanilla.** Fold the chocolate mixture into the whipped cream. Pour into a serving bowl. Chill. Serve with whipped cream. Serves 15-20.

Mrs. Michael (Sharon) Love

SUGARLESS MACAROONS

1 (7 oz.) pkg. shredded coconut
½ cup unsifted flour
⅛ tsp. salt
⅔ cup Milnot
1 tsp. vanilla
1 pkg. Nutra-Sweet (Equal)

Preheat the oven to 250 degrees. Grease cookie sheets. Combine the coconut, flour, salt, and Nutra-Sweet. Stir in the Milnot and vanilla until thoroughly moistened. Drop the dough by teaspoonfuls about 1-inch apart on the prepared cookie sheets. Bake at 250 degrees for 35 minutes. Cool on wire racks.

Mrs. John (Millie) Yoder

DUTCH BOTERKOEK

1¼ cups flour
1¼ stick butter or margarine (or half each)
⅔ cup sugar
1 tsp. vanilla
¼ tsp. salt
1 egg, beaten
Grated lemon peel, optional

Mix all the ingredients, except ¼ of the egg, in a mixing bowl. Blend with a fork, or better yet, with your hands until a smooth ball forms. Press the mixture into a 9 or 10-inch pie pan until flat. Brush the remaining egg over the top of the dough. Bake in the center of a 375 degree oven for about 30-35 minutes.

Sue Stratigos
From a Dutch co-worker

FRUIT PIZZA

1 18-oz. roll refrigerated sugar cookie dough
1 8-oz. pkg. cream cheese, softened
4 Tbsp. sugar
Fruits in season (strawberries, blueberries, peaches, apricots, pineapple, etc.)
½ cup orange marmalade
1 Tbsp. water

Pat the cookie dough into a foil-lined 12 or 14-inch pizza pan. Bake in a 375 degree oven for 12-15 minutes. Cool. Carefully remove the foil and return the cookie crust to the pizza pan or to a serving platter.

Combine the softened cream cheese and sugar until smooth. Spread over the crust, covering well. Arrange the fresh fruits in a circular fashion over the cream cheese. Glaze with a combination of orange marmalade and water. Chill. Cut in wedges to serve. (For parties or special occasions, cut and serve at the table; it makes a lovely presentation.) Yields 10-12 servings.

NOTE: Select fruits that go well together in flavor and color. A nice arrangement might include strawberry halves around the outer edge, next a row of blueberries, a row of apricot halves, a pineapple row, and the center filled with kiwi slices.

Charlotte Smith

GOLDEN SUGAR COOKIES

2½ cups flour, sifted
1 tsp. baking soda
1 tsp. cream of tartar
¼ tsp. salt
1 cup butter or margarine
1 tsp. butter flavoring
1 tsp. vanilla
2 cups sugar
3 egg yolks

1. Sift together the flour, soda, cream of tartar, and salt; set aside.
2. Cream together the butter and flavorings until softened.
3. Add the sugar gradually, creaming until fluffy after each addition.
4. Add the egg yolks one at a time, beating well after each addition.
5. Add the dry ingredients in fourths to the creamed mixture, mixing just until blended.
6. Form into small balls about ½ inch in diameter. Place them 2 inches apart on an ungreased cookie sheet.
7. Bake in a 350 degree oven for 10-15 minutes, or until golden brown. Makes 6 dozen.

Mrs. Brian (Carolyn Rohleder) Straup

CREAM CHEESE MINTS

1 pkg. (3 oz.) **cream cheese,** at room temperature
Color and flavor as desired (For example, green food coloring and peppermint extract)
2½ cups confectioner's sugar
Granulated sugar

Beat the cream cheese until softened. Add the color and flavoring as desired (start with about ¼ tsp. of flavoring). Gradually beat in the powdered sugar. Knead until the consistency of pie dough. Pinch off a small piece and roll into a marble-sized ball. Roll in granulated sugar and press into a soft rubber candy mold. Remove the excess and unmold the mint at once onto waxed paper. Yield: about 40-50 mints.

Mrs. Lee (Jill) Brummett

The South Bend Tribune, March 19, 1971.

GLAZED APPLE COOKIES

½ cup butter
1⅓ cups brown sugar, firmly packed
1 egg
2 cups sifted flour
1 tsp. baking soda
½ tsp. salt
1 tsp. ground cinnamon
½ tsp. ground cloves
¼ tsp. ground nutmeg
1 cup coarsely ground nuts
1 cup peeled and chopped apples
1 cup raisins
¼ cup milk

GLAZE:
½ cup confectioner's sugar
1 Tbsp. butter
½ tsp. vanilla
2½ Tbsp. milk

Beat the butter and sugar till fluffy. Add the egg and beat. Sift together the flour, salt, soda, and spices. Stir half of the dry ingredients into the creamed mixture. Stir in the nuts, apples, and raisins, then stir in the rest of the dry ingredients and the ¼ cup milk. Mix well. Drop from a tablespoon 1½ inches apart on a lightly greased baking sheet. Bake in a hot oven (400 degrees) for 9-10 minutes. Spread with the glaze while the cookies are hot. (You may want to double or triple the glaze recipe.)

Mrs. Charles (Mary) Taylor

PEANUT BUTTER BROWNIES

6 eggs
3 cups sugar
1½ cups brown sugar
1 cup peanut butter
½ cup shortening
1 Tbsp. baking powder
1 Tbsp. vanilla
4 cups flour
1½ tsp. salt
½ cup chopped peanuts

Combine the eggs, sugar, peanut butter, shortening, and vanilla; blend. Add the dry ingredients and mix only until the mixture is smooth. Spread the dough into 3 lightly greased 13 x 9 x 2-inch pans. Sprinkle with the peanuts (if desired, press the peanuts into the dough with your fingers). Bake at 350 degrees for 25 minutes; test for doneness with a cake tester. Cut into 80 bars and cool in the pans. (Use your favorite frosting, if you desire.)

This recipe can easily be cut in half; use a 10 x 14-inch pan.

Mrs. Ronald (Georgianne) Compton

SUGAR-FREE BANANA OATMEAL COOKIES

3 bananas, mashed
⅓ cup salad oil
2 cups uncooked oatmeal
1½ cups chopped dates
½ cup chopped walnuts
1 tsp. vanilla
¾ tsp. salt

Mix the ingredients and drop onto ungreased cookie sheets. Bake at 350 degrees for 20 minutes. Makes about 30 cookies.

Mrs. John (Millie) Yoder

AMISH SUGAR COOKIES

1 cup sugar
1 cup powdered sugar
1 cup butter
1 cup oil
2 eggs
4½ cups flour
1 tsp. soda
1 tsp. cream of tartar
1 tsp. vanilla
½ tsp. almond extract

Mix all the ingredients together. Chill the mixture. Roll into balls. Press with a fork that has been dipped in sugar. Bake at 375 degrees for 10 minutes.

Mrs. Lester (Aileen) Borough

SUGAR AND SPICE NUTS

3 cups mixed unsalted nuts
1 egg white
1 Tbsp. orange juice
⅔ cup sugar
1 tsp. ground cinnamon
½ tsp. ground ginger
½ tsp. ground allspice
½ tsp. salt

Preheat the oven to 275 degrees.
Grease a 15 x 10 x 1-inch jelly roll pan. Place the nuts in a large bowl and set aside. In a smaller bowl, beat the egg white and orange juice with a fork until frothy. Add the sugar and spices; mix until well blended. Pour over the nuts, stirring to coat well. Spread the mixture onto the jelly roll pan. Bake, stirring every 15 minutes, for 45 to 55 minutes. Cool. Store in an airtight container.

Mrs. Harrison (Lola) Lyons

FRUITCAKE CUPS

1 cup pecans, broken
1 cup walnuts, broken
½ cup red candied cherries, chopped
½ cup green candied cherries, chopped
¾ cup candied pineapple, chopped
½ cup citron, diced
¾ cup golden raisins
½ cup butter or margarine
¼ cup firmly packed light brown sugar
¼ cup thick maple syrup (you may also use corn syrup)
3 eggs
¾ cup unsifted all-purpose flour
1 tsp. cinnamon
½ tsp. salt
¼ cup whiskey or Cognac

Preheat the oven to 300 degrees. Place paper cups in muffin tins. Combine the first 7 ingredients in a medium bowl and set aside. Cream the butter, sugar, and syrup in a large mixing bowl. Beat in the eggs, one at a time, blending well after each addition. Combine the dry ingredients and add alternately to the batter with the whiskey or Cognac; mix thoroughly. (The batter will be quite thin.) Stir in the fruit and nuts. Fill the paper cups to just within the top. Bake for 35 minutes. Cool on wire racks. Store in a tightly covered container.

These cookies are always such a hit with my family that I have to double the recipe.

Diane Barts

DANISH BARS

Sift together in a bowl:
2½ cups flour, sifted
1 tsp. salt

Add **1 cup shortening**. Cut in with a pastry blender or 2 knives until it resembles corn meal. Place **1 egg yolk**, slightly beaten, in a liquid measuring cup. Add enough **milk** to make ⅔ cup liquid.

Slowly add the egg-milk mixture to the flour mixture. Blend just until the dry ingredients are moistened. Divide the dough in half. Roll one-half into a rectangle about 12 x 7-inches. Place in a greased 15½ x 10½ x 1-inch jelly roll pan, bringing the pastry up to the sides.

Sprinkle over the pastry **1 cup crushed corn flakes.** Arrange evenly over the corn flakes, **4 large cooking apples** which have been peeled and sliced. Sprinkle over the apple slices **1 cup sugar** and **1 tsp. cinnamon** which have been mixed together.

Roll out the other half of the pastry into a 10½ x 15½-inch rectangle (big enough to cover the top of the mixture). Moisten the edges with milk and pinch the top layer to the bottom. Place **1 egg white** in a small bowl and beat until stiff

peaks form when the beater is lifted. Brush this evenly over the top crust. Bake in a 400 degree oven for 1 hour. While still warm, ice with a confectioner's sugar glaze.

SUGAR GLAZE:
1 cup confectioner's sugar, sifted
1 Tbsp. water
½ tsp. vanilla

Mrs. Brian (Carolyn Rohleder) Straup

The fruit rich Lane Cake has been a favorite Christmas dessert for many years. This simplified version may be used as a sheet cake or a bar cookie. It would be an elegant addition to any tray of holiday goodies.

LANE BARS

COOKIE BASE:
1 cup butter, softened
2 cups sugar
8 egg whites
1½ tsp. vanilla
2 cups flour
1 cup nuts, chopped
½ tsp. baking powder

LANE TOPPING:
½ cup butter
1 cup plus 3 Tbsp. sugar
¼ tsp. salt
8 egg yolks
⅓ cup bourbon whiskey
1 cup candied red cherries, quartered
1 cup pecans, coarsely chopped
1 cup raisins
1 cup coconut

Preheat the oven to 350 degrees.

COOKIE BASE:
Cream the butter and sugar until light and fluffy. Add the egg whites and vanilla; beat well. Stir in the flour and baking powder. Fold in the nuts. Pour into a greased and floured 13 x 9-inch baking pan. Bake at 350 degrees for 30-35 minutes. Cool.

LANE TOPPING:
In a medium saucepan, melt the butter. Stir in the sugar, salt, and egg yolks. Cook over medium heat until the sugar is dissolved, butter melts, and the mixture begins to thicken (about 5 minutes). Be careful that the egg yolks do not become scrambled in appearance. Remove from the heat and add the whiskey; mix thoroughly. Add the cherries, pecans, raisins, and coconut. Spread over the cookie base.

Diane Barts

SOUR CREAM PASTRIES

1 cup butter or margarine
2 cups sifted all-purpose flour
1 beaten egg yolk
½ cup dairy sour cream
1 12-oz. jar apricot preserves
1 cup flaked coconut
1 cup finely chopped pecans
Granulated sugar

With a pastry blender, cut the butter or margarine into the flour until the mixture resembles fine crumbs. Combine the egg yolk and sour cream; blend into the flour mixture. Chill the dough several hours or overnight.

Divide the dough into 4 equal parts, keeping each part refrigerated until ready to use. Roll each part to a 10-inch circle on a lightly floured surface. Spread each with one quarter of the apricot preserves, the coconut, and the nuts. Cut each circle into 12 wedges with a knife or a fluted pastry wheel. Starting from the wide end, roll each wedge into a crescent. Sprinkle with a little granulated sugar; place on an ungreased cookie sheet. Bake in a 350 degree oven for 15 minutes or until lightly browned. Remove from the cookie sheet and cool on racks.

Diane Barts

Christmas 1973, was the year Jerry discovered the joy of creating and sharing homemade candy. Although we both have a hand in making our candies, he became the "candy chemist" -- knowing if the ingredients were in the proper proportion and just how long to cook and stir. Pralines were a favorite from the beginning, and we try to include them each year. They're a sweet, rich little candy that reminds us of how "rich" we are and makes us thankful for all of our blessings . . . even the snow.

PECAN PRALINES

3 cups sugar
1 tsp. baking soda
⅛ tsp. salt
1 cup buttermilk
¾ cup light corn syrup
2 Tbsp. butter
2 cups pecan halves

In a large saucepan, combine the sugar, baking soda, and salt. Stir in the buttermilk and corn syrup. Bring to a boil over medium heat, stirring constantly. Cook and stir to the soft ball stage (234 degrees). Remove from the heat; add the butter. Stir in the pecans; beat till the mixture is thick enough to drop from a spoon, 5-6 minutes. Quickly drop from a tablespoon onto waxed paper. If the candy becomes too stiff, add 1 tsp. hot water. Makes about 45 pralines.

Jerry and Sheri Wiener

CHRISTMAS CASSEROLE COOKIES

2 eggs
1 cup sugar
1 cup snipped dates
1 cup flaked coconut
1 cup California walnuts, chopped
1 tsp. vanilla
¼ tsp. almond extract

Beat the eggs well. Add the sugar gradually, beating until fluffy. Stir in the remaining ingredients. Turn into an ungreased 2 qt. casserole. Bake in a 350 degree oven for 30 minutes. Remove from the oven and while hot, stir well with a wooden spoon. Cool. When cool form into small balls and roll in **granulated sugar.**

Mrs. Maxine Bowers

What is a "sugarplum"? What vision is really dancing in our children's heads on the night before Christmas? Every family has foods that are the special "sugarplums" of their holiday feast. In our family, it's a sweet mixture of dried plums (prunes), raisins, nuts, and sugar.

SUGARPLUMS

2 cups pitted prunes, finely chopped (12 oz. pkg.)
2 cups raisins
1⅓ cups chopped walnuts
2 cups sugar
½ cup light corn syrup
½ tsp. vanilla extract
¼ tsp. salt
2 cans (3½ oz. size) **flaked coconut, very finely grated** .

1. Lightly grease a 9 x 9 x 2-inch pan. In a medium bowl, combine the prunes, raisins, and nuts; mix well.
2. In a small, heavy saucepan, combine the sugar, corn syrup, and **½ cup water.**
3. Cook over medium heat until the mixture starts to boil, stirring constantly.
4. Boil to 238 degrees F. on a candy thermometer, or until a little in cold water forms a soft ball that flattens on removal from the water. Remove the pan from the heat; cool for 10 minutes.
5. Pour the mixture into a small bowl of an electric mixer. Add the vanilla and salt. Beat at high speed for 5 minutes, or until the mixture is white and creamy.
6. Stir in the fruit mixture. Mix well.
7. Turn into the prepared pan; press evenly with a spatula. Refrigerate for 1 hour.
8. Cut into 64 squares. Form each square into an oval and roll in coconut.
9. Store in an air tight container, using waxed paper between the layers. Makes 64.

Jerry and Sheri Wiener

BOURBON STREET BANDWAGON

The Grouse Club's own Special Vision of New Orleans in the Spring
Tuesday, May 15, 1962 — Ponchatrain Room, Hotel LaSalle, Downtown South Bend
Absinthe Hour, from 6:30 - 7:30 P.M., when more than the heart grows fonder.
At 7:30 P.M. we'll enjoy a sumptious dinner in the best French tradition.
There will be downbeat and upswing, New Orleans jazz with **Art Hodes**
and his Tailgaters. Monsieur Hodes is known as the Dean of Dixieland
and is currently appearing at the Bourbon Street Cafe in Chicago.
This will be a great night for the tailgate jazz buffs.
Come and burp on Bourbon Street!

MENU

Shrimps Remoulade	B. and G. Sauterne
Green Turtle Soup, Madeira	Roast Sirloin of Beef, Flambe
Truffles, Periqueuz	Lattice Potatoes
Bib Lettuce Salad, Vinaigrette	
Cherries Flambe	
Demi Tasse	

The Grouse Club was an all-male social club composed of some of South Bend's leading citizens.

CURRY PICKLES

24 medium cucumbers, sliced or cubed
½ cup salt
8 cups water
1 tsp. curry powder
2 cups vinegar
2½ cups sugar
¼ cup mustard seed
1 Tbsp. celery salt

Wash the cucumbers; drain. Combine the salt and water. Pour over the cucumbers. Let stand for 5 hours. Drain and rinse. Mix the remaining ingredients. Heat to boiling and pour over the cucumbers. Bring to a boil again and pack in sterilized jars. Seal. Makes about 6 pints.

Mrs. Charles (Wava) Apelgreen

SPICED PEACH BUTTER

Peel and pit **peaches.** Cook to a pulp using very little water. Press the pulp through a sieve. Add **¼ cup lemon juice to each cup of peach pulp;** add **one-half as much sugar** as pulp. (2 quarts of peach pulp usually takes 6 cups of sugar.) Add **½ tsp. cinnamon** and **½ tsp. nutmeg.** Cook until thick. Pour into sterilized jars and seal.

Mrs. Charles (Wava) Apelgreen

When Kenneth Van Allen retired 20 years ago, he devoted some of his spare time to developing excellent pickle and candy recipes. We were introduced to one of these, Kenny's Sweet Pickles, on our first visit with the family of our sister-in-law, Gae Wiener. Gae's father, Kenny, spent some time with Jerry explaining how he made these candied pickles. When we returned home, we had not only some delicious memories, but a pickle recipe to keep those memories alive.

KENNY'S SWEET PICKLES

Slice 1 gal. cucumbers (about 8 lbs.). Heat to boiling **11 cups water** and **1 cup salt;** cool. Pour over the pickles. Let stand for 2 weeks, skimming scum off as needed. Drain; rinse the pickles.

Dissolve **2 Tbsp. alum** in a small amount of water. Add enough cold water to cover the pickles plus the dissolved alum. Let stand for 24 hours and drain.

Add **2 qts. vinegar** and **2 Tbsp. pickling spices;** let stand for 24 hours. Drain well.

Add **3 cups sugar each day** until you've added 9 cups.

Place in canning jars; seal with wax paper in lids. Label and store in a cool place.

NOTE: Use a 2-3 gallon stone crock to make the pickles. Weight the pickles down with plates to keep them from floating to the top of the crock.

Jerry and Sheri Wiener
From their friend,
Kenneth Van Allen

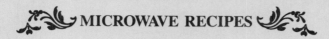

MICROWAVE RECIPES

The real charm and interest of curry involves the side dishes. Curry is served over rice, then topped with a variety of things. For a first rate curry, serve at least 7 different toppings. Since, in its early days, each topping was served by a house boy, offering 7 toppings showed that the household had at least 7 servants and was a well-to-do family. I usually serve coconut, crumbled bacon, raisins, chopped hard boiled eggs, chutney, chopped tomato, and chopped peanuts.

CURRIED SHRIMP
(Microwave)

1½ lbs. medium-size fresh shrimp
2 Tbsp. oil
1 onion, finely chopped
½ green pepper, finely chopped (optional)
1 tsp. curry powder (adjust to taste)
¼ tsp. cumin
Dash of cayenne pepper
2 Tbsp. flour
1½ cups chicken broth
1 tsp. lemon juice
1 Tbsp. tomato paste

Peel and devein the shrimp. Leave off to one side. Heat the oil in a 1½-qt. glass or ceramic casserole on the HIGH for 30 seconds. Add the onion and green pepper; cook for 1 minute. Stir in the curry powder, cumin, and cayenne pepper. Cook for 20 seconds. Stir in the flour. Stir in the chicken broth, lemon juice, and tomato paste with a wire whisk. Cook for 3 minutes. Add the shrimp and cook for 3 minutes more. Serves 4.

Cheryl Haas

MICRO PEANUT BRITTLE

1 cup sugar
½ cup white corn syrup
1 cup peanuts.
1 Tbsp. margarine
1 tsp. vanilla extract
1 tsp. baking soda

In a casserole, blend the sugar and syrup. Microwave on HIGH for 4 minutes, stirring occasionally. Stir in the nuts; cook for 3 minutes. Stir in the butter, vanilla, and soda. Cook 1 more minute. Spread on a baking sheet (greased). Cool. When hard, break the candy into pieces.
(Mrs. Sipocz uses a 15½ x 10½ x 1-inch jelly roll pan.)

Miss Jenny Sipocz
From her mother,
Mrs. Josephine Sipocz

MICROWAVE CORN PUDDING

2 eggs
2 Tbsp. sugar
2 Tbsp. flour
1 can (16 oz.) cream-style corn
1 can (16 oz.) kernel corn, drained
1 cup milk
¼ tsp. salt
⅛ tsp. pepper
2 Tbsp. butter or margarine
Nutmeg

Beat the eggs well in a large bowl. Stir in the sugar and flour. Add the corn, milk, salt, and pepper; blend well. Pour the mixture into a greased 1½-qt. casserole or microwave tube pan. Dot with the 2 Tbsp. butter and sprinkle with nutmeg (freshly grated nutmeg is best).
Microwave on HIGH for 4 minutes. Rotate a quarter turn and microwave at MEDIUM-HIGH for 18-20 minutes. (Rotate a quarter turn every 5 minutes.) The center will be soft, but will firm up after standing for 2-3 minutes; this problem will not occur if you use a tube pan. Serves 4-6.

Mrs. Roger (Louise) Barts

The Reuben sandwich has been an unquestioned favorite ever since it won the National Sandwich Idea Contest in 1956. This casserole blends the popular Reuben flavor with the convenience of microwave cooking.

REUBEN CASSEROLE

1 lb. sauerkraut, drained
12 oz. corned beef
2 cups shredded Swiss cheese
½ cup Thousand Island salad dressing
2 medium tomatoes, sliced
2 Tbsp. butter or margarine
½ cup bread crumbs

Place the sauerkraut in a 1½-qt. casserole. Top with the corned beef, then the shredded cheese. Spread the Thousand Island dressing over the mixture and top with tomato slices. Set aside.
Place the butter in a small glass bowl. Microwave for about 1 minute or until melted. Stir in the bread crumbs. Sprinkle over the casserole.
Microwave for 12-15 minutes or until the mixture is heated through. Let stand for 5 minutes before serving.

Mrs. David (Margie) Canfield

WHEN STUNG BY A BEE
To alleviate the pain, make a paste of meat tenderizer and water and apply it to the area of the sting.

GERMAN POTATO SALAD

**4 cups medium-sized potatoes, peeled and
sliced**
½ cup chopped celery
⅓ cup chopped onion
1½ Tbsp. finely chopped parsley
⅓ cup water
7 slices bacon, diced
2 Tbsp. flour
2 Tbsp. sugar
1½ tsp. salt
½ tsp. celery seed
⅛ tsp. pepper
½ cup cider vinegar
¾ cup water
3 hard boiled eggs

1. Combine the first 5 ingredients in a 2½-qt. casserole. Cover and microwave on HIGH for 15 minutes. Stir every 5 minutes. Let stand, covered, while cooking the bacon.
2. Place the diced bacon in a 1½-qt. casserole, cover with a paper towel, and microwave on HIGH for 5 minutes. Stir after 2 minutes. Remove the bacon with a slotted spoon and place on a paper towel to drain.
3. Stir the remaining ingredients (except the eggs) into the bacon drippings until smooth. Microwave on HIGH for 3 minutes, stirring well after each minute.
4. When thick and smooth, pour the hot dressing over the hot cooked potatoes. Add the crisp bacon and 2 diced hard boiled eggs. Mix well until the potatoes are separated and coated with dressing. To decorate the top of the dish, slice the remaining egg and arrange it with sprigs of parsley. Cover the dish and let stand a couple of minutes before serving.

Mrs. Roger (Louise) Barts

South Bend has changed a great deal since the 1870's, but the heart of the city still remains the St. Joseph River.
Courtesy of The South Bend - Mishawaka Area Chamber of Commerce.

GLOSSARY

AL DENTE
To cook pasta, rice, or vegetables until firm, but not soft.

AU GRATIN
To cover with a sauce, breadcrumbs, and sometimes cheese, then brown in an oven.

AU JUS
Meat served with its own juice or gravy.

BAKE
To cook with dry heat, usually in an oven.

BARBECUE
To roast meat on a spit or grill over charcoal or wood. The meat is often basted with a highly seasoned sauce.

BASTE
To moisten food while cooking to add flavor and prevent drying out.

BEAT
To mix rapidly with a spoon or electric mixer in order to make a mixture smooth.

BLANCH
To boil briefly in water or to pour boiling water over food for a few moments. This loosens skins or peels, sets colors, seals in juices, or prepares food for freezing or canning.

BLEND
To combine two or more ingredients.

BOIL
To cook in liquid at boiling temperature (212 degrees F. at sea level).

BONE
To remove bones, leaving the original shape.

BOUQUET GARNI
Soup seasoning generally added to the soup in a cheesecloth bag which is later discarded.

BRAISE
To brown in a small amount of fat and then cook slowly on top of the stove or in the oven in a small amount of liquid.

BREAD
To coat with crumbs or a mixture of beaten egg and milk and then crumbs.

BROIL
To cook over, under, or in front of direct heat in an oven or live coals.

BROWN
To sear in order to seal in juices and provide good color.

BRUISE
To partially crush therefore releasing flavor.

BUNGED
To plug with a stopper in the bunghole (which is used for emptying or filling a cask.)

CANDY
To cook in sugar or heavy syrup.

CARMELIZE
To melt sugar slowly over low heat to turn it brown and give it a special flavor.

CHOP
To cut into pieces.

CLARIFY
To clear a liquid by separating and removing the solids.

CODDLE
To poach gently in simmering water.

CONSOMME
Clear soup of beef or fowl.

CREAM
To rub together or stir fat and sugar or to beat fat in order to soften.

CRIMP
To seal the edges of a pie crust by pinching.

CURE
To preserve meat, fish, or vegetables by drying, salting, smoking, or some other method.

CUT IN
To mix shortening into dry ingredients until distributed in small particles using two knives or a pastry blender.

DEGLAZE
To heat stock or wine together with the sediment left in a roasting pan or pan to form gravy (after first draining off any excess fat).

DEMI TASSE
Small cup of after dinner coffee.

DICE
To cut into small cubes.

DREDGE
To cover food with flour or some other dry ingredient by shaking in a bag or sprinkling on.

FLAKE
To break lightly into small pieces.

FLAMBE
To sprinkle with brandy or a liqueur and igniting.

FOLD IN
To combine a whipped substance with another taking care to retain lightness and volume.

FRICASSEE
To cook gently in liquid; generally applies to poultry.

FRY
To cook in hot fat.

GARNISH
To decorate with colorful or flavorful foods.

GLAZE
To coat with a syrup or thick liquid to add a sheen to a food's surface.

HALF & HALF
Combination of half milk and half cream.

JULIENNE
To cut food in thin strips.

KNEAD
To work dough by pressing with the hands and turning.

MARINATE
To cover and allow foods to stand in a seasoned liquid. This tenderizes and adds flavor.

MINCE
To cut into very fine pieces.

MIX
To combine two or more ingredients, generally by stirring.

PARBOIL
To boil until partially cooked.

PARE
To peel.

PICKLE
To preserve by immersing in a brine solution.

PLUMP
To cook or soak dried fruits in liquid until they swell.

POACH
To cook gently in hot liquid.

(continued)

GLOSSARY

PROOF
To test yeast for strength or effectiveness.

PUREE
To mash until smooth.

RAGOUT
A thick, well seasoned stew.

REDUCE
To boil a liquid so that volume will be reduced by evaporation.

RENDER
To melt or clarify.

ROAST
To cook by dry heat in an oven.

ROUX
Mixture of melted fat and flour, generally for thickening sauces, soups, or liquids.

SALERATUS
Baking soda (sodium bicarbonate) used in cookery.

SALT PORK
Side of a hog which has been cured; fattier than bacon and with no smoked flavor. Used for flavoring and adding fat to dishes such as baked beans, stew, etc.

SAUTE
To cook in a small amount of fat, turning frequently (to pan fry).

SCALD
To heat a liquid to just below the boiling point.

SCALLOP
To bake in a sauce or other liquid.

SCANT
Not coming quite up to the stated measure.

SCORE
To make shallow cuts through the outer covering of food to tenderize and help maintain the shape.

SEAR
To brown quickly over very high temperature to improve color and seal in juices.

SIFT
To use a strainer or sifter to remove any lumps or to lighten dry ingredients.

SIMMER
To cook slowly in a liquid that is kept below the boiling point (about 185 degrees F.).

STEAM
To cook or heat over boiling water without touching the water.

STEW
To cook slowly in a small amount of liquid over a long period of time.

STIR
To mix ingredients in a circular motion to blend or prevent from sticking.

TOAST
To brown until crisp over direct heat.

TOSS
To mix ingredients lightly.

TRUSS
To tie poultry meat with skewers so that it will hold its shape during cooking.

WHIP
To beat rapidly in order to increase volume and lighten the mixture.

MEASUREMENTS

Dash = ⅛ teaspoon (or less)
3 teaspoons = 1 tablespoon
16 tablespoons = 1 cup
4 saltspoons = 1 teaspoon
2 teaspoons = 1 dessert spoon
4 tablespoons = 1 wineglass = ¼ cup
4 tablespoons = ½ gill = ¼ cup
1 tablespoon = 1 ounce
1 gill = 1 ounces = ½ cup
2 gills = 1 cup = ½ pint
2 wineglasses = 1 gill
4 gills = 1 pint
¼ cup = 4 tablespoons
⅓ cup = 5 tablespoons plus 1 teaspoon
½ cup = 8 tablespoons
2 cups = 1 pint
4 cups = 1 quart = 32 ounces
2 pints = 1 quart
1 cup = 8 ounces
4 quarts = 1 gallon
8 quarts = 1 peck
4 pecks = 1 bushel
16 ounces = 1 pound
Butter size of an egg = 2 ounces
Butter size of a walnut = 1 ounce

1 jigger = 3 tablespoons
1 medium lemon = 3 tablespoons of juice
1 medium lemon = 1 tablespoon grated peel
1 medium orange = ⅓ cup of juice
1 medium orange = 2 tablespoons grated peel
1 medium lime = 2 tablespoons of juice
1 large onion = ¾-1 cup chopped onion
1 cup regular rice = 3 cups cooked rice
8 ounces sour cream = 1 cup
8 ounces cottage cheese = 1 cup
1 cup whipping cream = 2 cups whipped cream
¼ pound cheese = 1 cup shredded cheese
1 slice of bread = ½ cup bread crumbs
1 pint of berries = ¾ cup
1 cup macaroni = 2 cups cooked
1 envelope unflavored gelatin = 1 tablespoon
1 (6 ounce) package chocolate chips = 1 cup
5 whole eggs = 1 cup
12-14 egg yolks = 1 cup
8-10 egg whites = 1 cup
15 marshmallow = ¼ pound
4 teaspoons vinegar or 1½ tablespoons lemon juice added to 1 cup of sweet milk = 1 cup of sour milk
1 stick of margarine = ½ cup

INDEX

This olive green long-sleeved knee length evening dress has a black silk attached Mandarin-style overdress. Small pleats around the hem peek through the black silk, which has rhinestone and black rose-shaped buttons at the cuffs, collar and connecting the four sections of the overdress. Appliqued black silk leaves on the sleeves and the panel down the front of the dress add to its attractiveness. The dress was donated by Mr. & Mrs. Herald Hershman. Circa 1926.

INDEX

INDEX

INDEX

INDEX

St. Mary's College students await the start of a cooking class -- circa 1916.

Aspic and Old Lace

Please send _____ copies of Aspic and Old Lace at $19.95 each plus $2.00 postage and handling per book. For Indiana delivery add $1.00 sales tax per book. Make checks payable to Northern Indiana Historical Society, 112 South Lafayette Boulevard, South Bend, Indiana 46601.

NAME _____

STREET _____

CITY _____

STATE _____ ZIP_____

VISA or MASTERCARD #_____

Exp. _____

Allow 4-5 weeks for delivery — Price subject to change.

- -

Aspic and Old Lace

Please send _____ copies of Aspic and Old Lace at $19.95 each plus $2.00 postage and handling per book. For Indiana delivery add $1.00 sales tax per book. Make checks payable to Northern Indiana Historical Society, 112 South Lafayette Boulevard, South Bend, Indiana 46601.

NAME _____

STREET _____

CITY _____

STATE _____ ZIP_____

VISA or MASTERCARD #_____

Exp. _____

Allow 4-5 weeks for delivery — Price subject to change.

- -

Aspic and Old Lace

Please send _____ copies of Aspic and Old Lace at $19.95 each plus $2.00 postage and handling per book. For Indiana delivery add $1.00 sales tax per book. Make checks payable to Northern Indiana Historical Society, 112 South Lafayette Boulevard, South Bend, Indiana 46601.

NAME _____

STREET _____

CITY _____

STATE _____ ZIP_____

VISA or MASTERCARD #_____

Exp. _____

Allow 4-5 weeks for delivery — Price subject to change.

All copies will be sent to same address unless otherwise specified. If you wish one or any number of books sent as gifts, furnish a list of names and addresses of recipients. If you wish to enclose a gift card with each book, please write the name of the recipient and we will include it with your gift.

All copies will be sent to same address unless otherwise specified. If you wish one or any number of books sent as gifts, furnish a list of names and addresses of recipients. If you wish to enclose a gift card with each book, please write the name of the recipient and we will include it with your gift.

All copies will be sent to same address unless otherwise specified. If you wish one or any number of books sent as gifts, furnish a list of names and addresses of recipients. If you wish to enclose a gift card with each book, please write the name of the recipient and we will include it with your gift.